COMMON WRITI

In a series of penetrating and attractively readable essays, Stefan Collini explores aspects of the literary and intellectual culture of Britain from the early twentieth century to the present. *Common Writing* focuses chiefly on writers, critics, historians, and journalists who occupied wider public roles as cultural commentators or intellectuals, as well as on the periodicals and other genres through which they attempted to reach such audiences.

Among the figures discussed are T.S. Eliot, Graham Greene, J.B. Priestley, C.S. Lewis, Kingsley Amis, Nikolaus Pevsner, Hugh Trevor-Roper, Christopher Hitchens, and Michael Ignatieff. The essays explore the variety of such figures' writings—something that can be overlooked or forgotten when they are treated exclusively in terms of their contribution to one established or professional category such as 'novelist' or 'historian'—while capturing their distinctive writing voices and those indirect or implicit ways in which they position or reveal themselves in relation to specific readerships, disputes, and traditions. These essays engage with recent biographies, collections of letters, and new editions of classic works, thereby making some of the fruits of recent scholarly research available to a wider audience. *Common Writing* will appeal to (and delight) readers interested in literature, history, and contemporary cultural debate.

Stefan Collini was Professor of Intellectual History and English Literature at Cambridge until 2014. Educated at Cambridge and Yale, he taught at the University of Sussex for 12 years before moving to Cambridge in 1986. He is a frequent contributor to *The London Review of Books, The Times Literary Supplement, The Guardian, The Nation*, and other periodicals. He is a Fellow of the British Academy and of the Royal Historical Society.

ALSO BY STEFAN COLLINI

As author

Liberalism and Sociology: L. T. Hobhouse and Political Argument in England 1880–1914

(with Donald Winch and John Burrow) *That Noble Science of Politics: A Study in Nineteenth-Century Intellectual History*

Public Moralists: Political Thought and Intellectual Life in Britain 1850–1930

Matthew Arnold: A Critical Portrait

English Pasts: Essays in History and Culture

Absent Minds: Intellectuals in Britain

Common Reading: Critics, Historians, Publics

That's Offensive! Criticism, Identity, Respect

What Are Universities For?

As editor

John Stuart Mill, *On Liberty and Other Writings*

Umberto Eco, *Interpretation and Overinterpretation*

Matthew Arnold, *Culture and Anarchy and Other Writings*

C. P. Snow, *The Two Cultures*

(with Richard Whatmore and Brian Young) *History, Religion, and Culture:* and *Economy, Polity, and Society: British Intellectual History Since 1750*

F. R. Leavis, *Two Cultures?*

COMMON WRITING

ESSAYS ON LITERARY CULTURE AND PUBLIC DEBATE

Stefan Collini

Great Clarendon Street, Oxford, OX2 6DP,
United Kingdom

Oxford University Press is a department of the University of Oxford.
It furthers the University's objective of excellence in research, scholarship,
and education by publishing worldwide. Oxford is a registered trade mark of
Oxford University Press in the UK and in certain other countries

First published 2016
First published in paperback 2018

Published in the United States of America by Oxford University Press
198 Madison Avenue, New York, NY 10016, United States of America

British Library Cataloguing in Publication Data
Data available

Library of Congress Cataloging in Publication Data
Data available

ISBN 978–0–19–875896–9 (Hbk.)
ISBN 978–0–19–881311–8 (Pbk.)

For Geoffrey Hawthorn, uncommon friend

CONTENTS

To criticize is to appreciate, to appropriate, to take intellectual possession, to establish in fine a relation with the criticized thing and to make it one's own.

(Henry James, Preface to the New York edition of *Portrait of a Lady*)

There's a cool web of language winds us in.

(Robert Graves, 'The Cool Web')

I essay much, I hope little, I ask nothing.

(Edward Elgar, inscribed at the end of *Enigma Variations*)

Introduction

The title of a book of essays can, given the plural nature of its contents, only provide an approximate indication of the character and range of its subject-matter. In choosing *Common Writing* as my title here, I am partly signalling that this volume is intended as a companion to the collection entitled *Common Reading*, published in 2008. As I remarked then, although 'common' may be understood in various ways, my main purpose in using the word was to emphasize an activity 'that is both shared and everyday'. The present collection focuses less, or at least less explicitly, on reading publics, but in its attention to forms of writing the emphasis on what is 'shared and everyday' remains constant. Beyond that, the two titles frankly acknowledge, rather than seeking to disguise, that these volumes belong to a long tradition of selected essays. Without presuming to stand alongside such classics of the genre as, say, Virginia Woolf's *The Common Reader* or Philip Larkin's *Required Writing*, I hope that the title phrases do suggest the presence of a literary form that is deeply familiar. The kinds of essay included here should not need any elaborate introduction or justification: most of the likely readers of this book will already be practised readers of the genre in its periodical form.

The phrases in the subtitle, 'literary culture' and 'public debate', are themselves so familiar that the mind easily can slide over them without picking up any clear meanings on the way. 'Literary culture' is, in my view, the less problematic of the two. It is now used very generally to refer to all that pertains to the writing and reading of books in a given society, which can include publishing, reviewing, and studying them, but can also include such currently fashionable cultural forms as literary festivals, literary prizes, and so on. The sense of 'literary' here is the broad, older sense, meaning all kinds of extended or considered writing, not the narrower one in which it picks out what is sometimes now called 'creative' or 'imaginative' writing—meaning, usually, novels, poems, and plays. For example, it would obviously be right to say that in Britain the Orwell Prize is part of literary culture, even though the kinds of writing it embraces include history, reportage, journalism, social analysis, and so on. 'Public debate' can be a more treacherous term, not merely when it seduces us into thinking that there is only one form or level of such debate, but also when the noun misleads us into imagining a conflict or exchange between two sides with opposing views. Most of what interests me in these essays is not part of any formal 'debate', with an identifiable motion and two teams, but, rather, modes of writing which attempt to attract and persuade by more indirect means. Questions of tone or 'voice', rather than of insistent propositional statement, then become central, and many of these essays concentrate on trying to characterize the quiddity of an individual writing voice without losing sight of the argumentative or rhetorical contexts that shape all attempts to sway public discussion. In bald terms, all the pieces included here deal with aspects of twentieth- and early twenty-first-century British literary and intellectual life, with the occasional European or transatlantic sortie for comparative purposes. Mostly, they are about authors who, while making a mark in a particular literary genre or intellectual discipline, have also figured, however indirectly, in wider public discussion, or else about some of the media that have enabled such contributions.

Review-essays in the intellectually more ambitious periodicals are often spoken of as being part of a larger 'cultural conversation'. In some ways that is a more appealing metaphor than 'debate'—conversations can be enjoyable, informal, responsive, open-ended—but from another perspective it, too, is misleading: in ordinary life, delivering four thousand words of uninterrupted, carefully chiselled prose is hardly a recipe for conversational success. Perhaps one way in which the metaphor is nonetheless apt lies in its acknowledgement that we never start from scratch: these matters have been talked about before, and how a review-essay is pitched, where it starts, and what it takes for granted, depend in part on a shared familiarity with some of that previous discussion, even if in certain cases (or for certain readers) that assumption is no more than a necessary fiction. A good review-essay, after all, is not like a chapter in an introductory text which is obliged to assume as little as possible and to regard simplification as more of a virtue than a vice. Implicitly presuming a culturally sophisticated and widely informed reader, the review-essay treads a fine line between telling and reminding. In this respect, the premise of the form is a little like that of a committee at which the minutes of the previous meeting can be taken as read. The speaker who now holds the floor may from time to time tactfully jog the other members' memories, but it is the difference made by recent developments or new information that is properly the focus. For example, a review-essay may be hung on the peg of a new biography or major edition of an author's writings (as several in this collection are); in such cases it seems appropriate to assume some basic familiarity with their work while standing back and taking stock, perhaps offering a more general reappraisal.

In Britain, though obviously not in Britain alone, there is a rich tradition of this kind of extended, serious, literary journalism. In practice, the longish review-essay—somewhere between, say, three and six thousand words—constitutes a distinctive sub-genre within that wider form. No doubt most writers and reviewers naturally gravitate, when they have any choice, to a sub-set of the available types of periodical writing. For example, I have in the past tried my hand at doing much shorter book reviews in the daily or Sunday broadsheets, but I found the form unsatisfying (as I often do, I must admit, as a reader). I felt that the genre required me to be too brisk, too purely judgemental; there was not enough space to build up at least the beginnings of that verbal world which communicates in ways that are beyond the reach of simple expressions of taste. Of course, there are notable reviewers who excel at this kind of writing, and I can admire them for talents I do not possess without wishing to try to emulate them. I'm encouraged in my preference by the fact that regular newspaper book-reviews are prone to fall into puffing and back-scratching—or else into their mirror-image, the hatchet-job. The longer forms, by contrast, tend to make the topic or subject-matter more the focus of attention than the reviewer's approval or disapproval, and that helps to reduce those vices. No doubt it is good that in Britain there are still some daily newspapers willing to carry reviews in any quantity at all (their number has declined over the past decade or so), but for the most part they confine themselves to the shorter lengths, ranging from six hundred to twelve hundred words.

The original versions of many of the essays gathered and re-worked in this volume come, therefore, from those publications that encourage the longer and more considered review-essay: the majority were written for either the *London Review of Books* or the *Times Literary Supplement*, with a smaller number having appeared in the *Guardian Review*, *Prospect*, and (in the United States) the *Nation*. It would be an exaggeration to describe the business of selecting pieces for inclusion as in any way akin to finding the statue in the marble, but the process has allowed me to give this collection a broad thematic and substantive identity. (In practice, the process of selection starts even earlier, when turning down commissions or invitations that are too far outside one's range.) No one could claim that the contingent selection of figures discussed in these essays is fully representative of either literary culture or public debate in Britain in the past century or so. A cast that is largely male, university educated, and with ready access to mainstream forms of publishing and literary journalism clearly belongs to a privileged stratum of society, the stratum that dominated intellectual and literary culture in Britain until the later decades of the twentieth century. In recent years, a variety of figures from less favoured categories have, quite rightly, received increasing attention, and attempts to challenge the traditional orders of prominence serve an important corrective purpose. But however much later scholars may focus on previously neglected or occluded figures, we cannot retrospectively alter the distribution of attention that obtained at the time in what was, from many points of view, a more homogeneous and self-confident public culture for the greater part of the period covered here. We cannot retroactively promote figures to a public standing they did not then possess, however fundamentally we may revalue their ultimate significance.

These essays, then, engage with figures who both enjoyed some prominence in their own time and have, mostly, continued to receive various kinds of critical or scholarly attention. While their principal identities may have been as poets, critics, novelists, historians, or journalists, they are also considered here in terms of their wider public roles as cultural commentators or intellectuals (to use a tricky term that I have repeatedly urged we need to be wary of but which is nonetheless indispensable). In some cases, I re-examine the arc of their careers, trying to identify the different ways they achieved the standing necessary to be licensed to provide such public commentary; in others, I explore the variety of their writing, something that can get overlooked or forgotten when they are treated exclusively in terms of their contribution to one established or professional category, such as, say, 'novelist' or 'historian'. And throughout I try, within the necessarily limited space available, to capture something of their distinctive writing voices and those indirect or implicit ways in which they position or reveal themselves in relation to specific readerships, disputes, and traditions. The last three essays in Part II push this engagement in a more overtly political direction, but although my own allegiances will be evident here, the primary focus is still on the ways in which particular uses of language inform or cajole, seduce or excite, distract or mislead, even when dealing with issues that are ordinarily thought to be largely 'matters of fact'.

For many years, the title of my academic post has yoked together the terms 'intellectual history' and 'English literature'. Though rather a mouthful, this is reasonably accurate about my main scholarly interests, except for the suggestion carried by that innocent-looking conjunction. Far from being two distinct entities, literary-critical and intellectual-historical approaches are, in my view (and certainly in my practice), hard to distinguish. I tend to regard them as two aspects of the attempt to understand and characterize various pieces of past writing, some of which may conventionally be classified as 'literature', some not. As I argue in the final essay in this volume, there can be no escape from the toils of everyday language when describing and assessing human experience, and therefore there can be no adequate recovery or re-description of that experience without being alert to the semantic unruliness of language and to the power words have over us as well as we over them.

In addition to that general preoccupation, these essays manifest a recurring concern with several more substantive themes. The making of literary and intellectual careers in twentieth-century Britain is one such topic, including the role of inherited or acquired cultural capital and the ways it can be deployed or squandered, an issue that bears directly on the relative paucity of women in my cast. This entails, further, a frequent return to the relations between academic and lay intellectual culture: universities were becoming steadily more prominent in national life during this period, yet we should, even so, not allow the insidious metaphors of 'inside' and 'outside' to mislead us into treating the division between academic and non-academic as more absolute or unchanging than it actually was. Then there is the interest in forms of cultural criticism (taking the term in its loosest and most encompassing sense) that engage with politics without according the political any automatic or universal primacy. Most frequently of all perhaps, these essays display an antipathy or even allergy to various forms of reductivism, oversimplification, or plain-mannish philistinism on the part either of my subjects or those who write about them. English culture has often been seen, and sometimes praised, as emphatically, maybe distinctively, un-intellectual or even anti-intellectual ('English' may be less inaccurate than 'British' where this trope is concerned). I have analysed and contested these claims more systematically in *Absent Minds* and elsewhere; here I have tried to resist these stereotypes in more local ways, a commitment always likely to entail moments of impatience or asperity.

The reasons why writers and scholars come to focus on a particular subject-matter or theme are various, often involving a large element of contingency, especially in the form of available educational or career options at a given historical moment. But by the time they are several decades into their writing lives, it is usually safe to assume that the type of work they do bears a more than accidental relation to the kind of person they are. I may have come rather late to a recognition of the sorts of literary and intellectual work that most attract me, but for some time it has been clear that I am more drawn to the irregular particularity of the portrait than to the clean outlines of the theory, that I am sceptical of explanations but hospitable to characterizations, that I privilege writers' own words, quoted exactly and examined closely, over paraphrase or reductive summary, and, generally, that I am more in danger of being a nuance bore than a concept nerd. Needless to say, all worthwhile intellectual work depends, at some level, on formulating theories, concepts, abstractions, and I draw on such ideas, in a secondary or parasitic way, all the time, but generating or testing such theories is not my primary purpose in these pieces.

It is not, therefore, altogether surprising that, as both writer and reader, I like essays and have a long-standing partiality for collections of them. Part of what, as a reader, I find appealing about the genre is that the very diversity of subject and occasion makes them the opposite of Procrustean. A book of essays may, in some cases, have a unifying set of perspectives or preoccupations (as I like to think this one does), but it can, in the nature of the case, not really be the medium of a theoretical or uniform treatment. The attention to the individuality of the figures and topics discussed in the various pieces is almost bound to lean in the direction of nominalism rather than realism, in the loose philosophical senses of those terms. There are judgements aplenty scattered across such volumes and, one would hope, lots of ideas; but they do not sustain a single argument, still less elaborate a system. Naturally, I like to think that in the present case the reader will find that points made in one essay are supported and amplified in others, and that the experience of reading them in the presented sequence is in some way cumulative rather than merely aggregative. But authors of such collections have to be wary of being taken in by the propaganda of their own suasive titles. There is an honesty about those volumes simply called *Selected Essays* for which I have a sneaking admiration, as well as a self-confidence behind them that I can only envy. So it is right to acknowledge that, while these essays are some of the most recent instalments of my long-running efforts to explore and understand the intellectual and literary life of Britain over the past century or so, the choice of topics partly just represents the writer various review-editors have imagined me to be.

As in earlier collections, I have lightly revised each of the original pieces, eliminating the intrusive stigmata of various journals' house styles, restoring some passages omitted on grounds of length or editorial misjudgement, correcting one or two stylistic solecisms that I (and my usually keen-eyed advisers and editors) had previously overlooked. I have also, obviously, combined them so as to form a series of larger essays and I have occasionally added a little introductory or connecting material. But I have not attempted to 'update' them in any more fundamental way: they still represent what it seemed relevant to say at the time they were originally written, which, in all but a couple of cases, was between 2007 and 2015. In a few instances I return in these essays to figures or topics I have discussed on earlier occasions. This highlights another property in the buried metaphor of a 'cultural conversation': just as such conversations have no fixed starting points, so they can never really end. New books, new evidence, new claims can and should lead to reassessments, or at least to further discussion focused on different aspects of a topic or of a writer's career and achievement. For these reasons, I have here revisited figures such as T. S. Eliot, Isaiah Berlin, Herbert Butterfield, and Raymond Williams, while the appearance of the first full biographies of their subjects occasioned a return to William Empson, R. H. Tawney, and Richard Hoggart. In all cases, details of the books or other prompts to the original writing are given at the foot of the first page of each essay. In addition to this Introduction and the linking passages just mentioned, substantial sections of Chapters 8, 9, and 10 have not previously been published in any form.

Part I

Literary Culture

1

Notables

J. B. Priestley, C. S. Lewis, Maurice Bowra

I

In 2009, I visited the Birmingham suburb of Bournville for the first time. Planned and developed by the Cadburys in the 1890s, the heart of the estate is explicitly modelled on an ideal of the English village, and the houses, mostly semi-detached, play a series of variations on the theme of the cottage. Consulting Pevsner as I walked around, I was a bit surprised to find that he, normally rather sniffy about the various forms of imitation and revival that make up most modern English domestic architecture, sounded almost enthusiastic about the style of these placid, unambitious dwellings. 'Gradually', he noted of the growth of the Bournville development, 'a few satisfactory basic types of house were evolved to suit the way people want to live.'

Driving out of Birmingham later that day on the peculiarly modern Dantesque nightmare that is the inner ring road, I found myself returning to that last, rather uncharacteristic phrase: types of house were evolved 'to suit the way people want to live'. But how could one know that *this* was the way people wanted to live, rather than being, say, the way they'd inherited and more or less unwillingly adapted to? Looking out of the car window, I would have had to conclude that the way an awful lot of people want to live must be to spend much of their time driving in and out of Birmingham on a badly designed race-track bordered by establishments that will fit a new exhaust on your car while-U-wait, sell you a leather three-piece suite for nothing (at least, nothing today), or stuff your family with a day's worth of unnutritious calories for less than a tenner—and all housed in structures whose pedigree was, at best, out of warehouses by sheds. I could feel myself beginning to work up a good

J. B. Priestley, *English Journey* (Great Northern Books, 2009; first published 1934).
Alister McGrath, *C. S. Lewis: A Life. Eccentric Genius, Reluctant Prophet* (Hodder, 2013).
Alister McGrath, *The Intellectual World of C. S. Lewis* (Wiley-Blackwell, 2014).
Leslie Mitchell, *Maurice Bowra: A Life* (Oxford University Press, 2009).

Ruskinian lather, finding texts for conscience-awakening sermons inscribed in the very structures and materials of the buildings around me. After all, wasn't this how it was done, the 'Condition-of-England' genre? Observation plus indignation equals cultural critique?

The fit passed, but it was a reminder that such critique always relies, in effect, on some idea of 'how people *ought* to want to live', something that can't simply be inferred from looking out the car window. But even while indulging, inwardly, the urge to rant, I never found myself saying of Bournville, as J. B. Priestley did after his visit there in 1933, 'it is one of the small outposts of civilisation, still ringed round with barbarism'. Taken in isolation, that comment sounds unappealingly superior and windily apocalyptic. Yet isn't that, I thought to myself, true of so much writing in this genre, always finding portents of aesthetic vulgarity and moral squalor in a handful of dust, or at least in a handful of carefully selected examples from both high street and back alley? Traditionally, the genre hasn't allowed much standing to 'the way people want to live', and if the phrase I've just quoted was representative of Priestley's contribution to the genre, then *English Journey* seemed likely to confirm my impression of him as a predictable and not very interesting writer. However, the truth about both this book and its author, and perhaps about the genre generally, turns out to be more complicated than that, as the full report of his encounter with Bournville reveals.

That encounter had been part of a journey around England made expressly for the purpose of writing an up-to-the-minute 'Condition of England' book. Born in Bradford in 1894, Priestley, after extensive service in the First World War and three years at Cambridge, had embarked in the early 1920s on the precarious career of a man of letters, turning his hand to criticism, essays, and novels, all written in haste, none enjoying much success. The income from a collaborative work with the much better-known Hugh Walpole enabled him to embark on a more ambitious third novel, *The Good Companions*, published in 1929. Its huge sales, together with those of *Angel Pavement* the following year, transformed his life. He became wealthy, sought after by publishers, loved by a wide readership, and reviled by Bloomsbury. When he succeeded to Arnold Bennett's reviewing pulpit in the *Evening Standard* in 1932, it confirmed his place in the national culture as the spokesman for what was sometimes denigrated as a plain-mannish or middlebrow taste for social realism in literature. As the literary hot property of the moment as well as a writer firmly identified with both 'the North' and 'the people' (the two could sometimes appear hard to distinguish when viewed from upper-middle-class literary London), he seemed to his publishers to be the ideal figure to take the national temperature at the depth of the slump. When the resulting book, *English Journey*, was published the following year, it, too, was an immediate success—displacing *Thank You, Jeeves* at the top of the best-seller list—and it was reissued several times during Priestley's life (he died in 1986). Here was a version of Cobbett's *Rural Rides* for the age of the motor-coach.

The genre of the travel narrative as cultural criticism has a distinguished history, stretching from Defoe and Cobbett up to Iain Sinclair and Bill Bryson. In the nineteenth century, such writing was both overlain and enriched by a style of critique that was less topographical and more frankly ethical or existential—extended essays on what a few carefully chosen examples of contemporary crassness and complacency, whether embodied in architecture or advertising, revealed about the moral quality of the culture as a whole. The great names here, whom Priestley admired, included Carlyle (who coined the term 'Condition of England'), Ruskin, Arnold, and Morris. In the closing decades of the nineteenth and the early years of the twentieth century there were several related attempts, by writers such as Richard Jefferies and Edward Thomas, to identify 'England' with 'the countryside' (largely for an urban readership), while the inter-war decades tended to throw up more quizzical searches for 'the real England', assumed to have been submerged by the shoddy detritus of 'progress' and requiring the skills of the then-fashionable figure, the anthropologist, for its proper identification and recovery. H. V. Morton's best-selling *In Search of England* (1927) was *English Journey*'s immediate predecessor, a rather whimsical attempt to locate the ghosts of nobler ages in surviving relics and ruins. Its best-known successor was, of course, Orwell's *The Road to Wigan Pier* (1937), a first-hand (or, given the prominence of smell in Orwell's reporting, first-nose) account of the degrading squalor in such 'depressed areas' as Wigan and Barnsley, and an indictment of the callousness and self-deception that enabled the comfortable classes to ignore such appalling conditions.

It may surprise many people to find Priestley in this company, since he currently seems to be regarded as a third-rate novelist and second-rate playwright, even though (perhaps partly because) he has provided so many readers and playgoers with so much ready pleasure. I have to admit that I came to *English Journey* expecting sentimental uplift mixed with anecdotal illustration of the claim that there's nowt so queer as folk. The book does, it has to be said, contain a certain amount of that, but it's far from being the whole story. And his rumination on Bournville encapsulates the book's strengths and weaknesses in a particularly revealing way, not least because of what it says about the recurring tension for cultural criticism between the claims of 'how people want to live' and how people *ought* to want to live.

For the most part, Priestley was impressed by what he saw in Bournville. The Cadburys' plan, he acknowledged, has 'proved very successful'. The dwellings and public spaces are 'infinitely superior to and more sensible than most of the huge new workmen's and artisans' quarters that have recently been built on the edge of many large towns in the Midlands'. Personally, he rather regretted that they are all detached and semi-detached: it would have been less 'monotonous' if there had been more terraces, quadrangles, and so on, 'but I was assured by those who know that their tenants greatly prefer to be semi-detached'. That, it seems, is how people want to live. Those of them who were employees at the chocolate works also seemed to want to live in the Cadburys' pockets:

> Their workpeople are provided with magnificent recreation grounds and sports pavilions, with a large concert-hall in the factory itself, where midday concerts are given, with dining-rooms, recreation rooms, and facilities for singing, acting, and I know not what, with continuation schools, with medical attention, with works councils, with pensions . . . Once you have joined the staff of this firm, you need never wander out of its shadow.

So, here are 'nearly all the facilities for leading a full and happy life'. What's more, the firm insists that no compulsion is involved, and it 'never moves to provide anything until it knows that a real demand exists'. The workers are getting what they want, and what they are getting is a lot better than most workers get elsewhere.

Nonetheless, Priestley can't help feeling a bit uneasy about the workers' sunny compliance with this generous paternalism. He notes that when the Cadburys tried to offer the same benefits to employees at a new site in Australia, 'they met with a decided rebuff'. The Australian workers wanted to get away from the shadow of the works and provide their own amusements, and though they may as a result have been worse off materially, 'it is clear', concludes Priestley, 'that the Australian employee as a political being is occupying the sounder position'. But here the question of 'the way people want to live' becomes more complex: the English employees, it seems, want one way, the Australians another. Priestley confidently prefers the latter as 'the sounder position', and this provokes him to a little riff on the 'spirit of independence' that can make him sound like the sternest Victorian moralist, even a latter-day civic humanist. All this paternalist provision creates 'an atmosphere that is injurious to the growth of men as intellectual and spiritual beings'. Almost before you know it, a visit to a chocolate factory has turned into the occasion for a sermon on 'character' and on the moral dignity of the 'free citizen'. 'I for one would infinitely prefer to see workers combining to provide these benefits, or a reasonable proportion of them, for themselves, to see them forming associations far removed from the factory, to see them using their leisure, and demanding its increase, not as favoured employees but as citizens, free men and women.'

But, this being so, the sense in which he regards Bournville as 'one of the small outposts of civilisation' must not be altogether straightforward. What he admires about it is not just that the architecture and layout of the estate are superior to the standard jerry-built barracks of other suburbs, but also that it is 'neither a great firm's private dormitory nor a rich man's toy, but a public enterprise that pays its way'. In effect, the ethical quality he admires in Bournville the estate is the opposite of the ethical quality he deplores in Bournville the works: the former embodies a healthy relation between independence and cooperation, the latter an unhealthy one between paternalism and contentment. But what if, more generally, provision of 'the facilities for leading a full and happy life' is inimical to fostering the 'spirit of independence' rather than favourable to it? Would England be better or worse if it were one big Bournville?

As one reads on in *English Journey*, these tensions come to seem structural rather than confined to this case. At the conclusion of his tour, Priestley reflected that he had discerned three 'Englands': 'Old England'; the 'England of the Industrial Revolution'; and 'Postwar England'. Definition by enumeration is a familiar trope of this genre, issuing in some memorable, and rhetorically effective, lists—think of Orwell's in *The Lion and the Unicorn* which runs from 'the clatter of clogs in the Lancashire mill towns' to 'the old maids biking to Holy Communion through the mists of the autumn morning', or Eliot's in *Notes Towards the Definition of Culture* which moves from 'Derby Day, Henley Regatta, Cowes' through 'Wensleydale cheese, boiled cabbage cut into sections', and on to 'nineteenth-century Gothic churches and the music of Elgar'. Priestley, looking to differentiate his 'three Englands', mostly focuses on what can be seen through the window of the motor-coach.

The first 'England' is gestured at in perfunctory terms: 'the country of the cathedrals and minsters and manor-houses and inns, of Parson and Squire; guide-book and quaint highways and byways England.... We all know this England, which at its best cannot be improved upon in this world.' While he makes clear that he is all for 'scrupulously preserving the most enchanting bits of it, such as the cathedrals and the colleges and the Cotswolds', he also recognizes that there can be no 'going back' to the way of life represented by these enchanting monuments.

Then there is nineteenth-century England:

> the industrial England of coal, iron, steel, cotton, wool, railways; of thousands of rows of little houses all alike, sham Gothic churches, square-faced chapels, Town Halls, Mechanics' Institutes, mills, foundries, warehouses, refined watering-places, Pier Pavilions, Family and Commercial Hotels, Literary and Philosophical Societies, back-to-back houses, detached villas with monkey-trees, Grill Rooms, railway stations, slag-heaps and 'tips', dock roads, Refreshment Rooms, doss-houses, Unionist or Liberal Clubs, cindery waste ground, mill chimneys, slums, fried-fish shops, public-houses with red blinds, bethels in corrugated iron, good-class drapers' and confectioners' shops, a cynically devastated countryside, sooty dismal little towns, and still sootier grim fortress-like cities.

Although overt ethical appraisal starts to intrude before the end ('cynically devastated', 'dismal'), this is by and large a list of material objects, above all architectural—the Lit and Phil Societies, like the Liberal Clubs, get in for their buildings. The period is characterized by what is most visible to the modern traveller, not by its ideas and social practices except as implicitly embodied in such artefacts. But the very exuberance and excess of the list bespeaks something like affection: these sights may not all be objectively beautiful, but they start to sound not merely familiar but treasured. This is, of course, the England in which Priestley grew up, and it clearly still tugs at his emotions.

The list he chooses to represent the third 'England', the England of the post-1918 years, aspires to offer something similar, but social criticism starts to short-circuit the description at an earlier stage:

> This is the England of arterial and by-pass roads, of filling-stations and factories that look like exhibition buildings, of giant cinemas and dance-halls and cafés, bungalows with tiny garages, cocktail bars, Woolworths, motor-coaches, wireless, hiking, factory girls looking like actresses, greyhound racing and dirt tracks, swimming pools, and everything given away for cigarette coupons.

This is not only a shorter list, and a notably cooler one, but it also includes a higher proportion of activities to buildings, bespeaking a sharper edge of social criticism. This was the Americanized England Priestley, in his early middle age, saw taking over, and the curl of the lip is palpable.

He is adamant that it makes no sense to think of 'going back' to the first England, and, for all his admiration for aspects of Industrial England, he regards it as on the whole 'a wrong turning', a condition where 'money and machines are of more importance than men and women'. Yet the England that has succeeded it he clearly judges to be ersatz and shallow, as cultural critics nearly always judge contemporary life to be. There is some of the same dividedness on this larger scale as was detectable after his visit to Bournville: he acknowledges that the third England is 'a cleaner, tidier, healthier, saner world than that of nineteenth-century industrialism', and that these are important improvements. But maybe a bit too clean, too tidy: the improved sewerage that now carries away the more plentifully available bath-water perhaps carries off some irreplaceable babies, too. 'I cannot help feeling that this new England is lacking in character, in zest, gusto, flavour, bite, drive, originality, and that this is a serious weakness.'

So where is his ideal 'England'? If it is projected into the future, as the radical strain in Priestley suggests it should be, then it looks as though it would have to combine the beauty and tranquillity of the first, the vigour and independence of the second, and at least the positive aspects of the democracy and widespread prosperity of the third. This is a familiar mix, characteristic of that strain in English sensibility from the late nineteenth to the late twentieth century which combined (among other things) social progressivism and love of old churches. Priestley is not a medievalizing romantic, certainly not any kind of agrarian fundamentalist, and he disclaims Golden Ageism in typically robust terms. But, as with so many writers in this tradition, such disclaimers do not mean that certain kinds of nostalgia aren't at work in his responses. Insofar as he has a consistent target it is, in true Carlylean or Ruskinian vein, industrialism rather than capitalism. And, as with Ruskin, the politics of the eye predominate. He is revolted by squalor and ugliness, but less acute about those forms of injustice that are structural and whose effects are not readily visible. Correspondingly, his method relies on the vivid portrait and telling anecdote rather than on economic history and sociological analysis. The focus of his critique of contemporary society appears to be 'standardisation' not exploitation. In his anxiety that the people are losing their 'natural vigour', he can sound like an antique moralist.

At the same time, part of the appeal of the book comes from the way Priestley's prose also exhibits a knowing sense of its own charms. This collusiveness is in play from the first page. Taking the motor-coach to Southampton, he rhapsodizes on the luxurious comfort of this relatively new means of transport, concluding: 'They are voluptuous, sybaritic, of doubtful morality.' Here he throws out his little strip of verbal excess like a rug-merchant theatrically unrolling an old Baluch. The author of *English Journey* is the winking, practised raconteur who deliberately allows his audience to see him enjoying his own rhetorical ornaments. From time to time he even stages a little inner conflict to show us what a human fellow he is. More generally, there is nothing pinched or chilly about Priestley's prose, nothing guarded or finicky. He tucks his napkin into his collar and sets to. There was good reason for him to be so frequently compared to Dickens, or at least to one strain in early Dickens, though these affinities also suggest the qualities that have attracted charges of cosiness and sentimentalism.

One of the staples of this style of social criticism involves citing a complacent and celebratory announcement of the country's prosperity and good fortune by some official or public person, and then juxtaposing to it a pointed, vivid instance of actual squalor and misery. Matthew Arnold had milked this device in 'The Function of Criticism', exhibiting the fatuity of politicians' eulogies on national greatness when placed alongside a news item recounting how a young workhouse mother had been driven to murder her illegitimate child in the Mapperley hills ('Wragg is in custody'). *English Journey* contains several such set-pieces, the best known being his visit to the street he calls 'Rusty Lane' in West Bromwich at the end of his tour of Birmingham and the Black Country. One source of the popularity of Priestley's writing lay in his readiness to pull out all the emotional stops. He was not frightened of the hackneyed or obvious. Thus, his visit to Rusty Lane has to take place in 'foul weather': 'the raw fog dripped . . . it was thick and wet and chilled.' The street is no ordinary hell: 'I have never seen such a picture of grimy desolation as that street offered me.' Local urchins throw stones onto the warehouse roof while he is visiting: he understands why they do it. 'Nobody can blame them if they grow up to smash everything that can be smashed.' Then he cranks the handle on his portable moralizer:

> There ought to be no more of those lunches and dinners, at which political and financial and industrial gentlemen congratulate one another, until something is done about Rusty Lane and West Bromwich. . . . And if there is another economic conference, let it meet there, in one of the warehouses, and be fed with bread and margarine and slabs of brawn. The delegates have seen one England, Mayfair in the season. Let them see another England next time, West Bromwich out of the season. Out of all seasons, except the winter of our discontent.

This does not really pretend to be proposing a policy: he has no idea what kind of 'something' needs to be 'done'. It is, instead, intended to prick the balloon of complacency and to puncture the thick skin of unawareness that allows the comfortable classes to maintain their habitual moral indifference when surrounded by suffering and injustice. Yet it is the depressingness of the scene as much as the underlying injustice that provokes this particular little cadenza; we're left feeling that 'something' needs to be 'done' about that dripping 'raw fog' while they're at it. If only those eminent gentlemen could be brought here to *see* this, all would follow. And the closing trope could hardly be more hackneyed. Making 'Mayfair in the season' the contrast is rather like wheeling on a cardboard cut-out of a stage villain complete with curling mustachios, while the heavy play on 'season' at the end sounds like an out-of-work Shakespearian actor declaiming to an indifferent shopping centre.

English Journey avoids the structural cliché of terminating at Jarrow (we ease down the east of England and on to the continuing civic vigour of Norwich), but it is certainly true that its account of the north-east contains some of his most memorable writing, weeping for a people 'without work or wages or hope'. 'I had seen nothing like it since the war.' Today we may think that it took no great powers of observation or sympathy to feel outraged by the condition in which a wealthy country allowed people to live in Jarrow in 1933, though it would seem that the greater part of the population at the time managed to remain either unaware of the reality of that condition or insufficiently moved by it, just as we mostly avert our gaze, deliberately or by self-protective habits of inattention, from the systematic waste of life that goes on around us in the present. Condition-of-England writing constantly reminds us that the nurturing soil of social injustice is inattention, ignorance, and unconcern. The moralist calls upon the reader to look and to focus. Ruskin had reminded the wealthy that they could only enjoy their feasts by literally averting their eyes from the starvation that was all around them, just as Orwell had drawn up a memorable list of comfortable pontificators whose peace of mind depended on refusing even to imagine the poor wretches who crawled underground to fetch coal for their fires. Priestley took his place in this tradition, and if his writing seems blowsy at times, that may have been a small price to pay for having a book containing such scorching pages at the top of the best-seller list. He may allow himself to do some stretches of the journey in his chauffeur-driven Daimler, but he writes as 'the people's' champion when angrily repudiating the claims of comfortably off moralists that the fecklessness of the poor is the cause of their shoddy surroundings, and he becomes fiercely indignant at Tory clap-trap about the unemployed living in luxury on the dole.

The England I looked at through the car window on the Birmingham ring road is in some respects unrecognizably different from the England Priestley observed from the top of a tram in the same city—vastly more prosperous, visibly more diverse, somewhat more egalitarian in attitude, and so on. Yet reading *English Journey*, especially in the depths of another slump, it is easy to feel that less has changed than meets the travelling eye. Priestley can sound uncannily contemporary when expressing bewilderment at the way the lives of whole communities have become the plaything of the global economy, or, for that matter, when complaining that money is ruining football. And he, too, has been told for years that various socially destructive things just had to be done because 'the City' required them. 'The City, then, I thought, must accept the responsibility. Either it is bossing us about or it isn't. If it is, then it must take the blame if there is any blame to be taken. And there seemed to me a great deal of blame to be taken.'

This new edition of *English Journey* seems a bizarrely misconceived enterprise. The book was not only a best-seller in the 1930s, but, as I noted above, it has been reissued several times in the past seventy-five years. The 1984 version was abbreviated (Swindon must have been thought too exciting for modern tastes), so this edition proudly claims to provide 'the fully restored original 1934 text', as though tireless scholars had unearthed some bibliographical jewel. Apart from a number of prefatory pages by current admirers of Priestley such as Beryl Bainbridge and Margaret Drabble, the chief novelty of this edition is that it has been printed in large coffee-table format to accommodate the numerous photographs that have been interspersed through the text. The addition of these photos, a curious mixture of unidentified 'period' images and recent shots, threatens to turn the book into something quite different, a patchy guidebook to the beauties of England. Thus, alongside the account of visiting Boston in Lincolnshire, we now have a photograph which is clearly not Boston but which, to judge from details of dress and transport, comes from the inter-war period. The caption, in its entirety, reads: 'A typical English market scene. Rural and urban markets are still popular today. Most county towns still have a weekly market where farmers and traders sell their products.' (There are several captions in this style, apparently written by a graduate of the Borat School of Tourism Studies.) In many cases, the connection to Priestley is negligible. Under a modern photograph of a thatcher on a cottage roof in Wiltshire we are told,

'Priestley would perhaps have seen this man's grandfather at work.' A picture of the Selfridges building in Birmingham, completed in 2003, is described, correctly but inanely, as 'far removed from anything Priestley would have come across in 1933'.

One begins to wonder whether the publishers are hoping the British Council might adopt *English Journey* as a handy introduction to the UK for the enquiring foreigner. For example, although the book only mentions Sheffield in passing, we are given a modern picture of a Sheffield mosque and told, 'Most major towns and cities in England now feature Moslem places of worship' (as a matter of fact most of them feature lap-dancing clubs as well, but presumably these would be too 'off-message'). Most asinine of all is the placing in the last chapter of a fetching photo of the village of Finchingfield in Essex, 'one of England's prettiest and most photographed villages'. 'Alas', the caption burbles, 'Priestley travelled home in thick fog so would have missed this lovely spot.' Have the editors and publishers actually read the book? Priestley makes quite clear that on leaving Norfolk he decides to curtail his travels and head straight back to London as fast as his chauffeur-driven Daimler will carry him. It was when coming down the A1 from Baldock into London that he encountered fog, which no more accounted for his having 'missed' Finchingfield (not mentioned in the text) than it did for his having missed, say, the Empire State Building, similarly hard to spot, even on the clearest day, from just north of Potter's Bar.

This edition is part of a larger programme for the re-publication of Priestley's major works by Great Northern Books. It remains, of course, easy to be lofty about Priestley, to see him as, at best, the poor man's Arnold Bennett or, even less charitably, as Wilfred Pickles between hard covers. (In attempting to correct this, it is not necessary to go as far as one later admirer who wrote a book about him as 'the last of the sages'.) One deterrent to taking too patronizing a view is provided by his own self-awareness of just this public image, as expressed, for example, in a letter to his American publisher about the misleading representation of him in American reviews of *English Journey*: 'Here is Priestley, who became popular (undeservedly) by writing a lot of sentimental novels, watery imitations of Dickens; he's a bovine hearty sort of ass; but about a third of the way through this book he suddenly discovers (and about time too) that all is not well with everything in this world.' On this occasion, he was hoping that the publisher might be able to do something to make clear that his writings were 'serious pieces of work and not sentimental catch-penny tushery'.

Perhaps a modified version of that case needs to be made again. In his preface to this new edition, Roy Hattersley, a predictable admirer, calls the book 'a masterpiece'. That is puffery, but when he characterizes it as 'a social commentary, a polemic, and a love story', he seems nearer the mark, and the way in which those identities are interwoven is part of what makes the book more than journalistic opportunism. There is a good deal of sentimentality in *English Journey*, and a certain amount of cheap writing, too. But it is, in its fashion, a serious and even moving book about the tensions between 'the way people want to live' and the way they *ought* to want to live, and seventy-five years later we cannot complacently conclude that we have made much progress in resolving these tensions.

II

It is difficult to write about C. S. Lewis without giving offence. Most authors have their admirers, of course, and literary sectarianism is hardly rare, but Lewis is unusual in being at the heart of more than one cult, having excelled in genres where attachments are warmest and where the cool touch of analysis can be most resented, such as popular religious writing and children's literature. That he was also a noted scholar and academic only makes appraisal of his achievements more perilous, since one group of loyalists will fear that focusing on his celebrity among various kinds of 'ordinary reader' signals an undervaluing of his contribution to the study of medieval and Renaissance literature, while those who claim to speak for the legions of passionate admirers will be suspicious of any intellectual perspective liable to be perceived as unsympathetic to the elemental readerly needs assuaged by his writing.

These passions show no sign of diminishing with the passage of time; quite the contrary. When he died in 1963, it seemed that his star was waning, following a peak of popularity in the 1940s and early 1950s, but his standing has enjoyed an extraordinary resurgence in the past couple of decades. In 1998, on the centenary of Lewis's birth, the Royal Mail issued a set of commemorative stamps, and when in 2011 a set of eight stamps was printed celebrating magical figures from all of English literature, two of them were from his best-loved children's book, *The Lion, the Witch, and the Wardrobe*, published in 1950. His standing as a Christian apologist has risen even more remarkably during these years. At the time of his centenary, *Christianity Today* announced that he had come to be 'the Aquinas, the Augustine, and the Aesop of contemporary evangelicalism', a list suggestive of deep alphabetical reserves of praise to come. Recent polls of American Christians apparently reveal that *Mere Christianity* (a re-worked selection of short talks he gave on the BBC during the Second World War) 'is regularly cited as the most influential religious book of the twentieth century'. Quite why the recycled wartime spiritual pep talks of a lapsed Church of Ireland Ulsterman turned myth-cultivating Oxford don should, over fifty years later, now be a best-seller among born-again American Evangelicals constitutes a pretty little question for cultural history.

Partly because Lewis was an inveterate if selective autobiographer, and partly because there have been several previous biographies of him, the outlines of his life are assumed to be fairly well known. Since both his scholarly and popular writings are often taken to exemplify a stereotypical Englishness, it is important to remember that he was originally not English, or at least that his adopted identity grew out of the 'more British than thou' soil of Ulster Protestantism. Lewis (known to family and friends as 'Jack') grew up in Belfast and was schooled partly in Northern Ireland, partly in England. He retained his early attachment to the Ulster countryside, always his preferred holiday location, and he is reported to have remarked that 'Heaven is Oxford lifted and placed in the middle of County Down' (thus uniting three places each of which may be thought to have its own kind of dodgy reputation). His mother died when Lewis was 10, confining him to an emotionally strained and distant relationship with his father, a Belfast solicitor who was a pillar of his local congregation, and encouraging an unbreakably strong bond with his elder brother, Warren ('Warnie'). He mostly hated his schooldays in England, but flourished under the supervision of an eccentric private coach, sufficiently so to gain a place at Oxford. For a healthy British male, November 1916 was not the best moment to have one's eighteenth birthday, universal conscription having been introduced earlier that year and the Battle of the Somme having just come to its murderous end. By spending a term at Oxford in the Officers' Training Corps Lewis qualified to get a commission in the army, thus increasing his chances of being killed (the mortality rate was highest of all among junior officers). He was sent to France in November 1917, then invalided home with a shell wound in May 1918. His undergraduate career began in earnest in January 1919.

During his training, Lewis had developed a close friendship with another fresh-faced future subaltern, Paddy Moore, and his relationship with Paddy's mother, Jane Moore, was to be arguably the most important relationship in his life. She had separated from her husband in Ireland and had recently moved to Oxford (accompanied by her 12-year-old daughter) to be close to her son. When they met in 1917, Lewis was a young 18, she a handsome 45. They formed a close attachment whose exact character remains a matter of speculation, but it was a relationship that was only intensified by Paddy's death in action in 1918. Mrs Moore began to take lodgings wherever Lewis was convalescing, following him around the country, and when he returned to Oxford to resume his studies, he partly lived in the house that Mrs Moore rented in Headington, explaining, when necessary, that she was his landlady. Having distinguished himself with a First in 'Greats' in 1922, Lewis then took the still newish honours school of English Language and Literature the following year, gaining another First. After minor setbacks and a year or two of hand-to-mouth existence (always accompanied by Mrs Moore), in 1925 he landed a tutorial fellowship in English at Magdalen College, and this became his base and home-from-home for the next twenty-nine years.

Publicly, Lewis lived the life of a bachelor don, but he combined this with a limited form of settled domesticity with Jane Moore and her daughter. From 1932 onwards, Lewis, Warnie, and an increasingly fractious Mrs Moore shared a house in Headington, though Lewis retained his rooms in college. Warnie had taken early retirement from his military career, probably because he was already on the way to the alcoholism for which he later received repeated treatment. Despite their obvious differences, the brothers remained remarkably close, Warnie often sitting in Lewis's inner room at Magdalen, typing some of his brother's work or correspondence, while Lewis gave a tutorial in the outer room.

Quite what the nature of Lewis's relationship was with Mrs Moore has become one of the cruces of a growing body of biographical studies. In his stylish Life published in 1990, A. N. Wilson declared: 'That he fell in love with Mrs Moore and she with him . . . cannot be in doubt', adding, 'while nothing will ever be proved on either side, the burden of proof is on those who believe that Lewis and Mrs Moore were *not* lovers—probably from the summer of 1918 onwards'. Well, maybe, but the direct evidence appears to be inconclusive. There was clearly a lot of arrested emotional development in the young Lewis, even by the standards of his time and class, and there are hints of an early interest in sado-masochistic pleasures (to one friend he confessed his flagellant fantasies, signing himself 'Philomastix', i.e. 'lover of the whip'). He also seems to have needed and wanted a substitute mother, a role Jane Moore certainly played. In the early phase he wrote to her every day, even though he was visiting her most afternoons (she later burned his letters). Whatever the inner emotional character of their relationship, it lasted in some form until her death in 1951. Latterly, she had become even more demanding and difficult and in her last years had been in poor physical and mental health. Through all her ailments, real or imagined, Lewis had cared for her (and walked her dogs, one of her obsessions); when she had to spend the last seven months of her life in a nursing home, increasingly demented, Lewis visited her very day. She had not been a particularly intellectual woman, nor, according to some witnesses, a particularly nice one. Whether Lewis mostly worshipped her or mostly suffered her, or both or neither, we don't really know. He began by needing her and ended by looking after her; perhaps it was not such an unusual relationship.

In 1926 Lewis began a friendship that was to have a formative influence of a different kind on his life, especially his imaginative life. J. R. R. Tolkien was six years older and already the Professor of Anglo-Saxon at Oxford. He and Lewis shared interests in Norse mythology, 'Old English' literature, religion (Tolkien was a devout Catholic, Lewis at this point a self-described agnostic), fantasy, and beer. Tolkien played some part in Lewis's rediscovery of his Christian faith at the beginning of the 1930s, though he was disappointed that his friend stopped at the half-way house of Anglicanism (insofar as Lewis adopted any fixed denominational identity). These two became the centre of a small group of (male) friends in Oxford with similar tastes, later known as 'the Inklings', who met regularly in a pub or in college rooms to talk and sometimes to read and discuss drafts of work in progress. The leading members of the group, which included the Anglican writer Charles Williams during the years of the Second World War, also seem to have shared a form of conservatism that was more cultural than political (and was the more conservative for seeing itself as apolitical, albeit with Tory anarchist leanings). Tolkien and Lewis encouraged each other in their forays into the genres of fantasy and children's writing, though the relationship could become strained, especially over Lewis's domestic arrangements. The enormous later celebrity of the two principal members of this group has led to some mythologizing of the intellectual character of their regular meetings; in reality the atmosphere seems to have been marked more by a kind of learned heartiness, summarized as 'beer and Beowulf'.

Perhaps because of the success of his popular writings, Lewis was not held in universally high regard in Oxford and was twice passed over for a professorship. In 1954 Cambridge created a new chair in Medieval and Renaissance English, and Lewis seems to have been widely regarded as the obvious first holder. After a brief episode of comedy in which he turned down the offer for laughably inadequate reasons (he feared that moving to Cambridge would mean losing his Headington gardener and handyman), he was appointed from October 1954 and began a routine of spending week-nights during term in his rooms in Magdalene and otherwise maintaining his established ménage in Headington.

All seemed set for a personally quiet final phase to his career, a prospect that was disrupted by what is probably now the most famous episode of Lewis's life, especially as represented, and perhaps somewhat travestied, in Richard Attenborough's 1993 film *Shadowlands*. In 1952 Lewis met and developed some form of relationship with (was single-mindedly pursued by?) a noisy, unhappily married, not very successful, American freelance writer sixteen years his junior. In 1955 Joy Davidman and the sons from her now-ended marriage moved into a house in Headington, not far from Lewis's. He seems to have supported her financially, and then in 1956 in a civil ceremony he married her, perhaps principally in order to allow her to remain and work in Britain. Months later, she was diagnosed with advanced cancer. Faced with her imminent death, Lewis went to some lengths to find a clergyman willing to conduct a Christian marriage, a ceremony that took place in Joy's hospital room. But then she made an unexpected recovery and lived for a further three years, during which time Lewis, according to his own later account in *A Grief*

Observed (1961), truly fell in love with her. Characteristically, he put the experience to the service of Christian apologetics, pondering yet again the place of pain and suffering in the world. The emotionally needy Lewis had always constructed settled forms of life for himself with people whose appeal was, shall we say, not obvious to outsiders—with Warnie the bluff alcoholic; Jane the demanding drama-queen; Joy the over-assertive gold-digger. But in these matters outsiders are just that; the inference from Lewis's behaviour must be that these three individuals helped him to know certain kinds of happiness, however inscrutable their contribution must remain. Lewis died on 22 November 1963, at about the time John F. Kennedy's motorcade began to leave the airport in Dallas.

Alister McGrath provides an accessible account of the life without aspiring to detailed comprehensiveness; his book is a sympathetic, readable portrait that concentrates primarily on the Christian apologetics. He maintains an amiable, slightly didactic tone, reminiscent of the evening-class lecturer conscious that his audience want the pleasures of feeling they have been stretched without actually having to absorb anything too taxing. At one point he, rather surprisingly, announces that his book is 'not a work of synopsis, but of analysis', and that he aims 'to explain, not simply why Lewis became such a figure of authority and influence, but why he remains so today'. Even granting him his terms (though Lewis is now surely a figure of 'authority' only in the most metaphorical sense, and then only for those of a particular religious inclination), answering these questions would require forms of historical and sociological analysis that McGrath stays well away from.

Lewis's life has already been documented with unusual fullness. There are several biographies, scores of studies of his work, and a massive (almost 4,000-page) edition of his letters, completed in 2006, not to mention the constantly autobiographical (or ostensibly autobiographical) and confessional nature of Lewis's own writings. Yet, faced with his prolific and disparate output, it is still not easy to put the pieces together or to arrive at a clear-eyed view of his achievements, and reading some of his work alongside McGrath's biography (together with his companion volume of essays on various aspects of his subject's thought) only increases one's feeling that Lewis could be both impressive and irritating—at times a witty and powerful writer, but at times seeming to use surface depths to mask deeper shallows.

By the late 1930s, Lewis was a well-regarded scholar and teacher, but not any kind of public figure. Wider fame came suddenly and unexpectedly. In the early months of the war he wrote his first piece of popular apologetics, a little book simply called *The Problem of Pain*. The informal clarity of its plain-man's answer to the traditional theodicy problem struck a popular chord. There was evidently a hunger for such consolation, one the BBC felt impelled to try to assuage. The war years marked the peak of radio's influence, and producers were conscious of the need to use their monopolistic power with impartiality, especially on such a sensitive subject as religion. Lewis seemed appealing as a possible speaker precisely because he was a layman who could speak to other laymen without being too closely identified with one particular denomination. Beginning in August 1941, his series of talks making an informal and personal case for Christian belief were a huge success: it became common to refer to him as 'the voice of faith' for the nation, alongside other broadcasters labelled as 'the voice of gardening' and so on. Between 1941 and 1944 he gave four series of talks, the texts of which were finally brought together, in only lightly revised form, as *Mere Christianity* in 1952.

His radio talks alone brought Lewis a kind of national celebrity. The publication in 1942 of *The Screwtape Letters* brought him international fame. Initially published as weekly articles, these ruminations on the everyday sources of spiritual experience were archly disguised as the advice of a senior Devil to his nephew, Wormwood, on how to prevent gullible humans from falling into faith. This slight book was an immediate publishing phenomenon, selling over a million copies and being translated into fifteen languages. It enjoyed particular success in the United States, the beginning of Lewis's cultish following in that country. McGrath tells us that the first Ph.D. thesis written about Lewis's work was completed as early as 1948 at the Northern Baptist Theological Seminary in Chicago. However, McGrath also reports that some fundamentalists in the United States now regard Lewis as a dangerous heretic, with one website declaring: 'C. S. Lewis was an impostor, who corrupted the Gospel of Jesus Christ, and led multitudes of victims into Hellfire with his doctrines of devils. Lewis used profanities, told lewd stories, and frequently got drunk with his students.' Which just shows that you can't be too careful, whether mildly experimenting with literary forms or offering students the odd tutorial sherry.

In Britain, the arc of Lewis's reputation seems to be clearly linked to the revival of Christianity, both among intellectuals and more widely, in the 1940s and early 1950s. When William Empson returned to Britain in 1953 after having spent his teaching career up to that point in the Far East, he professed to be shocked by the predominance of 'neo-Christian' perspectives in the teaching of English literature. It is easy to dismiss this observation as an example of that higher persiflage with which the belligerently agnostic Empson liked to pepper his contemporaries, but there was some historical basis to it. When one looks, to take a relevant illustration, at the board which elected Lewis to the Cambridge chair, one sees, in addition to his old friends Tolkien and Stanley Bennett, such leading Christians as Dom David Knowles, Benedictine monk and ecclesiastical historian, and Basil Willey, lifelong Methodist and member of the literary panel for the translation of the *New English Bible*. Perhaps it's small wonder that the electors' second choice, to whom they offered the chair during Lewis's initial dithering, was that devout Anglican Helen Gardner. Empson could make his case sound crankily paranoid, but he wasn't altogether imagining things. As in the wider culture, such literary Christianity fell sharply out of fashion in the 1960s and 1970s, and Lewis's reputation dipped correspondingly, though it may be that his children's books maintained their standing in these decades better than his apologetics. Once again, his reputation in the USA (which he never visited; but then he never went anywhere) took a distinctive form and seems to have benefited from his association with Tolkien, a commercial success there on a quite other scale.

Lewis's religious identity is what most interests McGrath (and a lot of other people, it must be said). Brought up in the respectabilities of Ulster Protestantism, Lewis became an agnostic for a decade or so from his student years, and then, at the beginning of the 1930s, underwent a celebrated conversion. But conversion to what, exactly? To some kind of theism in the first instance, it seems, and only subsequently to Christianity. He began to attend Church of England services, and gave that as his denominational identity when required, but the distinctiveness of his religious position, such as it seems to have been, lay in his endorsement of what he called 'mere Christianity'. That's to say, Lewis came to think that the basic mythical or quasi-historical story shared by all forms of Christianity was true and that the spiritual experience to which an individual was awakened by belief in this story was more important than all the matters which divided one denomination from another. Lewis skilfully represented himself as the Christian-in-the-street: not overly churchy; not preoccupied with the finer points of theology (though as a medievalist he was in fact deeply learned about such matters); but a suffering soul with a personal relation to God.

One reason why Lewis was an apologist of genius was his capacity to persuade readers that the wisdom and humanity of his views came from looking deep into himself and not flinching from what he found. In his most popular writings he was a cracker-barrel theologian, a purveyor of religious wise saws, a pedlar of spiritual quack-medicine—and hugely successful as a result. There is often a dash of Chesterton about these apologetic writings—that use of the natty phrase to jolly the reader into following him into an unjustified logical conclusion. However much latitude we grant Lewis on account of the diversity of his talents and the heterogeneity of the genres he cultivated, the truth is that he could be a kind of ideologue. The shallowness of the 'modern world' was relentlessly denounced (though in truth his experience of that world was, it would seem, strictly circumscribed); all secular beliefs were, ultimately, inadequate or false; the truth of Christianity was, plainly, inescapable. When writing in this mode, Lewis can come across as one of those highly intelligent people who are willing to encourage the embrace by others of not very intelligent views when it suits their argumentative purposes.

Part of what gave Lewis's essays and popular spiritual writings their appeal was that he appeared to write with the authority of the man who has shared, still shares, the common human failings and perplexities, but who is able to draw a helpful moral from the experience. He is the constant autobiographer in part because he does seem to find his own inner life so interesting. It is one mark of a bore, of course, to presume that what he finds interesting will be interesting, at length, to others, but Lewis has a lighter, wittier touch than that. More damaging is the unrelenting, if sometimes covert, didacticism. This may be inseparable from the genre of apologetic writing (and possibly from certain kinds of writing for children, too), but it can make Lewis seem bullyingly middlebrow—which, at his best, and above all at his scholarly best, he certainly is not. This suggests an obvious comparison with Priestley, another figure who had great success as a wartime broadcaster. Unalike in so many ways, they both managed to communicate a deep reassuringness, a feeling that the travails of common experience were familiar to them yet also ultimately surmountable—a message, or tone, that found an especially responsive audience during wartime. Priestley cultivated the middlebrow identity with polemical gusto, an identity that sat more easily with being a Bradford lad than an Oxford don. But Jack Priestley and 'Jack' Lewis both excelled at using an informal conversational tone in print and on air, and both succeeded in inducing just enough reflectiveness in their readers and listeners to enrich their lives without threatening to change them.

Several of Lewis's scholarly books still matter to the kind of reader to whom such writing matters, but the two on which his reputation largely rested in his lifetime were *The Allegory of Love* (1936) and *English Literature in the Sixteenth Century* (1954). The first of these focused on the tradition of 'courtly love', culminating in an extended discussion of Spenser's *Faerie Queene*, while the second, commissioned as a volume in the old Oxford History of English Literature, offered much detailed scholarship on lesser works to support Lewis's central denial of a sharp break between the Middle Ages and the Renaissance. His Oxford colleague Helen Gardner wrote of *The Allegory of Love*: 'Lewis recovered for the ordinary reader what had been lost for centuries, the power to read allegory and to respond to the allegorical mode of thinking. He was able to do this because he was a born allegorist himself.... He was, besides, a moralist to the depths of his being, and was deeply moved by allegory's power to embody moral concepts and illuminate moral experience.' Allegory—the representation of abstract ideas or principles by characters, figures, or events in narrative, dramatic, or pictorial form—constantly threatens to become a didactic mode involving a potentially patronizing relation to the readership or audience deemed to be in need of such help. Lewis's habitual allegorizing marks an interesting point of contrast with Tolkien, who sharply rejected any suggestion that *The Lord of the Rings* was an allegory about contemporary political conflicts, adding (in a much-quoted passage from the preface to the second edition of *The Fellowship of the Ring*): 'I cordially dislike allegory in all its manifestations, and always have done so since I grew old and wary enough to detect its presence.'

For all the elegance of Lewis's scholarly writing, a kind of ideological agenda makes its presence felt there, too. He was hostile to stories of 'progress', hostile to anything that seemed to represent a cultural fashion, hostile (more stereotypical Englishness here) to 'intellectuals'. As his erstwhile colleague George Watson observed: 'The chief purpose of his critical writings, in a negative sense, was the discrediting of sixteenth-century Humanism and twentieth-century Modernism, both of which he saw as dry, starved and stultifying.' It says something about Lewis's imaginative powers as well as about a curious limitation in his tastes that though he worked on English literature at the high points of its involvement with the cultures of southern Europe, he never visited either France (war service aside) or Italy. 'Northernness' is what moved him, not the Mediterranean; and anyway, his annual holiday always involved a return to the Ulster hills he had known in his youth. He seems to have had an almost Larkinesque aversion to 'abroad'.

It is noticeable that recent scholarly discussion of the part played by literary critics in public debate in Britain in the middle decades of the twentieth century focuses on such figures as T. S. Eliot or F. R. Leavis or Raymond Williams, usually without mentioning Lewis at all. This may seem surprising, given the scale of his popular success, but two features of his work help to explain his omission. First, he wrote practically nothing that directly addressed current cultural and political issues. He deliberately estranged himself from many of the concerns of the society around him, retreating into the worlds of his imagination, much of the time not even reading a newspaper (as a result, McGrath notes, 'even his friends sometimes found him worryingly ignorant of current affairs'). Second, his popular writing was not presented as any kind of self-conscious application of literary-critical methods to other kinds of material. In fact, Lewis rather scorned the vogue for 'criticism': he saw himself as a literary scholar, deeply learned in the writing and thought-worlds of earlier periods, not as any kind of textual technician or substitute therapist. As he put it in a revealing letter to Priestley late in his life, he had been disappointed by the way in which the discipline of 'Eng Lit' had developed in recent decades: 'My hope was that it would be primarily a historical study that would lift people out of (so to speak) their chronological provincialism by plunging them into the thought and feeling of ages other than their own.' In his Cambridge inaugural he presented himself as a dinosaur, 'Old Western Man', a messenger from the culture of the two millennia before industrialism, a culture he saw as rapidly becoming not just unfamiliar but unintelligible to a younger generation. This could be seen as an honourable role for a scholar, but as a job-description it fell some way short of offering, as some other contemporary critics appeared to offer, to solve the problems of the modern world.

Lewis was a university teacher his entire adult life. More memorably successful as a lecturer than a tutor, he nonetheless won the hearts of a number of his abler pupils. The huge three-volume edition of his letters contains a good deal of dross, but every so often there is a letter that allows us to catch a glimpse of his tutorial manner. For example, in 1941 an 18-year-old schoolboy who had just been admitted to read English at Magdalen wrote to Lewis, his future tutor, to ask for advice on what to read before starting his course (which was anyway likely to be interrupted or truncated because of war service). The kindly response he received included the following paragraph:

> Chaucer, Shakespeare, Milton are certainties whatever shortened course or ordinary course you take. Next to these in importance come Malory, Spenser, Donne, Dryden, Pope, Swift, Johnson, Wordsworth. After that it becomes more a matter of taste. The great thing is to be always reading but not to get bored—treat it not like work, more as a vice! Your book bill ought to be your biggest extravagance.

Lewis's lists, and his confidence in them, reflect not just his own tastes but the traditions of early 'Eng Lit' as they had grown out of the literary culture of the later nineteenth century (though Malory's prominence may have reflected Lewis's medievalist priorities and perhaps not everyone would have included Swift in this company). Essentially, the subject meant the line of poets (and poet-dramatists) from Chaucer to Wordsworth: the complete absence of novelists may seem surprising to modern readers, but Lewis had imbibed the view of an older educated class that novels were things a gentleman could read in his spare time. In addition, he was rather scornful of secondary critical works, and this list—like his weekly tutorial directives, apparently—was devoid of reference to such studies. As guidance to an earnest sixth-former, the whole reply may now seem quaintly anachronistic, and yet, for all its man-to-man downrightness, the reply surely gave the future undergraduate an invaluable steer: 'treat it not like work, more as a vice.' This is the literature teacher as drug-pusher, slyly nudging the student to lifelong addiction. And in this case it worked: the student in question, Derek Brewer, became one of the leading medievalists of the next generation.

At the same time, Lewis's manner could so often cheapen a good point by overdoing the counter-suggestible down-to-earthness. For example, though he may engage the reader's sympathies by some of his comments (in an essay about teaching) on the degree of intellectual autonomy that university students need to be allowed if anything deserving the name of 'education' is to happen, he then squanders that sympathy when he concludes his argument in terms reminiscent of a hearty country squire giving his son a manly talking-to: 'In the great rough countryside which we throw open to you, you can choose your own path. Here's your gun, your spade, your fishing-tackle; go and get yourself a dinner.' Such tones almost succeed in making the leaden-footed categories of the modern bureaucratic 'teaching quality assurance' process seem an advance.

Witnesses concur that in person Lewis enjoyed arguing, but in his published prose he mainly seems to have enjoyed argument in the way that people who like winning enjoy argument. There was a Johnsonian strain in him that could make it difficult to distinguish downrightness from dogmatism. What might have been bracing in his scholarly writing could come across as mere harrumphing in his more popular writing. One judgement about Lewis likely to cause offence among his devotees is that voiced by his admirer and former pupil, John Wain, when he observed in 1964 that 'his writing improves as it gets further from the popular and demagogic'. That latter adjective may at first seem harsh and inexact, but there surely are moments in reading Lewis where it feels as though he wrote to please the crowd—wrote down, wrote beneath himself—and the effect can be cringe-making. By way of illustration, Wain quotes a passage from Lewis's popular little book on the psalms which laments the decay of moral standards in contemporary society compared to a time when sinners were ostracized:

> It may be asked whether that state of society in which rascality undergoes no social penalty is a healthy one; whether we should not be a happier country if certain important people were pariahs as the hangman once was—blackballed at every club, dropped by every acquaintance, and liable to the print of a riding-crop or fingers across the face if they were ever bold enough to speak to a respectable woman.

The image of a bullying squire striding the streets with his riding-crop to protect the purity of respectable women would be comic were the coercive moralism of the whole passage not so repugnant—and so collusive with the all-too familiar phenomenon of intolerance dressed up as nostalgia.

Perhaps it is to be expected that the Lewis who emerges from my (admittedly spotty) sampling is less impressive than his admirers claim and less shallow than his detractors allege. But I have to confess, putting all attempts at balanced portraiture aside, that there is something about him and his circle that gives me the screaming heebie-jeebies. Even at this distance I find their company narrowingly coercive, in the way certain unspoken yet rigid codes of respectability usually are (and are meant to be). I feel myself struggling for air, suffocated by the beery male bonhomie of the Inklings and by the mock-humility of Lewis's accounts of his spiritual experience.

And yet, even as I run from the atmosphere of arrested development and conservative prejudice, I trip over a scattering of the kind of elegant, learned, perceptive sentences that he was capable of writing, and I am abashed—abashed at the too-ready deployment of my own prejudices, abashed that I was ever tempted to condescend to a mind that could be so subtle when it wasn't intent on parading its blunt scorn for all self-conscious forms of subtlety. And I have to remind myself that it is not altogether Lewis's fault that he has become the poster-boy of Evangelical Christianity (albeit these admirers probably fantasize his looking more like Anthony Hopkins than the ruddy-faced Farmer Giles whom he actually more resembled). More generally, Lewis's disciples may not be his best advocates: Lewis-and-water is a mass-produced characterless drink that lacks the pungent tang of the Ulster-plus-the-Classics original. Reading bits of Lewis alongside this enthusiastic but somewhat bland biography, I am reminded how much unhappiness and denial of unhappiness went into the too-bonhomous social style and the too-genial writing voice. I am not sufficiently drawn to his work to want to try to construct a more penetrating account in any detail, but even I do not want to see him diminished by shallow praise, so I cede the last word to Tolkien, who wrote to a mutual friend less than a year after Lewis's death when misleading or simplifying accounts of him were already beginning to appear: 'I wish it could be forbidden that after a great man is dead, little men should scribble over him, who have not and must know they have not sufficient knowledge of his life and character to give them any key to the truth.'

III

What is the best case that can be made for Maurice Bowra? In his day, and it was a long day, he was the most celebrated don in Oxford, and therefore in England. Born in 1898 (the same year as Lewis and four years after Priestley), he became a Fellow of Wadham in 1922; he was elected its Warden in 1938, holding that office, astonishingly, until 1970; he died a year later. He wrote or edited some thirty books, mostly semi-scholarly, semi-popular expositions of the imperishable qualities of the ancient Greeks, though also studies of, and translations from, modern European poetry. But, as his friend Isaiah Berlin later wrote, 'those who knew him solely through his published works can have no inkling of his genius'.

What Bowra did best was talk. 'I hear you are the funniest man in the world,' was the opening gambit of one visiting politician, who, predictably, was rudely snubbed. All accounts of Bowra emphasize his wit: quick, sharp, sometimes riotously inventive, often savagely satirical, much of it (to judge by quoted specimens) exhibiting a rather Wildean posiness. But the talk could also be serious, learned, and cultivated as well as incisive, frank, and shocking (he liked to shock). Accounts by admirers, of whom there were many, stress his role in 'liberating' them. Once installed in Oxford, Bowra applied his formidable force of personality to liberating young English men from the conventionality, philistinism, and moralism of their backgrounds. This involved a good deal of talk about the Greeks, about European literature, and about sex.

Bowra was widely renowned for his talk, which was not at all the same thing as being noted, as some suaver operators often used to be (still are?), as 'a good conversationalist'. Bowra talked *at* you; if, unwisely, you tried to interrupt, he talked over you. His preferred goal was intellectual seduction; that failing or being out of the question, he talked for victory; in cases where that might seem altogether too benign, he pressed on to annihilation. When he was at the top of his game, as he often was in the 1920s and 1930s, it could be, the admiring accounts concur, thrilling, heady stuff. And it was not as though the inner circle of his admirers was composed of woodenly talentless dummies: Berlin, John Betjeman, Kenneth Clark, John Sparrow, as well as, a little later, Noel Annan and Stuart Hampshire—all capable of the odd spot of talking themselves. But they acknowledged Bowra as their master, which was fortunate since no other terms were on offer.

With the young, Bowra's preferred pedagogical resource was the select dinner party. The chosen young men were not so much being instructed in a 'subject' as inducted into a civilization. The Greeks had taught us how to live: it was an aristocratic code, one requiring a lot of leisure (there were servants to do the messy bits); and it expressed a stoic view of life, meeting the arbitrary cruelties of existence without flinching. Above all, it was a civilization that accorded pre-eminence to poetry, the perfect fusion of form and meaning. Bowra cared passionately about poetry and he led others to care, too. His best writing was invariably about poetry, ancient and modern, and some of the leading poets of the age seem to have reciprocated his regard. Edith Sitwell, thought by some (including herself) to come into this category, hailed his *The Heritage of Symbolism*, published in 1943, as 'the most important work of criticism of our time'. There may have been few others, especially among professional literary critics, who would have concurred with this judgement: even by the 1930s his belletristic appreciation was beginning to seem old-fashioned and amateurish. But several of his books, including *Sophoclean Tragedy* (1944) and, especially, *The Greek Experience* (1957), met a need in communicating some of the flavour of Greek literature to an increasingly Greekless readership.

Yet even as one is trying to make out the best case for Bowra, he has a way of emerging as a complete monster. It was already clear while he was an undergraduate, as Leslie Mitchell acknowledges in this stylish, indulgent biography, that 'Bowra's company was not for the squeamish'. He 'aimed to be the arbiter of everything that was said and done' in his circle. It was emphatically *his* circle: he recruited to it, and he excommunicated. Only those who bent the knee could be admitted, and he was implacable in dealing with those who crossed him. As Mitchell neutrally observes: 'To Bowra, these contests of will were of supreme importance.' He aimed to dominate any gathering he attended. 'Maurice entered a room "like a naval vessel", with all the guns run out', or, perhaps more tellingly still, a character in an Elizabeth

Bowen novel who is partly based on him is said, when entering a room, to be always 'delighted to see himself'. He spoke with a booming voice, which got louder as he got deafer; 'he really ought to be fitted with a silencer', winced one friend.

Mitchell spends some time denying that Bowra was a snob, but there is a good deal of incidental evidence for the prosecution to hand in this biography. Though officially the champion of intelligence over status, Bowra proved quite susceptible to titles, including for himself, and he loved to shine in the salons of famous hostesses such as Margot Asquith and Ottoline Morrell. 'Part of the fun of life was "to cause pain" to enemies,' Mitchell records; cattiness about the dull and untalented was de rigueur. A rival elected by another college was denounced as a man 'of no public virtues and no private parts' (you see what I mean about the Wildean inheritance). In his day heads of colleges could exercise largely unconstrained powers over undergraduate admissions, and Bowra's hierarchy of preferences was said to be 'clever boys, interesting boys, pretty boys—no shits'. When it came to university business, especially anything to do with elections and appointments, Bowra schemed and bullied mercilessly to get his own way: 'integrity was an empty concept to him,' recalled Berlin. Yet this cannot be the whole story for, as Mitchell reports, Bowra was a capable administrator and an admired, if intimidatingly brisk, chairman, qualities that earned him spells as Vice-Chancellor of Oxford and President of the British Academy.

Admirably cosmopolitan in his literary tastes, Bowra was extraordinarily parochial in his sphere of operations. Oxford was what mattered, and what mattered went on in Oxford; this focus may (and, from another perspective, may not) have served him well during his apparently successful stint as Vice-Chancellor of the university in the early 1950s. Apart from writing his accessible books about the ancient world, his energies were not directed to reaching out beyond the walls. He was in some respects the protégé of Gilbert Murray, whom he hoped (and failed) to succeed in the Chair of Greek in 1936, but he played none of his mentor's public and political roles. He was an occasional signatory of letters to *The Times*, but he never set himself up as a commentator on contemporary society and politics. He lived through what some have seen as the golden age of media opportunities for well-connected Oxford dons, but he mostly didn't write for newspapers and periodicals and he wholly eschewed appearances on radio or, later, television. Bowra remained the kind of scholar-aesthete whose heyday fell between the 1890s and the 1920s: cultivation was his forte. Inevitably, this involved a taste for Mediterranean life, but, that apart, most of what interested him in the present took place within a few hundred yards of the Warden's Lodgings.

In the 1920s, one might have been forgiven for thinking that Bowra had elements of a minor English Nietzsche in him. He represented an antique paganism, at once austere and hedonistic: conventional morality was dismissed with a contemptuous wave of the hand, to be replaced by a strenuous ethic of intellectual rigour, aesthetic responsiveness, and unswerving loyalty to one's friends. Vitality was to be cherished: all forms of deadness were to be shunned, including social conformity, dreary scholarship, and most aspects of public life. Any attempt to make writing about literature impersonal was a mistake (no other kind of writing seemed to matter much). The most prized literary genre was the epigram. There was even the hint of a Nietzschean scheme of history: the human spirit had soared in ancient Greece, but had then pretty much gone underground for over two millennia, only starting to resurface in the 1880s with Symbolist poetry. However, such a comparison soon turns into another of those attempts to make a good case for Bowra which end up instead drawing attention to how far short of these heights he actually fell.

Perhaps surprisingly, Bowra's own writing (at least, such of it as I have read over the past few weeks) neither scintillates nor rhapsodizes: it is clear, serviceable prose which, while not parading its author's considerable learning, devotes itself to enlightening an educated but non-specialist readership about the matter in hand. This is a perennially important task, but fulfilling it did not place Bowra at the cutting edge of his discipline, which was tending to become either more minute in its focus or more analytical and sociological in its approach. He did, it is true, value exact scholarship, and he was not slow to point to inexactness in the scholarship of others; but he saw his business as the shaping of the whole human being, not the manufacture of pedants. Mitchell reports a revealing episode when T. W. Adorno, having met Bowra in Oxford in the mid-1930s and been impressed by his talk ('one of the most intellectual and cultivated men I know'), invited him to contribute an article to the *Zeitschrift für Sozialforschung* which Max Horkheimer was by this date editing from New York. Alas, when the article duly arrived it was found to be inadequate: 'It is much too general and has only the tone of good journalism,' Adorno told Horkheimer, and it failed to relate its material 'to the underlying social reality'. (In the end, a revised version of Bowra's article was accepted, so he became one of the less likely names to have appeared in the house journal of Frankfurt-school social theory.) It was not only exigent German social critics who found Bowra's belletrist approach wanting. Mitchell writes, with palpable sympathy, that 'in his academic studies Bowra suffered the inconvenience of becoming old-fashioned', but the situation was worse than this suggests. From the outset of his career, Bowra wrote in a manner that had more in common with the critical essays of Edwardian men of letters than with the *Quellenkritik* of the leading European classical scholars, though in this respect he may not have been unique among British classicists of his time.

His tastes in contemporary literature had at first made him seem far more up-to-the-minute as a critic, promoting the claims of Eliot, Joyce, and company in the 1920s, but his cultural pessimism soon came damagingly to the fore here, too, as he insisted (dropping into the local examining argot) that there had subsequently been no new 'first-class' names in literature. In most respects, he found the 1930s a sad come-down from the 1920s, and the post-war world was even less to his taste; the 1960s, though they were full of the 'liberation' he was supposed to favour, were simply unspeakable. In writing his memoirs, he defiantly stopped at 1939: nothing of importance had happened since, he liked to maintain—partly to annoy the *bien-pensants*, but chiefly because that expressed a truth about his own inner life. His exclusive devotion to the masterpieces of past literature earned him the soubriquet 'Big Stuff Bowra'; in the last decade of his Wardenship, the undergraduates referred to him as 'Old Tragic'.

It is notoriously difficult to recapture good talk, and Bowra's reputation during his lifetime now seems far in excess of his achievements. Mitchell, a retired Oxford history tutor, makes a spirited effort to bring 'Maurice' back to life: he draws a perceptive and sympathetic portrait, one which allows us to hear distant echoes of the voice and to persuade ourselves that we now have some inkling of his power and his charm. Mitchell has been enormously diligent in tracking down correspondence by, to, or about Bowra, and whole swathes of the book consist in snippets from these letters sewn together with minimal commentary. If you are fascinated by what Isaiah wrote about what John thought about what K felt about what Maurice said, then you will find this book deeply rewarding. There is very little analysis of the wider context of Bowra's activities, and practically nothing on the social and cultural forces that made possible Oxford's enormous sense of its own importance throughout his lifetime. The life of a minor classicist, however amusing, who had spent his entire career at, say, Leicester or Hull would never have attracted the quantity of published commentary that has been devoted to Bowra. Come to that, such a figure would surely not have been knighted at the relatively early age of 53 (just before his stint as Vice-Chancellor) or made a Companion of Honour the year before his death. Bowra rode the Oxford chariot across English society with imperious confidence, and that society duly accorded him its plaudits and its prizes.

One would, presumably, need to be quite engaged by the minutiae of Oxford life, and quite drawn to a certain kind of donnish performance, to undertake the biography of such a figure in the first place, but just occasionally Mitchell does seem culpably complicit with the idiom. Just how complicit (and how culpable) is suggested by the following passage about Bowra's election as Warden:

> On the day of Bowra's election, the omens were not propitious. During a thunderstorm, one of the Fellow's wives retired to a gardener's shed and committed suicide with the assistance of 'a large saw'. Someone as knowledgeable about the Greek world as Bowra might have found the episode daunting. Instead, he thought the coincidence of all these events mildly comic and dined out on retailing them. In fact, his insouciance in the face of sinister events was fully

> justified. Bowra would be Warden for thirty-two years. It would be one of the most talked-about reigns in Oxford's history.

It's hard to know where to start. The suggestion that there was one Fellow with many wives may just be a printer's slip, but the non-sequiturs are more substantial. And then there is the faux-scholarship of the quoted phrase; a footnote attached to it tells us that the evidence for the size of the saw comes from Noel Annan's commonplace book, so at least we're on solid ground there, then. But it's surely the willed effort at comedy that is most chilling. No doubt Bowra did dine out on the story and no doubt toadies and others with similarly arrested development laughed—I say, Warden, jolly funny story about old Snooks's wife being so maddened by unhappiness that she killed herself in an almost unimaginably painful and bloody way. But would it be tiresomely moralistic to think that, if there is any truth in this silly, horrible story at all, then it involved savage extremes of human distress and self-destruction that surely need to be talked about in other ways?

'Bowra was allowed the licence that overwhelming personalities always command.' Mitchell's book does not question this truth, and more generally it allows its subject, and the Oxford of his time, a great deal of licence. But it is worth asking why people who behave appallingly but in a dominating and entertaining way should be allowed any licence at all. Why do we in effect make special rules for those egocentric individuals who always hold the floor, hold the opinions, hold the rest of the company hostage with their combination of wit and assertiveness? At this distance, the overwhelmingness of Bowra seems rather to compound than to reduce his dislikeableness, but that reaction clearly fails to register something to which a lot of people, including some extremely clever people, were susceptible, and which allowed the Bowra legend to grow. In 1954 Isaiah Berlin put to John Sparrow what sounds, even now, like an unnervingly frank question: 'How much are you prepared to pander, and for how long? I am, quite a lot; for quite a long time. But why? Affection? Habit? Gratitude? Can you answer?' They none of them could, it seems, beyond registering that Maurice was Maurice.

One of the saddest passages in this inadvertently sad book comes in another letter from Berlin to another long-time Bowra disciple celebrating the fact that 'the Old Boy' (a couple of years before his death) had *not* come to stay with the Berlins that summer:

> Every day this freedom, this marvellous freedom from the pathetic, oppressive, demanding, guilt-inducing, conversation-killing, embarrassing, gross, maddening, at once touching and violently repellent, paranoid, deaf, blind, thick-skinned, easily offended, presence is a source of relief and almost joy: how disloyal, how awful.

Even allowing for Berlin's pleasure in his own rhetorical excess, it's a pretty sobering indictment, coming not from a sworn enemy but from one of

Bowra's oldest and closest admirers. Like the outlines of a skull becoming clearer as the flesh falls away, Bowra in his late sixties, largely stripped of his winning qualities, revealed his essential structure in its dreadful starkness.

It would obviously be reductive to try to explain Bowra's social monstrousness entirely in terms of early trouble with girls, but it's tempting. He spent his first years in China, where his father worked in the Chinese Maritime Customs Service, rising to the top of that European-staffed organization as Chief Secretary (and thus becoming, though Mitchell can be forgiven for not remarking the connection, Perry Anderson's father's immediate superior). Sent back to England to boarding school, the child was starved of affection, and he built his defences early and strong. He was always conscious of being short, with hardly any neck; one observer saw him as Humpty-Dumpty, another compared him to 'one of Beatrix Potter's pigs'. The dazzling talk, as Nietzsche irreverently suggested about Socrates, may have developed partly as compensation for lack of conventional attractiveness. Mitchell has uncovered one or two early crushes on young women which may have been more than that, and later there were his sadly comic proposals to some of the few eligible women in his milieu. But, in best Greek fashion, he mainly reserved his attentions for young men, though his passion was rarely if ever requited, it seems. Buggery in Berlin in the early 1930s met some needs; he became more circumspect in Britain as he became more prominent. He never lived anywhere but in all-male institutions from the age of 12 till his death. The centre of a glittering circle, he may have lived a life of profound loneliness.

To the credit of both Bowra and Mitchell, we do get one or two peeks beneath the carapace. A year or so before his death, he acknowledged the thought that 'life would have been happier if I had known any girls in my youth'. Stuart Hampshire, who knew him well (and succeeded him as Warden), declared flatly that 'he was frightened of women'. A whole world of high-table maleness might be read into these and similar remarks about others of Bowra's generation. Most poignant of all, a fragment of an undated letter to Cyril Connolly, written late in life, finds Bowra lamenting that he had never known enough love: 'Life without it is a terrible, impoverished affair, and the older one gets, the worse it is. I find myself drying up, without lust or rage to sting me on.' Rage seems to have had a better airing than lust in Bowra's life, though it's hard to know. But this sobering admission stirs one's human sympathies and provokes uneasy thoughts about what might count as living a successful life. Did Bowra, returning to his college rooms after another evening spent shining and dominating, exult in his triumphs and look forward to the pleasures of the next day's combat? Did he take down a volume of Pindar or of Wilde and contentedly pass the closing minutes of the day in unfailingly congenial company? Or did he silently howl like a lone beast in a frozen forest, racked by the boundless immensity of his own solitude?

2

Modernists

Ezra Pound and T. S. Eliot

I

In the summer of 1908, a 23-year-old American who had recently been dismissed for 'immorality' half-way through his first year of teaching at a small college in the Midwest found himself, like many other cultured or indigent Americans before and since, in Venice. He had brought with him little money, a soaring literary ambition, and the manuscript of a collection of his poems. He arranged for an Italian printer to run off 150 copies of this little volume, entitled *A lume spento* ('With Tapers Quenched'), and he drew up a list of people to whom copies were to be sent. The first four names on the list were Hilda Doolittle, A. C. Swinburne, William Carlos Williams, and W. B. Yeats. Such confidence, or presumption, was already characteristic of this singular young man, and the four names neatly represented the main aspects of the identity he had chosen for himself.

Fired up with fantasies of becoming a latter-day Dante, Ezra Pound thought he had found his Beatrice in Miss Doolittle, and the couple had become engaged three years earlier, when she was 19. The engagement was soon broken off (she chafed at having the script of her life written for her, and anyway her well-connected family disapproved), but a poetic as much as emotional bond endured: as 'H.D.', Hilda was to be at the heart of Pound's later (and also short-lived) attempt to make *Imagisme* the fashionable poetic of the day in London. One of the poets the young couple read together with rapturous intensity was Swinburne, a late Victorian whose lush, honeyed verses mingled aestheticism and atheism in a way that still made him seem

A. David Moody, *Ezra Pound: Poet. A Portrait of the Man and his Work. I: The Young Genius 1885–1920* (Oxford University Press, 2007).
Valerie Eliot and Hugh Haughton (eds.), *The Letters of T. S. Eliot. Vol. 2: 1923–1925* (Faber, 2009).
Valerie Eliot and John Haffenden (eds.), *The Letters of T. S. Eliot. Vol. 3: 1926–1927* (Faber, 2012).

thrillingly modern to some Edwardian readers. Pound's own early poetic sensibility was largely formed in the afterglow of Nineties' decadence; Ernest Dowson, for instance, commanded more respect than the would-be poetic revolutionary showed to most of those he chose to regard as relevant predecessors, and Swinburne was the still-living representative of this inheritance (he was to die the following year). William Carlos Williams had been a fellow-student at the University of Pennsylvania, where Pound, reacting violently against the aridity of the Germanic philology that dominated the study of literature, had pursued an idiosyncratic route through Latin and early Romance-language poetry, before abandoning a projected doctoral dissertation. Williams had been one of the few who got to know the eccentric Pound and took him seriously as a poet—a rival poet, it soon turned out, as Williams, less precocious and flamboyant than his younger friend, doggedly cultivated his own distinctive combination of the experimental and the everyday. But in some ways the recipient of the little collection of poems who mattered most to Pound was Yeats. When at the end of that 1908 summer Pound moved to London, one of his chief ambitions was to meet and learn from the man he described, with characteristic hyperbole, as 'the only poet worthy of serious study'.

His larger ambition was to conquer literary London, a task he set about with his typical energy and lack of social inhibition. He immediately placed poems in the *Evening Standard* and *St James's Gazette*; he began negotiations for the printing of a second collection, *A Quinzaine for this Yule*; he got himself invited to dinner at the Poets' Club, and shamelessly buttonholed writers at every opportunity. By June 1909 he had already made enough of a splash by his writing and his social activities to be granted the accolade of a lampoon in *Punch*. And two months earlier Pound had achieved the goal that mattered to him above all others: he had met Yeats. The older poet was welcoming, and the relationship between the two men developed to the point where from 1913 onwards they spent part of three winters closeted together in a cottage in Sussex, with Pound notionally fulfilling some secretarial duties, but with the real business being the writing and discussion of poetry.

The manner of the arrival in England in August 1914 of another American college graduate with poetic aspirations might have seemed, at first sight, to augur less well for literary success than Pound's confident assault. T. S. Eliot, having completed his course-work for a Harvard Ph.D., was committed to writing his dissertation on the philosophy of F. H. Bradley, but although he had come to England ostensibly to pursue his philosophical studies, and although he spent much of 1914–15 in Oxford where Bradley was a resident Fellow of Merton, the socially unconfident Eliot never attempted to invade the privacy of the notoriously reclusive philosopher. Indeed, it is not clear how well Eliot would have made his way in the London literary world (his real ambition, even if one not yet fully disclosed to his parents) had he not been taken up by Pound, only three years his senior but seemingly a decade ahead of him in terms of publication and social experience. And yet by 1920, the end of the period covered in the first volume of David Moody's new biography of Pound, their roles were to be comprehensively reversed. Eliot was by then highly esteemed as both poet and critic, especially by the serious young, and was well on his way towards the almost papal authority he was to exercise over English literary life in the middle decades of the century. Pound's career, by contrast, seemed to have run aground on the reefs of his own impatient literary experimentation and tactless self-advertisement. The rejection was mutual: England, he declared more than once (and more than tactlessly), now exhibited nothing but a 'dead mentality', and he decided to give up on the project of civilizing it by means of establishing a purer poetry, leaving for Paris in December 1920. He was to move to Italy in 1924, never to live in England again.

Many of the things that Pound did and said and wrote in the remaining five decades of his life (he died in 1972) so damaged his reputation that even now he can be dismissed in some quarters as—the emphases vary—a Fascist, a traitor, an anti-Semite, or a lunatic (he spent twelve years in an American military mental hospital after the war, having initially been tried for treason for having made pro-Fascist broadcasts from Mussolini's Italy). In other quarters, the huge, sprawling collection of the *Cantos*, whose composition was spread across these later decades, is regarded as one of the major literary achievements of the twentieth century. These contrasting assessments have in common a tendency to scant Pound's early life and work, merely mining them for anticipations of whatever is seen as his defining later identity. One of the merits of Moody's detailed narrative is that it eschews hindsight as far as possible and tries to recapture the excitingness and literary brilliance of the colourful young troubadour in a floppy tie who made such an impact on London literary society in the years immediately before and after 1914.

The main title of Moody's book may at first suggest that he is trying to repeat the success of his highly regarded *Thomas Stearns Eliot: Poet*, first published in 1979 and in a revised edition in 1994. But that book was explicitly not a biography: though arranged chronologically, it consisted of close critical commentary on the major phases of Eliot's poetry. The present volume is, without question, a fully researched biography, but it retains enough of the literary-critical emphasis of the earlier work to set it somewhat apart from the dominant genre of contemporary literary biography. In the course of the narrative, Moody allows himself lengthy interludes of critical analysis of successive instalments of Pound's poetry, analyses which certainly do not shirk that poetry's allusiveness and rhythmical complexity. Scholars may welcome these learned exegeses, though it has to be said that they make the reading hard going in places.

One of the extraordinary things about the first thirty-five years of Pound's life is his utterly single-minded and autonomous self-creation as a poet, and a poet of a self-consciously revolutionary kind. He did not come from a particularly literary background. His father had a fairly routine job in the Philadelphia mint, and Pound went to a local school which catered for boys of his class. But already by the time he entered the University of Philadelphia at the age of 16, he had ceased to have much truck with the conventional requirements of education. What he wanted to learn was how the great poets of earlier centuries, especially the medieval and Renaissance centuries, had achieved their strange and beautiful effects, and how he could deploy such knowledge to create a new poetic which would sweep away what he already saw as the accumulated sentimentalities of the intervening centuries. The intensity, exclusiveness, and unshakeable self-belief with which he pursued his chosen course did not endear him to most of his teachers or contemporaries, but Pound was, early and late, largely indifferent to others' judgements, whether of himself or anything else. When in February 1908 he was dismissed—or willingly resigned—from Wabash College, Crawfordsville, Indiana, leaving him free to set out for Europe (subsidized by a small allowance from his father), it was a merciful release for both parties. Neither dutiful academia nor small-town America knew how to cope with someone so unabashedly set upon becoming the new Dante.

Pound's London years were certainly not short of incident or achievement. He married Dorothy Shakespear, daughter of one of Yeats's former lovers (Yeats later married one of Dorothy's friends, with Pound as best man); he stage-managed or was at the heart of several short-lived but important literary movements, most notably *Imagisme* and Vorticism; he played a crucial role in furthering the careers of Eliot, James Joyce, and Wyndham Lewis; and more generally he made himself an unignorable presence on the London literary scene. His declared ideal in the years leading up to the First World War was a poetry that was 'austere, direct, free from emotional slither', as 'much like granite as it can be' (an indication of how far he had already moved from the Swinburno-Dowsonism of a few years earlier). In his desire to establish a 'purer' poetry, he was constantly tilting at windmills. One of the most celebrated examples of his manner of proceeding with his crusade was his letter to the Georgian poet Lascelles Abercrombie when the latter had called for a return to Wordsworthian simplicity: 'Stupidity carried beyond a certain point becomes a public menace. I hereby challenge you to a duel . . . my seconds will wait upon you in due course.' As Moody tells the story: 'the challenged poet, having the choice of weapon, proposed that they pelt each other with unsold copies of their books. Pound enjoyed the comic riposte and the affair ended in laughter. All the same, he really did mean to give no quarter to public stupidity.'

Only a very select group of writers were held by Pound to be free from the general stupidity—Eliot, Joyce, and Wyndham Lewis were the trio in whom he had abiding faith—and he tended to be dismissive of, or inattentive to, almost everyone else. This purism is evident in his despairing reflection in 1920 on the state of letters in Britain and America. Commenting on how some of H.D.'s recent poems had a 'touch of the real thing, *in spots*', he concluded: 'Suppose we ought to be thankful for what there is . . . A touch in her, in Williams—a touch of something very different in T.S.E., and elsewhere desolation.'

The connection, and contrast, with Eliot has been very fully explored over the years, and Moody does not try to revise the established account, though the relationship retains its fascination. Pound published, or helped to publish, Eliot's early poems, taking pains to get an uncut version of 'The Love Song of J. Alfred Prufrock' into print since he thought it 'the best poem I have yet had or seen from an American'. His decisive editing of the draft of *The Waste Land* a few years later was the most striking demonstration of his critical talents, as well as an indication of a mutual respect and affection between the two men that was often to be put to the test. But there was no disguising their differences in social style and literary manner. Pound could tease 'the Reverend Eliot' and regret that some of his compatriot's judicious critical essays sounded like coded applications for membership of the Athenaeum Club. Pound abhorred respectability, but he knew how deep the craving for it went in Eliot and he was amused at the latter's self-effacing, self-promoting conformism. In turn, Eliot was to stay loyal, after his fashion, to his old friend through thin and thinner, though often deploring his excesses. His much later characterization, in his edition of the *Literary Essays of Ezra Pound* (1954), of Pound's polemical manner strove to be sympathetic: 'Every change he has advocated has always struck him as being of instant urgency,' and for this reason 'he often presents the appearance of a man trying to convey to a very deaf person the fact that the house is on fire'. But 'Ole Ez' could never have adopted the tactics of 'Old Possum'. Pound didn't do lying low.

Pound's tirades against the parochialism and philistinism of English culture were often self-defeatingly exaggerated and intemperate, but there are details in *Ezra Pound: Poet* which every so often remind us of what he was actually up against. There was, to begin with, the constant prudery and the associated fear, on the part of publishers and booksellers, of prosecution. In 1916 a publisher was jibbing at some of the (far from indecent) poems Pound wished to include in his new collection on the grounds that 'not only men come into this shop, *but ladies*'. Conventional prejudices of other kinds also impinged on him. In 1914 he had published a long and well-informed article on Noh theatre in the conservative though still prestigious *Quarterly Review*, but after his appearance a year later in the first number of *BLAST*, Wyndham Lewis's Vorticist assault on received opinion, the self-consciously respectable, not to say stuffy, editor of the *Quarterly*, G. W. Prothero, wrote to Pound to say that henceforth its pages would be closed to him since to be 'associated publicly with such a publication as *BLAST* . . . stamps a man too disadvantageously'. All very pompous and unwarranted, no doubt, though one has to imagine the impact on a man of Prothero's pin-striped conventionality of Pound's having apostrophized *The Times* as 'You slut-bellied obstructionist, you fungus, you continuous gangrene' and his having assailed 'the state of mind which *The Times* represents' as 'a loathsome state of mind, a malebolge of obtuseness'.

A large part of the surface narrative of Pound's life during these years can be told in terms of his attempts to get control of a journal in order to promote the kind of new writing of which he approved. He successively played a prominent, or even in one or two cases a directing, part in the *English Review*, the *New Freewoman*, the *Egoist*, the *New Age*, *Poetry*, the *Little Review*, and the *Dial* (all the while inveighing against 'the villainy of contributors to the front page of *The Times Literary Supplement*'). He had some notable successes, securing the publication of several early Eliot poems in *Poetry* and the first publication of instalments of Joyce's *Ulysses* in the *Little Review*, but in the end there were always fallings short and fallings out. For example, he tried to exercise a dictatorially selective policy over submissions to Harriet Monroe's Chicago-based journal *Poetry*; after she had successfully insisted upon a more inclusive line, he, always the purist, would refer disparagingly to 'Harriet's *Home Gazette*'. He alienated several other erstwhile allies in the same way. 'He was not made for compromise or cooperation,' observed Herbert Read; others would have put it less understandingly.

And yet one kind of cooperation at which Pound excelled was that of providing a fellow-writer with detailed reconstructive suggestions for the improvement of a particular piece of work. Moody emphasizes the disinterestedness of Pound's devotion to furthering the cause of good poetry, not just of his own poetry: for a few years in the early twentieth century, Pound was the man you called in when you were having trouble with your lines. To have performed this service so successfully for poets of the calibre of Yeats and Eliot is already an unusual claim to fame. Helping, more than once, to raise funds for a habitual sponger such as Joyce was less distinctive, but it is still impressive to see Pound engaging in such cheerful benevolence when he was himself in pretty dire financial straits. On meeting Pound in 1920, Joyce recorded his impression of 'a large bundle of unpredictable electricity', 'a miracle of ebulliency, gusto, and help'. 'One of the kindest men that ever lived' was the considered judgement of one minor writer whom Pound assisted. Overall, Moody largely succeeds in conveying the attractive sides of Pound's personality, above all his exuberance, generosity, and eye-poking irreverence.

But there is another, more subterranean, and ultimately much more important, story to be told which can only be followed in the slim volumes and fugitive pieces of verse Pound published between 1908 and 1920. Moody's critical analyses go some way towards chronicling the rich and strange history of Pound's dealing with the music of words, but even these compressed commentaries are in some ways too doggedly exegetical and literary-historical quite to convey the distinctiveness, and the fertility, of

Pound's craftsmanship through the years that run from early volumes such as *Personae* and *Canzoni* to the later *Homage to Sextus Propertius* and *Hugh Selwyn Mauberley*. Quotation helps, but the biographical proprieties have to be observed, and those proprieties leave us little the wiser about the astonishing drama of Pound's poetic development in these years, as he moves from 'The Tree' of *c.*1906:

> Naetheless I have been a tree amid the wood
> And many new things understood
> That were rank folly to my head before.

to the celebrated 'In a Station of the Metro' of 1913:

> The apparition   of these faces   in the crowd:
> Petals   on a wet, black   bough.

to the opening of *The Fourth Canto* in 1919:

> Palace in smoky light,
> Troy but a heap of smouldering boundary stones,
> ANAXIFORMINGES! Aurunculeia!
> Hear me. Cadmus of Golden Prows!

It is hard to know how to talk about all this within a conventional biographical framework, so we fall back on summary judgements, such as Eliot's, in his best chairman-of-the-meeting manner, that 'Mr Pound is more responsible for the XXth-century revolution in poetry than is any other individual', or William Carlos Williams's more downright opinion, quoted in Humphrey Carpenter's still readable *A Serious Character: A Life of Ezra Pound* (1988), that Pound had 'the best damned ear ever born to listen to this language'.

For Pound, poetry was everything, and before quoting any of his all-too-quotable prose pronouncements against him (which is mostly the use they seem to have lent themselves to), one should recall his declaration to his mother in 1909: 'I should never think of prose as anything but a stop-gap, a means of procuring food. Exactly on the same plane with market-gardening. If a thing is not sufficiently interesting to be put into poetry, & sufficiently important to make the poetic form worth while, it is hardly worth saying anything at all.' A few months later he followed this up with a no less revealing piece of self-characterization: 'My mind, such as I have, works by a sort of fusion, and sudden crystallization, and the effort to tie that kind of action to the dray work of prose is very exhausting. One should have a vegetable sort of mind for prose.' Blessed, or cursed, with the opposite of a 'vegetable sort of mind', Pound wrote a wearying quantity of prose during his London years. In 1917 he sighed that he had been 'turning out an article a day for weeks': 'My present existence is that of a highly mechanized typing volcano.' It was not just that he never had any kind of salary to rely on, as Eliot did during his years working in a bank, but, more importantly, Pound lacked Eliot's strategic calculation about only writing pieces that would enhance his standing as a serious critic. To Pound, literary journalism was not merely secondary: it was, as a medium, of no account compared to the real business of writing good poetry. But others took it more seriously, and marked Pound down as a wild man, altogether too free with his (fast-changing) opinions and sweeping dismissals of other writers. 'See what he has become,' wrote Vivienne Eliot in 1919, 'a laughing stock.' Throughout Pound's career he seems to have failed to anticipate the harm, to himself above all, that he might do by his casual and not always well-judged prose excursions. Even A. R. Orage, the sympathetic editor of the *New Age*, had to acknowledge Pound's self-destructive tendencies when he saluted the poet's departure from London at the end of 1920:

> Mr Pound has been an exhilarating influence for culture in England; he has left his mark upon more than one of the arts, upon literature, music, poetry, and sculpture; and quite a number of men and movements owe their initiation to his self-sacrificing stimulus; among them being relatively popular successes as well as failures. With all this, however, Mr Pound, like so many others who have striven for the advancement of intelligence and culture in England, has made more enemies than friends. Much of the Press has been deliberately closed by cabal to him; his books have for some time been ignored or written down; and he himself has been compelled to live on much less than would support a navvy.

In the decades after 1920 he was, of course, to go on to make enemies on an altogether different scale; hence some of the continuing difficulties in doing justice to him. But even taking his early decades in their own terms, it is hard to know quite how to draw up a balance-sheet: for all the interest of his own poetic experiments and despite his success in promoting the work of the few writers he believed in, there was also something self-defeating about his crusading zeal, something about the man and his manner that provoked resistance and disdain rather than issuing in that opening of minds which he claimed as his goal. Grappling with this problem, Moody at one point observes that Pound believed he had been 'the sole entrepreneur of intellectual renewal in England—an outrageous delusion, one might think, until one thinks of his part in what has endured from these years'. This is generous, which is becoming in a biographer, but surely too indulgent. The exaggeration of 'sole' wrecks the claim (was no part played by Ford Madox Ford, by T. E. Hulme, or by Wyndham Lewis, not to mention by patrons such as Harriet Weaver or John Quinn?), and anyway 'intellectual renewal' is too tendentious to be allowed to pass unchallenged.

The better ground is not the actual effect of Pound's various cultural campaigns—most of which, for all their occasional spectacular success, ended in rejection and ruin—but his undeviating absorption in the *craft* of poetry. And for doing justice to this, the conventions of biography are, if not exactly irrelevant, at least maladapted. Even those who remain baffled by, or sceptical of, the achievement of the *Cantos* would have to concede that Pound *stretched* poetry in English in a way few have done. He heard the sounds and rhythms of words and lines so vividly, having cultivated his ear by his single-minded study of the poetry of other traditions and other languages (and ultimately, with Chinese, of other calligraphies, too). And he did not, at least during the period covered in this volume, give a damn about anything else—that was all just so much market-gardening, fit employment, after all, for 'vegetable minds'. This means it is not easy to be Pound's biographer, or even to be a reader of Pound's biography, for what justifies so much attention to all his bluster and wrong-headedness is really going on elsewhere, all but inaudibly to many of us. But Pound wouldn't have given a damn about that either. Perhaps he might have extended the sentiment he, still only 23, cheerfully expressed to his long-suffering father: 'Being family to a wild poet ain't no bed of roses but you stand the strain just fine.'

II

'I have written nothing whatsoever for three years and I do not see any immediate likelihood of my writing. The writing of poetry takes time and I never have any time.' That, alas, is an all-too-accurate summary of T. S. Eliot's life during the three years covered by the second volume of his correspondence (1923–5). Its 800 pages document in dispiriting detail the life of a writer who was doing hardly any writing. There was just too much else to do, and much too much else to worry about.

There was, to begin with, his wife Vivienne (sometimes spelled Vivien). As a lonely, shy American graduate student in philosophy at Oxford, Eliot had married Vivienne Haigh-Wood in June 1915, not many weeks after meeting her. By 1923, the disastrousness of the marriage for both parties was becoming all too apparent. Vivienne was plagued by almost constant ill health, often severe; it may now be impossible to say how much of this was psychosomatic, and it may not really matter. The signs of mental instability were by this point hard to explain away. Eliot, with a highly developed sense of his responsibility to provide for his wife, repeatedly made himself ill worrying about her, looking after her, and needing to get away from her.

Then he had to worry about international exchange rates, the bond issues of foreign governments, and the payment of war debts. Since March 1917 Eliot had worked in the Colonial and Foreign Department of Lloyds Bank in the City, rising to a position of some responsibility, overseeing the analysis of information about the financial activities of European governments. By 1923 the strain of his divided life was becoming unendurable, and various possibilities were canvassed that would buy him out of the black-coated army, but the regular salary from the bank, even the distant pension prospects, mattered more and more as Vivienne's future became increasingly uncertain.

And then he had to worry about *The Criterion*, the intellectually ambitious literary and cultural quarterly review that he edited, more or less single-handedly, in his 'spare time'. The review had been launched in October 1922, financed by Lady Rothermere, wife of Harold Harmsworth, first Viscount Rothermere. (Harold had helped his brother Alfred, Lord Northcliffe, establish the press empire whose flagship was *The Daily Mail*.) Eliot aspired to make *The Criterion* the most prestigious literary review of the day, promoting his favoured blend of Modernist literature and reactionary politics, but he soon discovered the scale of the labour this required. After a while a typist was taken on to handle some of his correspondence, and there was a brief period during which the poet and translator Richard Aldington acted as his assistant, but, as the successive deadlines rolled remorselessly around, it was Eliot who seemed to be responsible for everything from commissioning contributions to correcting proofs and arranging payments.

It was all too much. 'I am worn out, I cannot go on,' he lamented a little histrionically as early as March 1923, but he still had a long way to go on. February 1925 found him 'at the blackest moment of my life', but in reality there were blacker moments still to come. 'So life is simply from minute to minute of horror,' he wrote to Virginia Woolf the following month, perhaps hearing a draft line of poetry forming itself somewhere in his mind. But, as far as we can tell from the letters, during these years not many lines of poetry were forming in the mind of the figure who was arguably the most important English-language poet of the twentieth century.

It is Eliot's poetry, of course, that represents his principal claim on the modern reader's attentions, for all his influence as a critic, playwright, editor, and cultural commentator. In the month before this second volume of letters was published, he was voted Britain's favourite poet—perhaps a surprising choice when one considers the notorious difficulty of his verse, but maybe less so when one remembers that the inspiration for the hit musical *Cats!* was provided by his light-hearted *Old Possum's Book of Practical Cats*. However, his standing as a poet does not, of itself, account for the frisson of anticipation that has for some time been building up in advance of the appearance of this second volume of his letters. The mild sense of drama attending the publication (writers and publishers lead sheltered lives for the most part) has been heightened by Faber's unusually elaborate security measures, with reviewers having to sign legal agreements binding them not to reveal the contents of the volume to 'any third party' before the day of publication.

A brief historical re-cap may help to explain some of the fuss. In 1957, when Eliot was 68, he married his secretary Valerie Fletcher, who was thirty-eight years younger (Vivienne had died ten years earlier). Following Eliot's death in 1965, Mrs Eliot and the publishing firm of Faber and Faber (of which he had been an active director for almost forty years) controlled his estate, carefully regulating both the re-printing of published work and citation from unpublished material, including letters. In 1971 Mrs Eliot published her facsimile edition of *The Waste Land*, complete with Ezra Pound's annotations. She had also undertaken the huge task of collecting and editing his letters, with the first volume (covering the years up to the end of 1922) finally appearing in 1988. In the introduction to that volume, she explained that she had intended it to go up to 1926, but that there had proved to be too much material for a single volume. Therefore, she announced, the second volume would be published 'next year'. The literary and scholarly worlds waited, but 'next year' never seemed to come.

This delay was particularly unfortunate because, in the four decades following Eliot's death, many scholars had difficulty in getting permission from the estate to consult or quote from unpublished material. When in 1984 Peter Ackroyd published what is still the only serious approach to an adequate intellectual biography of Eliot, he had to record that 'I am forbidden by the Eliot estate . . . to quote from unpublished work or correspondence.' (He had to paraphrase his sources.) Some individual scholars could be more fortunate—I was given permission some years ago, I should record, to quote from a few letters in an essay about Eliot's social criticism—but a policy that could seem to be somewhat capricious was obviously an unsatisfactory situation, especially when it was known that the estate held or had amassed a considerable collection of material, not all of which had yet been seen by scholars. Just recently there have been encouraging signs of a thaw. Plans have been announced for a multi-volume edition of Eliot's prose, under the general editorship of Ron Schuchard, to be partnered by a complete edition of his poetry, edited by Christopher Ricks. And now, at long last, twenty-one years after its predecessor, we have the second volume of the letters, co-edited by Hugh Haughton, with the project henceforth under the general editorship of John Haffenden.

Given this history, the stock phrases about a book having been 'eagerly awaited' or its publication being 'a major literary event' are in this case understatements. For, in addition to the already considerable interest in Eliot's poetry and criticism, other aspects of his life and his views have attracted broader media attention and even controversy in recent years. It has, for example, been widely known that Eliot suffered acute anguish over his decision, first, to separate from Vivienne and, second, to have her committed to a 'sanatorium'. His own responsibility for his wife's physical and mental problems has sometimes been assessed in hostile terms, a line of popular speculation fuelled by Michael Hastings's 1984 play *Tom and Viv*, which was subsequently turned into a film. In addition, Eliot came in for some rough handling in the wake of Anthony Julius's 1995 book *T. S. Eliot: Anti-Semitism and Literary Form*, which mounted, with great forensic vigour, the case that Eliot's *œuvre* as a whole was irremediably tainted on account of a handful of allegedly anti-Semitic references. These controversies cannot have been welcome to the Eliot estate and may have fuelled its apprehension about the possible public response to any further 'revelations'.

Anticipation has been increased by the fact that the first volume of the letters was full of matter for those with a serious interest in Eliot's work and career. It covered the years in which he, arriving in England in 1914 as an unknown 26-year-old graduate student, had emerged as the most startling poet of his time, from the publication of *Prufrock and Other Observations* in 1917 up to *The Waste Land* in 1922. This was also the period in which he established himself as the critic most admired by the intellectually serious young, notably through the publication in 1920 of *The Sacred Wood*, a slim volume of critical essays that managed to be at once offhand, exciting, and authoritative. The letters, therefore, had allowed us to glimpse the inside story of nothing less than the making of Modernism. What could the second volume offer that would be of comparable interest?

'Not a lot' is the short and only partly misleading answer. After all this fanfare, these letters will, I fear, be a disappointment to many readers. Though they document the tribulations of his and Vivienne's illnesses and unhappinesses in heart-bludgeoning detail, they contain no great revelations, nor are most of them captivating pieces of writing in the way in which, say, the recently published early Beckett letters are. Eliot scholars, not a small tribe, will doubtless mine them for illustrative or corroborative detail, but in truth they throw little light on the poetry, not least because he was not writing any (except for sections of 'The Hollow Men' and the verse drama *Sweeney Agonistes*, written towards the end of this period). Nor did he write any of his major critical essays during these years, and the letters say very little about his own critical, as opposed to editorial, practice. However, if what you want is a practical handbook on how to edit, single-handedly, a high-end cultural and literary periodical, then this is a must-have guide. Overwhelmingly, the letters from this period were written by Eliot in his capacity as editor of the *Criterion*, and if this is something that interests you (I must warn you that it interests me a lot), then this volume is rich in fascinating detail.

Much of Eliot's editorial correspondence deals with what, to anyone who has any experience of literary journalism, will be bound to appear as the familiar constants, almost the universals, of the trade. Here, over and over again, is the desperate last-minute scramble to meet (or sometimes not quite to meet) the deadline for the current issue, followed by repeated resolutions to have the material ready in good time for the next issue. Here, in dispiriting quantity, are examples of the various ways of sucking up to eminent potential contributors, of well-meant evasiveness with lesser supplicants, and of tactful dealings with impossibly difficult authors (Wyndham Lewis wins the prize). Here, too, are the familiar grumblings about the inefficiencies of printers, the usual unrealistic fantasies about circulation, and the vehemently expressed regrets at ever having taken on such a doomed and life-destroying enterprise in the first place.

Apologizing to one contributor for the fact that, a year after being accepted, his article had still not been published, Eliot tried to enlist his sympathies:

> I can only say that there are others—in fact nearly all of my contributors at one time or another—whom I do not dare to meet in the street. Conducting a review after 8pm in the back room of a flat, I live *qua* editor, very much from hand to mouth, get myself into all sorts of hot water and predicaments, and offend everybody. At the end, the review is squeezed together somehow, and is never the number that I planned three months before.

In this case, he promised the article would be published 'early next year'; in the event, it never appeared.

Hand to mouth it may have been in practical terms, but Eliot had a pretty clear idea of the kind of review he wanted to produce. It appealed, he insisted without any defensiveness, only to 'the cultivated': he reckoned that there were about 3,000 such persons, though the basis for this high-handed piece of intuitive sociology is not clear. It was to be essentially a literary review, but 'its scope is wide enough to include almost everything of interest to people of culture with the exception of economics and contemporary politics'. Lady Rothermere, who had hoped for something with rather more appeal to the *beau monde*, is reported as finding the journal 'a little high-brow and grave' (but, madam, if you appoint T. S. Eliot as editor . . .). Though it is true that *The Criterion* did not deal with day-to-day party politics, it nonetheless had a very marked political character. It was explicitly intended to provide a counter to 'the usual Whig and semi-Socialist press of London'. It was hostile to all forms of liberalism, Whiggism, romanticism, and subjectivism; in its severe, aloof way it upheld what Eliot came to call 'classicism'. It is from this standpoint that we find him here dismissing Arnold Toynbee as 'a noxious humanitarian' and sneering at John Middleton Murry as 'this apostle of suburban free thought'.

In trying to establish the reputation of the new journal, Eliot had to perform the usual delicate balancing act: he wanted to publish high-quality original work of the kind he admired, but he also needed contributions from established names, which sometimes meant accepting work which was neither high quality nor original. The correspondence of any editor might catch him out saying different things to different people, but there are some arrestingly immediate juxtapositions in these letters. When, as the editor of a new journal, he is sedulously courting the 77-year-old George Saintsbury, Eliot hastens to tell him that he is 'the most eminent English critic of our time'; two years later, the journal now established, he frankly confides to another correspondent: 'Saintsbury, for all his merits, now has little point'. Similarly, Eliot is to be found writing to several authors in flattering terms explaining that he may be able to double the normal rates of payment to a truly exceptional contributor, 'one of whom is of course yourself'. Having already confided this, in turn, to Wyndham Lewis, Ezra Pound, and Virginia Woolf, he then writes to W. B. Yeats's agent saying: 'For such an important contribution from so distinguished a writer I would make an exception' to his usual rates and pay double. 'This is the only occasion on which I have ever offered more than the standard rate; but I have very great admiration for Mr Yates' work . . . ' and so on, a profession whose sincerity, already doubtful, was made more doubtful still by the misspelling of Yeats's name.

The question of two-facedness surfaces most awkwardly in his tricky friendship with Leonard and Virginia Woolf. While jockeying to establish himself in literary London, he had been grateful for the Woolfs' patronage: their Hogarth Press published *The Waste Land* in book form (after it had appeared in the first number of *The Criterion*), and in 1924 they were to publish three of his review-essays as a Hogarth pamphlet entitled *Homage to John Dryden*. In 1923 the Woolfs seem to have helped to persuade Maynard Keynes to offer Eliot the position of Literary Editor on the Liberal weekly the *Nation*. The position, though attractive, would not have provided Eliot with the financial security he needed, but it is not clear whether the paper's uncongenial political identity played a part in his eventual refusal (Leonard Woolf himself took on the post). At a less public level, Eliot shared some common ground with Leonard as a man who had considerable experience in handling the moods of a mentally unstable wife, but his direct relationship with Virginia was always shot through with distrust and a kind of literary rivalry. Neither Eliot nor Virginia Woolf gets high honours for consistent candour, and the very full annotations to these letters indicate a little of the discreditable backbiting that went on off-stage. Having cajoled Virginia to publish her (soon to be celebrated) essay 'Character in Fiction' in *The Criterion* for July 1924, Eliot enthuses to her that the presence of her piece alongside those by Proust and Yeats means 'the July number will be the most brilliant in its history'. But some months later he praises the next issue to Lady Rothermere by saying 'there is nothing of the costly showiness of Proust and Virginia Woolf (neither of which I cared much about myself)'.

At one point Virginia Woolf confides to her diary (quoted in the editorial annotations) the conviction that 'There is something hole-and-cornerish, biting in the back, suspicious, elaborate, uneasy, about him.' There was truth in this, though there was more than a touch of pot-and-kettle, too. At the end of this volume, Eliot leaves his job at Lloyds to join Geoffrey Faber's new publishing firm. Part of his private understanding with Faber was that the new firm would henceforth publish Eliot's books, beginning with *Poems 1919–1925*, which included *The Waste Land*. Eliot continued to write to the Woolfs in affectionate terms while somehow managing not to tell them that the Hogarth Press had just lost one of its star authors.

But it must be said that Eliot, by fair means or by sharp professional practice, made a success of the *Criterion* during these years. He was justified in boasting in October 1924: 'I think that at the end of the third year it will have as brilliant a record of contributors as any magazine could have in the time.' He had secured original contributions from most of the leading Modernist writers of the time, including Joyce, Woolf, Pound, Lawrence, and Wyndham Lewis, and the review could boast a particularly impressive array of European contributors, a deliberate policy on Eliot's part, one that was not matched by the habitually parochial established journals. The critical essays and, later, the book reviews generally maintained a high, if at times highly ideological, standard. Publication in *The Criterion*'s pages, he informed prospective contributors, ensured 'more intelligent attention than a contribution to any other review'. Only the circulation remained stubbornly resistant to Eliot's blandishments, sales never exceeding 800–1,000 copies per issue.

Beyond documenting his life as an editor, these letters add a little thickening detail to some of the already well-worn themes of Eliot biography and criticism. There is, for example, his view (to be trusted no further than several other ostensibly revealing confessions in these letters) that there were only 'about thirty good lines in *The Waste Land*'. It is somewhat more winning to find him acknowledging that his own prose has 'a rather rheumatic pomposity', and a knowingness about his early critical performances is suggested by his advice to a young would-be review essayist: 'You must begin by being or pretending to be an authority on some subject or other.' Every so often the letters will contain some remark in the lapidary style of his best literary journalism: 'Good verse is only recognised after five years at least. Good criticism is noticed at once. The cultivated public prefers critical to creative work.' His correspondence with his mother and brother over investments shows him fully sharing the family penchant for cautious capitalism (even though he was a banker). Part of his qualification for becoming a director of Faber's new firm was that, in addition to being one of the best-connected writers and editors of his day, he was 'a man of business'. And, inevitably, we get a few asides about 'Jew publishers' when his dealings with his American publishers were particularly vexed. No one could pretend that the writer of these letters emerges as consistently likeable or admirable, but it is hard not to feel sympathy for a man so cornered by personal unhappiness, financial anxiety, and professional frustration.

Eliot often affected the identity of the 'metic' or 'resident alien'; perhaps he came to feel that that label accurately described his relation to earthly existence as a whole. As a young man, he was not short of reasons to feel ill at ease in the world, and many of those who met him during his early years in London remarked this characteristic. Alternating between shyness and attitude-striking, he made others feel ill at ease with him, uncertain how far they could trust this now smooth, now angular, chameleon. Disguise, camouflage, adaptation: Eliot was rich in the strategies of self-protection. V. S. Pritchett later called him 'a company of actors within one suit'. Several members of the company are on show in these pages; the one constant is the suit, literally as worn to the bank every day, metaphorically in the pin-striped casing of so much of his epistolary prose.

If all of Eliot's surviving letters are to be edited on this lavish scale—and, as he became more famous in later years, presumably even more letters will have survived—one has to wonder a little about the rationale, in this electronic age, of the policy of printing annotated versions of practically every letter he ever wrote. With almost forty years of his life still to go, there could, at this rate, easily be fifteen volumes of similar dimensions to come, perhaps more. Eliot is, beyond question, a hugely important writer and an intriguing man, but the spirit does not leap at the prospect of so many thousands of pages of elaborate politeness.

This edition, it should be emphasized, presents Eliot's own letters; it does not provide both sides of the correspondence, even where such replies exist. But just occasionally the text of a letter from one of his correspondents is included, and the gain in our sense of the exchange is immediate. There are, in addition, a few impressive letters from Geoffrey Faber setting out the terms on which Eliot was to work for the new publishing firm, as well as Faber's own conception of the kind of periodical the new *Criterion* was to be (quite like the old, as it turned out). And there are several letters from Vivienne to other correspondents which vividly illuminate Eliot's predicament, though it is not immediately obvious why they and not others have been included.

Vivienne's letters have both a directness and an incoherence that rip apart that smooth surface of life which Eliot's guarded prose was always trying to maintain. Two of these raw, disturbing scribbles, from late 1925, suggest something of what Eliot had to contend with, but both are also mind-searing in the glimpse they give us of Vivienne's tortured, disturbed, unendurably miserable life. The first is to the Eliots' maid, Ellen Kellond, a desperately inappropriate choice of recipient; it is a panicked and plungingly despairing wail from a woman who felt herself to be held in a 'sanatorium' against her will, keening for the love she believes her husband has withdrawn, and ending: 'I mean to take my life . . . It is difficult here, but I shall find a way. This is the end.' The second is to Eliot himself. It begins calmly enough but soon degenerates. Amid illegible words and inconsequential remarks about various possessions, she suddenly throws herself into an anguished apology: 'I am sorry I tortured you and drove you mad. I had no notion until yesterday afternoon that I had done it. I have been simply raving mad. You need not worry about me.' But he did worry about her, ceaselessly, and this great slab of mostly unrevealing, practicality-driven letters depicts in harrowing detail a man almost drowning in the busyness he needed to stop himself from being driven 'mad'.

III

Writing in his best haughty-provocative manner, T. S. Eliot described Coleridge as 'one of those unhappy persons . . . of whom one might say that if they had not been poets, they might have made something of their lives, might even have had a career'. Although the syntax allows a little ambiguity about whether the unhappiness is independent of, or consequent upon, being a poet, the obvious reading suggests a somewhat laboured archness about how the propensity for writing poetry can blight the exercise of other talents, talents that might otherwise have led to success in more orthodox careers. Coleridge had, according to Eliot, been 'visited by the Muse' during his early manhood, but, the visitor having departed, he was 'thenceforth a haunted man'. He had a talent for metaphysics and similar studies, but 'he was condemned to know that the little poetry he had written was worth more than all he could do with the rest of his life. The author of *Biographia Literaria* was already a ruined man. Sometimes, however, to be a "ruined man" is itself a vocation.'

Eliot himself, it could be said, 'made something' of his life largely by not being a poet. His published poetic output was not large, and for long periods of his adult life he seems to have written no poetry at all. At the same time, there were various pressures on him, internal as well as external, to make something of his life, and the greater part of any biography has to be devoted to those other somethings. But were there moments along the way when he felt himself to be not just 'a haunted man'—that he certainly was—but 'already a ruined man'? It could scarcely be said that he made a vocation out of being a ruined man: in his later years he was garlanded with recognition of several kinds and he became a byword (or, to more critical eyes, notorious) for his cultivation of social respectability and worldly status. However, at the beginning of 1926, the start of the period covered in the third volume of his letters, the shadow of more than one kind of ruin still hung over him. Ten years earlier he had abandoned his promising academic career as a philosopher in order to stay in England to 'write', the start of a decade of economic insecurity that had been only partly alleviated by his job at the bank. More ruinous still had been his hasty marriage: by 1926 it was becoming ever clearer that Vivienne's psychological and physical problems were deep-seated, requiring long-term professional treatment. Whatever his feelings for his wife by this point—some commentators may have come to firmer conclusions about this than the evidence quite warrants—worry and guilt were substantial elements in the mix. And then there were the uncertainties arising from his own irregular relations with the Muse. He had already experienced several long periods of poetic drought, completing practically no verse between mid-1915 and mid-1917, again from early 1919 to early 1921, and then for a couple of years following *The Waste Land*. After the appearance of 'The Hollow Men' in 1925, it seemed as though another period of estrangement was beginning and perhaps this time the break might be permanent. He had recently given up his bank job (at the time, we should not forget, the epitome of secure and respectable employment) to take on a somewhat experimental role within Geoffrey Faber's new publishing firm, and he was about to expose the patchiness of his scholarship by giving a set of lectures to an exacting audience of Cambridge dons. Ruin was still a possibility, even if not a vocation, and the main interest of the third volume of his letters lies in the untidy immediacy of the daily evidence of Eliot's attempts to make something of his life.

The first sentence of the editors' introduction says this volume 'brings the poet to the age of thirty-nine', but in truth he is as little in evidence as a poet in these 900 pages as in the previous volume. Writing to Wyndham Lewis in January 1926, Eliot acknowledged that his recently issued *Poems 1909–1925* would not do much to alter critics' views of his work: 'But I wanted to collect all my stuff and get rid of it in one volume so as to get it out of my own way and make a fresh start.' Even if we don't take this quite at face value (he sometimes resorted to this reductive idiom to ward off any suspicion of self-importance; he was in fact delighted that Faber's new firm were willing to publish, in effect, an interim 'collected'), the felt need to make a fresh start poetically seems genuine enough. But it didn't come easily; in fact, in the years covered here it didn't come at all. Practically the only poetry he completed was the short 'Journey of the Magi' (the first of the 'Ariel' poems). 'I wrote it in three quarters of an hour after church time and before lunch one Sunday morning with the assistance of half a bottle of Booth's gin', or so it pleased him to tell his old Harvard friend Conrad Aiken, with more than a touch of drinking-buddy braggadocio. He also tinkered with some fragments intended to form part of a (never completed) drama of modern life called 'Sweeney Agonistes', as well as a translation of Saint-John Perse's prose-poem 'Anabase', which did not appear until 1930. He later acknowledged that 'I thought my poetry was over after "the Hollow Men"'. It was to be some years before he discovered that this was not the case.

So, in the meantime, what kinds of 'something' was he making of his life? Overwhelmingly, these letters, like those in the previous volume, give us Eliot as editor. Following his move in mid-1925 from Lloyds Bank to Faber and Gwyer, the *Criterion* was put on a new business footing (and Eliot paid a salary), though Lady Rothermere remained co-proprietor. Re-launched early in 1926 as *The New Criterion*, the journal continued to make a loss, leading to the experiment of appearing as a monthly early in 1927. This involved more editorial labour but scarcely any greater commercial success, and at the end of 1927 relations with Lady Rothermere, who had long been disappointed that the journal was not more of a chic high-society arts magazine, reached a crisis. Finally, she withdrew all support, and contributors were told in early December that the journal might have to cease publication.

The move to Faber and Gwyer meant that Eliot now had some proper secretarial support, but in effect he still edited the journal single-handedly. Inevitably, this means that the bulk of his surviving correspondence has the character of office memos, never the most exhilarating reading. To all contributors and (even more) would-be contributors, Eliot is unfailingly polite: variants on 'However, it is not quite suitable for the *Criterion*' would probably top any phrase-search of these pages (closely followed by 'I am sorry that I had to hold over your article'). There are a number of meatier, or more revealing, or just more personal, letters, but they are few and far between. Eliot scholars will no doubt find much grist for their finely grinding mills here, just as historians of literary journalism will be able to bulk out a largely familiar story; but readers with less specialized interests, particularly those drawn to the volume by their admiration for Eliot's poetry, may find themselves doing a great deal of skipping.

Writing to Pound in December 1926 to try to discourage him from starting yet another 'little magazine', Eliot declared: 'All reviews are worse than useless and my only excuse is that I derive the larger part of my income from this source.' When reading Eliot's obiter dicta of this kind, it's advisable to keep supplies of salt handy. He had, after all, slaved at his editorial task for the first three years without deriving any income from it, and elsewhere in his letters, as well as in his published writings, we see him taking the whole thing much more seriously. Eliot well knew that it only reached a small readership, but he believed it was important to sustain a journal of the highest literary and critical standards that would combat the slack, back-scratching puffery that dominated mainstream London literary journalism. But what gave the journal its distinctive identity was the way in which such standards were held to entail that elusive thing, a 'point of view', initially inimical to various forms of progressivism but increasingly marked by a frankly reactionary political and religious stance. Although the *Criterion* 'certainly does not associate itself with any existing political party', he explained to one potential contributor in June 1927, 'it has I think a definite character in the world of ideas'.

To help develop and sustain this character, he gathered round himself a small nucleus of like-minded younger contributors with whom he discussed books, ideas, and policy for the journal at regular '*Criterion* dinners' at a Soho restaurant. The most constant members of the group during this period were Bonamy Dobrée, F. S. Flint, Herbert Read, and Orlo Williams, all of whom were frequent contributors (and, therefore, frequent recipients of letters from Eliot), with several others participating more sporadically. In practice, Eliot still seems to have made the decisions and carried on the editorial business himself, but the idea that this was a more than merely personal enterprise clearly mattered to him. It could also be convenient to invoke the collective persona when communicating editorial decisions, as when he turned down some essays by Laura Riding because 'they are not closely enough in relation to the point of view of the *Criterion* and its principal collaborators'. The weaselly formulation here ('not closely enough in relation to') gestures towards unexpressed criticisms, just as his careful reference to 'the *Criterion* and its principal collaborators' signifies that something more than individual taste is involved.

He put the point more emphatically in a letter to his friend Richard Aldington, who had initially been a very close collaborator but who by this date was showing signs of the touchiness and divergence of views which would eventually lead him to break with Eliot entirely. Aldington had submitted a somewhat wayward, impressionistic essay on D. H. Lawrence, to which Eliot responded, apologetically though firmly, that 'I do not think that it falls in with the general position of the *Criterion*'. This, he went on to explain, might be thought of as 'the consensus of opinion of the people who attend the *Criterion* dinners', and so not just a matter of Eliot's own preferences. He emphasized that he himself refrained from publishing in the journal 'any opinions of my own with which others of our more important colleagues would be in real opposition', continuing: 'If I want to say such things, I try to say them elsewhere; even in the *Times* [i.e. the *TLS*] I can say things which I would not say in the *Criterion*.' He would, he conceded, occasionally be willing to carry a piece expressing a contrary position by someone acknowledged to be in opposition to the *Criterion* line, such as Middleton Murry, but he feared that Aldington, given his known connections with Eliot, would be taken rather to be speaking for the *Criterion* group itself, and this would be damaging. It is an exceptionally careful letter, even by the standards of this habitually careful writer, and its mixture of precision and deliberate vagueness perfectly captures Eliot's sense of the journal as a concerted cultural campaign. (This and many other letters here thus bear out the contention in Jason Harding's valuable 2002 book on the *Criterion* that critics have too readily taken everything in the journal to be the expression of Eliot's personal views.)

If Eliot as editor is familiar ground, one of the rather more surprising 'somethings' that these letters show him almost making of himself was an academic. *The Cambridge History of Literary Criticism* says of Eliot that 'he is the first non-academic critic who sounds like an academic critic'. It is an intriguing tag, catching something of the air of learning and scholarly precision (as well as asperity) in his early critical essays, but its force obviously depends on the fact that Eliot wrote as a literary journalist and man of letters, not as a university teacher. However, at this period these roles were not as sharply distinguished as they were to become, and it is clear that at times in the mid-1920s Eliot imagined himself, and was imagined by others, as a possible candidate for an academic appointment.

He had, of course, been working towards a career as a philosopher when he came from Harvard to spend the academic year 1914–15 at Oxford, but, having burned those bridges by staying in England and not returning to defend his dissertation, he embarked on an institutionally unanchored life as a poet and freelance man of letters. Yet, in less than a decade, he was being thought of for academic posts in English literature, despite having no formal qualifications and having made no scholarly contribution to the field. But 'scholarly' is both the puzzle and its solution here. It's true that Eliot had only published a series of review-essays in literary periodicals, but the best of these pieces managed to suggest that reserves of learning underwrote his casually authoritative prose, especially when writing about Elizabethan and Jacobean drama and poetry. His judgements had an *ex cathedra* finality about them even though their author occupied no chair. The slim gathering of such pieces that he published as *The Sacred Wood* in 1920, and the still slimmer pamphlet *Homage to John Dryden* that the Hogarth Press issued in 1924, acquired near-cult status among the advanced young. His reputation stood highest at Cambridge, where he already seemed to figure as one of the informing spirits of the newly founded English course despite never having studied or taught there. The fact that his friend I. A. Richards, the most evangelical of the young lecturers, energetically championed his cause obviously helped, but Eliot's impact on younger academic critics in the 1920s remains a striking and, in some respects, under-explained episode in the history of English as a discipline.

Much his most substantial engagement was the delivery of the Clark Lectures in English Literature at Trinity College, Cambridge. Between late January and early March 1926 he gave eight lectures on 'The Metaphysical Poetry of the Seventeenth Century with Special Reference to Donne, Crashaw, and Cowley', lectures which, almost in passing, proposed an ambitious re-interpretation of the intellectual and literary history of Europe, but more especially of England, from the thirteenth century to the present. His correspondence for this period is full of his weekly trips to Cambridge to deliver his lectures on Tuesday afternoons and then to be available for discussions with students over coffee on Wednesday mornings. Various reminiscences of these latter occasions have long been in the public domain, not least because the young William Empson occasionally attended (he did so, with characteristic Empsonian brio, without actually going to any of the lectures). The lectures were eventually published, in an exemplary edition by Ronald Schuchard, in 1993, and since Schuchard had access to letters that were at that point unpublished (and, for most scholars, inaccessible), the present volume does not add much to our understanding of this particular episode, though Eliot's subsequent exchanges with H. J. C. Grierson and Mario Praz show how anxious, and deferential, he could be when exposing his work to the critical eyes of the real professionals in the field.

This third volume of his letters is more revealing about an episode in which Eliot came even closer to academia, albeit in the rather peculiar form of All Souls College, Oxford, where Geoffrey Faber was a Fellow (and Estates Bursar). It has long been known that in the spring of 1926, Faber proposed Eliot for a research fellowship at the college, but this edition now makes available Faber's well-judged letter of support, Eliot's statement of his intended research, and testimonials from Bruce Richmond, editor of the *TLS*, and Charles Whibley, conservative literary journalist, stalwart of *Blackwood's Magazine*, and Fellow of Jesus College, Cambridge. In his research proposal, Eliot explained how he would extend and—perhaps with an eye to the college's reputation in History—substantiate the case that he had sketched in his Clark Lectures, a project he characterized as lying 'in an unexplored territory where the frontiers of philosophy, history, literature and the technique of verse meet'. He was, of course, not the first, and far from the last, applicant to try to describe his interests in terms he hoped might fit a particular academic slot, but this buffed-up scholarly pitch goes considerably beyond his faux-humble self-description (when declining an invitation from another institution to lecture on aesthetics) as 'only a writer of verse and a literary critic'. In pressing Eliot's case, Faber had already had to counter the objection of one Fellow that Eliot was merely a 'light skirmisher' rather than a true scholar, but the truth was that during these years Eliot opportunistically shuttled between these identities, trying to fend off expectations while simultaneously pulling rank.

Hitherto, our understanding of the All Souls episode has largely been dependent on A. L. Rowse's entertaining account of Eliot's eventual rejection. According to Rowse, who had recently been elected to a prize fellowship at the age of 22, Eliot's application was being regarded favourably until Rowse lent his copy of Eliot's verse to two or three elderly Fellows who were so scandalized by the 'indecency' of some of the early poems that they blackballed his candidature. This story is now partly supported by Faber's soberer post-mortem analysis, though he laid more weight on the (dispiritingly familiar) reservations of a number of senior historians about whether Eliot's proposed work on the seventeenth century in relation to its medieval inheritance would be 'properly' historical. Many years later, Eliot the Grand Old Man of letters could wave the episode aside: 'I am happy to say that the college was spared the ignominy of electing an unscholarly member and I was spared the waste of energy involved in pretending to a scholarship which I did not possess.' In 1926, however, he had been altogether needier, and had also, perhaps, persuaded himself (if not sufficient Fellows of All Souls) that he did possess, or would in the right circumstances acquire, the necessary scholarship. Although prone to present himself, when convenient, as 'a plain man of letters', Eliot was responsive to the claims of literary scholarship and went some way towards satisfying them. 'I do not suppose there is any need to collate the *Tenne Tragedies* text with the original texts of the separate plays?' he wrote to Whibley when preparing his edition of the Senecan plays for a volume in the series the latter edited, 'but I shall in any case examine the first editions at the [British] Museum.' It was with some pride that he later referred to his introduction to this edition as 'the most scholarly piece of work that I have done'. In his reviews written during these years he is insistent that 'literary criticism must be judged in relation to the scholarship of its time', confiding to Aldington: 'That is certainly a point which I want to hammer as much as I can.'

These letters contain several further, slightly tantalizing, instances of contact and attraction between Eliot and academia, with much mock-modest eyelash-fluttering on his part. We see him acting as an external examiner for both Ph.D. and fellowship dissertations; he gives several talks to undergraduate societies; he prevaricates over invitations to give lectures or even to consider some more permanent attachment. 'I had much rather get a job at Cambridge than at Oxford,' he confided to his mother in November 1927, perhaps to reassure her that some kind of conventional career was still a possibility, but perhaps also because he had not entirely ruled out the idea himself. In his very next letter to her he talks of lunching with the Master of a Cambridge college and of an upcoming visit to Oxford to address undergraduates; ten days later he is corresponding with Richards about the latter's celebrated lectures on 'Practical Criticism'; the following week he receives another invitation to speak at Oxford; Richards at one point draws his attention to a vacant post at Liverpool; the New School in New York repeatedly extends an invitation to him to give a course of lectures there; and so on. The possibility that he might one day have become 'Professor Eliot' does not, during these years, seem an absurdity, however much the next couple of generations grew used to thinking of 'Mr Eliot' as representing the pinnacle of non-academic literary culture.

It is important when considering Eliot's case to remember that in the 1920s only the rudiments of a career path as a professional scholar in English literature existed, and several of the (still few) professors of the subject had first made their mark as men of letters—George Saintsbury, Walter Raleigh, and Arthur Quiller-Couch were among the more prominent examples. In this connection, it is revealing to see how Eliot characterized the class of contributor whom he believed reviews such as *The Criterion* had to rely on, describing them as 'doing *two men's work*. That is to say, they are supporting themselves and their families in the Civil Service, or in museums, or in universities, or in banks and commercial houses; and are thus able to think, and read, and write independently of a livelihood.' For his purposes, Eliot is more or less equating these 'day jobs', all of which provide a man of literary inclinations with economic security and at least enough time to write well-informed essays and book reviews (as he himself had done during his eight years working in a bank). This accurately described the situation of his inner circle of contributors during these years: Bonamy Dobrée became a professor in Cairo, F. S. Flint worked in the civil service, Herbert Read was a curator at the V&A, Alec Randall served as a diplomat, and Orlo Williams was Clerk to the House of Commons. Several kinds of social and economic change thereafter combined to bring about a much sharper contrast between a university post and these other occupations; in the early twenty-first century we hardly think of a job in a bank or commercial house, or even perhaps in the civil service, as allowing much leisure to 'think, and read, and write' about literary and intellectual matters. Whether universities will remain distinct in this respect has, alas, recently come to seem uncertain.

The letters also throw an interesting light on the relations between Eliot's literary journalism and his volumes of essays, demonstrating how, by this stage of his career, he accepted commissions with an eye to composing a future collection. For instance, having published his article on Lancelot Andrewes in the *TLS* in September 1926, he replied to the editor of another journal later that year that he would be willing to write something 'if the subject fitted in with my general programme.... Two persons whom I have in mind to write about (with a view to a volume in which the essay on Andrewes would be included) are Hooker and Laud.' The volume in the making here is *For Lancelot Andrewes*, which appeared towards the end of 1928. In the event, he wrote about Archbishop Bramhall on this occasion rather than either Laud or Hooker, but he clearly still has his planned volume in mind in April 1927 when he asks Bruce Richmond if he could review a biography of Laud and the reissue of Bradley's *Ethical Studies*, the latter request yielding one of the best essays in that uneven collection. *For Lancelot Andrewes* contains, in addition to the Andrewes piece itself, five essays written during 1927 and two from the first half of 1928, and re-reading them alongside the letters gives sharper focus to the picture of Eliot making, or re-making, something of himself. We can, for example, watch his attack on various forms of secular liberalism, including its roots in the proto-individualism of earlier centuries, becoming more sustained and unyielding. Much of the essay on Bramhall is, in this vein, given over to denouncing Hobbes, including this memorable piece of social and intellectual condescension: 'Thomas Hobbes was one of those extraordinary little upstarts whom the chaotic motions of the Renaissance tossed into an eminence which they hardly deserved and have never lost.' This is the sound of Eliot walling himself in his chosen cell. Conrad Aiken's unsparing review of *For Lancelot Andrewes* identified the dominant note of the essays written during this period: 'Mr Eliot seems to be definitely and defeatedly in retreat from the present and all that it implies. A thin and vinegarish hostility towards the modern world is breathed from these pages.' In writing to members of his 'phalanx', urging them to pursue and cut down some liberal quarry, Eliot sounds a good deal less vinegarish than he does when posturing in print, but the same animus is repeatedly in evidence.

There is a fair amount of other meat here for biographical carnivores, from the fond yet carefully controlled letters to his mother to the camped-up obscenities of his elaborate 'Bolovian' letters to Dobrée (the Bolovians were an invented primitive people; 'Dear Buggamy' gives the tone of the larking). There are his reports that Vivienne is in a sanatorium in France 'by her own wish' (which may not have been Vivienne's entire view of the matter), and the undeniable evidence of how much more settled and contented he seemed when living a de facto bachelor existence. His passing admission, in the course of a rather philosophical set of reflections on 'the good life' in which 'saintliness' and a good dinner both feature, that 'I remember also minor pleasures of drunkenness and adultery', will no doubt set some biographical hares scurrying.

The exchange with Geoffrey Faber in which this phrase occurs is one of the most engaging things in the book, partly because Faber took the risk of pushing beyond the usual polite pleasantries. While on holiday in September 1927, he sent Eliot a long rumination on his own understanding of 'the good things of life', casting himself a little as *l'homme moyen sensuel*, but actually displaying exceptional reflectiveness, including some thoughtful warnings to Eliot about where his work and his life were heading. Having warmed up with some plain-mannish objections to aspects of Eliot's poetry, he took his courage in both hands and plunged further:

> Lastly, I will be even more impertinent, and make a personal criticism—one which I feel strongly, but am rather at a loss to phrase. I do think that, for whatever reason, you are putting yourself in some danger by the rigidity of your way of life. It is not right that you should chain yourself to a routine—it will cramp your mind, and ultimately be fatal to you both as poet and critic, if for no other reason than that it will divorce you further and further from the common man.

Taking a long view of Eliot's writing career, we may feel that Faber's anxiety was not groundless, but at this point Eliot desperately needed the security of a rigid routine if he was not to relapse into one or other kind of ruin (his own admiring description of Tennyson may be pertinent; 'the most instinctive rebel against the society in which he was the most perfect conformist'). In his reply, Eliot does not seem to have addressed this affectionately intended criticism, keeping (self-protectively?) to a more abstract level of analysis, though throwing in the occasional dictum that might be thought also to bear on his own situation: 'If anyone asked me what I take to be the good things of life, I should say, primarily, heroism and saintliness.' For the most part, the two men, working in the same building each day, had little cause to write letters to each other, but the marked rise of intensity in this exchange compared to most of the letters gathered here makes one hope that in future volumes Faber will be taking many more holidays.

Still, it would have needed more than a bit of good-natured chaffing to pierce the many protective layers Eliot placed between himself and the world, and it is expressive of this deep guardedness that the two most dramatic decisions he took during 1927 leave scarcely any trace in his correspondence. A letter to Whibley in November thanks him for his support in enabling Eliot to become a British subject, surely a momentous decision for a free-born American, albeit one who was shortly to describe himself as a 'royalist in politics'. 'I was only disappointed to find the oath of allegiance a very inferior ceremony' is his single, designedly sardonic, reference to the event: 'I expected to be summoned to the Home Office at least, if not before the Throne.' And similarly, when this lapsed Unitarian was received into the Anglican Church, his letters largely confine themselves to the practicalities of dates and places. Having been baptized by his friend William Force Stead and confirmed by the Bishop of Oxford the following day, Eliot sent the kind of polite bread-and-butter letter that made the whole thing sound as though it had been a slightly stiff lunch party: 'My dear Stead, Besides my gratitude for the serious business and the perfect way you managed every part of it, I must say how thoroughly I enjoyed my visit to you, and meeting several extremely interesting and delightful people.' We must look elsewhere for evidence of both the turmoil and the hard-won joy that were part of this troubled man's spiritual life.

Two concluding thoughts. First, in his retrospective tribute to Bruce Richmond, written in 1961, Eliot observed: 'Good literary criticism requires good editors as well as good critics.' Richmond must have performed some such role for Eliot, who did much of his best critical writing for the *TLS* (he was a notably frequent contributor during these years, with 14 reviews and other pieces in 1926 and 15 in 1927, several of them substantial essays of 3,000 words or more). Eliot, in turn, was an able occupant of the office for his stable of *Criterion* regulars, and these letters provide further documentation of his careful blending of thoughtful commissioning, timely encouragement, and tactful correction, as when praising a review by the young Dadie Rylands as 'learned, allusive, and indirect', before adding 'rather too much so perhaps for a critical review, in which directer if cruder methods, though always according to the Queensbury rules, are more effective'. One can see, more clearly than ever, why he was once ironically described as 'the last great periodical editor of the nineteenth century'. And now his own letters have benefited from enormously thorough yet judicious editing. The installation of the experienced and learned John Haffenden as General Editor of this sometimes vexed edition has brought a new level of authority and precision to the annotation and other editorial matter.

And second, Eliot, already aware in 1927 that future generations might have an interest in 'the man behind the poetry', urged his mother to make sure that his letters to her were to be destroyed after her death. 'I don't like reading other people's private correspondence in print, and I do not want other people to read mine.' One might, pedantically, try to argue that there are very few 'private' letters here: the proportions reflect his working life and the chance of what has survived rather than editorial decision, though the fact that his secretary kept carbon copies of his typed office correspondence means that that category was almost bound to predominate. But some letters are included that are, by any standards, 'private', not least letters by and about Vivienne that speak of utterly desolating unhappiness on both their parts. And Eliot's letters to close friends—Pound, Aiken, Aldington, and increasingly Faber, as well perhaps as Read and Dobrée—shift from the playful to the serious to the heartfelt to the business-like and back to the bawdy in the way letters to friends will and should. But no one, I think could object to or regret their publication now. Eliot has not thus far been well served by biographers and other speculators about his 'private life' (the restrictions on access to much of the unpublished material have not helped), and if the letters, at least those included in these two volumes, do not throw much direct light on the poetry, they do enable us to run our fingers over the texture of his public life and to witness him exercising his considerable talents as businessman, polemicist, and networker, as well as getting glimpses of him as son, brother, husband, and friend.

Poets have to do something in the many hours that writing poetry does not fill (a plight they share with mathematicians, logicians, sprinters, and other specialists in intensity). In these pages we see Eliot—former poet, future poet, but for the moment largely a resting poet—beginning to assemble around him the stockades of a life that would protect him against the various kinds of 'ruin' (economic, social, sexual, spiritual) he had flirted with in the previous decade. We leave him at the end of December 1927 writing to one contributor in reassuring terms about the future of the yet again imperilled *Criterion*—'we are hopeful of enlisting sufficiently powerful support to enable the review to continue indefinitely'—while also confiding to his Anglican spiritual adviser that he now took communion three times a week. With these pit-props in place there seemed some prospect that he might yet make something of his life.

3

Hierophants

C. Day-Lewis and Graham Greene

I

What are poets good for? Are all attempts to speak of 'the function of poetry', with that reductive definite article, doomed to pompous and empty failure? In response to these questions, the sentence which immediately precedes Shelley's over-quoted dictum that 'poets are the unacknowledged legislators of the world' is rarely cited, and one can see why. 'Poets', he huffs and puffs, 'are the hierophants of an unapprehended inspiration; the mirrors of the gigantic shadows which futurity casts upon the present; the words which express what they understand not; the trumpets which sing to battle, and feel not what they inspire; the influence which is moved not, but moves.' It is a daunting job-description, or would be if we didn't suspect that this was Shelley doing his regular rhetorical workout, the literary equivalent of feeling the burn. But although it may not have been common in the past century or so for poets to speak of themselves as 'hierophants of an unapprehended inspiration', the idea of a special bardic role (with markedly didactic, even priestly, overtones) did not disappear in the post-Romantic generations. It was still present, in suitably modern dress, in the 1930s, particularly in the actions and pronouncements of a group of young poets who did indeed see themselves as 'the mirrors of the gigantic shadows which futurity casts upon the present'. Their writing assumed that there was a substantial public which expected poets, above all others, to take the pulse of the age. That age has, in literary-historical terms, been labelled 'the Auden generation', and this narrow identification reflected, as Chris Baldick observed in his excellent volume in the Oxford English Literary History, *The Modern Movement 1910–1940*, 'a traditional yet

Peter Stanford, *C Day-Lewis: A Life* (Continuum, 2007).
Jeremy Lewis, *Shades of Greene: One Generation of an English Family* (Jonathan Cape, 2010).

increasingly unreliable assumption that the true voice of any generation will be heard from its poets. The Thirties were the last years in which that assumption was widely shared.'

Quite how widely is hard to say, of course, just as it would be rash to assume that it has altogether died out, even now. But it's true that a small group of poets do dominate popular conceptions of 'the Thirties' as a literary period, above all the four roped together in Roy Campbell's spiteful caricature 'MacSpaunday'— Louis MacNeice, Stephen Spender, W. H. Auden, and C. Day-Lewis—a composite creature marked by its blend of glib Marxism, shameless self-advertising, and large quantities of indifferent verse. As the popular label for the period suggests, Auden was from the start the dominating presence, and poetically he increasingly came to be seen as in a class of his own. MacNeice was, in truth, always an awkward recruit to this team, both poetically and politically, and he has enjoyed a revived standing in his own right in recent decades as a result of discerning attention from a later generation of Ulster-born poets and critics. Getting attention had rarely been Spender's problem, but even before his death in 1995, column inches had long ceased to be matched by critical esteem. Still, all three of these poets have in recent years been the subject of very full critical biographies, exhumations that have helped rescue their individuality from the homogenizing group identity.

In the 1930s, that identity seemed to be incarnated in its purest form in Cecil Day-Lewis (as an author, he only used his initial, and for a while he even experimented, driven by self-consciousness of class, with omitting his hyphen). Of the four, it was Day-Lewis who came closest to fulfilling the ancient bardic role of recording in verse the major collective experiences of his tribe. This may, in turn, have contributed to his having suffered the most dramatic decline in poetic reputation among the quartet (Spender might run him close here); the fact that no full-scale biography of him had been attempted in the three decades following his death in 1972 also meant he was less likely than his contemporaries to be seen in his full complexity and thereby reassessed. Peter Stanford, prompted and supported by Day-Lewis's widow, the actress Jill Balcon, has now undertaken the work of recovery, and he makes clear that he believes this biography should provide the occasion for a major reappraisal of his subject's standing as a poet.

Having just read a lot of the poetry, I have to say that I find it hard to imagine Day-Lewis's reputation being swept to new heights by a surge of critical acclaim. From this distance, it is rather his career as a poet that seems of greater interest than the poetry itself, providing a revealing illustration of several of the major features of the sociology of literary life in mid-twentieth-century Britain: the smallness and relative social homogeneity of the dominant literary circles in the 1930s; the peculiar circumstances of the book-starved, reading-hungry 1940s; the importance of radio as a patron of new writing in the 1940s and 1950s; and, from beginning to end, the partly successful attempts to keep alive a traditional idea of the cultural centrality of poetry and the public role of the poet.

There is nothing novel in noting that 'the Auden gang' (in *Scrutiny*'s hostile idiom) all came from families which, while neither rich nor titled, were well established in the ranks of the genteel professional class. Both of Auden's grandfathers were clergymen and his father a doctor, eventually a medical professor; MacNeice's father was a clergyman, ending up as a Church of Ireland bishop; Spender's father was a well-known and well-connected Liberal journalist and man of letters. Day-Lewis's father was also a clergyman whose promising ecclesiastical career was initially blighted by the death of his first wife when his son was only 4. Eventually he was appointed to a comfortable living in Edwinstowe in Nottinghamshire and later married a comparatively wealthy woman. Cecil Day-Lewis grew up, therefore, as a 'gentleman' in a society in which that was still an instantly recognizable, and hugely consequential, social identity; even when he was struggling to live on his clerical stipend at the beginning of the 1920s, his father maintained 'the household staff of a gardener and two maids that he felt a man in his position required'. For his son, public school, at Sherborne, was followed by four years reading, or more often not reading, Classics at Oxford from 1923 to 1927. Friendships formed at Oxford in the 1920s seem so pervasive in the literary life of inter-war Britain that we may be in danger of forgetting how small the absolute numbers were: Day-Lewis was one of only just over a thousand undergraduates coming up to Oxford that year (well under 0.2 per cent of the age-cohort). The social confidence derived from belonging to this tiny gentlemanly elite was hugely important in sustaining the personally not very confident young Day-Lewis as he took his first steps towards his chosen career of being 'a poet'.

The most important thing Day-Lewis did at Oxford was to meet Auden, three years his junior but already behaving like a fully ordained hierophant. Together they edited *Oxford Poetry 1927*, and their poetic careers were to be closely linked for the next ten years, as much for the precocity of their success as for their shared commitment to left-wing ideals (Day-Lewis's first 'Collected' came out from the Hogarth Press when he was 30). Both had spells of prep-school teaching after graduation, and then in 1935 Day-Lewis embarked on the endless round of anxiety and over-production that is the lot of most freelance writers. Fortunately, he discovered in himself another talent beside that for poems and revolutionary manifestos, and under the pen-name of 'Nicholas Blake' he published a whole series of commercially successful detective stories, the classic genteel-class literary genre of the inter-war period.

At this point, Day-Lewis seemed even more of a whole-hogger for 'the Revolution' than Auden and Spender (MacNeice never subscribed to their Soviet enthusiasms), the peak of political commitment being reached in the years between the publication of his long poetic sequence *The Magnetic Mountain* in 1933 and his editing of a once-celebrated volume of essays on Socialism and culture, *The Mind in Chains*, in 1937. The fact that the Hogarth Press published all his early volumes of poetry was one sign of his good connections, and the fact that, alongside the main edition, Leonard Woolf arranged for the release of a limited, more luxurious, edition of 100 copies of *The Magnetic Mountain*, signed by the author, indicates one of the ways in which political idealism and commercial shrewdness could promote each other in the publishing conditions of the time. Though still in his twenties, Day-Lewis could be marketed both as a commodity and as a collectable. According to the *Partisan Review*, here living up to its name, *The Magnetic Mountain* was perhaps 'the most important revolutionary poem as yet written by an Englishman' (the 'as yet' hitting the authentic note of Thirties' progressive optimism). Other critics were more inclined to describe it as, in Stanford's summary, 'something Auden might have written on an off-day'. There does now seem to be a rather dreary clunkiness about much of this manifesto in verse, apostrophizing the 'victims | Of a run-down machine':

> You shall be leaders when a zero hour is signalled,
> Wielders of power and welders of a new world

looking forward to

> A day when power for all shall radiate
> From the sovereign centres.

Throughout the 1930s, Day-Lewis's work attracted the usual venom from Geoffrey Grigson and the usual unsparing criticism from F. R. Leavis, but his consecration in the eyes of a wider public had come with T. E. Lawrence's judgement in conversation with Winston Churchill, as reported in the *Evening Standard* in 1934, that Day-Lewis was the one 'great man' in the country—'present company excepted'.

However, by the late 1930s, his radical ardour cooling, Day-Lewis began to tire of being in the spotlight, and in 1938 he 'noiselessly slipped the painter' of public life, as he put it, retreating to rural seclusion in a cottage in Devon, just inside the border with Dorset. By this point he had been married to his first wife Mary for ten years, with two small children, and he was growing sexually restless. An energetic, carefree affair with the sexually eager wife of a neighbour put a strain on his marriage that it seemed able to withstand, though it was a portent of greater strains to come. The affair, which stirred some of Day-Lewis's gayest, most lyrical pieces, soon acquired the golden glow of a lost Eden for another reason when Hitler invaded Poland.

Day-Lewis had a good wartime, though not much war. At first, his contribution involved little more than drilling a handful of Devon farm-workers in the rituals of the Home Guard, while otherwise getting on with his writing. From 1941 he spent his weekdays in London, working at the Ministry of Information. As Stanford neutrally comments: 'Of all the 1930s poets, he had shown the greatest capacity for producing propaganda and propaganda was the business of the ministry.' His main literary task in the opening years of the war was a translation of Virgil's *Georgics*, a nostalgic celebration of the rhythms of farming and rural life in the first century BC. In Day-Lewis's version, this became what Stanford calls 'a rousing hymn of classless patriotism at a time of national emergency'. (Rebecca West commented more tartly that it was 'the East Mediterranean edition of the *Farmers' Weekly*... two thousand years out of date'.) The translation sold over 11,000 copies, an index of the general appetite for reading matter during the war as well as of Day-Lewis's dexterity in recruiting Virgil to a Home Guard of the mind. He enjoyed similar success when his little collection of *Poems in War-time* appeared in 1941; indeed, the war years may have been the peak of his critical standing, as attested by the enthusiastic reviews for a 'Selected', published in the same year, which was one of the first titles in John Lehmann's 'New Hogarth Library' series.

The exceptional circumstances of the war not only contributed to Day-Lewis's literary success; they provided the enabling conditions for the most significant love-affair of his life. The novelist Rosamond Lehmann reviewed *Poems in Wartime* in the *New Statesman*, proclaiming that Day-Lewis was 'a writer with a profound and happy experience of love'. Day-Lewis responded to the review by inviting her to dinner, as one would. By this point, Lehmann herself had had considerable experience of both love and its absence, and her experience had been far from happy. She was 40, he 37: their passionate and very public relationship was to last nine years, initially pursued through the falling bombs in a number of London flats, later taking on a more settled domestic rhythm when he spent part of each week at Lehmann's house in Berkshire, returning no less regularly to his wife and children in Devon. It is always something of a surprise to be reminded how much of the conventional literary round of launches and parties continued in wartime London, and Lehmann and Day-Lewis's life of snatched nights and open appearances together at such gatherings reflected an atmosphere that was both nerve-twangingly on edge and sexually relaxed.

This mixture of heightened emotions seems to have elicited some of his best poems, several of which are to be found in his 1943 volume *Word Over All*, another commercial success, going through five impressions by 1946. By this point, his renunciation of the 'pylon poetry' and political sloganeering of his youth was complete: this was the poet Doing His Bit. For example, 'The Stand-To', evoking his time with his little platoon of Devon Home Guardsmen, repudiated 'Destiny, History' and similar rhetorical abstractions as 'the words of the politicians', while he more humbly asks the autumn wind to 'sing through me for the lives that are worth a song'—though, of course, this is only mock-humility, since he is still taking bardic responsibility upon himself. This sinking of political energy into the common enterprise was caught in what may be his most quoted quatrain:

It is the logic of our times,
No subject for immortal verse—
That we who lived by honest dreams
Defend the bad against the worse.

Little actual defending had been called for in the lanes and fields of Devon in 1940 and 1941, but the lines hit the right note for the time. Stanford suggests that Day-Lewis was here taking his cue from Yeats in 'On Being Asked for a War Poem':

I think it better that in times like these
A poet's mouth be silent, for in truth
We have no gift to set a statesman right.

But arguably Day-Lewis was shifting the register rather than altogether putting off his hierophant's robes; indeed, something similar was, arguably, true of Yeats, too. In times of public clamour, neither poet was naturally given to 'silence'.

War and war's alarms furnished Day-Lewis with a theme adequate to his high conception of the poet's place in society. In 'Ode to Fear', from the same collection, the sky is filled with 'a throbbing cello-drone of planes', that familiar wartime sound,

When Fear puts unexpected questions
And makes the heroic body freeze like a beast surprised.

Such fear may in time serve 'cleansing' functions, but meanwhile the scribe goes about his modest business:

Today, I can but record
In truth and patience
This high delirium of nations
And hold to it the reflecting, fragile word.

Day-Lewis's habitual self-consciousness about the poet's role finds another voice here. For all its parade of weakness, the poem actually expresses a continuing confidence that 'the reflecting, fragile word' will prove adequate when faced with the 'delirium of nations'.

In the second half of the 1940s, Day-Lewis took on more and more of those roles which successful poets undertake in the hours when they are not writing poetry. Stanford observes that Day-Lewis had 'refined his position of the 1930s into a broader support for the public role of poetry'. 'Refined' rather slides over the evident discontinuities between his pre- and post-war personae, but the concern with the 'role' of poetry was indeed a constant. One sign of his standing was the invitation to give the Clark Lectures at Cambridge, published in 1947 as *The Poetic Image*, one of his several attempts to lay down the law about the lawless nature of poetry. He and Lehmann tried their hand at founding a new literary journal, a fever that comes upon so many writers at some point in their careers: *Orion* folded after four, irregular, numbers. In 1949, the BBC commissioned him, for a sum equivalent to a year's salary, to translate Virgil's *Aeneid*. It was broadcast in 1951 as part of the Festival of Britain, and published, to considerable acclaim, the following year. This was an important and effective way of maintaining poetry's high office at a time when the proportion of the reading public that had been Classically educated to some level was not negligible and when the Classics still enjoyed a wider cultural deference. His success in these roles was signalled by the award of a CBE in 1950, and in 1951 by his election as Professor of Poetry at Oxford, the first lecture of his tenure being broadcast on the Third Programme. In the same year a selection of his work appeared as a volume in the 'Penguin Poets' series, Eliot having at that point been the only other living poet to have received this particular accolade.

The end of the 1940s may have marked the end of his best poetry; it certainly saw the end of his increasingly fractious relationship with Lehmann, as well as, in a gesture of fresh starts and new springs, his divorce from Mary. The immediate stimulus to this unusual spate of decisiveness in matters of the heart was meeting Jill Balcon, twenty-one years his junior, with whom he fell urgently in love after the briefest acquaintance and whom he married in 1951. (It is a pity his courage didn't extend to telling the distraught Lehmann to her face that their relationship was over, rather than resorting to the cowardly medium of a letter.) There were one or two sexual forays still to come—he was, all reports concur, extremely attractive to women, and old habits are hard to lose—but it seems to have been a happy marriage, producing two children, the younger of whom is the actor Daniel Day-Lewis.

The speaking engagements and committee memberships that increasingly took up the last two decades of his life may have been, in their way, expressions of what Stanford calls 'his continuing belief that the poet had a public, civic role', but from the 1950s onwards the public seemed less disposed to recognize that role, or at least to find him a compelling occupant of it. For his part, he continued to repudiate the fashionable cultivation of difficulty and the deliberate address to a minority audience. As he put it in his Norton Lectures at Harvard in 1964: 'We are so inured nowadays to accepting poetry as an art for the minority that it is difficult to put ourselves in the minds of the people who knew it as a popular art.' Perhaps it was part of both his achievement and his failing that he wrote as though poetry were still a popular art, even though it mostly wasn't. His practice was informed by a neo-Wordsworthian commitment to simplicity, sincerity, purity, 'complete truth to feeling', and by the attempt, as he put it, 'to discover images and rhythms which convey the elemental states of mind a man shares with all other living men and has in common with his remotest ancestors'.

Day-Lewis's poetic reputation might have been higher in his final decades, as well as since his death, had he published less. However, not only was he a professional writer with a living to make, but to the writer's ingrained habit of turning experience into words was conjoined a striking (perhaps class-based?) confidence that the world was waiting for those words. John Masefield, the aged Poet Laureate, perhaps had less of this confidence by this date: Stanford reports the endearing fact that when, following some royal or public event, a poem by Masefield would arrive unheralded at the offices of *The Times*, it was always accompanied by a stamped self-addressed envelope. In the 1960s, Day-Lewis increasingly acted as Masefield's unofficial deputy, giving, for instance, the address in Westminster Abbey to mark Shakespeare's 400th anniversary. When Masefield finally died in 1967, Day-Lewis was appointed to succeed him. Letters of congratulation even included an effusion from his bank manager ('The whole Midland is rejoicing with you'). Others reflected that the Laureateship is more often the kiss of poetic death, 'by appointment to HM the Queen' rarely proving the guarantee of quality goods in this particular trade. Day-Lewis seems to have recognized that much of what he turned out in this capacity was hack work, but his defence was consistent with the conception he had had of his role from the outset: 'The important thing is to keep the idea of poetry before the public eye.' One response to this might be to think that he was better at the *idea* of poetry than at the thing itself; another might be to think that the public *ear* would be the appropriate organ to aim at. It could be said that he managed that, indirectly, by dying: his memorial service from St Martin's-in-the-Fields in October 1972 was broadcast live on BBC radio.

Day-Lewis is presumably doomed to be forever cast as 'a poet of the 1930s', but if such period labels are needed it seems to me more illuminating to consider him as 'a poet of the 1940s'. That decade not only saw much of his best work and the high point of his popularity, but its peculiar circumstances nurtured both a sense of civic responsibility and an appetite for elevating, consoling reading that suited Day-Lewis's rather old-fashioned sense of poetry's rightful presence in society. It was also the decade in which radio enjoyed a more important role in British life than it ever had before or, possibly, ever has since. Day-Lewis wrote well for radio, though perhaps not as well and certainly not as much as MacNeice, who was employed by the BBC for most of the 1940s and 1950s. MacNeice's appreciative judgement (quoted in John Stallworthy's fine biography) that BBC radio was 'one of the least interfering patrons there have ever been' seems borne out by Day-Lewis's experiences, and it is worth remembering how much of this enlightened and imaginative commissioning pre-dated the founding of the Third Programme in 1946 and was continued by the Home Service thereafter.

It is something of a critical commonplace to diagnose the chief weakness of much 1930s poetry, particularly that of 'the Auden gang', as arising from its subordination to political ideology, as though it provided mere rhyming programme notes for a performance starring History, Class, Dialectic, and similar capitalized abstractions. There is something to this charge, but even in Day-Lewis's case—he is usually singled out as the most doctrinaire and consequently the most flawed poetically—this could only be alleged of a small proportion of his *œuvre*, and anyway it is not clear that his poetry did not gain as well as suffer from its political ambitions if one takes a wider view of the things poetry might try to do. I wonder whether the complaint that some of what he wrote was 'oratory, not poetry' (in this case the words are Virginia Woolf's) isn't what we should expect from critics, who are, after all, usually acting as prosecuting counsel in the case of Art v Social Purpose. According to the Aestheticist creed, it is not only better to write one immortal line than to rally the troops, but all attempts at the latter goal are bound to produce merely shallow, drum-banging, formulaic stuff, not the charged intensity of 'felt experience'. Well, maybe, but maybe there is also something to be said for the idea of trying to use verse to rally the troops in the first place—for, that is, believing that different types of poetry might perform different types of function, and that there is something admirable in the idea of wanting it to be as normal to use verse as to use prose in order to address fellow-citizens about matters of shared public interest. In this period one might identify a parallel ambition in the attempts by T. S. Eliot and Christopher Fry to write verse drama—not altogether encouraging examples, to be sure, but efforts similarly animated by a desire to see poetry as a recognized, familiar medium for communal as well as private experience.

In the 1930s Day-Lewis and his friends had wanted to write poetry that was modern but not Modernist. As his programmatic commitment to the future softened, sloughing off the association with technology and shiny novelty in general, his distance from Modernism's formal experimentation became more evident. He acknowledged the element of 'pastiche Auden' in his early work, but it became clearer in the 1940s that his real poetic masters were Hardy and, more indirectly, Wordsworth. By the 1950s this could have made for recognition of unobvious continuities with the disciplined mundanity of a younger poet such as Larkin rather than with either the metaphysical disjunctions of post-Eliotic Modernists or the cascading syllables of Dylan Thomas's 'New Romanticism', but 'Movement' writers were allergic to the whiff of self-importance they detected in poets too at ease on public platforms. When Day-Lewis's *Collected Poems* was published in 1954, it met with a muted reception. George Fraser confined his praise to the 'dexterity' and the 'many skilfully absorbed influences' visible in the work. As Day-Lewis became more and more of a panjandrum (he chaired the Arts Council's Literature panel in the 1960s), younger poets became more dismissive: Eavan Boland mocked his 'cool dejected, rose-water poems, with their flowery symbols of transience'. That doesn't seem quite right: yearning, and its bafflement, is far more present than dejection, and there are echoes of Robert Frost in the ways in which his conversational prosiness rises to its own kind of lyricism. But he does, poetry and prose taken together, now seem very much of his period, standing for a kind of Reithian ideal of poetry that would inform, educate, and entertain. Like so much of the literary and intellectual life of the 1940s and 1950s, he was part of an old-fashioned social elite that profited from cultural deference while taking advantage of new ways to reach wider publics. He outlived the days when poets could still hope to be treated as hierophants or unacknowledged legislators, but in his way he tried to embody the 'public service' ideal, contributing to the cultural aims of the welfare state by becoming the Virgil of the Third Programme.

Stanford does a decent job of narrating the life, and he is to be congratulated on resisting the elephantiasis that infects so much contemporary literary biography. But the endnotes to the book are a shocking example of some trade publishers' condescending attitudes towards their readers. First, the 'references' are so scarce, brief, and entirely lacking page numbers that they provide no help in tracing any particular quotation or piece of information. But, worse, a large number of these 'notes' are not references at all, but minimal identifications of some of the famous names mentioned in passing in the text. For example, in the chapter on Day-Lewis's schooldays at Sherborne we are told that the boy showed little interest in the surrounding county, but later 'he was to grow passionate about Dorset, and especially about Thomas Hardy'. That, as the attached note will tell you (if you can find it) is 'Thomas Hardy (1840–1928)'. And that is all it will tell you. Similarly, we are told that the headmaster, Nowell-Smith, was 'a distinguished Wordsworth scholar'. An endnote number attached to the poet's name has us again turning to the back of the book where, after some rummaging (there are not even any running heads with page numbers to make the hunt easier), we find the note: 'William Wordsworth (1770–1850), Poet Laureate from 1843.' It is almost impossible to reconstruct the conception of readers and their needs that must have led to the insertion of these otiose, patronizing 'references', which are pervasive. The irritatingness is compounded at moments of emotional drama, such as this early encounter with Jill Balcon: 'He walked Balcon home past what had once been George Eliot's house in Chelsea's Cheyne Walk. They carved their initials in the tree outside. That night they became lovers.' A superscripted number hovers officiously around the famous name, simply so that we can break off to discover among the endnotes 'George Eliot (1819–80)', and nothing more—not that she was a novelist, not even what her real name was. What possible justification can there be for this inane mixture of intrusiveness and uninformativeness? Both Stanford and Day-Lewis deserve better, and so do the rest of us.

II

Graham Greene was more than half in love with easeful failure. He chose to end *A Sort of Life*, the sly memoir of his early years that stood in for an autobiography, with 'the years of failure which followed the acceptance of my first novel', adding the characteristic gloss that 'failure too is a kind of death' and so may conclude the story of a life as appropriately as one's last breath. Greene had famously gambled his adolescent life on the odds that one of the five empty chambers of the revolver he held to his head would be more likely to come up when he pulled the trigger than the one loaded with a bullet (or so he later wished us to believe). In his case, it is not clear which outcome should more properly be regarded as 'failure' here: 'winning' at Russian roulette could be seen as condemning him to more years of unbearable boredom, as yet another drug started to lose its power. A typical character from one of his novels would presumably have put the gun to his head but been unable to pull the trigger, thereby generating further grounds for the self-loathing which had driven him to this desperate act. Desperate and sinful: suicide, even attempted suicide, perhaps even the stagey simulation of possible suicide, is, according to traditional Christian teaching, a sin against the Holy Ghost, and although Greene, who converted to Catholicism when he was 22, may have had no orthodox belief in the Holy Ghost, he devoutly believed in sin. And sin, too, is a kind of failure, a confirmation of man's fallen state as well as a welcome escape from the tedium of virtue. It is easy to come away from Greene's books with the thought that the deepest form of human inauthenticity is to be a worldly success.

But that, of course, is precisely what Graham Greene became—a huge success. He became a best-selling author who was also critically acclaimed—indeed, something of a hierophant in prose; he became a very rich man; and he became that indefinable but recognizable thing—a public figure (he appeared on the cover of *Time* magazine, a major form of consecration in the decades after the Second World War). This was success as members of his family and class understood it, albeit that Greene inhabited his fame in an idiosyncratic and reclusive way. But it was, he always felt, just a series of disguises; he was driven on, he claimed, 'by this damned desire to be successful that came from a sense of inferiority'. The wealth, fame, and independence that he came to know in the 1950s could never still the itch of self-disgust. During that decade he roamed the world with even more than his usual restlessness: 'I had no employer from whom to escape—only myself, and the only trust I could betray was the trust of those who loved me.' Escape and betrayal were something to hold on to when one's life seemed to be slipping into a bottomless abyss of success.

Greene had gambled with his life in a different way when in 1929, at the age of 25, he had resigned his secure job as a sub-editor on *The Times* in order to try to convert the unexpected success of his first novel, *The Man Within*, into a career as a writer. Three years and two woeful flops later, it looked as though the chamber with the bullet was spinning into place. He wished, he later reflected, that he had had an experienced mentor to call upon for advice—someone such as Robert Louis Stevenson who 'had always seemed to me "one of the family"'. Greene was distantly related to RLS through his mother's cousin. 'Names which appeared in his Collected Letters were photographs in our family album. In the nursery we played on the bagatelle board which had belonged to him. Surely from my relative in Samoa I might have received better and more stringent counsel than from my publisher.' This sense of connection, even identification, with Stevenson stirred his imagination. Wishing in retrospect that he had been the beneficiary of the right kind of avuncular counsel, his mind instinctively moved to 'my relative in Samoa', a writer who had capped success in his thirties with voluntary exile and early death at the age of 44. As a boy playing on Berkhamsted common, Greene had cast himself as David Balfour, and as novelist he can be thought to have given his own bleak twist to the kind of 'adventure story' with which Stevenson's name was for so long associated. In 1949 he began to write a biography of Stevenson, only abandoning it when he discovered that another biographer was well ahead of him. For such a determined loner, Greene had a pronounced streak of family piety.

Commenting on young Graham's first novel, his rich uncle 'Eppy' (Edward) told him: 'It could only have been written by a Greene.' In his memoir, Greene stages his puzzlement at this remark:

> I thought of my parents, I thought of all those aunts and uncles and cousins who had gathered together at Christmas, and of the two unknown Greene grandfathers, . . . and then I thought of the novel, the story of a hunted man, of smuggling and treachery, of murder and suicide, and I wondered what on earth he was driving at. I wonder still.

But he didn't really, because in his mind he had already constructed a pleasing line of descent. There was 'something at least of the Greene character in *The Man Within*, if only that irrational desire to escape from himself which had led one Greene grandfather out of the Church and the other to die in St Kitts'. Much later, he was to call the episodic volume which served as the second half of his autobiography *Ways of Escape*, but he knew that one never could escape, and that even through the fug of sex and drink in low dives in far-off ports he could find ways to torment himself. In the later decades of his life, he lived abroad permanently in an attempt to escape from success, or at least some of the undesirable consequences of success such as being buttonholed by strangers or having to pay a lot of income-tax. Antibes wasn't exactly the South Seas, but it tickled the vestige of English upper-middle-class conformity that lurked beneath his bohemian exterior to feel that he was maintaining something of a family tradition.

Family is, ostensibly, the organizing theme of *Shades of Greene*. Jeremy Lewis has not attempted to add yet another Life of the most famous Greene, instead writing a narrative account of aspects of the lives the more prominent Greene siblings and cousins, Graham included. The bloodstock details are quickly stated. Grandfather William Greene came from a family with West Indian and brewing interests; we are told that 'he qualified as a solicitor but never practised; he dabbled in scientific farming, but was unable to retain his interest'; and then, rather magnificently, that he 'abandoned full-time employment'. He married the daughter of a master mariner, and they had nine children between 1855 and 1870. The fifth was called Charles and the sixth was called Edward (lots of Greenes were). Charles became a schoolmaster, eventually the headmaster of the public school in Berkhamsted. He married his first cousin, Marion Greene, and between 1896 and 1914 they produced six children. His brother Edward went into the coffee business in Brazil, becoming quite a rich man. In Brazil he met and married a young German girl, Eva Stutzer, and between 1901 and 1914 they also had six children. Edward moved his family back to England, buying a large house in Berkhamsted in 1910, so that the two families saw a good deal of each other when the children were growing up.

'Large house' doesn't really do justice to The Hall: when it was put up for sale seventeen years later, the estate agents' particulars (Lewis hasn't stinted on the legwork) recorded that it was set in 25 acres of parkland and boasted 'seventeen bedrooms, three bathrooms, a billiards room, a "Tudor-style dairy", a vegetable garden, "a garage for three large cars", an orchard, a walled garden, tennis courts (two grass and one hard), stables, a home farm producing milk, cream and eggs, and three cottages for members of staff'. This establishment, adds Lewis with his customary twinkle, 'employed eleven indoor servants, as well as a carpenter, several gardeners, a chauffeur called Collins who, according to Barbara [one of the children], had been brought up on a farm and "was far more used to animals and never understood the workings of a car", and a very old man, the chauffeur's father, whose sole job was to mow the lawns with a horse-drawn mowing machine, and remove every weed in the process.' As this suggests, the book takes an indulgent view of local colour. When one of the Greenes (Hugh) was involved in interviewing captured Luftwaffe pilots during the war, we are told: 'His life was made easier by the fact that Luftwaffe crews often carried diaries and letters in their pockets, and he made use of his fluent German and his knowledge of their country; a dead Luftwaffe officer on Chesil Beach was found to be wearing pink silk women's underclothes and carrying lipstick and a powder puff.' A good thing Hugh was on hand to bring his knowledge of the country to bear. If only Ian McEwan's knotted protagonists had known of this particular *genius loci* it might have got their juices flowing to better effect.

Four of the 'School-house Greenes', as they were known (to distinguish them from the 'Hall Greenes'), made enough of a mark on history to merit extended discussion in this book. Raymond, the eldest brother, became a leading doctor and mountaineer, taking part in the 1933 Everest expedition. Graham became a writer. Hugh Carleton became a journalist and eventually Director-General of the BBC. And Elisabeth helped to recruit people into MI6 (including, predictably, Graham). Of the 'Hall Greenes', three receive extended treatment. Ben was active in the Labour Party in the 1930s, playing a leading part in reforming its constitution, but his extreme opposition to war with Germany led him to be classed with the far-right British People's Party, and as a result he was interned during the war. Barbara knocked about a good deal, accompanying her cousin Graham to Liberia, and then spending the entire war in Germany (she inherited excellent German from her mother). And Felix, too, became a journalist, the BBC's first North American correspondent, and subsequently a great authority on China, as well as an adept of various forms of Californian new-age twaddle. They could be ruthless in their appraisal of each other, especially the School-house Greenes of the Hall Greenes, and being interesting was de rigueur. 'He had a dull life', commented Barbara after her cousin 'Tooter's' death in 1990, 'and his wives were all dull too.' There is also the obligatory black sheep, Herbert, who drank and lost jobs yet who nonetheless managed to do the odd spot of spying along the way (for the Japanese, as it turns out, but still, the important thing is not to be boring, and old Herbert was frightfully entertaining in his frightful way). One thing the Greenes did not do was die young: in this particular inter-family competition, the Hall Greenes (I calculate) just beat the School-house Greenes, with an average life-span of 82 as opposed to the latter's 78. The score of the winning team was perhaps disproportionately boosted by the contribution of Eva, otherwise one of the less enterprising siblings, who was the last to die, aged 98, in 2001.

I expect this book will give a lot of people a lot of pleasure. It is not hard to imagine reviewers finding it 'readable', 'entertaining', 'the story of a remarkable family', 'a panoramic account of English society', and much else besides. It helps that the leading Greenes knew nearly everybody who was anybody in Britain in the 1930s and 1940s, and it helps even more that the life of the best-known member of the clan involved lots of religion, lots and lots of drink, and lots and lots and lots of sex. In addition, it won't do the book any harm that not only does Jeremy Lewis write an agreeable sentence and have a shrewd eye for amusing quotations, but he is also a senior figure in British publishing, having worked at Collins and at Chatto, as well as being an editor-at-large at the *Literary Review* and a former deputy editor of the *London Magazine*. He has written well-received biographies of Cyril Connolly and Allen Lane, and he has already published three volumes of autobiography, the last entitled *Grub Street Irregular*. Now he has written a book which is, the blurb tells us, 'both a riveting exercise in group biography and a masterly account of English society in the twentieth century'.

Perhaps I'm just not that easily riveted. The book is amiable enough, and full of interesting details, but the protocols of the genre seem to require that a wearyingly unbroken narrative pace be sustained, with any larger analysis or questioning of sources strictly forbidden, and that the more the text can be crammed with well-known names the better. Thus, when Graham's soon-to-be-estranged wife Vivien is parked in Oxford early in the war, we are told: 'she had begun her collection of dolls' houses, and included among her Oxford friends A. L. Rowse, Lord David Cecil, Maurice Bowra, Roy Harrod, Neville Coghill, and A. J. P. Taylor and his wife Margaret.' Graham's elder brother Raymond was principally an endocrinologist, but when his career in the 1930s is under discussion we are told that 'he enjoyed obstetrics and, years later, took a retrospective pride in having delivered Antonia Fraser'. Even the background fact of Uncle Eppy's having worked, when first in Brazil, for the firm of Edward Johnston prompts the tit-bit 'a scion of the family was Brian "Johnners" Johnston, the much-loved cricket commentator'. Fortunately, the occasional appearance in these pages of a hitherto unknown name serves to stir one's flagging interest.

In practice, the significant aspects of the seven main characters' careers did not overlap very much (at one point Lewis frankly concedes 'there was not much contact or even much liking between the two families'), so that what we have in effect is a series of episodic mini-biographies. The book's chief technical device as far as the narrative is concerned involves having a longish section on some colourful Greene followed by a paragraph beginning 'Meanwhile, another Greene . . . '. Lewis concentrates on the 1930s and 1940s, a period he obviously finds attractive, so the subsequent decades get rather brisk treatment, though there is a good account of Graham's later career among, and entanglements with, publishers, a topic on which Lewis writes with particular authority. There is also a very fair discussion of Hugh Carleton's controversial tenure as Director-General of the BBC, from 1960 to 1969. This Greene (six years Graham's junior) had a generous measure of the family self-confidence, but also a genuine and unstuffy liberalism about social and cultural matters, and he encouraged and defended much that was good about the corporation's broadcasting during that liberating decade against a variety of narrow-minded, philistine, and downright self-serving complaints.

If we try to adopt a slightly more analytical perspective on the wealth of interesting period detail in Lewis's book, the main organizing themes would have to be social class and cultural capital. Lewis claims that one of the things his cast had in common was 'an ability to make their own ways in the world with the self-confidence that was once so typical of the English upper-middle classes'. Only this book's blithely individualist focus could suggest that they 'made their own ways' in the world. Their ways were smoothed by caste connections and class privilege at every turn. They mostly exude a sense of entitlement, which their experiences as narrated here would have reinforced. At the mere approach of a confident young Greene, doors to promising careers opened themselves.

The Greenes grew up on the lower slopes of those peaks of privilege and gentility that dominated English society until the 1950s. Even though Graham tried heroically to turn himself into an isolated outsider, removed from any kind of 'Establishment', the family, actual as well as imagined, helped him on his way at many points. He twice failed to win a scholarship to Oxford, but, as he coolly explained, 'we still lived in a world of influential friends', and the History tutor at Balliol was 'an old pupil and disciple of my father's' and awarded Graham an Exhibition on very slender evidence. As an undergraduate, he was the contemporary of Evelyn Waugh, Cyril Connolly, Harold Acton, and other gilded youths who expected the world to pay attention to them. As the editor of *Oxford Outlook*, he asked his father to try to persuade their Berkhamsted neighbour, the eminent historian G. M. Trevelyan, to contribute, while sending his first book of poems to another Berkhamsted contact, Walter de la Mare. Edith Sitwell was gratified by an article on her poetry, but the terms in which she wrote to thank its undergraduate author suggest she also had other reasons to be well disposed: 'Do remember me to your aunt, whom I knew when young.' While still an undergraduate, Graham was introduced to many of the leading figures of literary London, and he managed to persuade the BBC to allow him and a group of student friends to read their poems live on air. Perhaps most strikingly of all, when he was 20 he successfully wrote to the German Embassy in London suggesting that they might care to subsidize a visit by him to the French-occupied Ruhr in order that a case sympathetic to Germany might be presented in the pages of those mighty organs *Oxford Outlook* (a student mag) and *Oxford Chronicle* (a local paper).

His father extended the normal parental subsidy of the day by paying off his son's drinking debts at Oxford (not small) and helping to keep him afloat financially during the lean years that followed. Having been part of the tiny elite of English society who went to Oxford in the 1920s meant that Graham thereafter had a social passport valid for entry to a series of influential networks. A friend got him some reviewing on the *Spectator* when he was hard up, another acquaintance helped him to get a publishing contract, and on it went in the small world of London literary life in the 1930s. When in 1937 Chatto tried to found a smart literary weekly, *Night and Day* (the launch party for 800 people was held at the Dorchester), Greene became its literary editor, but the paper folded within a year. During the war, several people in addition to his sister helped 'to pull the requisite strings' to get him taken on by MI6, thus initiating him into a world for which he seemed so well fitted by inclination. His immediate superior was the double-agent Kim Philby, whom he liked and later refused to condemn when Philby defected to the USSR. Philby in turn found Greene a 'tonic' for his section, 'the equivalent of a lot of stiff whiskies'—not, presumably, an innocent comparison (but then perhaps Philby didn't really do innocence). Before the war had ended, another friend had recommended Greene for a job with the publishers Eyre and Spottiswoode, and by the early 1950s his books were so successful that he no longer needed a regular job. Nonetheless, having an eminent Harley Street doctor and a future Director-General of the BBC among his brothers could still come in useful at times. Whenever life threatened to scorch him, he could usually find a spot of Greene shade.

Later in life, Greene liked to portray himself as something of a misfit, but he was in fact a recognizable representative of the English literary elite of his time, shaped by his liberal upper-middle-class family even as he rebelled against its more herbivorous tendencies, with an entrée to embassies, clubs, and rich men's houses around the world. When Hugh learned, at the age of 28, that he was to be included in the next edition of *Who's Who* (presumably on the strength of his being *The Daily Telegraph*'s Berlin correspondent), his first thought was, 'I should think Da will be able to claim a record with himself and three sons in it.' Even when most disgusted with himself, a Greene was always Somebody.

Lewis says that Graham Greene has been 'badly served by his biographers', though 'the facts of his life have been well covered', which suggests unspoken reservations about Norman Sherry's vastly detailed but calamitously self-advertising three-volume account. I'm not sure that setting a much briefer (if much better written) narrative of the novelist's life alongside parallel accounts of selected siblings and cousins changes the story much. Graham does emerge, perhaps unsurprisingly, as by some way the most interesting member of his family, partly just because he was a much better writer than any of the others, and partly because in his case the common class insouciance was shot through with a haunted, remorseful sense of evil.

The genial but slightly relentless bonhomie of Lewis's prose drove me back to reading Greene himself, not something I had done much of since I had mooned around the Surrey suburbs in my late teens fantasizing that I, too, was a writer used to drinking too much and having frank and unillusioned sex in exotic locations (not that I then knew what frank and unillusioned sex was). As others have long noted, he is an uneven writer, and the spiritual melodrama that mars some of his better novels now grates more than ever (even my teenage self thought that the ending of *The End of the Affair* ruined what was otherwise a powerful depiction of properly adult lust). But his autobiographical writings, perhaps because deliberately offhand in manner, have a spare, laconic elegance which is rare among autobiographers. A tiny illustration: as a 19-year-old he fell in love with the family's 30-year-old governess, and he tells how 'every evening of the winter vacation I would go upstairs to the nursery where she sat alone and the slow fire consumed the coals behind an iron guard'. This minor, passing instance of the pathetic fallacy has an almost Flaubertian or Nabokovian concision, a reminder of what Greene's best prose can be like when not striving for dramatic or religious effect. Or, slightly longer, his memorable description of arriving in 1920s Nottingham to work on the local paper, the tone of which is far from Lawrentian romanticism. For Greene it was 'a town as haunting as Berkhamsted' (high praise indeed), with a bleakness that sang to him. 'Like the bar of the City Hotel in Freetown which I was to know years later it was the focal point of failure, a place undisturbed by ambition, a place to be resigned to, a home from home.' The deceptive ease of the slide from, or equation between, 'the focal point of failure' and 'a home from home' neatly captures the way the dialectic of belonging and escape maps onto that of failure and success in an attempted reversal of conventional patterns.

At the end of *A Sort of Life*, Greene is drawn back to the flame of failure. In the early 1950s he visited, and smoked opium with, an old Oxford contemporary who had lived for many years in Siam. As an undergraduate, the friend 'had written poetry of great promise, but for long now he had given up any attempt to write. Unlike myself he had accepted the idea of failure and he had discovered in lack of ambition a kind of bleared happiness.' Greene did not 'accept' the idea of failure: he both courted and resisted it, strove for success and strove to undercut any conventional estimation of success. On the occasion of this visit, he had his weapons ready. 'For a writer, I argued, success is always temporary, success is only a delayed failure.' Eventually the work will be forgotten; eventually the loaded chamber will spin round. The poppy-mellowed author could afford to take the long view, following the huge success of *The Heart of the Matter* and *The Third Man*. He was much the most successful of the successful Greenes, yet also a more spectacular failure than any of the unsuccessful Greenes—a carnal, selfish, sinful man, incapable of regular family life. One is left feeling that Graham Greene mostly got what he wanted, and that what he mostly wanted was to have it both ways. In the end, failure might just be a form of delayed success. After all, there was always the possibility of eternal damnation to look forward to.

4

Critics (I)

William Empson and F. R. Leavis

I

William Empson 'invented modern literary criticism in English'. It is no small claim. Of course, we need, in the manner of the activity in question, to submit every word in that judgement (by Empson's biographer, John Haffenden) to close scrutiny. We would not ordinarily think of 'literary criticism' as something that could be 'invented', certainly not by one individual, so there is already a suspicion that Empson is here being credited with a more specific achievement than first meets the eye. 'Modern' raises another cluster of questions about how the activity Empson is alleged to have fathered differed from that practised by, say, Dryden, Johnson, Coleridge, or Arnold. And even 'in English' may be taken to signal that a distinctively English or perhaps Anglo-American tradition is at issue, to be distinguished from French or German or other European models for talking about literature.

When analysed in this way, the claim starts to become intriguing rather than self-defeatingly hyperbolic. Those who only recall Empson's name from text-book histories will associate him with the ingenious, perhaps sometimes over-ingenious, identification of multiple meanings in individual words and phrases within lines of poetry—the kind of dazzling virtuosity of interpretation that he exhibited in his first book, *Seven Types of Ambiguity*, published in 1930. But, as Haffenden's magnificent two-volume biography demonstrates, there was much, much more to him than that. Even so, any attempt at a more considered estimation of his achievement is likely to come up against a particular obstacle these days, especially in the United States, the result of a

John Haffenden, *William Empson, Vol. I: Among the Mandarins* (Oxford University Press, 2005).
John Haffenden, *William Empson, Vol. II: Against the Christians* (Oxford University Press, 2006).
Christopher Hilliard, *English as a Vocation: The 'Scrutiny' Movement* (Oxford University Press, 2012).

canard that was much put about in graduate schools in the closing decades of the twentieth century. This decreed that 'criticism' should be understood as one among several possible 'approaches' to the 'study' of literature, the approach associated above all with the distinctive, but (allegedly) unreflective and theoretically innocent, practice of the New Critics, who were dominant in the academic study of English in the United States from the 1930s to at least the 1960s, but who, it is claimed, were then superseded by the more analytical and systematic enquiries of 'literary theory'. 'Close reading' is thus supposed to have been discredited as a 'method', yielding to the superior knowingness of those deconstructive and politically sensitive 'reading strategies' known as 'the hermeneutics of suspicion'. So even if Empson could, in any intelligible sense, be credited with fathering modern 'literary criticism', that would simply confirm that his work is outmoded, an exhibit belonging to the palaeolithic period in the history of the discipline of literary studies.

Among its several failings, this tendentious piece of pseudo-history confused the activity of reading works of literature with the various claims made *about* that activity. The conceptual enquiries lumped together as 'literary theory' may illuminate aspects of the practice of literary criticism, and may especially uncover the grounds of its possibility, but they cannot 'replace' it. So-called 'close reading' is really just reading—attentive, intelligent, responsive reading. Its antithesis is not 'theory', but something like 'slack reading', which is certainly a much more widespread activity, even if not one actually recommended in those terms by supposedly rival approaches. Anyone seriously engaged with literature, whatever their theoretical allegiances, practises 'close reading'; it only becomes one 'approach' among others when the attempt is made to abstract some principles from it which are held to rule out the legitimacy of other ways of thinking about one's reading.

Text-book surveys, identifying Empson with the interpretative fertility of *Seven Types*, sometimes classify him as a British outrider of the New Critics. But this is a fundamental mistake. Indeed, Empson spent much of his later career vigorously polemicizing against the New Critics who, he believed, were attempting artificially to constrain criticism by declaring illegitimate any inferences from our knowledge of the author and his intentions, or our knowledge of the intellectual assumptions of the period, or of its generic conventions, and so on. The artificial purity of the exclusive concentration on 'the words on the page' meant, in his view, trying to rule out 'a process which all persons not insane are using in all their social experience'. Common 'social experience' was the final court of appeal in Empson's criticism. He may have displayed an exceptionally alert responsiveness to verbal detail, but it was always (at least after his first book) in the service of the enterprise of understanding a work of literature as a whole, of identifying the meanings its author intended to convey, of placing this particular artefact within the larger range of forms of human self-expression. Whether or not Empson can be said to have 'invented' anything about this activity, he practised it with a virtuosity recognized even by those with whom he most sharply disagreed: 'I believe that before he is done', John Crowe Ransom handsomely acknowledged in 1953, 'Empson will rank as the leading literary critic of our time.'

During his lifetime (1906–84), William Empson published four books that lastingly shaped the activity of criticism: *Seven Types of Ambiguity* (1930), *Some Versions of Pastoral* (1935), *The Structure of Complex Words* (1951), and *Milton's God* (1961). He is also generally regarded as one of the best minor poets of the twentieth century. His poetry, practically all written between the late 1920s and the end of the 1930s, has a cerebral exactness and a marked formal elegance (he excelled in unfashionable forms such as the villanelle). Several poets of the next generation claimed to take much of their inspiration from Empson: Robert Lowell wrote to him in 1958 to say, 'I think you are the most intelligent poet writing in our language and perhaps the best. I put you with Hardy and Graves and Auden and Philip Larkin.' Even before Empson's death in 1984, both his poetry and his criticism had already lost some of their appeal, the flame being kept alight by small bands of devoted admirers. But the fashionable orthodoxies in whose name he was demoted have in their turn now lost their glamour and started to fade, so it is possible that the publication of this weighty biography may help to gain him new readers and to restore him to his proper eminence.

Empson came of Yorkshire gentry stock; a certain patrician confidence sustained him through his geographically unsettled existence and his at times extravagantly penurious bohemianism. He went up to Cambridge in 1925 to study mathematics, which he did for three years (he is rare among literary critics in his level of scientific literacy). He then switched to the recently established course in English for an additional year, 1928–9. By virtue of being in the same college, he had the good fortune to be taught by I. A. Richards, then the intellectual pin-up of the Cambridge English Faculty who had recently embarked upon his legendary lectures on 'practical criticism'. Empson wrote an essay for his supervisor exploring how multiple meanings worked in poetry; the essay grew unmanageably large; recognizing the quirky brilliance of his pupil, Richards advised him to go away and work up the piece for publication. Thus it was that one of the landmark works of modern literary criticism began life as an undergraduate essay by someone who was only in his first year of studying English. When *Seven Types* was published, Empson was just 24.

Upon graduating in 1929, Empson had been elected to a junior fellowship at Magdalene College and looked set for an orthodox academic career. But that summer a member of the college staff discovered condoms in Empson's room. The conventional, and largely elderly, Fellows panicked; Empson's fellowship was rescinded and he was ordered to leave Cambridge. The scandal precipitated him into several years of a hand-to-mouth existence which may, indirectly, have enriched his thinking more than the predictable routines of an established academic post would have done. Short periods as a freelance reviewer in London punctuated longer spells teaching, first in Japan, and then, 1937–9, in China, where he endured considerable physical hardship and some danger as he shared in the retreat to rural southern China of his colleagues from Peking University in the face of the Japanese invasion. He returned to Britain in 1940, convinced of the need to do his bit in resisting Hitler. He spent some six years working for the BBC, mainly broadcasting to the Far East: during this time he wrote practically no criticism, cheerfully accepting that his talents should be directed towards making a modest contribution to a great cause.

In 1947, by then married and with two children, he returned to a British Council-sponsored teaching post in Peking, where he took a sympathetic view of the early years of Communist revolution (his own politics were always of a firmly social-democratic kind, though Hetta, his South African-born wife, was for a while a member of the Party). But the conditions required for the independent, disinterested teaching of English literature began to decline sharply from 1950, and Empson finally resigned his teaching post and returned to Britain in 1952, becoming Professor of English at Sheffield University the following year. This would not have been regarded as one of the plum appointments within British academic life, but he desperately needed a regular income to provide for his family and it pleased him to be teaching in his native Yorkshire. He had an unconventional way of being a professor, as he did of being a husband, father, and everything else; but he did the things that mattered well enough, and stayed in this post until his retirement in 1971. His later career included several spells teaching at American universities, including the Kenyon summer school of criticism in its heyday. Writing from Kenyon in 1950 he joked: 'My position here really seems to me very dramatic; there can be few other people in the world who are receiving pay simultaneously and without secrecy from the Chinese Communists, the British Socialists, and the capitalist Rockefeller machine. Practically a little friend of all the world.'

Towards the end of the second volume of Haffenden's huge biography, there are several extended descriptions, poignant veering towards dispiriting, of the increasingly frail Empson holed up in uncongenial quarters (and uncongenial isolation—he was a natural party animal) in various American universities as he tried to supplement his inadequate pension. It is hard not to feel a frustrating sense of waste about these episodes: Empson was by now one of the imperishable names in the canon of great critics, yet he spent several deeply unrewarding semesters dragging unwilling undergraduates through their five-finger exercises in English literary history, neglected by local scholars, drinking too much (as usual), lonely. Even here it is his indomitable and mostly uncomplaining cheerfulness that comes through, a kind of sunny resolution that was of a piece with the courage he had shown in the face of larger challenges. He was, by any measure, a singular man, yet one who did not protest too much when his later years dealt him more than his share of unrewarding labour and commonplace tedium.

John Haffenden's labours, though presumably more rewarding, have been on a heroic scale, even by the standards of devoted biographers, since he embarked upon this task as long ago as 1982. Along the way he has edited several volumes of occasional or unfinished writings by Empson, as well as a meticulously annotated *Complete Poems* in 2000 and a wonderfully usable *Selected Letters* in 2006. Now, finally, the biography itself has seen the light of day in all its amplitude. It is a quite magnificent work, far outstripping the conventional kind of literary biography so beloved of commercial publishers, those unanalytical narratives of daily trivia and sexual gossip whose chief function sometimes seems to be the indulgence of readers' nostalgic fantasies of belonging to a past social elite. Haffenden's research trips have constituted an Empsonian odyssey in themselves, extending across China and Japan as well as Britain and the United States, and his wide scholarly reading has allowed him to reconstruct his subject's milieux in fascinating detail, including absorbing accounts of Cambridge in the 1920s, the BBC during the Second World War, Peking during the Communist revolution of the late 1940s, and so on. In addition, these volumes, unlike those that only clumsily mine their subject's books for biographical material, are exceptionally perceptive and illuminating about Empson's writing and thinking.

If this biography has a fault, it lies in its very amplitude: it is simply too long. Haffenden has been a little self-indulgent in allowing himself to include too much information about, for instance, the remoter reaches of the family background (by which he is clearly charmed) or the minutiae of departmental life in Sheffield (where he has spent most of his own academic career). But this is a venial failing, forgivable in a biographer who has devoted a quarter of a century's labour to such a remarkable figure.

One of the most valuable things this biography helps us to do is to identify the *ethical* drive at the heart of Empson's criticism. He could be wonderfully scornful of the deformations of scholasticism in the study of literature, 'the vast facade of imbecility' created by theories that interposed barriers between reader and work. He may have been over-optimistic to think that his always learned and often elaborate works were actually going to be read by that 'ordinary tolerably informed reader' whom he professed to address, but it was an ideal that saved him from the more hermetic excesses of professionalism. And this in turn underwrote literature's educative power. 'The central function of imaginative literature is to make you realize that other people act on moral convictions different from your own.'

In terms of imaginative sympathy, Empson was a 'globalist' *avant la lettre*. He was, for example, far more knowledgeable about and sympathetic to both

Buddhism and Confucianism than most Westerners of his generation, and this 'worldmindedness', as he called it, helped to make him much more quizzical about those Christian beliefs and symbols that were so easily taken for granted even by non-believers. After his return to England in 1952, he became somewhat obsessed with the influence of 'the neo-Christians' among literary critics, and he embarked on a long and outspoken campaign to make readers alert to the ethically appalling nature of many Christian tenets (something that may cause greater difficulties for Empson's reputation in the contemporary United States than in more secular Britain). He took every opportunity to denounce the savagery and sheer horribleness of ostensibly familiar biblical teachings such as 'the doctrine that God is a sadist who could be bought off torturing all mankind by having his son tortured to death'. *Milton's God* is on one level an interpretation of *Paradise Lost*, but on another it is a sustained polemic against the humanly disfiguring consequences of the central teachings of Christianity about atonement, redemption, and damnation.

Although *The Structure of Complex Words*, his most forbidding and unshapely book, bristles with formulae and other bits of home-made quasi-scientific machinery, Empson was not primarily a theorist and it is a mistake to try to locate his significance in systematic or abstract terms. His critical *practice* is what matters above all else, a practice conducted in the light of what Haffenden nicely terms 'his belief that language is always answerable to intelligence'. And, going further, the *tone* in which he conducted that criticism is what constitutes the chief glory of his writing. Empson never lost either his patrician briskness or his intellectual assurance, but he seasoned the mix with a genuine cosmopolitanism and an openness to social experience that disregarded the usual boundaries of class and nation. The residue of this extended education in human sympathy is present in the calmly decisive way his writing from time to time sets bounds to the importance of the intricate details of literary interpretation that are its main business.

A particularly memorable instance of this occurs in *Some Versions of Pastoral* when he observes that the ideas he is discussing are compatible with Socialism but not with 'a rigid proletarian aesthetic'. He goes on:

> They [the ideas of pastoral] assume that it is sometimes a good thing to stand apart from your society so far as you can. They assume that some people are more delicate and complex than others, and that if such people can keep this distinction from doing harm it is a good thing, though a small thing by comparison with our common humanity.

The declarative simplicity of these sentences gives them a kind of moral grandeur, an effect enhanced by the confidently grounded sense of proportion expressed in the final clause.

This accepting spaciousness of view is what gives so much of his writing its force. 'In pastoral you take a limited life and pretend it is the full and normal one, and a suggestion that one must do this with all life, because the normal is itself limited, is easily put into the trick though not necessary to its power.' It is important not to be distracted by the quasi-demotic of 'trick' here: Empson is not belittling or rug-pulling. We 'pretend' in this way, but that is not a bad thing to do: it makes life liveable, enables us to cope with its inevitable limitedness. There is a subterranean affinity here with the final refrain from 'Aubade', one of his most frequently anthologized poems: 'The heart of standing is we cannot fly.' (As Paul Alpers, one of the best commentators on Empson, has put it: 'The strength of knowing how we stand is at the heart of the greatness of *Some Versions of Pastoral*.') One further passage from that book is representative in both its brevity and its pregnancy: 'The feeling that life is essentially inadequate to the human spirit, and yet that a good life must avoid saying so, is naturally at home with most versions of pastoral.' By this point, the connection with a particular literary genre comes to seem almost incidental; Empson has brought us to realize that pastoral is not fundamentally a matter of swains and shepherds but rather of obtaining a steadying, encompassing perspective on life. Yet that perspective is not complacent or inert: it allows room for 'the feeling that life is essentially inadequate to the human spirit', while at the same time registering the potential destructiveness of dwelling on that insight. But the insight remains, inducing both a sense of modesty or even humility and a sense of soaring, untrammelled potential.

I'm not so sure that Empson 'invented' anything. The 1920s and 1930s saw important changes in the ways that category of sophisticated readers we term 'literary critics' attempted to make their interpretations persuasive. Eliot, Richards, Robert Graves and Laura Riding, John Crowe Ransom and his followers all played their parts in these changes alongside Empson, and there is no easy way to disentangle his particular influence on subsequent critical practice. But perhaps no other critic displayed Empson's sustained alertness and fertility as a reader, especially of poetry, and certainly no other critic wrote with his dazzling mixture of sensibility, analysis, argument, and wit, though it may be that the ethical force of his writing, that steady solidarity with the core experience of being human, is still underrated or misperceived, partially hidden by the smoke from the firework display.

John Haffenden's remarkable biography now enables us to reconstruct the core experience of being Empson. His strangeness and eccentricity come through strongly; the unnerving mix of his remoteness from, yet centrality to, our contemporary concerns and values is made vividly present; and the social and intellectual world in which he moved and had his being is reconstructed in loving detail. But the qualities that seem to me to stand out, though Haffenden is too accomplished a biographer to parade them in the abstract, are Empson's courage, generosity of spirit, and—what may seem an implausible thing to say about a figure of such marked originality and at times wilful abrasiveness—lack of egotism. Finally, although it may seem either an obvious or, worse, a patronizing judgement, what leaps from the page throughout these long volumes is Empson's peculiarly pure, independent intelligence. The term 'literary criticism' has at different times been used to refer to a cluster of endeavours that are variously attendant upon the act of reading, but Empson may have been more incisively and sustainedly intelligent about individual works of poetry and drama than *any* of the other contributors to the incomparably rich corpus that makes up 'modern literary criticism in English'. It is no small claim.

II

'I'd like to take this opportunity of saying, in all sincerity, that I have learned more from you and from *Scrutiny*—far more—than from anyone else.' The 35-year-old adult education tutor who wrote to F. R. Leavis in these terms in 1953 clearly worried that the genuineness of his acknowledgement might be doubted. Leavis, then coming to the height of his reputation, could be notoriously prickly; the letter-writer had never met him, and he had dared to write on this occasion in mild correction of a point in one of Leavis's recent essays. Reason enough for nervousness, then, but somewhere at the back of his mind may also have been a memory of the view he had expressed to another correspondent seven years earlier when he had written about the excesses of the young 'Leavis boys' then moving into adult education who comprehensively denounced the 'debased language and sentiments' manifest in popular culture. Now, 'in all sincerity', he wanted to acknowledge what he had 'learned', though this was evidently no simple case of discipleship.

The tutor in question was Richard Hoggart, still four years away from being made famous by the publication of *The Uses of Literacy*. But his case illustrates some of the difficulties involved in charting the influence of Leavis and *Scrutiny* in British culture (and beyond). After all, Hoggart had never been taught by Leavis, and so was not part of the 'Downing diaspora', nor did he in any simple sense belong to those 'Leavisite networks' which, the media were by this date beginning to speculate, had infiltrated so much of British educational and cultural life. Hoggart had been educated at Leeds University just before the Second World War; his most important teacher, with whom he remained in close, semi-filial, contact for some years, had been Bonamy Dobrée, an elegant metropolitan man of letters who was a former contributor to T. S. Eliot's *Criterion*, thus combining several of *Scrutiny*'s favoured targets. Nor was it the case that Hoggart simply imbibed or even agreed with all of Leavis's views. Hoggart's first book (indirectly the reason for the letter quoted above) had been on W. H. Auden, by then firmly incarcerated in one of the inner circles of *Scrutiny* hell as an overrated writer. The work on which Hoggart was about to embark, which eventually became *The Uses of Literacy*, implicitly disputed the dismissal of 'popular entertainments' that was the stock-in-trade of *Scrutiny*'s jeremiads. Nonetheless, any adequate analysis of *Scrutiny*'s impact on British intellectual life would have to find room for Hoggart and also find the right terms in which to account for his heartfelt declaration of indebtedness.

'Influence' may be one of the least rewarding, yet most overworked, categories of intellectual history. From one point of view, it might seem to underwrite the claims of past ideas to be worthy of the historian's attention at all: they were important because they had been, in some sense, so influential. And yet, the more rigorously any individual claim of this kind is investigated, the more it dissolves and slips through the fingers. Ideas cannot simply be caught, like chicken-pox, and so their epidemiology inevitably starts to become a more complex story, or stories, of shared affinities, pre-existing needs, selective adaptation, and outright misinterpretation. The more fully the later ideas are characterized, analysed, and contextualized, the less they can be understood as any mere reproduction of the earlier ideas.

Labels derived from proper names often embody compacted claims about influence. When we speak of, say, Keynesians or Wittgensteinians (to stay with the middle years of the twentieth century) we are suggesting that some kind of intellectual affiliation seems undeniable, yet the balance of autonomy and discipleship in a given case may be complicated and difficult to determine with any exactness. The use of 'ite' rather than 'ian' as a suffix—as in, say, Namierite or, of course, Leavisite—usually conveys a more mocking or hostile attitude, with the suggestion that the followers are blinkered zealots (Graham Hough, one of Leavis's most implacable local enemies in Cambridge, preferred the mock-biblical 'Leavite' in order to accentuate the exclusiveness and rigidity characteristic of true believers). At the extreme, the sneer in 'Leavisite' could be inflected to suggest less a sect than an insect—a plague of Leavisites was gnawing away at the body cultural rather in the way that demonized immigrants are sometimes figured as hollowing out the body politic. Ultimately, the adjective became a useful piece of polemical or media shorthand, imputing the same narrow range of characteristics: puritan, priggish, intolerant; rabid persecutors of the mediocre and the popular (which were too readily equated); literary Roundheads who gave moral seriousness a bad name. Not surprisingly, discussion of Leavis's influence, during his lifetime and for a decade or more after his death in 1978, frequently provided occasion for name-calling rather than for detached analysis.

In *English as a Vocation*, Christopher Hilliard aims to cut through the mythology and to keep his distance from these ancient enmities by subjecting the available evidence to cool historical examination (as a thirty-something

Harvard-educated New Zealander who now teaches in the History department at the University of Sydney, he brings more than one kind of distance to the task). His admirable book is based on unusually wide research, drawing on archive collections across three continents as well as the published record. (The Leavis estate has not imposed any restrictions on access in Hilliard's case and its cooperativeness has been well rewarded.) It treats Leavis and his fellow-Scrutineers with proper respect while not being afraid to identify exaggerations or weaknesses in some of their diagnoses. And it is written in an attractively clear style which manages to be simultaneously measured and crisp. I have done a lot of work on this subject over the years, but, even so, in reading Hilliard I have often been impressed by the resourcefulness of his scholarship and the perceptiveness of his analysis, and I can say, in all sincerity, that I have learned a great deal from this book.

The book's eight chapters fall, in effect, into two uneven groups. The first two chapters summarize the *Scrutiny* project, concentrating principally on Leavis's pedagogic practice and on the journal's bleak cultural diagnosis. These chapters do their job well, though I suspect Hilliard would acknowledge that the originality of the book does not primarily lie here. One effect of these chapters, which may be deliberate (and is certainly defensible), is to identify Leavis and *Scrutiny* largely with the forms they gave to their concerns in the 1930s, with the result that Leavis's later skirmishing with various elements of what he identified as the metropolitan cultural elite is somewhat underplayed. In delineating *Scrutiny*'s cultural analysis, Hilliard argues that it depended less on some imagined rural past ('the organic community') than many later commentators have assumed. Denys Thompson, who collaborated with Leavis in compiling the widely used primer *Culture and Environment* in 1933, was the most responsive to an idealized version of a pre-industrial rural society, but many other contributors, including perhaps Leavis himself, were more preoccupied with the distinctiveness of the most recent phase of social development, marked by mass literacy, advertising, and 'standardization', where the key sources were the works of semi-popular American social scientists such as Stuart Chase or Robert and Helen Lynd. As Hilliard nicely puts it: 'The capital of the modernity that troubled *Scrutiny*'s core contributors was not Victorian Manchester but interwar Muncie, Indiana' (the original of the Lynds' 'Middletown').

The remaining six chapters then attempt to track down the routes—personal, institutional, intellectual—by which a broadly Leavisian way of thinking about literature and society came to have a marked presence in various cultural milieux, and it is in these chapters that the research is most thorough and the findings are most original. Hilliard begins with an intensive prosopographical analysis of those students who read English at Downing College, Cambridge, between 1932 and 1962, with details of schools and fathers' occupations garnered from college records. It has been common to assert that Leavis primarily recruited lower-middle and working-class boys from grammar schools who were already primed to adopt an oppositional stance, but Hilliard's meticulous documentation does not really support this picture. Fathers in middle-class occupations predominate, and even some of those from lower down the social scale had contrived to send their sons to fee-paying schools. However, this does not mean that Hilliard's lists yield no distinctive pattern. The major public schools, and the more traditional boarding schools, are conspicuous by their near-absence, in contrast to the pattern of Oxbridge entrance in the period more generally. Instead, several of the lesser or more liberal public schools that took day-boys figure quite frequently, as do Catholic schools and various forms of direct-grant grammar school (most of which probably became private after the comprehensivization of the 1960s and 1970s). Ordinary local-authority grammar schools do not seem to have provided the majority of Leavis's students. Intellectually serious sixth-form teachers were the key element, and as time went by, more and more of these had themselves been to Downing and encouraged their best pupils to apply there.

School-teaching was certainly the most popular destination for Downing English graduates, but, as Hilliard emphasizes, this was no less true of graduates of several other colleges and was even truer of those who read English at other universities during these decades. In practice, Leavis's students were to be found in many occupations, some of them scarcely the expected habitat of the species, such as advertising and industry. Having unearthed details of these sometimes unlikely future occupations, Hilliard observes drily: 'The due attention paid to the students who became teachers and critics in their own right means that the carpet-manufacturers escape notice.' It should also be said that considerable numbers of students at other colleges, and even some reading subjects other than English, were drawn to Leavis as a lecturer and supervisor, but it would of course be more difficult to identify them and their sociological profiles in a comparably systematic way.

This analysis is followed by a searching examination of what the early contributors called 'the *Scrutiny* movement in education'. Lesser Scrutineers figure more prominently here than does Leavis himself—figures such as Denys Thompson (a considerable force in promoting the teaching of English in schools), G. H. Bantock, Raymond O'Malley, and, particularly, David Holbrook, to whom Hilliard devotes several notably generous pages, including the wonderful nugget that 'Marvellously for someone in the *Scrutiny* tradition, Holbrook was descended from wheelwrights on both his mother's and his father's side' (George Sturt's threnody for the disappearing world of satisfying craft work, *The Wheelwright's Shop*, was an overworked point of reference among *Scrutiny* contributors). This leads naturally to a discussion of adult education and 'Left-Leavisism' (note the more respectful suffix), which emphasizes that 'the heyday of Leavisism in adult education was the fifteen years after the Second World War'. That *Scrutiny* was a source of intellectual inspiration for both Hoggart and Raymond Williams is well known, but Hilliard provides a wealth of detailed archival evidence about the content and style of their tutorial classes during these years, deftly highlighting those points where they deviated from their inheritance. There was considerable debate among adult education tutors about the merits or otherwise of 'practical criticism' (the young Williams was a fervent evangelist), and it is interesting to note how, by this date and in these circles, this method was associated overwhelmingly with Leavis rather than I. A. Richards or William Empson. As Williams put it in the preface to his primer on teaching 'reading and criticism': 'Mr F. R. Leavis has been largely responsible for the intelligent development of critical analysis as an educational discipline, and to his work, and that of *Scrutiny*, I am indebted.' (Curious that Williams should strip Leavis of the doctorate that was normally inseparable from his name and, in some subliminal way, so often part of the sneer at his alleged combination of academicism and self-importance.)

The sixth chapter is called 'Discrimination and the popular arts', a title combining elements from the two key publications it discusses: *Discrimination and Popular Culture*, a collection of essays edited by Denys Thompson, and *The Popular Arts*, co-authored by Stuart Hall and Paddy Whannel, which both appeared in 1964, both indirectly growing out of an NUT conference. 'Discrimination' was a key term for those intent on bringing a sensibility sharpened by literary criticism to bear upon contemporary cultural forms, and Hilliard reminds us of the large number of school-teachers in the 1950s and 1960s who saw it as part of their role to alert their pupils to the corrosive power of advertising and the newly identified consumer society. But Hall and Whannel, in particular, were unwilling to endorse *Scrutiny*'s relentless pessimism about contemporary popular culture, emphasizing the creative potential of art forms such as film ('no one needed defending from Antonioni'), and Hilliard discusses several instances of writers who were committed to making judgements of quality without, as one editor shrewdly put it at the time, 'using Q. D. Leavis's trick of comparing today's average with yesterday's best'. Despite such divergences, the movement represented by these two books may still be regarded, suggests Hilliard, as 'the last significant episode in the *Scrutiny* tradition of cultural criticism'.

His discussion of 'minority culture and the Penguin public' again brings detailed archival research to bear on a large, ramifying issue: at what public or publics did *Scrutiny* aim and how far did various groups of alleged Leavisites attempt to reach beyond this initial audience? The case-study at the heart of this discussion is the *Pelican Guide to English Literature*, edited by Boris Ford, which appeared in seven volumes between 1954 and 1961. Leavis's own position on this matter was more complex than is always recognized. He addressed his criticism to those for whom the truths to which he was pointing were 'plain' (one of his favourite coercive terms); such trained and responsive readers would only ever be a small minority, and Leavis could be magnificently intransigent in scorning any form of popularization that colluded with the debased norms of a corrupt culture. But he always allowed that these readers would in turn then help to educate, formally and informally, wider circles of readers who might well have, collectively, more impact in the society as a whole. Or, as Hilliard summarizes the case: 'minority culture presupposed relationships between multiple publics.' The *Pelican Guide*, by contrast, aimed to reach this wider audience directly, to use the power of mass paperback publishing to put Leavisian interpretations of works from all periods of English literature into the hands of any casually interested reader. As a result, as Hilliard rightly observes, chapters in the *Guide* may have resembled articles from *Scrutiny* in their evaluative judgements, but they differed from them in their 'performative force'. Writing in *Scrutiny* had been 'a particular kind of intellectual act', one whose insurgent and disruptive qualities were intrinsic to its point. For all that the *Pelican Guide* was conceived as a vehicle for disseminating his views, Leavis's curt disowning of the whole enterprise was consistent and wholly in character.

And then finally there is 'Scrutiny's empire', examining various instances of Leavisian influence in universities in colonies and dominions (and their successor states) across the world from Natal to Colombo to Wellington. The most detailed, as well as the most riveting, discussion here focuses on the career of the Australian critic S. L. Goldberg whose (characteristically forceful) attempt to introduce Leavisian ideas into the English course at the University of Sydney when he became professor there in 1963 led to such a fundamental split in the department that, after some even bloodier than usual hand-to-hand combat in committees, the university ended up with the embarrassment of having two entirely separate curricula in English. But once again Hilliard resists any easy mockery or reductive explanations. The quiddity of the local situation is fully allowed for, and the evidence is not twisted to fit any simplistic centre-and-periphery model. Goldberg and his circle were not slavish 'followers' of Leavis: for them, *Scrutiny*'s critical style had a uniquely energizing effect in an academic milieu caught between the pressures of dry Oxford historicism and a local version of coercive cultural nationalism. This is a reminder, from another angle, not to caricature Leavis's work as little more than the promulgation and transmission of a normative form of 'Englishness', as hostile accounts written in the 1980s so often did: what mattered in many of these geographically far-flung instances was an ideal of critical thinking and a sense of the importance and urgency of that calling.

When considering the impact of *Scrutiny* overseas, the large and unmanageable question, which Hilliard makes a brief stab at, concerns its uptake in the United States. This was not negligible in the 1940s and early 1950s, but it does seem, in historical retrospect, comparatively slight. It was, of course, true that there were native strains of criticism already occupying some of the cultural space which might otherwise have been filled by *Scrutiny*, most notably the 'Southern Agrarians' and their eventual academic extension as the 'New Critics'. John Crowe Ransom might be thought to have played a role not dissimilar to Leavis's, as both literary and cultural critic and as acknowledged leader of a school or movement. But perhaps another element in the explanation would have to be the difficulty of wholly domesticating the Leavisian temper within the more thoroughly professionalized ethos of American universities and colleges. Interestingly, Empson's critical writings, for all his maverick outrageousness as an individual, proved more assimilable as part of the enthusiastic embrace of 'close reading' in the decade immediately after 1945. In this connection, Hilliard includes a delightful fact that I hadn't known: when the teachers and students at the Kenyon School of Criticism in 1950 played softball in their off-duty hours, the two teams were captained by their two English guest lecturers: L. C. Knights's team was 'The Scrutineers', Empson's was 'The Ambiguities'. This surely signalled the high-water mark of the influence of English literary criticism upon its American counterpart.

Hilliard's careful and probing book will henceforth be the indispensable starting point for anyone wanting to think seriously about the role and influence of Leavis and *Scrutiny*. It does not displace, because it is very different from, *The Moment of Scrutiny* by Francis Mulhern, a pioneering, tough-minded critical analysis which concentrated on the journal's contents and questions of ideological identity. That book, published in 1979, was in some ways a form of political engagement in its own right, an expression of the New Left's urge simultaneously to recognize the genuinely oppositional character of *Scrutiny*'s project while berating it for its inadequate politics. Written thirty years later, Hilliard's book addresses a different set of questions, but it also expresses a moment when Leavisism and its cultural role are at last becoming available for detached scholarly analysis. It joins, for example, Guy Ortolano's valuable *The Two Cultures Controversy*, which came out in 2009 and which was similarly thorough in its archival and other research and similarly careful in sifting historical truth from memory and mythology.

Hilliard acknowledges that he has 'not dwelt on the history of university English departments', focusing instead on '*Scrutiny*'s impact in domains where its influence was most substantial and transformative'. This may have been a defensible decision within the economy of the book as a whole, but it will seem to many readers to ignore the very sphere in which *Scrutiny*'s impact was most pervasive, elusive, and problematic. Anyone who scans the pages of literary periodicals from the 1920s and again from the 1960s would be bound to remark systemic changes in the register, rhetoric, and critical address of a substantial proportion of the contents. And as part of these changes, the presence of a particular critical lexicon, shared by critics writing about different topics and different periods, would be inescapable—including phrases about 'realized values' and 'felt intensity', 'mature humanity' and 'genuine vitality', and so on. It would be no simple matter to disentangle the distinctively Leavisian contribution here from the wider impact of 'Cambridge criticism' (and, towards the end of this period, of American New Criticism, although that favoured a rather different lexicon centring on 'paradox', 'irony', 'tension', and so on), but the change itself is undeniable. Perhaps another kind of story would need to be told here, one that concentrates less on 'networks and institutions', as Hilliard rightly describes his own book, and more on the texture of the writing and thinking that constituted critical practice. This would, of course, make the project less manageable: it might require a more literary-critical approach and its results would probably remain more disputable. Hilliard does not altogether neglect such issues, remarking, for example, how '*Scrutiny* put into circulation an "economy of passages"—from Pound, Eliot, Lawrence, and others—the quotation of which was a marker of affiliation', and he provides several telling instances of this tic. But although he also quotes Boris Ford on 'the journal's "watermark": its patterns of vocabulary, quotation, and allusion', he does not attempt to trace these more elusive markers in the general criticism of these decades.

His own discussion of Sam Goldberg's role as the recognized leader of Leavisism in Australia indicates how the reliance on biographical and institutional evidence needs to be supplemented by more textual and interpretative forms of intellectual history. After all, the young Goldberg was directed by his Oxford-educated mentor to go from Melbourne to Oxford to do a B.Litt. where he ended up working on the sixteenth-century historian Sir John Hayward under the supervision of the impeccably traditional David Nichol Smith. His later responsiveness to Leavis's very different critical style cannot be attributed to educational formation or personal contact: no doubt temperament and local situation played their part, but ultimately the story would also have to be told in the apparently naive terms of one mind's contact with another via the printed page. And with a mind as acute and wide-ranging as Goldberg's, such an account would have to work with subtler instruments than that of the billiard-ball impact of master upon disciple. His first book was an appreciative study of Joyce's *Ulysses*, a work that was never part of the *Scrutiny* canon; Goldberg was deeply drawn to philosophy whereas Leavis liked to describe himself as an 'anti-philosopher'; Goldberg's last book, *Agents and Lives*, bore the marks of his (critical) reading of figures far removed from English studies, such as Bernard Williams and Martha Nussbaum. After a while, the use of labels such as 'Leavisite' starts to feel as though it obscures more than it illuminates, yet it is also true that Goldberg's indebtedness to Leavis is unmistakable. It is a strength of Hilliard's work that he sticks so closely to the documentary record, but maybe his historian's fidelity to one kind of evidence sets limits to the kind of story he can tell.

In the 1970s and 1980s, proponents of 'Theory' frequently operated with a crude stereotype of 'Leavisism' in order to trumpet the superiority of the new modes, and it suited their purposes to represent this derogated model as 'dominant' within English studies in the previous generation. But it was never that, even at the peak of its influence in the 1950s. Hilliard properly reminds us that 'most university English departments in Britain (and the empire) were established on the Oxford or London models', and the forms of literary scholarship broadly associated with those traditions remained the dominant presence there, albeit a presence that was less evangelical, less noisy, and less noticed than that of *Scrutiny*-affiliated critics. Hilliard pushes this truth a little further when he remarks: '*Scrutiny* occupies a much more important place in the genealogy of left literary criticism and cultural studies than it does in English studies at large.' Well, perhaps, at least if the provenance of later historical studies is any guide, but this may be to swing a bit too far to the opposite extreme in underplaying the wider *disciplinary* impact of Leavis and *Scrutiny*.

Hilliard's book having provided so much, it is bound to seem ungracious to ask for more, but a full analysis would need to go a little further still, towards exploring the place of literary criticism in British culture more generally during this period. Here it becomes very difficult to separate out the distinctively Leavisian impress. Within the unevenly professionalizing academic discipline of English, 'criticism' challenged and in some places dislodged philology and literary history from their earlier dominance. In part, this was achieved by offering demonstrably more attentive and illuminating readings of familiar texts; in part it came about because of the pedagogical advantages of close reading within an expanding university system (though literary history, and to a lesser extent philology, effortlessly retained a scholarly legitimacy that criticism had to struggle to be granted, as it was). But, beyond such explanations, the critical practice so closely associated with inter-war Cambridge recommended itself to successive generations of teachers and students partly because it promised to provide a more general form of cultural critique, ultimately a form of 'resistance' to the corrupting powers of modern society. This made English more than a 'subject'; it made it a 'cause'. Though others may have offered more original or eye-catching critical readings, Leavis was arguably more important than any other single figure in promoting this sense of a cause: more important than Richards, even though the latter could claim a kind of paternity of the pedagogic practice; more important than Empson, despite the unparalleled brilliance of his exploitation of the method; and, in a way, more important even than Eliot, who inspired them all but who, in addition to his carefully maintained distance from the academic world, came to represent a fastidious and largely ineffectual form of cultural conservatism.

And perhaps this is how the unremarked Weberian echoes in Hilliard's title should be heard. The idea of English as a calling, as an existential identity, ran counter to the norms of academic professionalism. In a curious way, the ethic of *Scrutiny* had more in common with 'Politik als Beruf' than with 'Wissenschaft als Beruf': it called for commitment, not abstention; for passion rather than patience. Yet, at the same time, it embodied a repudiation of the pragmatic instrumentalism at the heart of everyday politics. Like so much cultural criticism, it railed against the current form of society while also scorning the familiar mechanisms for changing it. Yet this, for those at all susceptible to its call, strengthened rather than diminished its appeal.

Ultimately, the measure of *Scrutiny*'s impact had less to do with whether Leavis's pupils and readers shared his (emphatically positive) judgements about Shakespeare or George Eliot or even his (relentlessly negative) judgements about *The New Statesman* or J. B. Priestley. Rather, it had to do with whether they thought that literary criticism mattered because it, uniquely, involved a disciplined engagement with fundamental judgements about what makes for 'life', for a fully human existence. This set it apart from, possibly even above, other disciplines and at the same time made it more than a purely 'academic' discipline. This view, so expressed, would have seemed eccentric or implausible before the 1920s and in most quarters it came to seem dated or naive from the 1970s. But in the intervening half-century it was not uncommon for 'English' to be seen, to be *felt*, as a 'vocation' in just this way, and Christopher Hilliard's excellent book helps us, more perhaps than any other work has so far done, to understand the part which Leavis and *Scrutiny* played in that remarkable story.

5

Critics (II)

Lionel Trilling and Raymond Williams

I

Do you turn to literary criticism to find out who you are or might be? To many readers now, this question may seem wilful, even perverse; to others it probably risks seeming blankly irrelevant. 'Literary criticism' has come to be widely thought of either as an elaborately sterile academic practice or else as a presumptuous (and possibly precious) attempt by a few self-appointed arbiters of taste to tell other people what they ought to like. But this cannot, of course, be the whole story even now. Reflective readers continue to find, in the essays and introductions and reviews written by the best contemporary critics, helpful prompts to reading more alertly and understanding their responses more fully. Still, it is doubtful whether any literary critic in the early twenty-first century commands the level of general cultural authority that Lionel Trilling exercised in the USA in the three decades between the end of the Second World War and his death in 1975. The fact that his best-known book, *The Liberal Imagination*, published in 1950, sold 70,000 copies in hardback (and a subsequent 100,000 in paperback) may already suggest a lost world, especially when we remember that it belonged to the genre that most mainstream publishers and booksellers now regard as virtually unsaleable: a miscellaneous collection of previously published essays in literary criticism.

In his day job, Trilling was a Professor of English at Columbia University, but his earliest ambition (like many English professors) had been to become, simply, 'a writer', and his constant practice (unlike many English professors)

Lionel Trilling, *The Liberal Imagination: Essays on Literature and Society*, introduction by Louis Menand (New York Review of Books, 2008; first published 1950).
Lionel Trilling, *The Journey Abandoned: The Unfinished Novel*, ed. Geraldine Murphy (Columbia University Press, 2008).
Adam Kirsch, *Why Trilling Matters* (Yale University Press, 2011).
Dai Smith, *Raymond Williams: A Warrior's Tale* (Parthian, 2008).

was to write in periodicals aimed at the public beyond the walls. As a result, his writing is learned without seeming self-importantly academic, and there is a conversable, ruminative quality to his essays that draws readers in and makes them collaborators in the enquiry at hand. One of the recurring sources of tension and conflict in literary culture since Trilling's time has been the disparity or mismatch between what are presumed to be the scholarly protocols of the academic study of literature and what are claimed to be the requirements of writing for non-specialist general readers. In reality, neither of these identities is as homogeneous and clear-cut as the polemical conventions assert. As I have argued elsewhere, there is never just one type of 'general reader' or 'non-specialist public': readerships can be divided and classified along several axes, and we also have to recognize that those who count as specialist readers for one purpose may also be 'non-specialist' readers for many other purposes. Similarly, there is no single, defining form of academic writing about literature: a piece of literary history expresses different possibilities and constraints from those governing a critical essay, just as a scholarly edition may operate at several removes from the introduction to a reprinted classic. The occasions for tension or conflict are increased by the fact that, in Britain at least, several of the most prominent contributors to the literary pages of broadsheet newspapers and similar publications are moonlighting academics, and it is a sad truth that few reviewers are more sweepingly dismissive of the alleged scholasticism and unreadability of academic literary scholarship than some of those professors who have access to a regular reviewing berth.

As a way of exploring some of these themes, this essay begins with an extended reconsideration of Trilling's writing, especially as represented by *The Liberal Imagination* but also as re-appraised by one of his most recent admirers. It then goes on to discuss a figure who, though one of the most influential and widely admired literary academics of the last generation, disowned the category of 'literary criticism' and constantly sought to connect his writing, which included both cultural analysis and fiction, to a much wider public beyond the walls.

II

There is, for many of us, something vaguely oppressive about the thought of having to re-read Lionel Trilling now. His elegant periods, always in danger of sliding into sonorousness; his confident, familiar invocation of the great names of modern European thought and literature; his cultivated superiority to all that might be tainted by provincialism or pragmatism—which, he concedes with the stoical air of the dutiful mourner at a funeral, amounts to most of American life; and above all, that elusive but pervasive note that runs through his prose—the note of mind taking stock of its resources and finding that they are, despite their fragility, adequate to its tasks. We can't help feeling that we should be improved by reading Trilling, and this feeling itself is inevitably oppressive.

The previous paragraph, as will have been evident to those familiar with Trilling's writing, deliberately blends characterization with homage and pastiche. His liberal use of the first-person plural to suggest a community of the like-minded was a much-criticized mannerism, as was his unembarrassed recourse to cultural name-dropping as a substitute for argument. Then there was his frequent use of the verb 're-read', signalling his great storehouse of literary experience. And finally, there was the characteristic structure of a Trilling sentence, with the clauses queuing up to make their restraining or amplifying comment on their predecessors. The blending of homage and pastiche in my tribute may itself be expressive of the ambivalence Trilling now excites. We, I might imitatively say, admire him; we may even sense that we need him; yet it remains true that we have ever so slightly to brace ourselves for a prolonged spell in his company. Reading him keeps us up to the mark, but we can't help but be aware that the mark is set rather higher than we are used to.

All this may seem puzzling to those for whom Trilling is little more than a name, especially those who have come to literary and intellectual awareness in the years since he died. It may be hard to understand why he was, a couple of generations ago, one of academia's most cherished culture-heroes, one of the few saints of modern literary criticism. It may be harder still to make the case for why Trilling, in his antique, mannered way, might matter now. But, if so, there can be few better places to start than with a reconsideration of his most celebrated book, *The Liberal Imagination* (first published in 1950), now reissued with a brief, deft introduction by Louis Menand, who may come as near as anyone can to being Trilling's successor today.

The scale of the book's success on first publication, referred to above, seems scarcely credible today. Menand remarks that the volume 'made literary criticism matter to people who were not literary critics', which is true enough but may understate its reach. A similar work that sold, say, 20,000 copies would already be doing that. *The Liberal Imagination* made Trilling's version of literary criticism matter to a readership that was in search of something more than criticism, perhaps more than literature itself. His essays spoke to a cultural or political moment in a way that is now hard to reconstruct and surely impossible to repeat. But why does it seem unimaginable that any work by a literary critic might have a similar impact now? Has 'the culture' changed too much? Has 'literary criticism'? Have 'we'?

Trilling, we should begin by remembering, was a native of a peculiar and distinctive territory lying just off the eastern seaboard of the United States. Born on the upper West Side, in 1905, to first-generation Russian-Jewish immigrants, he spent almost his entire life in Manhattan and was as closely identified with the peculiar, hot-house intellectual life of that skinny island as any avatars of Bloomsbury or the *quartier latin* ever were with that of their own geographically circumscribed milieux. He was Columbia, man and boy, and perhaps no figure better represented that university in its heyday in the first couple of decades after 1945. But he was also, from his earliest adult years, a contributor to the serious end of the literary and intellectual journalism that has cropped so abundantly in that fertile cultural soil. In his early twenties, exploring his Jewishness, he wrote for *The Menorah Journal*; in his early thirties, sharing in a broader political radicalism, he became a stalwart of *Partisan Review* (once it had sloughed off its initial Stalinist identity); by his early forties, cultivating his critical voice, he was one of the contributors most sought after by all the leading journals of opinion, including *The Nation*, as well as by the most highly regarded literary critical journals such as *The Kenyon Review*. The sixteen essays collected in *The Liberal Imagination* were mostly revised versions of pieces that had appeared in these last three periodicals, all initially published between 1940 and 1949.

It was during that decade that Trilling secured his academic career and began to build a scholarly as well as literary-journalistic reputation. In the late 1920s and right through the 1930s he had struggled to make ends meet with a series of temporary or part-time appointments, held back by the economic circumstances of the Depression, by his failure to finish his Ph.D., and by being Jewish. But in 1938 he did finally complete the dissertation, and its publication in 1939 as *Matthew Arnold* brought immediate recognition as well as appointment as an Assistant Professor (at the age of 34). Trilling became the first Jew to obtain a permanent position in Columbia's English Department, and thereafter his promotion was relatively rapid. A short book on E. M. Forster followed in 1943; the choice of Arnold and Forster as subjects indicated deeper intellectual and political affinities, as well as a lifelong Anglophilia.

Trilling brought academic authority to his forays into literary journalism, though his learning was by no means confined to English literature. The names he invokes so freely in his essays tend to be continental European more often than English, and many of them were not writers of 'literature' in any narrow sense. In common with others of that loose grouping known as the New York Intellectuals (such as Philip Rahv, Clement Greenberg, or, slightly later, Irving Howe), Trilling drew upon Romantic and post-Romantic literature and thought, and especially his intense engagement with European Modernism, in his efforts both to shame American parochialism and to redress the narrowness of radical politics. His range, as well as his name-dropping, are most strikingly illustrated by the opening pages of the essay in *The Liberal Imagination* entitled 'Freud and Literature'. By the second page there has already been mention of Diderot, Hegel, Marx, Nietzsche,

Schopenhauer, Goethe, and Shaw; the next page brings Rousseau, Blake, Wordsworth, Burke, Coleridge, Arnold, and Schiller, followed on the next by Mill, Shelley, Schlegel, George Sand, Ibsen, Tieck, and Stendhal, and quite soon thereafter Dostoevsky, Poe, Baudelaire, Nerval, Rimbaud, Proust, Eliot, Kafka, Mann, Joyce... Most of his essays do not attempt to mass the cultural cavalry on this scale, but his writing always implies that he is on familiar terms with the great names of the old world who could be called upon to make up for the failings of the new.

Trilling explains in his subsequently much-quoted 'Preface' that his essays are linked by their concern with 'the ideas of what we loosely call liberalism, especially the relation of these ideas to literature'. Notoriously, he nowhere defines what he means by his rather idiosyncratic use of 'liberalism'. Occasionally, he suggests a lineage stretching back to Bentham and Mill; more frequently he associates the term with the broadly radical or progressive political impulse prominent in American life in the 1930s and into the 1940s; later he was to claim that he had chiefly had in mind the fashionable enthusiasm for Stalinism. Perhaps his most interesting, as well as illuminating, comment on the subject comes in his essay 'The function of the little magazine'; he appears to be glossing his sense of 'liberalism' when he writes: 'Our educated class has a ready if mild suspiciousness of the profit motive, a belief in progress, science, social legislation, planning, and international cooperation, perhaps especially where Russia is in question.'

However, as the cumulative effect of the essays comes to be felt, the target expands until it seems to be the narrowness of practically *any* politics which is being chided and corrected. Trilling takes his place in the long line of cultural critics, Arnold pre-eminent among them, but stretching from Coleridge and Carlyle to Eliot and Leavis (to cite only some of the most obvious names), who have sought in literature an antidote to the mechanical and instrumental tendencies of political and economic reason—literature understood as (in Trilling's much-quoted phrase) 'the human activity that takes the fullest and most precise account of variousness, possibility, complexity, and difficulty'. The character (and presumably much of the impact) of *The Liberal Imagination* comes from his use of the genre of the critical essay to dramatize this conflict and to gesture towards some of the ways in which our sense of 'variousness, possibility, complexity, and difficulty' is extended and given content by great writers, above all by the novelists of the previous 150 years.

In these essays, Trilling writes as a literary critic, but so much of what he writes is not literary criticism, at least not in any of the stricter forms of that activity made familiar by Eliot, Empson, and the New Critics. The essay in the collection which is sometimes referred to as Trilling's most extended exercise in close reading, that on Wordsworth's 'Immortality Ode', is still far from being any kind of New Critical exercise in the detection of tensions and paradoxes in the verbal texture of the poem. Its energies are focused on the attempt to identify and translate 'what the poem says', and so even this, his most purely exegetical essay, concludes by telling us that the 'Immortality Ode' is about 'something common to us all, the development of the sense of reality'. Even here, and *a fortiori* in the more discursive essays, literary criticism serves the purposes of moral instruction. More generally, it is striking how little he quotes compared to most critics, nor does he have a great deal to say about the formal properties of particular literary works. 'The moral life' is really Trilling's home turf. Quite a lot of his writing was a kind of natural history of the moral life, a characteristic that comes most clearly into view in his last book, *Sincerity and Authenticity* (1972).

Trilling's use of literature for the purposes of moral pedagogy, as well as the drawbacks of such an exercise, are notably illustrated in his celebrated essay on Henry James's *The Princess Casamassima*. The novel is not normally regarded as one of James's finest, and Trilling does not sufficiently attend to the detail of the book to be likely to convert any resistant reader to a more positive view. Yet he manages to deploy aspects of James's tale to underwrite a probing, at times moving, meditation on the moral or human limitations likely to attend upon any over-zealous commitment to radical political change. The novel might be said to dramatize—or at least, more creakingly, to stage—the conflict between the claims of culture and of social justice, and its portrait of those who pursued the latter by extreme (anarchist) means was far from flattering. Tough-minded progressives scorned the book accordingly as an example of the inherently reactionary tendency of James's elaborate filigree-work and its lack of attention to the 'realities' of social and political conditions. In his essay, Trilling triumphantly turns the charge of 'unrealism' on its head. The novel, he argues, provides 'a brilliantly precise representation of social actuality'. But it does more than this, and more (and other) than its radical critics ever do: it understands and captures the essence of tragedy, the irresolvable conflict of fundamental values. This he terms, in a favoured phrase, 'moral realism'. 'Moral realism is the informing spirit of *The Princess Casamassima* and it yields a kind of social and political knowledge which is hard to come by.' It is a question whether this rather flawed James novel is actually as good as Trilling needs it to be to sustain his larger case, and this is not the only instance where one wonders whether his magnificent moral edifice has not been built on rather shaky literary foundations. Nonetheless, the essay, moving out from literary criticism, becomes a powerful secular sermon.

Writing that is this high-toned is also high-risk. At times, Trilling's characteristic emphasis on ethical education can seem out of proportion to the literary subject-matter, banging the drum too loudly in order to disguise the lack of rewarding melody. Consider, for example, his explanation of why *Huckleberry Finn* is a 'subversive' book: 'No one who reads thoughtfully the dialectic of Huck's great moral crisis will ever again be wholly able to accept without some question and some irony the assumptions of the respectable morality by which he lives, nor will ever again be certain that what he considers the clear dictates of moral reason are not merely the engrained customary beliefs of his time and place.' One response to this might be to say that anyone capable of this kind of 'thoughtful' reading is not likely to be a prisoner of social convention in the first place, and vice versa. The passage risks both patronizing the imagined reader and imputing an unrealistic power to Twain's book. In such passages, the adjective 'moral' appears overworked, now indicating the merely conventional social codes, now referring to the wider human vision offered by the critic.

The half-dozen best pieces in the volume are among Trilling's most admired writings, and justly so: 'Reality in America', 'The Princess Casamassima', 'Huckleberry Finn', 'Manners, Morals, and the Novel', 'The Kinsey Report', 'The Meaning of a Literary Idea'—these are all essays which stay in the reader's mind and work there more fruitfully than do whole books by most other critics. But if, to recommend him to a new generation of readers, one wanted to take a representative example of Trilling at work, one could hardly do better than the rather slighter essay on F. Scott Fitzgerald, the bulk of which appeared as a review in the *Nation* in 1945.

Fitzgerald may at first seem a surprising enthusiasm, but the basis for it becomes clear in the opening paragraphs where Trilling invites us to admire 'the moral force of the poise and fortitude which marked Fitzgerald's mind'. The essay proves to be yet another example of Trilling's propensity to use literary criticism as a vehicle for ethical reflection. Fitzgerald, we are told, 'really had but little impulse to blame, which is the more remarkable because our culture peculiarly honors the act of blaming, which it takes as the sign of virtue and intellect'. A casual reading of this sentence might suggest the perspective of a relaxed post-Freudian moralist, pardoning all because understanding all, but it is in fact Trilling who, characteristically, is adopting the more strenuous position. Real 'virtue and intellect', he is suggesting, require something at once more discriminating and less immediately gratifying than the slack disposition to confirm one's own self-righteousness by so readily apportioning blame.

When he goes on to begin a sentence with such an iteration of self-evidence as 'In the equipment of the moralist and therefore of the novelist . . . ' we know we are on home ground. Authoritative asides along the way reinforce the sense that we are in a rhetorical universe not afraid of wise saws and *sententiae*: 'The form, that is, is not the result of careful "plotting"—the form of a good novel never is'; or again, 'What underlies all success in poetry . . . is the poet's voice.' Nor is there any shrinking from the high notes in his praise of the 'voice' of Fitzgerald the novelist: 'It is characteristically modest, yet it has in it, without apology or self-consciousness, a largeness, even a stateliness, which derives from Fitzgerald's connection with tradition and with mind, from his sense of what has been done before and the demands which this past accomplishment makes.' Trilling's own 'voice' was perhaps neither so modest nor so free from self-consciousness, but otherwise the element of identification is surely clear. When, having quoted a longish passage, he says that it exemplifies 'the habitual music of Fitzgerald's seriousness', the warmth of the commendation is palpable. But Trilling's prose also incorporates a recurring note of self-criticism: 'I am aware that I have involved Fitzgerald with a great many great names', he writes at one point, catching himself, and so he changes the register. This is rather like what Arnold called Burke's 'return upon himself', and such arrests are part of the appeal of Trilling's writing, a style expressive of his balanced, dialectical mind.

Later scholars have offered various explanations for the remarkable success of *The Liberal Imagination*. These explanations have included: Trilling's subtle blending of the authority of the academic scholar with the address of the freelance critic; the stage reached in the growth of an educated reading public not yet cut off from the accelerating specialisms of the universities; the Cold War context in which even subtle or disguised critiques of Stalinism were assured of a ready welcome; the peculiar position of the New York Intellectuals in the cultural demography of the United States in these years, at once outsiders who intellectually outranked most insiders, and insiders claiming the licence of outsiders. But if for a moment we take an even wider view and consider the book's success in an international perspective, it is the prestige of literary criticism in these years, certainly in both the United States and Britain, that now seems such a remarkable historical phenomenon. What Randall Jarrell called 'the Age of Criticism' may only have stretched from the late 1930s to the mid-1960s, at most—the decade after 1945 was its true heyday—but the activity enjoyed a remarkable standing among a bookish public eager to find guidance about life in the meditations of critics on irony in Donne or self-realization in George Eliot, a public mostly not, or not yet, disposed to fret too much about the kinds of cultural homogeneity which such acceptance of a narrow literary canon depended on.

Reviewing *The Liberal Imagination* in *The Hudson Review* in 1950, R. W. B. Lewis shrewdly remarked that Trilling's 'noble sadness' provided 'sandbags for the will'. The essays are marked, though not disfigured, by the pathos of stoicism, that slightly stagey bracing of the brow for a buffeting from an indifferent universe that had been raised to an art form by Arnold. In Trilling's sensibility, stoicism is the natural partner to tragedy, not the least of their value being the way they convict more cheerful or more optimistic sensibilities of existential shallowness. Another reviewer, Clifton Fadiman, writing in the *New Yorker*, spoke of the way Trilling rehabilitated 'the Big Words that Hemingway's generation thought it had choked to death', and it's true that his readiness with terms like 'love', 'the imagination', 'the will', and so on is one of the things that now gives Trilling's prose an oddly archaic air. But the value that his work, early and late, speaks up for most convincingly is 'intelligence' (he liked to quote, as have many since, the line of his Columbia teacher John Erskine on 'the moral obligation to be intelligent'). In the 1930s and 1940s, with radical progressivism in the ascendant among the intellectuals of Trilling's Manhattan, this entailed being 'a dissenter from the orthodoxies of dissent'. But although he could be allergic to the coerciveness of intellectual or political fashion, his was never the facile and purely reactive identity of the 'contrarian'. Rather, his critical essays enact the effort to see the topical and the transient through the optic of a rich, subtle cultural tradition which has attempted to take the measure of the divided and frustrated nature of human experience. The result is sometimes merely portentous—as when he says of the Kinsey Report, with not quite enough self-irony, that 'the best thing about the Report is the quality that makes us remember Lucretius'—but at its best his writing makes the critical essay seem the genre in which a kind of wisdom is most naturally at home.

For most of his career, certainly its early decades, Trilling was reluctant to classify himself as a 'critic' or, less appealing still, a 'scholar': the self-image he craved and nurtured, in the face of an increasingly discouraging lack of achievement, was 'writer', which meant, above all, 'novelist'. By the mid-1940s he had published several short stories, including the much-anthologized 'Of this time, of that place', and his one novel, *The Middle of the Journey* (1947). That book, essentially a 'novel of ideas' about the demands of maturity in both politics and personal life, received a rather grudging reception, with several reviewers opting for the predictable complaint that the heavy load of the 'ideas' weighed down and eventually capsized the fragile narrative craft in which they were carried. Trilling never published another novel, and it has usually been assumed that the chilly reception of his first-born deterred him from further efforts in the genre. But among his papers deposited at Columbia there is the typescript of what seems to be the first third or so of an unfinished, and untitled, novel, apparently written shortly after he completed *The Middle of the Journey*. Geraldine Murphy has now edited this text for publication, giving it the title *The Journey Abandoned*, alluding both to the earlier novel and to *The Beginning of the Journey*, Diana Trilling's 1994 memoir of the life she and Lionel had shared.

The 150 printed pages are full of interest, testifying both to Trilling's gifts as a social observer and recorder of the eddies and velleities of the inner life and to his difficulty in subduing his reflectiveness to the demands of adequately pacy and dramatic action. There are overtones of Forster and of James in this story of the anxieties and temptations of the literary life—the expression of character through the niceties (and brutalities) of social exchange is one of its strengths. It is impossible to say what fate the completed novel might have assigned to its central protagonist—a variant on one of Trilling's favoured types, 'the young man from the provinces'—but the indications are that, compared to *The Middle of the Journey*, Trilling was struggling with a less directly political working-out of such characteristic themes as the corruption of ambition and the betrayals of desire.

For that reason, the appearance of this fragment may seem to support that interpretation of Trilling's later career which took his fastidious disdain for the inevitable crudities of politics to signal a move in an increasingly apolitical, and therefore conservative, direction. Trilling clearly did become culturally more conservative, especially in reaction to the perceived excesses of the 1960s, but he surely remained too political an animal to countenance any aestheticist withdrawal. The obligation to be intelligent included being intelligent about politics, and he knew that a lofty disdain for the difficult business of managing the conditions of collective life was crassly unintelligent.

Some writers who invoke 'complexity' are in practice as bleakly schematic as those they criticize. In their hands, 'complexity' just means 'my simplicity rather than your simplicity'. But that is not the case with Trilling. There is enough genuine ambivalence and dividedness in him to make the movement of his mind naturally dialectical. Diana Trilling later spoke of 'the grave energy' of her husband's middle years, and that almost oxymoronic phrase nicely captures something about the stretched tension discernible, not exactly 'beneath' the polish of his Augustan periods, but actually embedded *in* them, preventing them from slipping into weakly mock-Augustan imitation. This sense of him is deepened when we read in Diana Trilling's memoir about his anxieties and depressions, his long-drawn-out but inconclusive analysis, and the difficulties this effortlessly polished writer sometimes had in writing anything at all. Trilling, it seems, was a divided character, as would perhaps have to have been partly true of someone from his background who had turned himself into a facsimile of a courtly English gentleman at home in the tweedy world of Ivy League English departments in the 1940s and 1950s. 'The return of the repressed' would be an inaccurate as well as over-dramatic figure to describe this tension, but Trilling's prose benefits from those moments when a more bohemian, Greenwich Villagey voice threatens to disrupt the donnish calm of the Morningside Heights seminar room.

One anxiety that only rarely surfaces in *The Liberal Imagination* became more visible in his work in subsequent decades, the anxiety that, in drawing back from expecting too much from politics, we might end up expecting too much from literature. This is not quite the view commonly associated with the later Trilling—namely, that in installing the masterpieces of modern literature in the curriculum we routinize them and deprive the experience of reading them of its personally disorienting intensity. It is, rather, a more interesting 'return upon himself' in which he raises doubts about the efficacy of what he had once seemed most eagerly to propose. Perhaps Trilling the writer intermittently felt the need to rescue the anarchic energies of literature, the purposeless purposiveness of the aesthetic impulse, from the worthy ambitions of Trilling the moral pedagogue.

'Mind', 'culture', 'the moral life'—these Big Words make us a little uncomfortable nowadays, and we have difficulty in using them other than in a knowing, allusive way. But they are the notes which make up the habitual music of Trilling's seriousness. In allowing him the last word, I choose a passage from his great essay 'Manners, Morals, and the Novel' in which he reaches for the highest of high notes and holds it, unwaveringly, for just long enough: 'Some paradox of our natures leads us, when once we have made our fellow men the objects of our enlightened interest, to go on to make them the objects of our pity, then of our wisdom, ultimately of our coercion. It is to prevent this corruption, the most ironic and tragic that man knows, that we stand in need of the moral realism which is the product of the free play of the moral imagination.'

Trilling's engagement of and with the reader gives his best essays a charm and a persuasiveness that time has not altogether staled. One of the central insights of Adam Kirsch's thoughtful and unusual little book is that Trilling was more concerned than most critics have been with what certain sorts of literature *do* for their readers. His best critical energies were called out not by dwelling on the ambiguities of small details in the verbal texture of a poem, nor by highlighting the techniques through which novelists discharged their narratorial duties, but rather by 'treating literature as the medium of experience'. Reading, as Trilling understands that activity when true to its highest purposes, is bound to be strenuous: it is in the meeting and overcoming of various kinds of resistance—the resistance generated by not immediately graspable form as much as by difficult, uncongenial, or simply unfamiliar ideas—that readers encounter and go beyond the boundaries of their present mind and sensibility and start to shape themselves anew. This may not involve deciding, in any straightforward sense, questions of right and wrong, but it can be a kind of ethical self-education. Or as Kirsch puts it, more emphatically: 'Moral thinking, for Trilling, is finally thinking about the kind of character one wants to have.'

This may sound a bit daunting, even ponderous, yet the experience, in our turn, of reading a Trilling essay is more like a late-night conversation with an older friend than it is like either a lecture or a sermon. We can still be left feeling inadequate in the face of such sustained gravity—the fact that he was fond of the maxim about 'the moral obligation to be intelligent' reminds us not to lapse into any post-prandial slackness—but this is offset by surprising moments of self-revelation or self-identification in his criticism, such as his not wholly predictable admiration for Keats, less on account of his poetry than for the ethical example of a life and a character that managed to be so open to experience while not being simply scattered by it. And we surely warm to someone who, himself impeccably liberal and resolutely intellectual, could write: 'When the liberal intellectual thinks of himself, he thinks chiefly of his own good will and prefers not to know that the good will generates its own problems, that the love of humanity has its vices and the love of truth its own insensibilities.'

This is clearly the voice of a writer who, while learning from Nietzsche and Freud as well as from Mann and Proust, has managed to keep his balance. Trilling's own vulnerability to the frightening, disruptive power of the greatest Modernist literature coexisted with that air of all-comprehending serenity that is the familiar hallmark of his prose, as well as with an almost staid respectability in his life. And it is, as Kirsch rightly sees, the never wholly resolvable tension between Trilling's responsiveness to the darker or more purely Dionysiac elements of life and his constantly renewed effort to achieve an intellectual as well as emotional equilibrium that prevents his ethical earnestness from degenerating into the sententiousness of a modern Polonius. The struggle between id and ego (to use the metaphors provided by one of the writers whom Trilling most admired) must never be allowed to lapse into comfortable victory for either side. For all the much-remarked Augustan polish of Trilling's prose, ease is not what his criticism offers us.

That Kirsch, an American poet and critic in only his mid-thirties, should identify and appreciate so many of Trilling's strengths is no small achievement. He perhaps spends a little long making a space for himself by skirmishing with other critics; he slightly labours the question of Trilling's Jewishness; and at moments he can seem to equate the judgements that matter with literary and intellectual opinion in contemporary Manhattan (but then so, occasionally, did Trilling). Nonetheless, in the concluding sections of this book he has managed to convey, in a few spare, elegant pages, more about why Trilling matters than many admirers have succeeded in doing at several times this length.

Trilling does not dazzle; there are no Empsonian or Ricksian fireworks. Nor does he hector us: there is none of the Leavisian or Eagletonian certainty about the one right answer. Rather, he shares with us his own experience of finding certain books indispensable in reflecting on the mysteries and glories of being alive. As Kirsch finely concludes at one point: 'To Trilling, literature was above all the medium in which he made himself, and his essays, with all their dignity and vulnerability, are the record of a soul being made through its confrontation with texts. For this reason, Trilling may matter most of all as a representative of the virtue he admired in George Orwell: "the virtue of not being a genius".'

III

When Raymond Williams died suddenly, aged 66, in January 1988, estimations of him were sharply divided. There were those who thought that the intellectual and political life of not just Britain but the world had suffered a grievous loss: they regarded him as a deservedly influential literary and cultural critic, a major Socialist theorist, and an exemplary instance of the union of intellectual seriousness and political purpose. There were others who thought Williams had for too long enjoyed an inflated reputation, that he was a muddy thinker and verbose writer who had been swept to a form of cultural celebrity by the vogue for working-class sentimentalism in the 1960s and lefter-than-thou self-righteousness in the 1970s.

In the immediate aftermath of his death, it was, understandably, the positive assessments which predominated. Some moving tributes appeared as former comrades, colleagues, and students tried to take stock, emotionally and personally as well as in more public terms, of what his unexpected death deprived them of. The sense of having been abandoned by one to whom they were accustomed to look for intellectual guidance and moral leadership was strong. The next few years saw the publication both of posthumous collections of his work and of volumes devoted to discussion of his ideas and his influence. Reviews of these works were sometimes made the occasion for much less sympathetic assessments of his significance. A notable example of the genre appeared in the *London Review of Books* (8 February 1990) when R. W. Johnson sharply criticized Williams's political judgement and wrote in disparaging terms about the combination of uplift and unrealism allegedly characteristic of the Welsh labour movement from which Williams was assumed to have emerged.

This contested legacy, together with the fact that Williams had always made aspects of his own life and background central to both his political vision and his intellectual identity, meant that any attempt to write his biography was bound to be a more than usually delicate project, involving tangled issues of patrimony, possession, and partisanship. Shortly after her husband's death, Joy Williams entrusted the task to the prominent Welsh historian Dai Smith, who had known (and greatly admired) Williams in the last decade or so of his life, and who shared many of his political allegiances. Smith was given unrestricted access to Williams's papers; as, in effect, the authorized biographer, he was also able to draw on information from and interviews with a wide range of Williams's family and friends. Smith made good progress with the task into the early 1990s, it would seem, when he had largely to set it aside in favour of other demands—he was successively head of English language programmes for BBC Wales and Pro-Vice-Chancellor at the recently transformed University of Glamorgan.

At this point, another biographer set to work, but without access to Williams's papers. Fred Inglis, whose cultural bloodline was 'out of Leavisite literary criticism by New Leftish political conviction', had written several books in educational theory and cultural studies, and he, too, had known and admired Williams. Inglis's book appeared quickly, in 1995, attracting several favourable reviews but also some hostile, and in some ways damaging, criticism—again, most notably in the *LRB*, where the late Raphael Samuel itemized its failings in particularly unforgiving fashion (4 July 1996). Inglis's was an unusual biography, partly because it was based on relatively little research into unpublished or archival material: instead, he drew on extensive interviews with a range of people, not all of them close to Williams, whose reminiscences and opinions he reproduced in extenso. But much of the hostility with which it was received arose from two other unusual features. First, it was often sharply critical of Williams, at times even appearing to question his subject's good faith. And second, it allowed itself considerable liberty by way of imaginative re-creation and lyrical evocation, not always discernibly anchored in any documentary evidence or publicly available testimony. Samuel pounced on a notable instance of this creative licence when he pointed out that although the book begins with a vivid, detailed, apparently first-hand account of Williams's funeral, Inglis had not in fact been present.

I have to say that although my eyebrows were sometimes raised by these characteristics of Inglis's book when I first read (and reviewed) it, I thought they were partly compensated for by a stirring kind of political affirmation which attempted to capture, imaginatively and symbolically, the solidarities informing the labour movement, the commitment behind adult education in the period, the excitements attendant on the early days of the New Left, and so on. In addition, some of its criticisms of Williams struck me as refreshingly clear-eyed rather than (as they seemed to some other reviewers) unjustified carping. Re-reading Inglis's book now, I wonder if my response wasn't too indulgent: the evocative passages retain their power, but it has become harder, once alerted by the accumulating criticisms, not to feel uneasy with the apparent casualness and unreliability of parts of the narrative.

Meanwhile, in the last few years, Dai Smith, now translated to a research chair at Swansea (where the Williams papers have been deposited), has been completing his own biography. Given the sequence of events I have just summarized, there is, unusually, no exaggeration in describing his book as 'long awaited'. One immediate disappointment is that, even now, Smith's is not the full biography so eagerly anticipated: he covers only the first forty years of Williams's life, stopping in 1961 after the publication of *The Long Revolution*, which, together with his most famous work, *Culture and Society* (1958), and his first novel, *Border Country* (1960), represented the culmination of the first phase of his career. Nonetheless, what Smith has done he has done well: his book at once becomes the authoritative account of this period of Williams's life. We need to consider, therefore, how his treatment differs from Inglis's, and what difference, if any, it makes to our understanding and estimation of Williams.

The most immediately visible difference is the scale and pace of the two books. Smith takes 400 pages to get Williams into his mid-thirties, when he was finishing *Culture and Society*; Inglis gets there in 150. Smith draws on a far more extensive range of unpublished sources than Inglis, not just utilizing the rich hoard of Williams papers, but pursuing his subject into his wartime regiment's archives as well as the BBC's. He also brings a deeply informed historical discipline to the analysis of the relevant slices of British society during the first half of the twentieth century. And he writes, for the most part, in a cooler idiom than Inglis. Although the resulting book has its longueurs, this is a careful, fair-minded, and, above all, humanly sympathetic account of Williams before the years of his considerable fame.

The chief shift of emphasis that Smith wishes to effect in our view of Williams is to restore his fiction to the centre of his writing life. At the time of his death, Williams had published five novels (two volumes of *People of the Black Mountains* appeared posthumously). They have had their admirers, especially the first, *Border Country*, but on the whole they have seemed distinctly secondary to his theoretical and critical work, and many readers have returned a negative answer to the question that Ian Parsons, his publisher at Chatto, posed after having read the typescript of an early novel: 'Is Williams really a novelist?' Smith certainly demonstrates that Williams thought of himself as primarily 'a writer': 'Between 1948 and 1955 he worked at six separate projected novels, fully completing three of them and writing lengthy drafts of others.' As his widow later recalled, without any evident reproach: 'After the war, all he wanted to do was write.'

Smith professes great admiration for some of the unpublished novels, and even more for *Border Country*, which he regards as Williams's 'greatest creative achievement', his 'masterpiece'. What he praises in the unpublished drafts is, on the showing of extensively quoted extracts, certainly present and it is in its way admirable: an attempt, or series of attempts, to find an adequate form for representing the relation between individual experience and collective situation. But a solution to a theoretical or political difficulty is exactly how most of the extracts read. Williams's habitual reflex was to re-state particular cases in general terms: what was a strength in the theorist was a handicap in the novelist. His characters are too often assigned mini-lectures to deliver: abstractions hang heavy in the air as 'solutions' to the current 'crisis' are sought. Even in the quick punch and counter-punch of dialogue, the characters are too often debating, representing positions, and essaying a profundity which can be leaden when not comic (and which was wonderfully caught in Terry Eagleton's wicked pastiche of Williams's second published novel, *Second Generation*, quoted by Inglis). I respect Smith's sympathetic reconstruction of the various stages of Williams's thinking and writing, and it is historically right to place the fiction at the heart of his endeavours in this period. But I cannot honestly say that anything in these pages makes me regret that the early novels remained unpublished.

Smith's other chief emphasis is less revisionist, and it again echoes his subject's own estimate. Williams presented himself as able to sustain an essentially moral critique of contemporary society, with its disfiguring class-caused scars of deference, competitiveness, and distance, because he had grown up within the grounded solidarities and spontaneities of working-class life, an experience of 'finer living' (in a phrase of Leavis's he adapted) which served as his ethical compass or benchmark. Smith tries to put more historical flesh on this claim than Williams himself ever did, and he writes very well about the distinctive class structure of the semi-rural area on the Welsh border where Williams grew up, especially about the various categories of employee of the railway companies (Williams's father was a signalman, a fact frequently foregrounded in his writing). The railway did not simply pass through this area: other commentators have tended to speak of Abergavenny, the nearby town where Williams went to the grammar school, as a market town or small country town, but Smith brings out that at this period it was 'essentially a railway town'; in the 1920s around a third of the working male population was employed on the railways.

And Smith is too good a historian to overlook the changes that were constantly re-making these social and economic relations. Williams's father spent his entire working life as a railway employee, but in his later years, after his son had left home, he became prosperous enough to acquire a car (and, it's interesting to learn, to subsidize the ailing finances of his 'middle-class' son on several occasions). The car enabled him to take the produce he grew on his allotment and the honey derived from his bee-keeping to more distant markets, becoming in the process a small-scale entrepreneur. Smith quotes a nicely balanced entry in Harry Williams's diary (an important and rather affecting source throughout) for 7 February 1950: 'I decide to go to Hereford with honey and am hopeful of a contract for the rest of it. Went Tory heckling in the evening.' There is no single template for 'a working-class background', and Williams's later invocations of the values of 'his' class risked smoothing over even some of the variations that were close to home.

In other respects, Smith amplifies rather than modifies the familiar narrative. Williams got a scholarship to read English at Cambridge in 1939, the point at which he made the symbolically important transition from 'Jim' (his name within the family) to 'Raymond'. He became unsettled in his second year at university, throwing himself into political work for the student branch of the Communist Party, pursuing his growing interest in film, and being attracted to various women, especially Joy, whom he married in 1942. 'Never again', observes Smith, 'would he feel quite so imbalanced or his personality quite so divided' as in this difficult year—a fact which, when confronted with the granitic steadiness of his later personality, one feels almost tempted to regret.

His studies were interrupted by his call-up in the summer of 1941. Smith writes well about Williams's war, both on the inanities of camp-bound life between 1941 and 1944, and then on the terrifyingly immediate chance of being burned alive in an armoured vehicle while on active service. Williams served right through from the invasion of Normandy to the end of hostilities as an officer in an anti-tank regiment of the Royal Artillery attached to the Guards Armoured Division. As one might have predicted, he proved an impressive commander of men, calm and authoritative, while always keeping his innermost self well out of public view. In 1945 he returned to Cambridge to take Part II of the English Tripos: this was an intellectually formative year in which not only did he become absorbed in the study of Ibsen, the kernel of his 1952 book on *Drama from Ibsen to Eliot*, but, more enduringly, he also became an almost fanatical convert to the Cambridge style of 'practical criticism', and especially to F. R. Leavis's distinctive cultivation of that strenuous art. Williams later repudiated this critical approach with some vehemence, rather underplaying his own early attachment to it, but the evidence that Smith cites, sometimes only in passing, underlines just what a zealot the young critic was in these years.

In 1946 he was appointed to a post in the Oxford Extra-Mural Delegacy, responsible for tutorial classes across a broad area of eastern Sussex, and he remained an adult education tutor till his return to Cambridge and a lectureship in the English Faculty in 1961. Williams seems to have been respected by his fellow tutors, but also to have been a man apart, friendly though with few close friends; some colleagues saw him as someone who 'set out to plot a career', and even a well-disposed acquaintance could speak of 'an absolute ruthlessness at his centre'. When the Communist leanings of some adult education tutors occasioned controversy and the threat of witch-hunts in the late 1940s and early 1950s, Williams was criticized for remaining aloof, but Smith enters a humane plea: 'He did not, in these years, choose clear-cut positions intellectually or politically because the dilemma of irresolution lay within his own personality.' Resolution was only to be achieved by writing and more writing; the regular thudding of his typewriter keys was the rhythm to which Williams marched.

Along the way, Smith's narrative throws some incidental light on the germination of the ideas first fully explored in *Culture and Society*. In my view, this evidence provides further demonstration of just how crucial the second half of the 1940s was to Williams's intellectual and political development. Smith cites the script which Williams wrote towards the end of the decade for a projected Paul Rotha documentary film (which ultimately was never made) on 'The effect of the machine on the countryman's work, life and community'. The script spells out the way in which the historical part of the film would show 'how and why late eighteenth-century industrialisation altered everything'. For that reason, it was a mistake to sentimentalize present or recent village life: 'the village community', Williams declared, 'has gone.' Smith claims that 'there is little trace, in any of this, of the "nostalgia" for which he was later berated in the 1970s', but surely, at a fundamental level, there is. Williams may recognize, unlike more conservative critics, that the village of the nineteenth and early twentieth centuries was not an 'organic community' which had been disrupted only by the social and economic change of the past couple of decades, but there remains the structural nostalgia involved in believing that such community existed before the Industrial Revolution destroyed it. This was the historical story that underwrote the argument of *Culture and Society*: the idea of 'culture' develops from the late eighteenth century as a way of compensating for the ravages of industrialism and individualism. Williams maintained that only 'culture', understood not as art and literature but as 'a whole way of life' (and in practice, in his view, only working-class culture), could now restore the experience of living in genuine community with each other. The rhythm of Community Lost and Community Regained was inscribed in Williams's historical schema from very early on.

The success of *Culture and Society*—finally published, after long delays, in September 1958—changed Williams's life. When we leave him at the end of this book, three years later, intellectual celebrity beckons, and thereafter there are always readers ready to hang on even his most casual words—not that any of his words really were casual, though some of his later occasional pieces could be at once wordy and thin. Part of the great service done by Smith's biography is to take us back behind Williams's later fame, behind Williams-as-guru as well as Williams-as-professor, behind 'cultural materialism' and his engagement with fashionable forms of Marxism, back to the period of obscurity, tucked away in Seaford or Hastings as a promising adult education tutor, furiously filling notebooks with ideas, devoting his mornings to writing and rewriting novels and critical works ('he wrote incessantly'), some of which never saw publication, some of which were thriftily re-used as opportunities offered themselves, but always, always attending to that unceasing inner monologue.

In his later career that monologue seemed to spill out into various kinds of oral performance as unstoppably as it did onto the page, with the characteristics that regular readers and listeners came to recognize—fluent yet abstraction-laden, exciting but also somehow boring, astonishing in its range and command while rarely deviating from a few strong central themes. Perhaps for some of the same reasons, Williams has attracted oxymoronic labels: the solitary communitarian, the cheerless optimist, the detached activist. While it cannot be said that the younger Williams was consumed by uncertainty or hesitation, since few young writers or scholars could have been more focused and determined than he was, the glimpses we get of him struggling with conflicting senses of identity or experiencing difficulties and setbacks are, it has to be said, rather welcome. Inglis at one point described Williams's later manner, ever courteous as well as conscious of its own dignity, as 'ducal'. Smith occasionally enables us to see a more vulnerable and therefore more interesting figure.

It is not immediately evident why Smith titles his book 'A Warrior's Tale', a phrase that may suggest different things to different readers. Some might see Williams as a paid-up class warrior; others might note the centrality of his wartime experience; still others may think of him, more remotely, as a descendant of the kind of warrior traditionally found in borderlands, coming down from the Black Mountains to harass and repel English invaders (the maleness of the term emphasizing the subsequently much-remarked absence of attention to women in his work). Actually, the phrase cannot but seem oddly melodramatic applied to someone who spent most of his adult life hunched over a typewriter in a quiet study. It's true that 'struggle' was one of his favoured terms, yet in its frequent appearances on the parade-ground of Williams's prose it was usually accompanied by so many other abstract nouns—'structure', 'consciousness', 'form', 'process', 'crisis', and so on—that it lost any warrior-like associations and became an abstraction in its turn, 'the *concept* of struggle' more than the landing of any particular blow on any particular adversary.

Making a point in Williams's defence against those on the left who criticized him from a more theoretical or more internationalist position, Smith invokes Aneurin Bevan's remark about a local Socialist opponent in South Wales: 'Strong on India. Strong on Africa . . . But weak on the subject of New Pits.' But if the implication is that Williams was, in his own terms, 'strong on New Pits', then the sally doesn't seem quite apt. Although he celebrated the solidarities of working-class life in general, his writing during these years was short on concrete detail and for the most part far removed from the discussion of actual measures of policy. In addition, the South Walian allusion draws attention to the discomfiting fact that, in his critical writing (though not in his unpublished fiction), the Williams of the 1950s scarcely acknowledged his Welshness, blithely allowing the first-person plural that so liberally populated his prose to signal 'we in England'. Later, of course, he re-connected with his Welsh inheritance in various ways, especially as part of his repudiation of English culture and its ideological creature 'English literature', and he came to describe himself as a 'Welsh European' (the range and interest of Williams's later writing about Wales has been demonstrated in the collection edited by Daniel Williams (no relation) entitled *Who Speaks for Wales?*, to which Smith gives handsome acknowledgement). But the Williams of the period covered here was in some ways more Leavisite than Bevanite, stronger on 'our responses' to changes in 'English society since the late eighteenth century' than on New Pits or, for that matter, India.

The effect of the detailed scale and slow pace of Smith's biography, as well as of its attempt to place its subject's life in a wider social history, is to root Williams more securely than ever in the middle decades of the twentieth century. So many of the determining concerns and reference-points of his later work can be traced back to the 1940s and early 1950s, a series of efforts to come to some kind of terms with the disorienting trajectory of his own life in these years. It is true that even after all this patient accumulation of detail there remains something unplumbable about Williams's willed absorption, about what he termed the need to 'keep terms with one's own experience'. But, confining himself to his subject's first four decades, Smith has done all that we can ask the historian-as-biographer to do, and as a result we are now better placed to eavesdrop intelligently on that unceasing monologue.

Even so, not all Williams's admirers will be pleased by a biography that almost completely removes him from the larger anglophone world of contemporary literary studies as well as from the still more internationalized world of Socialist theory, and here we have to consider his posthumous reputation and current standing from a different angle. Williams pushed his thinking in new directions and engaged with new topics throughout the 1960s and 1970s and into the 1980s. During his lifetime, some commentators on his work, seeking to represent these diverse forays as a clear intellectual progress, had recourse to the once-fashionable Althusserian notion of an 'epistemological break' in the development of his thinking. This was usually taken to indicate the way he had sloughed off the 'pre-scientific' moralism of the literary-critical tradition in which he had been educated and replaced it with a 'materialist' analysis of the relations of literature and society which was both theoretically explicit and politically self-conscious. The central texts then became *Marxism and Literature* (1977) and the essays gathered in *Problems of Materialism and Culture* (1980) and *Writing in Society* (1984). The very category of 'literature' was called into question as an ideologically driven selection from the pluri-signifying abundance of 'writing in society'. The later Williams, extending and modifying the traditional Marxist emphasis on the primacy of productive labour, now termed his approach 'cultural materialism', and those taking their inspiration from this phase of his work became an important presence in the theory-riven world of Anglo-American literary studies in the 1980s and early 1990s. If Williams could at one point have been seen as 'the English Lukács', not least for his sustained engagement with the historical place of literary realism, he now came to be seen as 'the English Goldmann' or even 'the English Bourdieu' (such labels always exhibited a blithe disregard for the fact that he was not English, as he pointed out with increasing insistence). And indeed, since cultural materialism's attentiveness to non-literary contexts and its repudiation of 'evaluative criticism' was seen by many to have affinities with the academically still more powerful school of 'New Historicism', Williams could even be classified, at least when seen down the wrong end of a transatlantic telescope, as 'the English Greenblatt'.

Fortunately, Williams's standing was never confined just to the world of academic literary studies. His work, early and late, on 'communications', especially television, meant that he was a constant point of reference in the fast-expanding field of Media Studies ('the English McLuhan'), just as several of his books from *Culture and Society* onwards were regarded as founding texts, albeit frequently repudiated, in the diverse subject, or movement, now established as Cultural Studies ('the English Gramsci'). And, of course, his more directly political writing always engaged with a much wider, non-academic, left-leaning public, to whom he spoke inspiringly of the continuing value of 'community', of the imperative to pursue a thoroughgoing democratization of economic and cultural as well as political institutions, and of the need to cultivate 'resources for a journey of hope' towards a possible form of Socialism ('the English Habermas'?). In his concern with the natural environment, especially in the form of the relations between country and city, he provided the elements from which a 'Green Williams' could be constructed, just as his reflections on the consequences of colonial settlement and cultural dominance, here drawing explicitly on his Welshness, could even be made to yield a sketch of a 'postcolonial Williams'.

These multiple intellectual identities, or plausible appropriations, contribute to the combative possessiveness still noticeable among some of Williams's current admirers. But the inevitable effect of biography, at least of detailed biography on this scale, is to shift the focus from legacy to origins, from continuing relevance to initial context. Instead of speaking to current debates about race, gender, and 'the canon' (debates which are themselves now feeling pretty tired, it must be said), Williams is shown as sharing the angry revulsion, still so raw in the late 1940s, at the humanly deforming consequences of the Industrial Revolution. A version of Marx was undeniably important in the circles in which Williams the adult education tutor moved, but scarcely more so than William Morris, still a powerful living presence in the Labour movement into the 1950s. And although for a generation or more now, Leavis has, if mentioned at all, been routinely dismissed by literary theorists as irretrievably conservative and parochial, he takes his proper place here as a disturbingly intense, unacademic (indeed, anti-academic) reader of literature and an intransigently outspoken cultural critic.

The later Williams emphatically distanced himself from his work of this period. *Culture and Society*, he declared in 1979, 'is not a book I could conceive myself writing now. I don't much know the person who wrote it. I read this book as I might read a book by someone else. It is a work most distant from me.' Williams's autobiographical reflections of this sort are notoriously unreliable as guides to his actual development, but, when one re-reads that book now, it is easy to see why he came to feel uncomfortable with its left-Leavisite tone and assumptions. Nonetheless, *Culture and Society*, with its close examination of a long tradition of critics from Burke to Orwell, does provide a forceful reminder of what a good practical critic Williams could be when he chose. I realize that any indulgence to this aspect of his early work is now likely to be dismissed as a predictable piece of 'conservative recuperation', but I cannot help feeling that some of his later writing, which was always in danger of sinking into a midden of wordy over-abstraction, might have benefited from the crisp perceptiveness of his earlier literary-critical engagement with textual detail. On this score it will be interesting to see which of Williams's books best survive into the future. I suspect *Culture and Society* and, still more, *The Country and the City* will continue to have readers when *Marxism and Literature* and *Problems in Materialism and Culture* will be found only in the footnotes of the more recondite intellectual histories.

Nonetheless, once all the reservations have been registered, there remains something compelling about Williams. This is not just on account of his writing, which is variable in its quality and interest, and it is not just on account of his life, which was in many ways dull and unexceptional, as the lives of critics and scholars tend to be. What is compelling arises out of a peculiarly intense and hard-to-disentangle blending of life and work, personality and writing, background and purpose. That often-remarked deep centredness and confidence in who he was; that massive, calm certainty about central human values; that constant bringing-back of intellectual and literary issues to a half-remembered, half-idealized experience of genuine community, grounded in the everyday solidarities of working-class life; that unremitting effort to find an idiom and a form adequate to the representation of this experience: somewhere in the extraordinary ordinariness of this mix lies the source of his continuing force.

Perhaps Williams's greatest achievement by 1961 was to have fashioned a form and idiom in which to combat the dominant cultural pessimism without ceding the moral high ground. What he identified as the 'long revolution' was a record of 'actual growth', of a liberation of human potential rather than a dilution of 'standards'. As he put it in a never-published conclusion to the book of that name (which Smith reproduces in full): 'Everything that I understand of the history of the long revolution leads me to the belief that we are still in its early stages.' That was an important thing to say in Britain at the end of the 1950s; it's still an important thing to say, especially if given a properly internationalist application. Part of the value of Smith's painstaking account is that it shows that even Williams had to feel his way towards that conviction and towards the confident declarative terms in which it is expressed. Thereafter, he could easily sound *too* confident, *too* declarative, but, for all his later lapses into leaden abstraction and windy pomposity, he was right about this central matter, impressively and inspiringly right. Claims that everything is going to the dogs all too often rest on the hidden supports of parochialism, snobbery, class insouciance, and a wilful refusal of the intellectual effort required to try to draw up a more realistic balance-sheet of gain and loss. Williams fought against those things all along the line. It is hard to come away from this biography without admiring the way he made himself strong enough to fight that fight to such good effect.

6

Realists

'The Movement', Kingsley Amis, David Lodge

I

The poet and critic Craig Raine recalled that when the former Chairman of Faber and Faber, the genial Charles Monteith, encountered the suggestion that one of Philip Larkin's poems was indebted to the French poet Gautier, he was 'incredulous and dismissive'. To Monteith, the idea that Larkin might have been influenced by a *foreign* poet was 'ludicrous'. 'He had fallen', commented Raine, 'for the propaganda—Larkin's bluff, insular, faux-xenophobic, self-caricature.'

Compound terms using 'self-' often raise intriguing questions about agency and responsibility. When we speak of 'self-criticism' or 'self-restraint', we are calling upon ideas of dividedness where the 'self' that is doing the criticizing or restraining is in some sense more sophisticated or more knowing, as well as more in command, than the 'self' that is being criticized or restrained. But when we talk about being 'self-revealing' or 'self-destructive', the 'self' in question is precisely not in control of the process. More victim than agent, the 'self' in these cases is unknowing, unwitting; the behaviour involved is something that people, as we revealingly say, end up doing 'despite themselves'. In smiling at Monteith's gullible reaction, Raine obviously intended 'self-caricature' to be understood as an example of the first of these two categories. Larkin, he is suggesting, knew what he was at: 'propaganda' is something deliberately put about in order to persuade or mislead. The poet, we are invited to conclude, may have chosen to *appear* bluff, insular, and faux-xenophobic (it is an interesting question whether, if disguise is at work, he was

Zachary Leader (ed.), *The Movement Reconsidered: Essays on Larkin, Amis, Gunn, Davie and their Contemporaries* (Oxford University Press, 2009).
Zachary Leader, *The Life of Kingsley Amis* (Cape, 2006).
David Lodge, *Quite a Good Time to Be Born: A Memoir 1935–1975* (Harvill Secker, 2015).
David Lodge, *Lives in Writing: Essays* (Harvill Secker, 2014).

caricaturing himself as 'faux-xenophobic' or just xenophobic; double bluff, perhaps), but he wasn't *really* like that, or at least there was a lot more to him than that, and the 'more' included the subtler, knowing self who was responsible for designing the propaganda in the first place.

There is, however, an ambiguity lurking in the phrase 'self-caricature' which threatens to destabilize this comfortable conclusion. When we say of someone 'he's becoming a caricature of himself', we are, pointedly, not crediting him with masterminding a cunning disguise or laying down a smoke-screen; we are regarding his behaviour as increasingly 'out of control'. In addition, we are suggesting that the characteristics that are provoking our distaste or disapproval are not arbitrary or unprecedented: they are intensifications or exaggerations of qualities that have long been part of that individual's personality and social identity. (This is the sense in which it is sometimes said that as we become older we all become caricatures of ourselves.) So 'self-caricature' can be doubly threatening to our idea of conscious agency, both because it may be partly involuntary and because the direction it takes is already in some sense laid down. The most that can be said, and it is Larkin who said it, is that

> in time,
> We half-identify the blind impress
> All our behavings bear.

Much of our response not just to Larkin but to 'Movement' writers more generally turns on the question of how we construe the process of 'self-caricature'. There is a lot about their writing and behaviour, that of Larkin and his close friend Kingsley Amis in particular, which contemporary sensibility finds parochial, conservative, and sometimes downright offensive. For some years now, condemning these writers has been a way of affirming one's credentials as progressive and internationalist, as pro- or post- but definitely not anti-Modernist, and various other right-on identities. But there is always the suspicion that to respond in this way is to fall into a cunningly designed heffalump trap, a spectacle witnessed with rowdy delight by the shades of Larkin and Amis, drinks in hand. For it could be said that their critics had, like Monteith (if from the opposite side), 'fallen for the propaganda' and failed to recognize the elements of 'self-caricature'. Or—the question swings back—is that to credit Larkin and company with too much self-awareness and too much choice? Should we not emphasize, rather, the blind impress that, despite their knowingness, all their behavings bear?

Labels may be necessary in literary history, but they are also a great source of bother. From the outset, there has been incessant dispute over whether such a group as 'the Movement' ever existed, what its members were supposed to have in common, who belonged and who didn't, and so on. Many commentators have been tempted to concur with Thom Gunn's later weariness: 'The whole business looks now like a lot of categorizing foolishness.' Yet it is a label that has stuck, at once serviceable and misleading, much as we still speak of 'the Metaphysicals' or 'the Georgians', even though we immediately move on to dissolve any strong version of group identity. In the case of the Movement, the reasons for the success and longevity of the term probably have as much to do with the social history of post-war Britain as with poetic practice more narrowly conceived.

The story has no single starting point, but it is, as usual, easier to identify the date of the christening than the conception. In the early 1950s, there had been several attempts, by participants and observers alike, to identify a new tendency in contemporary writing, before, on 1 October 1954, J. D. Scott, the Literary Editor of the *Spectator*, published (anonymously) a leading article entitled 'In the Movement'. Modern Britain, Scott argued, was emancipating itself from the old social hierarchies of the pre-war years, and this new spirit was finding expression in a literature that deliberately distanced itself from the hitherto dominant styles of Modernism and Bloomsbury, as well as from the more recent 'New Romanticism' of 1940s poetry. Younger writers, taking their tone from Orwell as well as from Leavis and Empson, were adopting tougher attitudes and plainer idioms. 'The Movement', he wrote, launching the capitalized noun on its successful career, 'as well as being anti-phoney, is anti-wet; sceptical, robust, ironic, prepared to be as comfortable as possible.'

Although literary journalism was the medium through which this new tendency was identified and brought to wider public attention, its defining genre was the anthology. *Poets of the 1950s*, edited by D. J. Enright, appeared in 1955, followed a year later by *New Lines*, edited by Robert Conquest. Enright's volume contained work by eight poets: Kingsley Amis, Robert Conquest, Donald Davie, D. J. Enright, John Holloway, Elizabeth Jennings, Philip Larkin, and John Wain, to which list Conquest's volume added the name of Thom Gunn. Insofar as there has ever been agreement on the matter, the Movement has been taken to consist of these nine writers. They appeared in these anthologies as poets, but some of them, notably Amis and Wain, were already becoming better known as novelists, while others, such as Davie, Enright, and Holloway, went on to make a greater mark as critics.

Since they were challenging the old metropolitan literary elite and repudiating the authority of (European) high culture and (international) High Modernism, the new generation of writers was taken to represent not just an emphatically English identity but, within that, a 'provincial' perspective. In terms of geographical family origins, this was not wholly inaccurate, but it rather underplayed these writers' links with the institutions of established cultural power. All of them were Oxbridge educated, for example, and they enjoyed significant patronage from the BBC and the smart London weeklies. In the early 1950s, before they were at all well known, most of them had work published in the *Listener* and the *New Statesman*, and Blake Morrison calculated (in his still excellent 1980 study of the group, *The Movement*) that between June 1953 and July 1956 'there were over 240 Movement contributions to the *Spectator*'.

Almost immediately after the putative group identity was established, the denials and defections began. Although ties of friendship and some shared literary tastes remained, scarcely any of these writers thought of themselves as members of such a group by the early 1960s, and with the benefit of several decades' worth of hindsight, it is easier to see how their increasingly divergent later trajectories involved the working-out of dissimilarities that were present from the start. For example, Thom Gunn, who went on to become a substantial and much-admired poet, was always a little awkwardly placed in this company, even in the early 1950s when some genuine poetic affinities were discernible. His emigration to California in the late 1950s and his later poetry's experiments with syllabics (as well as its celebratory explorations of gay sex) increased this sense of distance. Something similar might be said, on a smaller scale, for Elizabeth Jennings, whose Catholicism and metaphysical yearnings likewise quickly came to seem at odds with the supposed style of Movement writers. John Holloway, never a central figure, soon drifted away and became better known as an academic. D. J. Enright, already marked out by his Scrutineering past, also pursued a university teaching career, in his case largely abroad. Robert Conquest was a hybrid: somewhat older than the others, he didn't fit any of the social stereotypes—he was from a wealthier, part-American background, and a Wykehamist to boot—and after working in the diplomatic service he moved to the United States where he wrote a series of books denouncing the Soviet Union. John Wain, it's true, corresponded to the identikit picture of a Movement writer better than any of these, and, having enjoyed early success with his 1953 novel *Hurry On Down*, he continued to publish fiction and criticism and to polemicize vigorously on behalf of traditional forms and plain sense, deliberately casting himself as a latter-day Dr Johnson. But time has not been kind to Wain's reputation: he still has his admirers, but in scholarly circles his role as a minor cultural broker in the 1950s now seems to be regarded as his apogee.

That leaves three very considerable literary talents as the core of the group: Philip Larkin, Kingsley Amis, and Donald Davie. Davie may be a rather neglected figure these days—critical essays that combine close reading with a somewhat stiff-backed Nonconformist Protestantism don't much recommend themselves to either academic or lay readers now—but for a while his critical prose constituted a kind of parallel scholarly manifesto for Movement writing. He was a more intellectually restless figure than the others, indeed a more intellectual figure *tout court*, and by the early 1960s he was writing some trenchant critiques of the literary manner he and his erstwhile associates were alleged to have cultivated (trenchant was Davie's natural mode). For this and other reasons, the later reputation of the Movement came to be almost wholly determined by the standing of Larkin and Amis. They were not innocents in these matters, of course. Reflecting in the mid-1970s on the recent anthologies edited by his friend and himself, Larkin could not resist self-satisfaction: 'We shall have stamped our taste on the age between us in the end.'

But the age had ideas of its own about that, and the literary and cultural tides were already running against what was increasingly identified as a distinctively 1950s sensibility. The new generation of poets, dominated by the Big H brands (Geoffrey Hill, Ted Hughes, Tony Harrison, and Seamus Heaney), were prosodically and thematically more ambitious. And the mood of the cultural politics of the later decades of the twentieth century was not indulgent to the perceived misogyny and little-Englandism of Larkin and Amis when biographies and editions of their correspondence began to appear in the 1990s. Their camped-up double act as 'old misery-guts and Jack-the-lad' did not, in the circumstances, seem likely to encourage appreciative and discriminating reading of their work. Even the cooler idiom of literary history now registered that work's diminished standing. In his wide-ranging volume of the *Oxford English Literary History* covering the period 1960–2000, published in 2004, Randall Stevenson complained of what he saw as the Movement's parochialism and unadventurousness, and he lamented 'the extent and longevity of its influence over English poetry in the decades that followed'.

As all this indicates, the ground which Zachary Leader and his platoon of contributors are attempting to occupy in *The Movement Reconsidered* has already been much fought over. One of the chief strengths of the many good essays in this collection lies in their cutting through these adventitious polemics to read the poetry itself with fresh attention, and the result is to make the writing, especially that by Larkin, Gunn, and, in parts, Davie, seem more interesting than its now stereotyped reputation allows.

The contributors fall into three main groups: the poet-critics (Blake Morrison, Craig Raine, James Fenton, Alan Jenkins, Clive Wilmer), the academics (Nicholas Jenkins, Terry Castle, Colin McGinn, Deborah Cameron, Deborah Bowman, William Pritchard, Eric Homberger, Michael O'Neill, Rachel Buxton), and the memoirists (Karl Miller, Anthony Thwaite, Robert Conquest), though several of them could, of course, lay claim to more than one of these identities. Varied though the essays are in both approach and theme, certain emphases recur. Perhaps the most interesting, urged by several of the poet-critics in particular, involves acknowledging the passion, the yearning, even the romanticism, half-buried under the world-weary or tough-guy personae. For example, Blake Morrison, brooding on the difference between Amis and Larkin as poets, observes parenthetically: 'Whereas Amis the poet writes what he knows, with confidence, and that's what makes him a light verse poet, Larkin yearns for what he doesn't know, and that's what makes him a Romantic.' Similarly, Raine, in the course of conducting a strikingly confident practical criticism class in his essay, remarks: 'We think Larkin is the unromantic, *l'homme moyen sensuel*, undeceived. But he is romantic. The yearning always gets under the wire, under the wary radar.' A generation or more ago, calling Larkin a 'Romantic' might have seemed perverse, but the attentiveness with which Morrison, Raine, and their fellow-poets listen to the yearning underlying Larkin's stagey bleakness earns them the right to apply this label.

This theme emerges in a different way in James Fenton's reading of Amis's poetry, a bravura performance which asks why so much prohibition and denial is so truculently thrust at the reader; is it that urges to which Amis fears he may himself be prey are being outlawed here? Fenton also reminds us of the strikingly uncynical conclusion to one of Amis's best-known poems, 'A Bookshop Idyll', about trying to

forget those times
We sat up half the night
Chockful of love, crammed with bright thoughts, names, rhymes,
And couldn't write.

A quieter, but wonderfully sure-footed appreciation of Thom Gunn by Alan Jenkins extends this theme. Jenkins is alert to the formal resemblances to other Movement writers in Gunn's early work, but he reminds us that Gunn never really shared the 'reasonable pubbable register' of early Amis and Larkin ('not so much a man speaking to men as a chap speaking to chaps'), and he is unpolemically responsive to Gunn's responsiveness to a wider world, both sexually and geographically. Among other illustrations, he turns to Gunn's 'Tamer and Hawk' from his 1954 collection *Fighting Terms*, a poem which ends:

You but half-civilize,
Taming me in this way.
Through having only eyes
For you I fear to lose,
I lose to keep, and choose
Tamer as prey.

Jenkins adduces the Yeatsian and Shakespearian presences in the poem, but concludes convincingly: 'It is Donne who sponsors the conceit, and the poem's relish for the paradoxes of falling in love: the willing submission to another, the loss of freedom that is experienced as freedom, the relinquishing of self-possession in the greater cause of possessing and being possessed.' On Jenkins's showing, the complex delights of love and desire are captured even in early, not always explicitly homosexual, poems by Gunn in tones that are more winning than either the sweaty frustration associated with Larkin or the coarse instrumentalism paraded by Amis.

It might have been helpful to have a separate essay on the rewriting of literary history entailed in the Movement's reaction against both Modernism and 'new Romanticism', and this would have been the place to do justice to Davie's two influential critical books, *Purity of Diction in English Verse* (1952) and *Articulate Energy* (1955), with their positive revaluing of, in particular, hitherto minor eighteenth-century poets (though there are some astute remarks in Clive Wilmer's sympathetic discussion of Davie). More generally, several of the essays contain some sharp thinking about literary forebears, especially Yeats, Auden, and Empson. Several of the most illuminating juxtapositions involve the work of the poet whom both Davie and Larkin explicitly evoked as the father of a plainer vernacular tradition that had been temporarily displaced or driven underground by the cosmopolitan experimentalism of the Modernists—Thomas Hardy. It is particularly interesting to find the young Thom Gunn invoking a writer with whom he might not, at first blush, seem to have much in common. Gunn reflected that although Hardy's 'mastering obsession' is loss and 'regret for the past', his apparently confessional poetry is in a sense 'impersonal': Hardy's first person speaks as a 'sample human being'. Alan Jenkins finds this 'misleading both about Hardy and about confessional verse', but the fact that this belief informed Gunn's verse was surely part of what made him a Movement poet in the early years, insofar as he was one, however much he subsequently developed other poetic identities. It goes with Wain's evocation of 'the common stock', and Davie's later characterization (in *Thomas Hardy and British Poetry*) of the 'social-democratic' character of the tradition of English writing descended from Hardy. And this is surely what we respond to in some of Larkin's most powerful poems, which conjure solidarity not in any transiently political, welfare-statish, way but by tapping into the deep common ground of human existence.

Several of the contributors prompt us to reconsider the question of the alleged 'narrowness' or 'limitation' of Movement writing, and the extent to which it may have been a matter of deliberate choice. No one, presumably, would want to say that Movement poetry is distinguished by its *terribilitá*, but that still leaves a pretty wide range of possibilities. A lot turns, perhaps inevitably, on how one assesses Larkin and his tonal bleakness. Clive Wilmer takes it one way: 'There is something narrow about his sensibility: not just the provincialism, but the ready defeatism and the resistance to all forms of literary adventure.' (Even if one is taking this line, suggesting he was resistant to 'all' forms of literary adventure may be less than fair.) Barbara Everett is quoted taking a different view: 'Larkin's great art is to appear to achieve the literal while in fact doing something other.' 'Achieving the literal' may sound a little unidiomatic, but it properly places the emphasis on the craft; 'appearing to achieve the literal' goes further still, suggesting, once again, a more deliberate and knowing strategy beyond merely local poetic effects. But what kind of 'something other' might he be doing?

So often Larkin captures our puzzlement about life, our 'wondering what to look for' (as 'Church Going' has it); something we shouldn't go on about too much but that nonetheless surrounds and threatens to make mock of our everyday activities. As Fenton nicely observes, Larkin can never approach this portentous theme head-on: 'It seems as if in order to get to the beautiful moments, like the beautiful moment in the last stanza of "High Windows", you have to pass through the very ugly first stanza, you have to pay a little ugliness tax.' That poem opens with these lines:

> When I see a couple of kids
> And guess he's fucking her and she's
> Taking pills or wearing a diaphragm

but it ends:

> And immediately
>
> Rather than words comes the thought of high windows:
> The sun-comprehending glass
> And beyond it, the deep blue air, that shows
> Nothing, and is nowhere, and is endless.

Only twelve lines separate these stanzas, yet the vocabulary and register seem worlds apart. Perhaps Raine is pointing in a similar direction when he speaks, improbably but in the end persuasively, about 'Larkin the secular mystic—or what you might call the Marriage of Heaven and Hull'. The characteristic way in which so many Larkin poems have some such existential, or even metaphysical, kick in the tail suggests something not quite allowed for in Thom Gunn's rather diminishing description of him as a poet 'of minute ambitions who carried them out exquisitely'.

To my mind, the issue of the narrowness of experience, or even absence of strong emotion, allegedly characteristic of Movement writing is not the main charge that needs to be answered. It is rather (and this would need to be supported by citation from their programmatic or occasional writings as much as from the main literary genres) that, in their horror of pretentiousness and insistence on 'writing to be understood', they risked encouraging a kind of anti-intellectualism. The insistence on the perspective of 'the plain man' by writers who are, almost by definition, rarely plain themselves should always be suspect. This is one of the places where the influence of Orwell was damaging as well as inspiring for the post-war generation. (Deborah Cameron's essay has some acute comments on the kind of bad faith involved in the way in which Orwell's claims about the debilitating effect of 'corrupt' language apply only to other people.) The register of blokeish, knocking negativity, exploited most insistently in Amis's criticism and journalism, was not just culturally destructive in itself, but at odds with the delicacy and, in its way, the intellectually rigorous character of the best Movement writing. In this respect, Empson provided a better model than Orwell, and one that encouraged a more authentic, because not wilfully plain-mannish, solidarity with the common human lot.

One of the things that is so heartening about the (mildly revisionist) arguments of the best of these essays is that they are sustained by attentive, discriminating literary criticism that gets away both from cod cultural history ('Rationing encouraged rationalism') and from reductive biography ('What will survive of us is love-letters'). Not that their criticism necessarily issues in a wholly positive estimation. Wilmer, among others, endorses Davie's later complaint that too much Movement poetry was preoccupied with the self-positioning of the poet and his relation to an audience rather than with looking at what was out there in the world. This brings us back to knowingness by another route. Demonstrating that they weren't naive, and certainly that they weren't gushing in the manner of the so-called 'New Apocalyptics' such as Dylan Thomas and George Barker, was an important element in the cultural identity of these writers in the early and mid-1950s. The bony intellectualism of Empson's poetry, in particular, encouraged a terse, argumentative idiom housed in tightly wrought formal structures. But Empson's example, especially when accompanied by familiarity with his criticism, may also have encouraged a somewhat intrusive self-consciousness about the rhetoric of poetic effects, and being explicit about rhetoric always leads to a focus on the relations between writer and readers.

Self-confident, self-conscious, self-caricature: there is almost a grammar to be parsed here, a progression (or degeneration) that is simultaneously logical and chronological. Movement writing encourages our comfortable sense that we know how its tunes go, and hence that we've got its number. But one of the things good criticism can do is to make us wary of underestimating writing with which we thought ourselves familiar. The palette of Movement writing may seem restricted, but the deliberate choice of monochrome can, as with photography, allow for subtle effects that full colour squanders in its pursuit of vulgar opulence. Allowing ourselves to feel superior to the 'narrowness' and 'limitations' of Movement poetry is a risky business. Questions about how far we are, any of us, authors of our own identities may come back to haunt us, and we should surely not be so confident that we have got the measure of how far a writer such as Larkin—by any measure the pre-eminent talent in this group—is the prisoner of a particular poetic voice rather than its knowing creator. Certainly, I wouldn't want to back my own puzzled musings on identity against the poet who could write the lines (partly quoted above) which conclude 'Continuing To Live':

And once you have walked the length of your mind, what
You command is clear as a lading-list.
Anything else must not, for you, be thought
    To exist.

And what's the profit? Only that, in time,
We half-identify the blind impress

All our behavings bear, may trace it home.
        But to confess

On that green evening when our death begins
Just what it was, is hardly satisfying,
Since it applied only to one man once,
        And that one dying.

II

Giving offence has become an unfashionable sport. Indeed, confusion about what 'toleration' requires has inspired something of an official crackdown on the activity, as if being 'offended' were one of the more grievous harms we can suffer, on a par with legal constraint or physical injury. Of course, for a few devotees of the habit, this has only added an extra *frisson*, both sharpening the satisfaction and bolstering the sense of justification. But in what, exactly, does the pleasure consist? Well, at least some of the following: discomfiting people we dislike; punctuating pomposity; the venting of impatience; taking revenge for having been subjected to absurdity, posturing, and tediousness; delighting in our own rhetorical inventiveness or command of hyperbole; an immediate sense of power, of impact on the world; a gratifying awareness of one's own daring, shading over into self-congratulation on one's greater robustness, honesty, freedom from cant; and, not least, a conviction of Duty to Truth nobly performed—after all, some people (a recognizable voice declares) simply *are* whey-faced wankers who wouldn't recognize a joke if it farted at them.

Kingsley Amis (the influence of whose idiom here is hard to resist) belongs in the Hall of Fame for the sport of giving offence, truly one of the all-time Greats. When Roger Micheldene, the central character in his 1963 novel *One Fat Englishman* is warned that he's about to say something he'll be sorry for, he replies, 'those are the only things I really enjoy saying'—and there's not much sign that Micheldene or his creator *did* feel sorry afterwards, either. The Cambridge historian Maurice Cowling, who overlapped with the circle around Amis in the early 1960s when Amis was in his pomp, spoke of their having 'a doctrine about being rude', a topic on which Cowling spoke with some authority. One of the phrases that crops up most often in recollections of Amis's social manner is 'fuck off!'—or, as he responded when somebody once had the courage to reproach him for his oafish behaviour: 'Fuck off. No, fuck off *a lot.*'

The issue of offensiveness is one of the recurring complications at the heart of any attempt to arrive at an overall assessment of Amis: of his quality as a novelist, his significance as a cultural figure, his appeal (or otherwise) as a man, and his symptomatic and influential expression of one powerful strain of Englishness. Closely linked to this is the question of the acceptable costs of humour. Both as a writer and a man, Amis could be, at his best, hugely and memorably funny. In the introduction to his excellent edition of *The Letters of Kingsley Amis*, published in 2000, Zachary Leader remarked that one of Amis's qualities that did not seem to decline much with age, among so many that did, was his 'comic aggression'. It's an accurate phrase, albeit leaning towards pleonasm, and it underlines the need for targets; giving offence cannot, by definition, be a victimless pleasure. There are also what might be called the 'opportunity costs' of humour: to be funny about something is not always to be unserious, but a compulsive drive to turn everything into hilarious absurdity is likely to shut out other idioms, other human needs. And then there is the egotism. Witnessing the giving of offence, like being part of the audience for someone else's humour, may have its enjoyment, but, tellingly, the real champions of comic abuse don't much care for this secondary role, and this points to another dimension of the pleasure involved: it's a way of performing, attracting attention, showing off, a form of the will to power.

This may seem to be getting a bit heavy as a way of talking about the author of *Lucky Jim* if that still-engaging novel is all one recalls of Amis, but reading or re-reading a wider selection of his work alongside Leader's sympathetic yet unsparing biography has repeatedly driven me to brood not just on the relation between Amis the comic novelist and Amis the serial offender, but on the *costs* (that word again) of his relentlessly mocking idiom, his increasingly wilful insistence on the priority of the laugh, and that streak of inner despair which initially finds expression in a kind of anarchic farcing but which progressively degrades into nihilistic bleakness.

No one writing about Amis's life (biographer or, for that matter, reviewer) can help but be intimidated by the dazzling presence of Martin Amis's *Experience*, published in 2000. An unclassifiable memoir-testament-album-apologia, this deeply clever book is also a love-song to his father, whose last years and death it selectively recounts, interweaving other episodes in the son's life, including anecdotes from the earlier years of his relationship with his father. It's much the best case that can be made for the later years of Kingsley Amis: yes, he was often impossible, but through all their arguments and rows (the verbals must have been classy indeed in their case), Martin manages to love and, mostly, to forgive. They couldn't, it seems, talk much about their writing, largely because Kingsley really hated all that clever-clever experimental Nabokovian crap he thought of his son as writing. *And* when young the poncey smartarse was a Leftie (by his father's standards, anyway), and would *go on* about it. But one is still left envying aspects of Martin's relation with his father, especially when thinking of such episodes as Kingsley buying his eagerly post-pubescent sons a *gross* of condoms or doing his imitation of the dog whose bark sounded just like 'fuck off!' ('when he made you laugh, he sometimes made you laugh—not continuously, but punctually—for the rest of your life').

Experience ends with an account of the comprehensive falling-out of the Amis family with Kingsley's first biographer, Eric Jacobs. In agreeing to take on the tasks of, first, editing the letters, and then writing the 'authorized' biography, Zachary Leader, a close friend of Martin Amis, was thus taking on a delicate and highly charged project, which makes it the more impressive that his biography is full, perceptive, and admirably even-handed. Leader clearly has a high regard for Kingsley Amis as a writer, but he does not shy away from documenting his failings as a man (to the less sympathetic eye, the second half of Amis's life seems largely to consist of failings). One benefit of Leader's diligence in tracking down papers and witnesses is that his picture of Amis corrects for the distorting power of what is, by any measure, the richest single source, the letters to Philip Larkin. Some 530 of these survive, almost half of which were printed in Leader's edition of the *Letters*, predominantly from the 1940s and 1950s, the period of their greatest intimacy.

The epistolary expression of that intimacy is precisely what makes the letters problematic as well as irresistible as sources. Amis and Larkin wrote to amuse each other but also, competitively, to outdo each other, especially in offensiveness. They cultivated the excesses of an undergraduate idiom: 'I love the *persistent mis-spelling* of author's names,' Amis confides at one point, 'it's amazing how it lowers the tone' ('Lord David Cess-hole', for example). Getting the tone down to sewer-level became an end in itself, with much verbal japing along the way, especially mistranscribing the sound of familiar phrases '(FUCKY NELL)', preferably for obscene effect (describing someone as 'a bit of an R-scrawler' and so on).

Above all, the Amis–Larkin correspondence was an abattoir specializing in sacred cows. There was blood everywhere ('Do you know who I hate? I hate T. S. Eliot. That's who I hate.'), and no established literary reputation emerged unbesmirched ('all those cheerless craps between 1900 and 1930—Ginny Woolf and Dai Lawrence and Morgy Forster'). It is perhaps not surprising that the publication of their letters did not exactly enhance the contemporary standing of either author, but, quite apart from the faux-naif priggishness of much of the disapproval, there was a failure to allow for the distinctive literary conventions of the genre. One of the many services rendered by Leader's biography is the way it reminds us, in the face of much contrary temptation, not to underestimate Amis's knowing self-awareness about himself and his writing. Or putting it more briefly (as he did in recording, for Larkin's delight, his response to an unimpressive poem by John Wain): 'COULD OF TOLD YOU THAT, SHITFACE'.

Amis was not born into the literary purple, as many of the Bloomsburyish or Bloomsbury-affiliated writers of the previous generation had been, and this humbler background was thought to be somehow explanatory of *Lucky Jim*'s distinctive tone when it was published in 1954. He was born (in 1922) into the clerical lower-middle class, his father commuting from Norbury in London's southern suburbs to his undemanding but respectable job at the Cannon Street offices of J. and J. Colman, the mustard firm. An only child of bookish disposition, Kingsley won scholarships that took him first to City of London School and then, in 1941, to St John's College, Oxford. Three years in the army interrupted his studies, such as they were (he and his new Oxford friends, including Larkin, spent a healthy amount of time keeping their distance from the boringly old-fashioned English course). Returning in October 1945, he came to recognize that getting a good enough degree to save himself from various dreary fates required some work; going too far, as usual, he got a First, and ended up staying on to do a B.Litt. While still a student, he got married, to Hilary Bardwell ('Hilly'), and had two children, Martin being the second (a third followed a few years later). Having failed to get any of the several academic jobs he had applied for, Amis was facing destitution at the end of the summer of 1949 when, to his surprise, he landed an assistant lectureship in the English department at Swansea, starting immediately.

Up to this point, poetry was the chief focus of his literary ambition. His later fame as a novelist has tended to obscure his standing as a poet, though by 1979 he had written enough, and was well enough thought of, to merit a 'Collected'. In the early Swansea years, Amis had been intermittently working on a novel, provisionally titled 'Dixon and Christine', but initial efforts to find a publisher met with rejection. His thirtieth birthday found him bewailing his lot as a poorly paid lecturer and father-of-two who had yet to publish a novel: 'What am I doing here? Or anywhere for that matter. If only someone would *take me up*, or even *show a bit of interest*. If only someone would publish some books of mine.' A Swansea friend, noting the Amises' financial hardship, remembers helping Kingsley load Martin's pram with empty beer flagons so that they could be returned to the pub to collect the deposits ('"Ah empties", Amis later recalled, "my only form of saving at the time".' Then Larkin (who had published two novels while still in his twenties) read his friend's typescript, making fundamental and detailed suggestions for improvement. Leader provides an excellent account of Larkin's contribution to the revising of what then became *Lucky Jim*—a contribution, Larkin was prone to feel later in his life, that was not properly recognized, perhaps not even by Amis.

Amis's life was 'utterly transformed' by the immediate success of *Lucky Jim*, published at the end of January 1954. Moreover, later that year he was raised to the dignity of spokesman for the *Zeitgeist* when 'the Movement' was first identified (in J. D. Scott's baptismal piece in the *Spectator*) as being, above all, 'anti-phoney'. Amis in particular had, as a later acquaintance put it, 'this laser pick-up for anything pretentious'. He made frankness and lack of pretension seem like a cause well worth giving offence for.

A lot of early Movement writing had a swing to it that partly arose from knowing their moment had come and partly from sensing that there was a large and responsive audience for writing that cocked a snook at both the social conventions of the drawing-room and the literary convention of High Modernism. This audience has been characterized in various ways—young, Penguin-reading, ex-services, 'provincial'—united by a delight in seeing ordinary human appetites and fallibilities treated sympathetically in contemporary fiction. The characteristic tone of the writing was, in a phrase Amis the reviewer used in speaking of one of the forerunners of this fashion (William Cooper's *Scenes From Provincial Life*), 'non-cosmic and non-operatic; entirely believable'.

Commercially, Amis was the most successful of the group. Success brought him more drinking companions in London and the money to keep up with them. It also brought him a lot of reviewing and other journalistic commissions (Leader calculates that Amis reviewed seventy-five novels within a year of *Lucky Jim*'s publication), throwing him into the career of all-round man-of-letters that he thereafter pursued with gusto. Karl Miller, a frequent commissioner of his reviews for the *Spectator* and the *New Statesman* during the late 1950s and 1960s, recalled Amis's impact in this role: 'To the older literati he *was* his jokes and sneers and funny faces, a low and vulgar fellow—which helped to endear him to readers of his own age. To his friends he seemed gifted, abrasive, condignly abusive, enjoyable, engrossing. He was the glamorous beauty of his circle.' Given what was to follow, it is important to emphasize his human attractiveness in his early years: several witnesses are reported as finding him 'natural', 'easy, amiable, unselfconscious'.

He remained at Swansea until 1961, an increasingly celebrated novelist and critic who maintained a sideline in university teaching, at which point he was tempted away by a fellowship in English at Peterhouse, Cambridge. This was not a successful experiment on the whole. He found Cambridge academics dull and conventional; they affected to be mildly scandalized by his excesses (F. R. Leavis didn't do mildness: he denounced Amis as a 'pornographer'). It is hard to know whose tongue was in whose cheek in the reported comment of the economic historian at Peterhouse, Michael Postan, that he didn't understand what was so funny about Jim Dixon writing (or not writing) on 'the development of shipbuilding techniques, 1450–1485': 'Fellow had a perfectly good topic.'

Amis remained in his Cambridge job for only two years, before, at the age of 41, setting out to live by his writing, which he did with great success until his death thirty-two years later. But 1963 marked a turning-point in his life in an even more fundamental way. During the fifteen years of their marriage up to this point, he and Hilly had each had a lot of sex with other people (I mean a *lot* of sex: he was 'a man who used to *live* for adultery' during these years according to his son's uncensorious recollection). The stormy bohemianism of their relationship was finally put under intolerable strain when Amis started an affair with the writer Elizabeth Jane Howard. Almost immediately, this affair threatened to be different from its innumerable predecessors because

Kingsley fell passionately in love with Jane. Hilly finally walked out on him; he and Jane set up together, marrying in 1965.

This seems to have been something of a golden period in Amis's life: he was in love, and with a fellow-writer (they read their day's tally of words to each other over pre-dinner drinks); he was a well-known author who was deliberately diversifying into various forms of genre fiction (James Bond thrillers, science fiction) and popular journalism; he was making money, and he and Jane lived a conspicuously comfortable life. But Leader's clear-eyed narrative leaves enough clues around for those disposed to look for the seeds of later decline. Amis expected people to look after him, especially if they were married to him. He held 'wholly traditional notions of the female domestic sphere' is Leader's dry summary. Amis organized the drinking, of which there was a lot; Jane did everything else, of which there was a lot more, including paying closer attention to his children than Amis always remembered to do. His writing included more and more meretricious or cheaply ideological journalism for publications such as *Penthouse* and the *Daily Mail*; he was gratified not only by the large sums this earned him, but also by 'the thought of how cross with me the intellectual Left will get'.

This last phrase signalled an important change in Amis's public identity. A not-very-political Labour voter in early adulthood (after a very brief flirtation with Communism at Oxford), he now became a vocal and even splenetic Tory. Or, at least, he became that kind of Right-winger, no lover of toffs and traditions, who may have been more common in American rather than British politics until Thatcherism crystallized some of the underlying social resentments. He denounced 'the sixties' (not that *he* had had to wait till 1963 for sexual intercourse to begin); he denounced 'liberal intellectuals', 'women's libbers', and associated demons; and he virulently denounced Communism and anyone suspected of not denouncing it with equal virulence. He noisily supported America's war in Vietnam. His close friend Robert Conquest ('Kingers and Conquers' as Martin recalled them) provided a lot of the stuffing for these views, and the two of them were at the heart of a group who for many years lunched together at Bertorelli's to hone their invective ('the fascist lunch' he liked, tauntingly, to call it). The combination of his increasingly dismissive hostility towards so much of the modern world and a flatteringly eager market for his views was not good for his writing. Even the ever-loyal Leader describes 'The Importance of Being Hairy' (1971) as 'a television play crudely and unfunnily satirising campus Lefties, perhaps the worst thing he ever wrote'.

None of this was a sudden change or without its roots in his earlier selves. An admirer from the late 1950s, when Amis could still seem attractively responsive to other people, shrewdly noted that he was 'a closer off as well as an opener up'; in the course of the 1960s and 1970s this negativity increasingly expressed itself as cultural truculence. He despised, for example, all 'fucking phoney foreign films', didn't read 'experimental crap', was increasingly dismissive of 'American crap', and so on. He became one of that tiresome kind of cultural pessimist who doesn't even try to distinguish his personal sense of nostalgia occasioned by the loss of the familiar from a generalized symptomatic reading of change as decline. The prejudices got uglier as he got older—'queers', 'blacks', 'Lefties', 'females'—or, as Leader puts it with teasing judiciousness: 'He was hardly without intolerant moments, especially in the later years of his life' (FUCKY NELL, steady on). As usual with self-conscious bigots, there are mitigating instances of individual kindness to members of these groups to be taken into account, as well as an allowance for the desire *épater les bien-pensants*. But, also as usual, Amis showed little sign of understanding the larger social-structural circumstances condensed into such labels nor much awareness of how intellectually lazy and humanly limiting the pleasure of provocation for provocation's sake can be.

By the mid-1970s his relationship with Jane was showing evident signs of strain. Leader's account is, as one has by now come to expect, carefully fair to all parties, but it's hard not to sympathize with Jane. Amis had gone off sex, perhaps as a result of his sustained drinking; in fact, he went off a lot of things other than the regular routines that he insisted on tyrannically. Finally, in 1980 Jane left him. He was, in his own way, badly shaken. Expressing it in his own way, he wailed: 'I've had a wife for 32 years.' Having one, of some kind, almost seemed more important than the particular woman. He hated living alone: he was a complete domestic dependant and he suffered various phobias and anxieties that were sometimes disabling when he was by himself.

It seems to have been his sons who hit on an improbable solution. Amis had a lot of money and needed someone to look after him. Hilly, by now happily re-married to an impoverished SDP peer, Lord Kilmarnock, had no money and needed somewhere to live. After negotiation, a curious *ménage à trois* was established on a partly commercial footing; Hilly had had a lot of practice in looking after him, after all, and at least now she was paid for it.

The other essential prop of Amis's later life had been in place since 1973, when he had been elected a member of the Garrick. Its bar now became the preferred stage for his regular lunchtime performances, which tended to stretch into brandy-fuelled matinées. He liked the Garrick, he reported in 1984, as 'somewhere to get pissed in jovial not very literary bright *all-male* company' (his emphasis). 'Pissed', 'jovial', 'not very literary', 'all-male': it's obviously possible that someone so at home in such company could be, as Leader claims, 'not only the finest British comic novelist of the second half of the twentieth century but a dominant force in the writing of the age', but it's somehow a depressing thought.

It would be easy to see the story as downhill all the way from this point, but that would be, once again, to underestimate Amis the writer. After a brief nose-dive following Jane's departure, his literary energy revived in the early

1980s. In 1984 he published *Stanley and the Women*, something of a revenge novel (revenge on 'females' generally), and then in 1986 *The Old Devils*, which won the Booker Prize. Leader alerts us to the Larkinian echoes in this book, from its title onwards ('The Old Fools', one of the latter's most unsparing poems); Larkin's emotional and imaginative presence seems to have been a feature of much of Amis's best work.

Amis's correspondence with Larkin had largely lapsed during the years of his great success and happy second marriage, but it revived in the 1980s, when they could compare ailments and share dismay at the decline of practically everything. There had always been a competitive edge to the friendship, and it is interesting to see how pleased Amis was to be invited to edit *The New Oxford Book of Light Verse* (1978), partly no doubt because Larkin had earlier been asked to edit *The Oxford Book of Twentieth-Century English Verse*. The will to power assumes another form in such projects, not least in their shared desire to displace the Modernist tradition: the anthologies were a particularly practical way in which they tried, in Larkin's satisfied reflection, quoted earlier, to 'stamp our taste on the age'.

Larkin died in 1985—in the funeral address Amis celebrated his friend's honesty and humour, always his touchstone qualities—but Amis himself went on for another ten years, publishing several more books. Even in his final, heavily criticized novel, *The Biographer's Moustache* (1995), he could handle the themes of selfishness and outrageous behaviour in ways that raise the possibility that he understood their place in his own life and had them to some extent under control. But so much of the evidence that Leader has assiduously compiled suggests otherwise. There are too many reports of his 'domineering' social style: he 'was determined to monopolise the conversation'; he could be 'very dictatorial'; 'he was full of fun but "if you took issue with him then you were in trouble"'; 'when Kingsley was arguing, he didn't just despise your opinions, he despised you personally'; he 'has a sadistic side to him and . . . he will look for your weak spot and then he will press it'; and so on. The will to power had hardened into a kind of bullying.

Kingsley Amis died on 22 October 1995, following, as Leader puts it, 'the loss of everything he needed to live—the ability to write, to drink, to joke, to laugh'. The ability to cause laughter lived on, of course, in his friends' memories as well as in his books. Leader reports Christopher Hitchens, at Amis's memorial service in 1996, recalling an occasion when Amis performed several of his most celebrated 'imitations': 'He made all his noises, and by all I don't just mean the Metropolitan Line train approaching the station at Edgware Road and I don't just mean the brass band approaching on a foggy day . . . or even the one described by Philip Larkin as unusually demanding and very seldom performed, of four British soldiers attempting to start a lorry on a freezing morning in Bavaria . . . ' With self-conscious design, the last word of this very long biography is 'fun'.

But that can't be 'the last word', of course. Considered as a narrative of the growth and decay of character, Leader's biography starts to assume the features of an Aristotelian tragedy, in which habits of selfishness, laziness, and self-indulgence undermine virtue and lead to nemesis. Strategies for avoiding difficult emotions are at the heart of the tale: turning them into material for jokes, not letting other people's needs impinge too much, keeping life superficial, amusing, manageable. One wouldn't be asking Amis to become Dostoevsky if one remarked that some of his fiction, too, might have benefited from a bit more intrusion by the humanly and emotionally unmanageable sides of life. Maybe some of Amis's vulnerabilities were too raw for exposure, but it is the deadly corrosion of the selfishness that is most in evidence as the narrative progresses: you start to feel that life can be made bearable for any of us only if we care enough about things other than our own ease and are willing to reveal or express this care at least some of the time.

One of the effects of Amis's tone and stance, it will already be clear, is that the critic is immediately cast into the waiting role of prig, disapproving of cakes and ale (the scorn is all too easily imagined: 'so what has ballsache COLLY KNEE done with *his* life that he's such a fucking expert?'). How many lives, after all, have produced as much laughter as Amis's? Shouldn't that alone guarantee access to the express lane at the Pearly Gates? But those (loosely) Aristotelian reflections I mentioned will keep coming back, here in the thought that one of the constitutive elements in much tragedy is waste. Amis could be 'an opener up', but he became a great 'closer off'. Negativity more and more became his modal form. And this, too, can be a mode taken by the will to power. Never venture onto terrain where you can't dominate. If you can't be the one in the spotlight, kick the fucking bulb out. And that 'laser pick-up for anything pretentious': why *was* it so alert, so acute, so savage? Pretentiousness deserves all it gets, but by becoming such a virtuoso in mockery Amis was shoring up his own impregnability, too; lots of fun at other people's expense, with no risk of having to expose his own deeper self.

Then there was the drink. Although in his early work Amis could write about being drunk in a way that makes you hurry to top up your glass, reading the latter part of Leader's biography almost makes you want to take the pledge. It's not just the amount, though he drank 'at least a bottle of whisky a day' in his later years, creating the need for a counter-balancing cocktail of pills to keep his bodily functions more or less working. It was the selfish rigidity of it all that is most dispiriting. Even as early as 1968, in his mid-forties and very happily married to Jane, a motoring holiday with another couple in Mexico was in effect organized around his drinking:

> In addition to suitcases Amis carried with him what amounted to a cocktail cabinet: a large straw bag with handles in which he packed bottles of tequila, gin, vodka, and Campari, as well as fruit juices, lemons, tomato juice, cucumber juice,

> Tabasco, knives, a stirring spoon and glasses. Amis insisted that wherever they were the car had to stop at 11.30 so that they could have a drink: only one drink, though a big one, carefully prepared. Everyone had to get out of the car while Amis fetched his drinks basket and mixed elaborate cocktails.

Later he became even more rigid in insisting on being at the pub when it opened, insisting on long pre-lunch drinks, insisting on long post-lunch drinks, always insisting, brooking no obstacle to his desires. Martin Amis suggests that, for his father, getting drunk was the thing rather than being drunk; hilarity rather than oblivion was the goal, at least for as long as he had any choice in the matter. But after a certain point he didn't have a choice: he just needed it, and finally, of course, he needed oblivion, too.

And then there were the women. For all Leader's sympathetic and perceptive remarks about his subject's relations with individual women, whether wives, lovers, or friends, there remains something I still find scarcely intelligible about Amis's attitude, though perhaps milder versions of it were common among men of his generation. He really did seem to think of 'females', collectively, as a separate species, maddeningly attractive though a few among them might be. When he was young, their chief function was to be on the receiving end of 'the old pork sword'; when he was older, especially after Jane had left him, he banged on about their general irrationality and vindictiveness (though at the same time confiding to his son that life without a woman was 'only half a life'). The *maleness* of so much of his idiom and sensibility as well as of his preferred social world is something of a deterrent in itself. Leader quotes from a John Carey review of Amis's *Memoirs* (1991): 'His prose style seems to exert masculinity at the expense of feeling.' That still seems dead right, and not just about that book. More generally, one is left feeling that the drive of too much of his writing as well as of his persona and habits is to *narrow* experience: too many kinds of feeling, too many kinds of reasoning, are shut out, mocked, pissed on, talked over. On my terms or not at all: fuck off!

The case for the defence has, in the end, to hinge on the quality of the best of the novels. Reflecting in *Experience* on the decline of his father's marriage to Jane, Martin Amis remarks: 'Penetrating sanity: they both had that, in their work.' It seems a rather uncharacteristic idiom at first, till one remembers that Amis *fils* had at one point stood up for Leavis against fashionable dismissal of him. It is also not an obvious, or even perhaps wholly persuasive, thing to say about Amis *père*: 'knockabout sanity' maybe; 'penetrating satire' certainly; but 'penetrating sanity'? 'In their work' is crucial, for as he goes on to editorialize, recalling the way these two penetratingly sane individuals drove each other to distraction and eventually divorce: 'But writers write far more penetratingly than they live.' Was this sufficiently true of the later Amis to outweigh any strictures on Amis the man?

In mounting his carefully argued case about the later Amis still being capable of writing fiction of a quality that not only contradicted the public perception of its author as a ranting curmudgeon, but could place and even satirize some of his own most unlovely characteristics, Leader makes much of *The Old Devils*, published when Amis was 64. Re-reading the novel now, I half-recognize what Leader is led to admire in it (and what, presumably, the Booker judges and enthusiastic reviewers admired), while nonetheless finding the experience on balance a lowering and disagreeable one. Yes, there are funny passages and portraits, mostly mordant and acidulous; and yes, one can read a kind of hope into at least one strand of the deftly restrained ending; and yes, a book portraying a group of limited and largely unappetizing individuals may be the work of an altogether richer and more generous sensibility than any represented in the book itself (creating the consummate representation of provincial small-mindedness does not make Flaubert a small-minded provincial). And yet, and yet.

The disagreeable aspect of the experience comes, at least in part, from the way in which Amis's humour presumes a matey collusiveness with the preoccupations of those it is satirizing. They may be shits, but they're our kind of shits. It's a social world in which, for example, petty point-scoring is prominent; this dispiriting trait is half-mocked, half-endorsed, as though to say: come on, we're all at that game, so don't get too high-and-mighty about it. Lack of honesty about oneself is mocked, but usually when it takes the form of pretentiousness or trying to disguise low motives: the greater emotional dishonesty of not confronting the paucity of positive, other-directed hopes and feelings passes largely unchallenged.

These reactions may seem ungenerous to the novel, whose satire is frequently penetrating and intelligent. But consider the effect of the narrative voice in the following small example. Peter is the one character who at the end has the possibility of finding something like late-life love, reunited with Rhiannon, a woman he had loved and behaved very badly to decades earlier. For the moment, however, he is still bound to Muriel, in a marriage in which almost everything seems to have died except the low flame of antagonism. The penultimate scene of the novel centres on the wedding of their son to Rhiannon's daughter and the reception back at Rhiannon's house. Here is Peter emerging from the house and catching sight of his wife:

> She was strolling along the edge of the lawn and, just as he noticed her, she half turned to run a superior eye over what was growing—nothing very much, perhaps—in the nearby bed. She let her gaze linger, making quite sure things were as bad as they had looked at first glance, then snatched it apologetically away, both in a style he felt sure he would have recognised with an inward yell of loathing at ten times the range. Seeing it, seeing it unseen, catching the old bitch out even on such a puny scale, was as good as a stiff one.

It matters to the intensity of Peter's reaction that it should be *Rhiannon*'s garden that is being condescended to, and it matters for the timing of the whole scene that Muriel had chosen the eve of their son's wedding to announce to Peter her decision to sell their home and move away, in effect to leave him. Even so, the passage is representative of those moments when Amis seems closest to sharing his character's emotion in part just because it records one person *triumphing* over another, 'even on such a puny scale'. And a nagging uncertainty about how deep the irony goes is partly the result of the way the prose, from the middle of the second sentence, starts to veer from impersonal third-person narration to something like free indirect style, with the final sentence being voiced very much in Peter's idiom. Or, should one rather say, in the idiom Amis often shares with Peter, the idiom of the chap familiar with the equally morale-boosting effect of 'a stiff one' and of 'catching out' a resented 'female'? It's the kind of collusive interiority Amis's fiction (not his alone, of course) tends to reserve for its more sympathetic characters. Peter is no Jim Dixon; he is sourer and pockmarked by disappointment. Still, he is the least depressing man in the novel.

And yet—the dialectic of one's reactions swings back again, prompted, properly enough, by Martin Amis once again. One of the many bravura passages in *Experience* describes the son struggling to get his paralytically drunk father safely home one night. 'On a traffic island in the middle of the Edgware Road', the older Amis falls over. 'And this was no brisk trip or tumble. It was a work of colossal administration. First came a kind of slow-leak effect . . . Then came an impression of overall dissolution and loss of basic physical coherence. I groped around him, looking for places to shore him up, but every bit of him was falling, dropping, seeking the lowest level, like a mudslide.' We seem to be witnessing one of his father's own legendary, exaggerated impressions, as though he were 'doing' Kingsley Amis falling down drunk; we are also reminded that we are reading a passage by the son of the author of the celebrated account of Jim Dixon's heroic, incapable, drunkenness. Martin does finally get his father home, of course. 'Dad, you're too old for this shit, I might have said to him. But why bother? Do you think he didn't know?'

And that's the larger problem facing anyone writing about Kingsley Amis, especially with *Experience* to hand, proprietorial yet also (to use his word) penetrating, tacitly challenging even the slightest slackness in judgement. You are not, you can sometimes feel, likely to say anything they haven't between them thought of already. So what if you do find something worse than unlovely in this man, and so what if you find yourself pondering the relation of that unloveliness to the limited but incontestable merits of his work (an appropriately 'unoperatic', almost suburban, version of the wound and bow)? What about it? Do you think he didn't know?

Reviewing a biography of Evelyn Waugh in 1975, Amis reflected that he was glad that he had never met the author of work that he so much admired, not least because he would probably have been on the receiving end of a savagely rude put-down. 'It was his nature to go too far, most of all in the direction of outrageousness,' Amis judged. 'At a safe distance, one can rather half-heartedly deplore all this, but without this compulsion to say the unsayable he would never have come to be the writer he was. There was the drink too.' Amis was 53 when he wrote this; the best period of his life was coming to an end, his habits and his persona were rigidifying beyond recall. But he never, quite, became one of 'the old devils', and his intelligence, including intermittent, often largely concealed, intelligence about himself, was part of what saved him from that fate. At the same time, one cannot help wondering whether that intelligence wasn't a burden, too, adding to the pathos of the later years. It is not, in the end, comforting, as one broods on the Aristotelian morality tale of his life, to hear that other, distinctive but uncannily resonant, Amisian voice asking: 'Do you think he didn't know?'

III

In the preface to *The Ambassadors*, written for the New York edition of 1909, Henry James insisted that although the whole conception of the novel required that the unfolding action must, in some sense, be seen through Strether's eyes, there had been no question of using first-person narration. That technique, he insisted, would have been too laxly self-indulgent: his treatment of Strether had 'to keep in view proprieties much stiffer and more salutary', demands that 'forbid the terrible *fluidity* of self-revelation'. Not all writers would share James's sense of the desirability of the discipline of free indirect style, but his slightly stagey horror at the likely excesses of the first-person mode might nonetheless strike a chord with readers of a variety of free-running or confessional forms, not just novels (think Christmas circular letters).

But what about autobiography or memoir? Surely here self-revelation might seem to be of the essence. Yet James's stricture still has purchase: any autobiographical account is no less the achieved effect of selection and arrangement, not some spontaneous or artless recall. At the same time, a salutary discipline cannot be achieved in this genre by submitting to the technical demands of third-person narrative. That the 'I' who writes and the 'I' who is written about are identical is the defining premise of autobiography. So what might constitute a comparable kind of 'terrible *fluidity*' here and how might an author guard against its perils?

Few writers may seem as well qualified as David Lodge both to diagnose and to overcome these potential difficulties. As one of the leading critics and literary theorists of the past few decades he has interested himself above all in the mechanics of narration, both the nuts and bolts of expository technique, the subject of his first critical book, *Language of Fiction* (1966), and the deeper structures of pattern and archetype, treated in several later works, notably *Working with Structuralism* (1981) and *After Bakhtin* (1990). As a novelist, he has exhibited a winning dextrousness in matters of form, from the parodies threaded into *The British Museum is Falling Down* (1965) through the filmic inter-cutting of *Changing Places* (1975) and on to the temporal dislocations and frame narratives employed in his most recent novel, *A Man of Parts* (2011), a fictional treatment of the life and loves of H. G. Wells. He has also, not coincidentally, long been a keen Jamesian, devoting an acute chapter to *The Ambassadors* in *Language of Fiction*, and later attempting a similar fictionalizing of James's life in his novel *Author, Author* (2004). Whatever else we might anticipate about an autobiography by such a writer, we can be sure it will not be artless.

Actually, we can also be sure that its main outlines will be largely familiar, since he has already told us the story of his life several times over. His early novels, in particular, were unashamedly autobiographical: *The Picturegoers* (1960) centred on a group of Catholic teenagers, *Ginger You're Barmy* (1962) dealt with national service, *The British Museum is Falling Down* (1965) riffed amusingly on life as a contraception-averse Catholic graduate student and budding novelist, and *Out of the Shelter* (1970) recorded the encounter with 'abroad' after growing up in austerity Britain. Even *Changing Places*, still his funniest book and the one that made him famous, clearly re-worked his own experience of going, as a lecturer in English at Birmingham, to be a visiting academic at Berkeley. And he has never hesitated to report directly on his own life in a series of confessional essays, reflective prefaces, and—a form in which he has been notably proficient—discursive review-articles (*Lives in Writing* reprints several examples of the latter, mostly from the *New York Review of Books*).

So we already know a lot about his growing up in a lower-middle-class family in an inner suburb of south-east London; about his inherited Catholicism and his struggles with it; about his time studying English at University College London; about his long-lasting marriage to a fellow-student and the fact that their third child was born with Down's Syndrome; about his having lived in Birmingham since he was appointed to his first teaching post there in 1960, though he retired from the university to become a full-time writer in 1987; about his several extended visits to the United States; about his close friendship and rivalry with Malcolm Bradbury; about the onset of deafness in late middle age; and about much, much more besides. Lodge said in a recent interview that the idea of his writing an autobiography had been suggested by a reader of *Lives in Writing*, given that collection's evident interest in the relation between lives lived and books written. But this seems a slightly odd inference on two counts: first, it is not obvious that the curiosity and attentiveness that fuel the best of this kind of biographical criticism have any necessary carry-over to the quite different task of writing an autobiography; and second, Lodge has already brought his own life into so much of this and other kinds of writing that we may wonder whether there is much left to say.

He has also been consistently reflective about the character of his own work. Writing as long ago as 1976, when he was 41, Lodge recalled that in his youth he had been attracted by the existential dilemmas treated in the fiction of Greene, Mauriac, and other Catholic writers, but that in his own novels 'I domesticated their themes to the humdrum suburban-parochial milieu that I knew best.' This was certainly true of his fiction up to that date: the baked dusty roads of Mexico or the sweat-soaked bedrooms of West Africa familiar from Greene's exotic morality tales are replaced by rows of identical terraces in south-east London, and instead of guilt-ridden whisky priests agonizing over damnation and redemption we have spotty young men wondering whether they will get to kiss the girls after ping-pong at the church youth club. But although he has continued to mine the material of fiction from the seam of his own life (*Deaf Sentence*, published in 2008, is the most recent example), Lodge is not as easy to classify as he may at first appear.

Despite having been admirably faithful to Birmingham, where he has now lived for fifty-four years, he is in no sense 'a regional writer': there is no great celebration of place in his work, no obeisances to local deities, no real attempt to capture or write in any local dialect, and so on. Nor is he an overtly political writer: there is some gentle satire on contemporary *mores* scattered through the novels, but such exasperation as it allows itself seems directed at individual instances of idiocy rather than larger structural failings. He is obviously not any kind of historical novelist: his fiction, like his criticism, mostly confines itself to the twentieth century and he has never seemed greatly interested in more distant periods. Although he has written several times about his Catholicism, which also provided the central theme of one of his most serious novels, *How Far Can You Go?* (1978), it would have to be said of him, as Greene said of himself, that he is a novelist who happens to be a Catholic, not a Catholic novelist. And although he is probably best known, and cherished, as a comic writer, neither his early nor his late novels comfortably fit this classification, and the range and seriousness of his critical writing suggest a deep and enduring interest in the potentialities of types of modern fiction far beyond the comic.

Indeed, it is a merit of considering his critical writing alongside his novels that it reminds us of his constant fascination with form. When thinking of the novelists who influenced him most, it is Greene and Kingsley Amis who come most readily to mind. He has written more than once about Amis, emphasizing his range as well as his comic invention, but also the importance of 'the Movement's' freedom from traditional metropolitan class snobberies. However, the fictional master to whom Lodge has given his most unstinting and undiminished allegiance is a figure who might well surprise the casual reader of one or two of Lodge's best-known novels, for it is James Joyce. There may be, it's true, a Catholic connection, especially with the author of *Portrait of the Artist*, but that is minor; the chief reason he can speak of Joyce as 'the writer I revered above all others' is on account of his linguistic virtuosity and the daringness of his experiments with form. Lodge's late novels, re-imagining Henry James or H. G. Wells, may seem like departures from his earlier work, which mostly stayed close to that 'humdrum suburban-parochial milieu', but they can also be seen as further instances of his interest in the ways the resources of fiction can be deployed to re-imagine the familiar. In a similar way, he has been appreciative of the work of writers as different (different from each other as well as different from him) as Muriel Spark or Truman Capote in part because in each case their work demonstrates that, where formal inventiveness is concerned, playfulness does not merely issue in comedy.

Still, it may be his fate to be celebrated as a contributor to the sub-genre now known as 'the campus novel' since his two best-known books must be *Changing Places* and *Small World* (1984). In the former, a British and American academic exchange jobs (and much else) for a semester, while the latter takes the form of a Grail-quest pursued through a series of international scholarly conferences; both depict academic life largely in terms of comedy, sex, and self-importance. Indeed, so little do the serious concerns of the scholarly world feature in these novels that some commentators have seen them, along with works such as Bradbury's somewhat darker *The History Man* (1975), as contributing to the decline in public regard for universities and academic life in the 1970s and 1980s. Significantly, Lodge himself has discussed the campus novel more in terms of literary form than social effect. In a 1982 essay, he described the genre as 'a form of stylised play . . . a modern, displaced form of pastoral'. That may be a helpful way to see his own two contributions (or three if one includes *Nice Work*, published in 1988), even while remembering that pastoral usually functions as a vehicle for social criticism. It would be a mistake, however, to define his *œuvre* exclusively in terms of this sub-genre: his fictional achievements are far more diverse and, in some respects, weighty than that.

Seen from another angle, the university has arguably been the key institution in Lodge's life, and here his biography is a microcosm of the much-vaunted social mobility experienced by many of those who came to adulthood in the decades immediately after 1945. At first sight, it might be tempting to say that he is not an academic novelist but a novelist who happens to be an academic. However, that might not only under-state the extent to which Lodge's critical and theoretical work has informed his fiction—his skilful exposition of the role of metaphor and metonomy in *Nice Work* is one obvious example—but it may also misrepresent his identity. Lodge doesn't just 'happen to be' an academic: he owed his writing voice to the university, just as in a more material way he owed the opportunity to establish himself as a writer to the financial security provided by his academic career.

His may not have been the most eye-catching or celebrated version of class ascent, nor has it involved continuing to find some kind of touchstone of authenticity in fidelity to one's origins even while rising into a more privileged stratum, as in the case of Richard Hoggart, his one-time Birmingham colleague. Still less does his life story make a classic *Bildungsroman*: his climb up the educational ladder does not appear to have involved formatively picaresque adventures or years of *Sturm und Drang*. Rather, his education and academic career seem to have stimulated and nurtured his natural intellectual curiosity and literary gifts in ways that have allowed him to develop a lucid, intelligent writing voice without either falling back on class resentment and chip-on-the-shoulder touchiness, or miming the affectations of traditional high culture (it may have helped that his education and career took place entirely outside Oxbridge).

Though his fiction is minutely observed and in that respect faithful to the conventions of traditional English social comedy, Lodge writes from a perspective that has been freed from inherited class associations as much by the corrosive of critical thinking as by the sheer fact of economic and professional advancement. At one point in *Language of Fiction*, where he is discussing the continuing contrast between the traditions of High Modernism and the conventions of social realism observed by work that is contemporary without being, in this sense, 'modern', he writes: 'Anyone who has had a literary education, who has experienced the work of the great moderns instructed by such education, will tend to feel dissatisfied with "contemporary" work, with its thinness of texture, its lack of complexity, its simplifications and evasions, its indifference to significant form.' In the passage as a whole, Lodge does not wholly endorse this Modernist credo, but his clear identification with 'anyone who has had a literary education' (implying an education well above the minimum) says something important about where he is writing from and who he is writing for. Lodge's writing voice, as opposed to the facts of his biography, can make him seem both classless and placeless, but the truth is that this relative freedom (or, more sociologically, displacement) has been enabled by the institution of the university and the part it played in opening up the world of the mind to new social strata in the three or four decades after 1945. In some of his fiction Lodge may have depicted academic life satirically, but in his life he has been a striking beneficiary of its world-opening power.

Writing about Kingsley Amis's early novels in *Language of Fiction*, Lodge declared that they 'speak to me in an idiom, a tone of voice, to which I respond with immediate understanding and pleasure'. I suppose I might say something similar about my own response to the best novels of Lodge's early and middle periods, in part because of coming from much the same stratum of English society, in part from having attended an almost identical school, and in part because of having been similarly nurtured and empowered by the institution of the university. But the difference of half a generation makes all the difference. Lodge went to university in 1952, in an England still subject to rationing, social deference, and the deferral of pleasure. Things had changed by 1966. For example, Lodge confides to us the surprising disclosure that 'I had no ambitions to have sexual intercourse as a teenager.' By contrast, I sometimes think that at that age I had no other ambition to speak of, but, further differences aside (notably Lodge's Catholicism), this may be a telling illustration of the development of the very category of 'teenager' between the late 1940s and the mid-1960s. And such reflections remind us how Lodge has in many ways been the chronicler of the expanding horizons of English society in the post-war decades, reporting the experience of prosperity as encountered by an austerity-conditioned sensibility.

He is also representative of a moment in the history of literary criticism in Britain that has almost disappeared from view. It might most economically be described as post-Leavis but pre-Theory. In publishing terms, its early natural habitats were periodicals like *Essays in Criticism* and *Critical Quarterly*, journals in which an undogmatic, conversable, but intensely serious form of literary criticism could be confident of reaching a like-minded audience. Published in 1966, when Lodge was 31, *Language of Fiction* was an important expression of this style of criticism, applying to the novel some of the same attention to verbal texture that close readers of the previous generation had addressed to poetry. He drew on eclectic older critics such as John Holloway, Ian Watt, and, above all, Frank Kermode—many of his circle, he reports, 'were covert Kermodians inasmuch as we regarded him as the most accomplished literary critic of his generation'—but also on outliers of American formalism such as Wayne Booth. He shared interests with near contemporaries such as Tony Tanner while his literary doppelgänger (and closest friend) was Malcolm Bradbury. Like Kermode and Tanner, Lodge was thereafter initially receptive to new theoretical ideas coming from Europe, particularly Russian formalism in his case but also early Structuralism, and he did much to show how concepts derived from these sources could illuminate the mechanics of fiction and indeed narrative in general. Drawing upon such sources did not mean abandoning his lucid, relaxed mode of writing, but it enabled him to supplement the kind of close reading he had been good at from the start with a broader grasp of patterns and archetypes, seeing beyond the surface texture of a novel to structuring design of its narrative choices. However, also like Kermode and Tanner and some others, he became uneasy with some of the more rebarbative or implausible applications of post-structuralist ideas, and he never became a card-carrying member of any of the most militant sects in the theory wars. In this respect, he has remained, if not exactly a traditional literary critic, then at least someone with too much interest in, and respect for, the ways his fellow-novelists have used their shared tools ever to feel quite at home in more strenuously ideological company.

The essays collected in *Lives in Writing* are for the most part nicely turned, workmanlike pieces of professional literary journalism, though in places lacking the engaged energy of the best of his earlier critical essays. But every so often he reminds us of what an acute and sympathetic reader he can be. In the course of an appreciative essay about Alan Bennett, he suddenly swoops on the passage in *Untold Stories* in which Bennett recounts a visit with his father to see his mother who has been committed to an unbearably awful mental hospital.

> Dad sat down by the bed and took her hand.
> 'What have you done to me, Walt?' she said.
> 'Nay, Lil,' he said and kissed her hand. 'Nay, love.'

Lodge responds tenderly to the pathos of the scene, singling out Bennett's north-country use of 'Nay': 'Semantically equivalent to "no", it has a quite different force here, freighted with inarticulate apology, deprecation and dismay.' That is acute and exact, a small example of the attentive reading, devoid of critical showiness, that Lodge at his best is so good at.

The essay as a whole is responsive to Bennett's writing, in part because Lodge is interested in how he achieves his distinctively flat yet engaging tone. 'Bennett writes very honestly about himself, or he creates the effect of doing so.' Lodge, too, creates the effect of seeming to write honestly about himself, though in a less mock-morose and downbeat manner than Bennett (being less downbeat than Bennett is, it must be said, scarcely an unusual quality). It is a pity that the end of this essay is marred by a quite unmerited ticking-off of Bennett for his failure to express the approved reaction to the events of 9/11; one can't help wondering whether Lodge would have felt inclined to add this reprimand if he had not been writing for a primarily American readership.

After such varied literary achievements as well as after so much re-working of episodes from his own life, *Quite a Good Time to be Born*, published to coincide with his eightieth birthday, is almost bound to be a bit of a disappointment. There is, to begin with, the question of how much of it really is new writing. He not only quotes fairly generously from his own earlier books, but he also re-works—and in some cases simply re-uses almost verbatim—whole passages from things he has published before, sometimes more than once. For example, he recalls first encountering Frank Kermode in 1961: 'At the Cambridge conference he [Bernard Bergonzi] introduced me to Frank Kermode and as a result I found myself sitting with a group late one evening in somebody's room, sipping whisky out of tea-cups and bathroom mugs, listening to Frank discoursing in his relaxed, drily amusing style. Unfortunately I cannot recall anything he said on that occasion except his enjoyment of the drive down from Manchester in his Mini, then a new and trendy vehicle.' After this, it is a little dismaying to find that *Lives in Writing* had already reported the same vignette in almost identical words, complete with the whisky and Kermode's Mini. But then it turns out that that piece is itself substantially a reprint of an essay that had appeared in *Critical Quarterly* in 2012, where the whisky and the Mini had previously done duty, and then that that piece in turn had largely reproduced Lodge's earlier contribution to a 1999 volume honouring Kermode, which seems to have been, as far as I have followed the trail, the first public appearance of the whisky, the Mini, and the otherwise defective memory. Autobiographers, like those holding forth round the late-night whisky, are allowed some slack in the matter of repetition, but such examples reinforce our sense that, where the main episodes of Lodge's life are concerned, we've heard it all before.

In addition, *Quite a Good Time to Be Born* contains too many passages that fall below what we have come to expect of Lodge. Thus, we are told of his visit to the United States in 1963–4: 'Life was not entirely trouble-free. I had to have a tooth extracted, the first since childhood . . . Then Mary was stung in the foot by a wasp . . . ' That 'terrible *fluidity* of self-revelation' is too much in evidence, and the dispiriting cadence of the Christmas circular letter echoes through whole stretches of the prose. For example, in the same year Christmas was spent with his sister-in-law and her husband: 'Eileen and John entertained us kindly in their suburban apartment, and Christmas day was enhanced by the excitement of the four children opening their presents. On Boxing Day we went to an open-air skating rink in the centre of the city so that Eileen's elder boy could try out his new skates, but the surface was wet with melting ice so that if you fell over you got soaked.' This may, of course, be a subtle parody of an Alan Bennett monologue, perhaps called 'A letter from Uncle David'. And maybe there is an untravelled elderly relative who needs to be told 'Rhode Island is not an island, but is the smallest state in the Union, with a history that goes back to colonial days,' though it is hard to imagine there will be many readers who will be gobsmacked by this revelation.

At times one wonders how deliberate is his frequent choice of a curiously old-fashioned, almost bufferish, diction: something is described as 'a thoroughly sound decision'; something else 'interested me exceedingly'; guests at his wedding were 'satisfied with the modest repast we gave them'; and so on. After such language, it is not altogether surprising to find him saying, when recalling his shock at the frequency with which his fellow national servicemen used 'fuck' and its derivatives: 'Needless to say, I had never uttered the word myself, and during my service I did not acquire the habit of doing so.' Quite so, quite so. All this, one has to remind oneself, comes from the creator of the immortal Morris Zapp, the self-appointed Crapfinder-General of academic life.

One of the many passages Lodge quotes from his own earlier writing is his playful parody, in *The British Museum is Falling Down*, of Molly Bloom's final, epically unpunctuated, soliloquy at the end of *Ulysses*, where he has his own female character shift the register from Molly's joyous, sexual 'I said yes' to an altogether more hesitant, sceptical 'I said perhaps'. Reading this again I said alright it was a nice idea but repeating it seems a bit like showing off or just not being able to think of anything so inspired these days not that I mind much and anyway its alright to do this because he is so cherished now and no one wants to say anything bad about him and thats alright because he is a good thing and over the years he has made me laugh and can still make me smile a bit and anyway its only an autobiography and its alright to go on a bit about yourself there in fact it wouldn't work if you didn't really but even so I wanted to say to him that its not really very good but I didn't quite have the heart and perhaps Im only disappointed because I used to enjoy him a lot when I was younger and when he was younger too and perhaps its never quite as good when youre older only alright and so thats what I said about his book I said it was alright though it isnt really but thats alright.

Interlude

7

Media

Little Magazines, the *TLS*, *New Left Review*, Radio Four

I

'The first function of a literary magazine is to introduce the work of new or little-known writers of talent.' There is an appealing modesty about this brisk declaration, even a kind of impersonality in subordinating editorial ego to the larger good; it seems likely to provoke a murmur of agreement, not least from new or little-known writers. But this is not, of course, the only way in which the function of such publications may be conceived. The editor of one of the many new literary periodicals established in the 1920s announced a no less definite sense of purpose in quite other terms: 'I shall make its aim the maintenance of critical standards and the concentration of intelligent critical opinion.' The goals expressed in these two quotations do not have to conflict: editors might, it is true, maintain 'critical standards' in a practical way by identifying new literary talent. But the tendency is for the pursuit of these two purposes to issue in periodicals of rather different types. One, often thought of as the classic 'little magazine', largely carries new poetry and fiction, mostly by as yet unrecognized writers, often exemplifying a style of writing that is self-consciously, even determinedly, insurgent and unfashionable. The other, committed to upholding the critical or reviewing function, is largely filled with essays and book-reviews; taking in the literature of both the past and the present as well as taking in more than literature; it aspires to shape intelligent

Peter Brooker and Andrew Thacker (eds.), *The Oxford Critical and Cultural History of Modernist Magazines: Vol. I, Britain and Ireland 1880–1955* (Oxford University Press, 2009).

Derwent May, *Critical Times: The History of the Times Literary Supplement* (HarperCollins, 2001).

'Fifty Years 1960–2010', *New Left Review*, 61 (Jan./Feb. 2010).

David Hendy, *Life on Air: A History of Radio Four* (Oxford University Press, 2007).

opinion and to combat the slackness and puffery characteristic of so much mainstream literary journalism.

Much of the history of literary periodicals can be written around the contrasts and tensions between these two types and their various hybrid manifestations. As it happens, both the above statements are by the same person—T. S. Eliot. There is nothing fortuitous about this common source: Eliot was not only a dominant, perhaps the dominant, figure in English literary life for roughly the half-century after the end of the First World War; he was himself the editor of a literary journal and one who frequently mused on the character and purpose of such publications. The first quotation comes from 1954, when, very much the literary elder statesman, he was wishing well to the new *London Magazine*, and hence could afford to affect the impersonal view. The second comes from 1922 when he was just about to launch *The Criterion*, and it faithfully catches that note of haughty self-importance characteristic of Eliot in his pomp (perhaps few editors of journals committed to maintaining 'critical standards' can be altogether free of it).

Taking a wider view, the importance of such publications in the literary or intellectual history of a period is tantalizingly hard to gauge, especially in the case of journals that were short-lived and erratically distributed. To the enthusiast for a particular coterie of minor poets, the yellowing pages of the few issues that appeared before debt and infighting took their usual toll may have the aura of holy relics. But to the literary historian, focusing on who read what and who influenced whom, the scale of attention given to such a publication will be largely determined by whether any of its contributors subsequently enjoyed a significant reputation. The social historian, in search of pattern and representativeness, may well conclude that such a source has the documentary value of school magazines or the annual reports of local horticultural societies, and allot space accordingly.

A brave attempt at addressing these difficulties and bringing some kind of order to the bewildering array of literary journals in the early decades of the twentieth century has been made by the Modernist Magazines Project, based at De Montfort University (not to be confused with the Modernist Journals Project at Brown University in the United States which is in the forefront of the change that is helping to revolutionize the study of this genre by making available fully searchable digitized versions). It appears that the British project will, in the first instance, issue in three large volumes of essays to be known as *The Oxford Critical and Cultural History of Modernist Magazines*, of which *Britain and Ireland 1880–1955* is the first (to be followed by volumes on the United States and on Europe). Any choice of defining dates for such a survey, as well as any definition of 'Modernist', are bound to be contentious: the present volume, it is safe to say, errs on the generous side on both counts. The Pre-Raphaelite journal *The Germ* (1850) figures as a 'precursor', before we launch into detailed discussion of journals relating to the 'Art-for-art's-sake' and the 'Arts-and-Crafts' movements, and then to the Celtic revival and the Georgians. We are a quarter of the way through the volume before we encounter the kind of journal more usually thought to be associated with the beginnings of literary Modernism, such as Ford Madox Ford's *The English Review* (1908–10), Dora Marsden's *The Freewoman* (1911–12), and Wyndham Lewis's *Blast* (1914–15). The logic behind 1955 as the closing date also seems a little hard to fathom, but perhaps it is an acknowledgement of the fact that the Hugh MacDiarmid-inspired journal *Voice of Scotland*, having appeared irregularly between 1938 and 1949, suddenly heaved itself into life again in that year (maintaining, with superb indifference, the continuity of issue numbers from six years earlier), although Cairns Craig's informative essay on Scottish journals seems to indicate that in fact it carried on appearing at least into the middle of 1956.

The definition and scope of 'Modernism' as a literary-historical label have long been a matter of debate, but there has been a marked tendency in recent scholarship to try to expand its range, employing it as a quasi-historical label for a whole period rather than for a cultural style or movement. Indeed, there is some risk that it is coming to embrace more or less everything post-Victorian. Thus, the present volume claims to operate with 'a more generous definition' of the term which 'defines modernism primarily as an engagement with the intellectual problems of modernity . . . in which the formal properties of literature are only one means to that end'. Or again, we are told that what qualifies a group of Cambridge-based politico-literary magazines of the 1930s for inclusion is their 'active contemplation of alternative modernities'. In such declarations (of which there are several in this collection), 'modernity' hovers between being a purely chronological term and being a way of picking out, analytically, certain developments which, taken together, allegedly characterize the defining novelty of the period. Whatever the merits of this usage, readers should be alerted to the fact that this volume discusses a lot of writing that would not normally be thought of as having any closer relation to Modernism than that of mere contemporaneity, as well as some that does not have even that.

In addition, all the tensions and uncertainties about the genre of the 'literary magazine' suggested by my earlier quotations from Eliot re-surface here in the form of intractable definitional issues facing the scholarly study of such publications. We may all have our own ideas of what constitutes a literary 'magazine', but I suspect many readers will find it odd to include, for example, a general political and cultural weekly such as *The New Age*, edited by A. R. Orage (1907–22), under such a label (at least in its British usage), as it does in a different way to include Eliot's own stately quarterly *The Criterion* (1922–39). This then raises inevitable questions about implicit criteria for inclusion and exclusion. There is an essay on the smart monthly *Life and Letters* (1928–35) but not one on, say, *The Bookman* (1891–1935), with which it was to merge in later years. *The New Age* is included, but not *The New English Weekly* (1932–49), which was also initially edited by Orage and which had the distinction of first publishing three of Eliot's *Four Quartets*, a not insignificant role in the dissemination of literary Modernism. By contrast, we have an essay on Sir John Squire's *London Mercury*, which, though it did publish one or two writers subsequently classified as 'Modernists', chiefly cultivated a rather more hearty, middlebrow version of Englishness and was regarded as 'the enemy' by the likes of Eliot and John Middleton Murry. The free-thinking, broadly feminist weekly *Time and Tide* is included, though not any of the more established weeklies with which its founder, Lady Rhondda, explicitly aligned the new journal—*The Nation*, *The Spectator*, *The New Statesman*, and *The Saturday Review*, periodicals with 'the highest office' in journalism of attempting 'not merely to talk but to think'. Only the first decade of *Time and Tide* is discussed in Jane Dowson's essay, reasonably enough, though it went on to have a long life in various incarnations, ending up, improbably, as *Time and Tide and Business World* in the late 1960s. (It even seems to have had a brief reincarnation under its original title in the 1980s.)

So, working with a generous if rather implicit remit, this volume consists of almost forty essays, treating in detail some eighty periodicals, the majority of them literary journals of either the 'creative' or the 'critical' kind, most of them publishing, discussing, or responding to 'Modernism' in literature and the arts, during the century between the 1850s and the 1950s, but heavily concentrated in the period from about 1910 to the 1940s. The high quality of several of the essays together with the sheer informativeness of the accounts of numerous relatively obscure publications make this an extremely useful publication, for all its ragged edges. (It has also been handsomely produced, in pleasingly readable layout, with footnotes at the bottom of the page; it contains more than 100 illustrations, mostly reproductions of periodical covers.)

The best essays, such as Michael Whitworth's outstanding contribution on the two journals edited by Murry, *The Athenaeum* (1919–21) and *The Adelphi* (1923–48), draw upon new archival research and combine sensitive content-criticism with attention to the journals' material properties. There are also authoritative accounts by those who have dealt at greater length with a particular journal elsewhere, such as Laura Marcus on *Close Up* or Jason Harding on *The Criterion*, while excellent essays of a different kind rescue short-lived journals from various kinds of obscurity, such as Rod Mengham's on a trio of Surrealist magazines in the late 1930s and early 1940s or Craig's, already mentioned, on a clutch of ephemeral outlets for new Scottish writing over several decades.

Much of the pleasure to be had from this volume comes from the accounts of periodicals that have not previously made large claims on the attentions of literary historians. These include *The Acorn* (1905–6), an 'Arts-and-Crafts' journal in which the contributors' names were not printed but signed by hand; *New Numbers* (1914), which had no editor or editorial matter and was 'published' from Lascelles Abercrombie's 'cottage in rural Gloucestershire, with his wife, Catherine, doing much of the work'; *The Decachord* (1924–31), which promoted a belated 'Georgianism' in poetry though 'it retained a focus on the West Country'; *Ireland Today* (1936–8) whose anonymous editor was 'a former bomb maker and Director of Chemicals with the IRA'; and *Arson: An Ardent Review* (1942), whose editor declared, ardently enough: 'N.B. It will be noticed that no poetry is printed in these pages for the simple reason we do not believe there is a single line approaching the nature of poetry being penned in English.'

One of the most fascinating themes to emerge is the repetitiveness of the terms in which the target readerships were imagined. There are constant invocations of a 'serious reading public', a public not defined by profession or level of education, whose needs are not being met by the shallow or coterie-led discussion of literature available in existing publications. *The Welsh Review* (1939–40) was representative in aiming to address 'men and women of mind', hinting in this case that Wales's more democratic educational traditions meant that, as in Scotland, such individuals were not to be identified with any one class or set of occupations. And the necessary rhetorical complement of this idealized public was the demonization of the dominant literary culture. *The Athenaeum*, for example, defined itself as the 'enemy of every form of intellectual cant and humbug, however eminent and established', while Geoffrey Grigson, never one for understatement, positioned *New Verse* (1933–9) in opposition to 'the poisonous and steaming Gran Chaco of vulgarity, sciolism and literary racketeering', an encompassing if somewhat unspecific characterization. Grigson's lusty wielding of the critical scythe receives winningly sympathetic treatment here from Stan Smith. Grigson's penchant for exaggeration does, it has to be recognized, make him very quotable: it's hard to resist his unfair description of *Scrutiny* as in danger of becoming 'the perfect body-builder for prigs'. Needless to say, these and other self-serving self-positionings are not all to be taken at face value. Several of the essays buttress their more quizzical treatment of these aspirations by referring to Mark Morrisson's argument, in his *The Public Face of Modernism* (2001), about the way in which some of the early Modernist journals were not in fact, as is often assumed, deliberately cultivating a withdrawal into a minority sphere of avant-garde culture, but shared, rather, 'an optimism about re-directing the public function of the press'.

In addition to the perhaps unavoidable self-dramatization involved in posing as the lonely beacon of artistic or critical integrity in a corrupt and commercial world, a kind of energizing pathos could be generated by the recurrent trope of being the last of a kind. Sean Latham rightly remarks that 'from the beginning, *Horizon* [1940–50] had established itself rhetorically as the last "little magazine"', but as with so many claims to being the last of a kind, the pleasures of elegy were here being allowed to displace the demands of accuracy. Almost every such journal is the last of the 'little magazines'—until the next one comes along. R. A. Scott-James, the last editor of *The London Mercury*, declared in 1939, in the kind of obituary-editorial common in journals announcing their closure, that there was no longer any hope of resisting 'the democratisation of culture and the mass-production of books, papers, films etc which stimulate or drug the popular mind'. As it happened, *Horizon* was launched later the same year, giving the lie to such pessimism. Of course, sometimes the ailing do actually die. When the venerable *Edinburgh Review* closed in 1929, *The Bermondsey Book*, a quarterly aimed at encouraging writing by 'working people', drew the familiar declinist moral: 'The passion of the modern reader for the topical, which is too frequently the ephemeral, is notorious, but we are surprised to learn that among the cultured classes there are not sufficient people with a sense of tradition strong enough to support a journal as famous as the *Edinburgh Review*.' Alas, the following year saw the realization that among the 'working people' there were not sufficient readers to support a journal as obscure as *The Bermondsey Book*.

Given that the nature of the various assumed readerships was as pivotal rhetorically as it was crucial economically, it is a pity that no systematic effort has been made to provide circulation figures. Some of the essays do attempt this, most do not (and there is no entry for 'circulation' in the index). We know that for the critical reviews, we are usually talking about the low thousands, while for the little magazines of new writing we are sometimes talking the low hundreds. Among the better-known examples, the range extended from Eliot's *Criterion*, which peaked at between 800 and 1,000 copies in the mid-1920s (at 3*s*. 6*d*. it was expensive, even for a quarterly), to Cyril Connolly's *Horizon* which, profiting from the paucity of competitors as well as the wartime hunger for reading matter, reached the dizzy heights of 8,000–10,000 copies per month in the early 1940s.

One way of making some, necessarily speculative, inferences about readership is from the kinds of advertising a journal carried (when 'commercial' enough to do so), and several essays attend to the semiotics of those pages that content-greedy literary and intellectual historians usually ignore. For example, Jane Goldman concludes that the advertisements in *Life and Letters* under Desmond MacCarthy's editorship (1928–34) suggest 'the caricature of a comfortably-off pipe-smoking, male, metropolitan reader, middle class, middlebrow, but with some highbrow literary aspirations as a serious reader, a book collector and literary connoisseur, and possibly a fledgling writer'. The fact that the advertisements seem to be aimed at male readers may say more about control of purchasing power than appeal of content; other kinds of (necessarily patchy) evidence suggest that many of these magazines had substantial female readerships.

Perhaps it is inevitable that a very large collection of essays on such a sprawling topic should seem, in the end, to add up to less than the sum of its parts. Repetition exacerbates this impression: for example, Connolly's celebrated contrast between 'eclectic' and 'dynamic' editors is quoted in at least five different contributions. It also has to be said that the attempts by the editors, in the general introduction and the introductions to each section, to impose a kind of coherence do not really help. The repeated deployment of Raymond Williams's schematic binary of 'emergent' and 'residual' conjures up a faux-sociology, and their insistence on celebrating the 'dissident' or 'oppositional' character of these periodicals obviously sits better with some examples than with others. Looking to identify an organizing developmental theme, they emphasize that the volume runs from *The Germ* of the Pre-Raphaelites

> to the discussion in the final chapter of F. R. Leavis's *Scrutiny*, no longer a magazine of art and creative writing, but of criticism, which closed in 1953. This movement over a century from an artistic to a critical formation is symptomatic of the emergence, consolidation, and institutionalisation of predominantly literary modernism.

Well, yes, a story can be told of the growing acceptance of 'literary modernism', though it cannot be told in terms of 'critical' journals replacing 'creative' ones (and it seems curious to date the 'movement' from the 1850s). But more curious still is the fact that the chapter on *Scrutiny* is *not* actually the 'final' chapter in the book. It is the antepenultimate chapter, the final one being a discussion of Tambimuttu's *Poetry London* (1939–51) and *Indian Writing* (1940–2), the former of which showcased new poetry by the younger poets of the so-called 'Apocalyptic' school. Not only is it surprising to find the editors misremembering the structure of their own book, but this slip seems symptomatic of their urge towards the schematic even when that is resisted by the riches surveyed in the constituent essays. Far from representing the 'institutionalization' of Modernism, the last chapter signals a fresh wave of creative energy on the part of poets who were mining other seams, exploring other idioms, and in this respect it serves as a properly open-ended ending, pointing to the continued vitality of the genre. The literary journal is dead. Long live the literary journal.

II

As the foregoing discussion suggests, literary journals tend to follow a fairly predictable life-cycle. Founded upon the insurgent energy of an individual or small group, they try hard in their early years to disturb what they see as the offensive placidity of the larger cultural pond which is their necessary habitat. Then, adolescent passion spent, they enjoy a period of respected eminence, disposing of opinions and reputations with a papal largesse: writers jostle to review in their now-glamorous pages, publishers court the editorial staff in the hope of easing their books into the limelight, circulation rises. Before long, however, the signs of ageing appear: the content becomes repetitive or stale, younger competitors steal the best writers, subscribers die, leaving their descendants to adhere to other churches. Eventually, a final issue carries a mournful and self-justifying threnody on the end-of-civilization-as-we-know it, and the title joins the category of what librarians expressively term 'dead' periodicals.

The *Times Literary Supplement* has been a remarkable exception to this pattern. It celebrated its 100th birthday in January 2002, and even the usual metaphors about looking 'spry' or 'well-preserved' seem out of place, since it still exhibits a youthful vigour—indeed, a pre-adolescent eagerness to embrace the abundance of the world. Every week it carries a score or more of essays and reviews on a dauntingly wide (though by no means limitless) array of books, including some not in English and many clearly not in very good English. And, by and large, it does not succumb to the review-page vices of puffery and back-scratching: indeed, it is sometimes reproached for carrying reviews that are too severe in their criticisms, though these bravura pieces of scholarly handbagging are an expression of its commitment to the highest intellectual standards and are among the pieces most enjoyed by its devoted readers, the unlucky victim apart. How has this particular paper managed to defy the laws of literary-journalistic mortality?

Derwent May's large centenary history provides a mass of material to draw upon in trying to answer this question, though this is already to co-opt the book into a more analytical kind of investigation than this genial, companionable chronicle of *Times* past really aspires to. By and large, May confines himself to recording the sequence of editorships and to summarizing some of the more notable contributions from each period of the history. If you want to look up what the *Lit Supp*, as it was generally known during the first half-century or more of its existence, made of, say, the late novels of Henry James (not much) or the early novels of Martin Amis (quite a lot, but then he did work for the paper for a while), you will find this book enjoyable and satisfying. If, on the other hand, you want to see some hard questions asked about its place in British (and increasingly Anglo-American) culture, or about the tensions between the scholarly and the literary worlds, or about comparisons and contrasts with rivals here and abroad, then the book may seem something of an opportunity missed.

What *Critical Times* does make clear is that the unique standing achieved by the *TLS*, as it has tended to be known since the 1960s, was principally the work of one man, Bruce Richmond, effectively its first, and incontestably its longest-serving, editor (1903–37). Looking back on its first couple of decades, Richmond shrewdly remarked that the paper had contrived to have 'two publics' which he characterized as those interested in 'books for the drawing room' and those concerned with 'books for the study'. The well-connected Richmond catered to these overlapping publics very skilfully: whatever the subject, the *Lit Supp* contrived more often than not to hit the note of impartial authority. Richmond tirelessly sought out those with relevant knowledge, but then cajoled them into writing accessibly for a non-specialist readership. The authority which came with being part of *The Times* obviously counted for a lot in the early years; more important still, perhaps, the house practice of publishing all reviews anonymously reinforced the impression of impersonal, collective canons of judgement at work. The *TLS* did not finally abandon anonymity until 1974, and it is only as a result of research on the back files carried out in recent years that the identities of those countless reviewers can now be revealed.

One, not entirely surprising, revelation is that the reviewers were not as countless as all that. In any period, there was a pool of regulars, most of whom were drawn from the same narrow social circles (it has been calculated that 20 per cent of the reviews during Richmond's editorship were written by members of the Athenaeum club). But it has also revealed that some of the brightest stars in the literary firmament contributed a great deal of unsigned prose to its pages (albeit in some cases 'anonymous, but signed in every line', as one wag put it). One of Richmond's discoveries, the kind literary editors dream of making, was the 23-year-old Miss A. V. Stephen. She proved to be a dexterous, beguilingly percipient, reviewer, with a great appetite for work, writing with the requisite air of accessible authority on almost any literary topic. She wrote for Richmond, almost always anonymously, for thirty years, through the latter part of which period she was becoming the leading English novelist of the day under her married name, Virginia Woolf.

Another talent spotted and nurtured by Richmond was T. S. Eliot, who, from 1919 onwards, reviewed regularly, publishing some of his most influential pieces on Elizabethan and Jacobean literature as 'lead' reviews. When first invited to write for the paper, Eliot rather over-excitedly told his mother that this was 'the highest honour possible in the critical world of literature'. One can see why this particular 31-year-old Ph.D. dropout and struggling writer might want to reassure his parent that he was making a go of his life, but even so his exaggeration is still a kind of testimony to the centrality the *Lit Supp* had already achieved. As with many other big and not so big names, the deal cut both ways: Eliot's astonishingly assured and stylish pieces contributed to the distinctive tone of the paper, while his prominence in its pages was a crucial element in the making of his literary career (it turns out that 'literary London' often had a pretty good idea who had written what).

The paper has had its blind spots, of course, from its patchy and often unsympathetic reception of the more experimental Modernists such as Pound or Joyce to the reviewer of *Wind in the Willows* who concluded, 'as a contribution to natural history the work is negligible' (it would be nice to think this was straight-faced irony). More recently, the champions of literary theory or of cultural studies may have felt that there were in practice pretty narrow limits to the *TLS*'s vaunted catholicity, and the more technical works not just (as one might expect) in science but in the social sciences, too, have proved hard to cover intelligibly. (The success of 'popular' science writing by the likes of Hawking and Dawkins has been widely remarked, but one wonders whether the social sciences are not now in need of similar intermediaries and translators.) The clearest trend in the last few decades has been for 'books for the drawing room' to be increasingly edged out by 'books for the study', and in practice for 'books for the study' to become more and more books for the unvisited stacks of university libraries or books on the tenure-hunting c.v. It would be interesting to know whether the use of greater numbers of academics as reviewers, as well as of more foreign contributors, has entailed more rewriting by the staff. After his piece had appeared in heavily edited form, Umberto Eco wrote wryly to the editor: 'I enjoyed your article, but I preferred my own.'

The *TLS* has shown a Whiggish capacity to adapt to these larger social and cultural changes, and when Ferdinand Mount took over as editor in 1991, he could still speak with some confidence of what he called the paper's 'bedrock virtues': 'the comprehensive coverage, the adventurousness, the readiness to cover any book, no matter how obscure or difficult'. It's a proud credo, though one not subject to much sceptical or probing analysis in this book. Birthdays are, after all, sentimental occasions; as the *TLS* received its telegram from the queen, Derwent May's attractive and well-illustrated volume no doubt made a fittingly generous and celebratory present.

III

New Left Review at fifty: no balloons, of course, and definitely no party-games. The very idea of 'celebration' smacks of consumerist pseudo-optimism. Mere chronology is, after all, an untheorized concept. We should see 2010 as not so much an anniversary, more an over-determined conjuncture.

It is hard not to be intimidated by *New Left Review*, and teasing is, as usual, a form of resistance as well as an expression of affection. At times, the journal can seem like an elaborate contrivance for making us feel inadequate. One's relation to it conjugates as an irregular verb: I wish I knew more about industrialization in China; you ought to have a better grasp of Brenner's analysis of global turbulence; he, she, or it needs to understand the significance of community-based activism in Latin America. For many *Guardian* readers (and others), the journal functions like a kind of elder brother whom we look up to—more serious, better informed, better travelled, stronger, irreplaceable.

Well, maybe a tiny bit solemn at times (we could draw lots for who gets the job of telling him to lighten up), and perhaps when we were out of touch for longish stretches life seemed if anything a bit easier. But then we meet up and it's a case of respect at first sight, all over again.

It hasn't always been like this, however: even elder brothers had rocky periods in their youth—misguided enthusiasms, failed relationships, moody withdrawals. Some readers may remember times when *NLR* seemed hell-bent on sectarian purism, theoretical slavishness, and a wilful opacity. It has been through several changes of identity in the past fifty years, and memories of some of these earlier phases may still hamper the efforts that it has made recently to reach out to a more diverse readership. Not that there isn't a lot in that history to be proud of. The journal has, in its own unbending fashion, registered and responded to huge changes in the world during this half-century, and in doing so has made a stock of ideas available well beyond the ranks of those who may at any point have shared its particular form, or forms, of Marxism (an allegiance that has itself modulated, possibly even attenuated somewhat, over the decades). Some things about the journal, however, don't change that much. What other publication, after all, could take out a full-page advertisement in a national newspaper with a bold headline announcing its 'quinquagenary issue'? *NLR* has been accused of many things, but never of populist dumbing-down.

The biography of the review cannot be reduced to a formula: its experience so far has been too rich and too contradictory. But it would be fair to say that a journal that began life hoping to animate and express organized popular movements on the left soon became a more emphatically theoretical enterprise, albeit with certain Leninist or Trotskyist longings held in reserve. Then, in the 1980s, it began to interpret its intellectual task in more expansive terms, and since 2000 it has been self-consciously a 'journal of ideas'—on the left, to be sure, but detached from radical movements in the present or any worked-out political blueprint for the future.

As a severely intellectual journal committed, in principle, to the radical transformation of society, *NLR* had few models to draw on in British history—and the journal grew out of, and was for some time rooted in, British culture, however internationalist it has since become. There had been a lot of small, usually transient, journals of the left, such as William Morris's *Commonweal* (1885–90) or the original *Left Review* (1934–8); there were political periodicals closer to the parliamentary fray, such as the *New Statesman* (1913–) or *Tribune* (1937–); and there had been more eclectic, radical-leaning reviews of art, culture, and politics, such as the *New Age* (1907–22). But to find another successful journal of ideas conducted at the highest level by a self-consciously radical group we may have to go back to the *Westminster Review*, the journal of the Philosophic Radicals of the early nineteenth century. In the present, the journal closest in spirit, despite all the obvious differences in form, may be the

London Review of Books (there is some overlap in contributors), but *NLR* is less literary, even more political, and committed to more systematic economic analyses and theoretical constructions. It also concerns itself very little with British politics and culture these days.

Insofar as there was a conscious model in the early years, it was Sartre's *Les Temps modernes*, and an idealized version of Parisian intellectual life in the 1950s seems to have retained something of a hold over several of the review's leading spirits. It takes quintessential black-polo-neck subjects such as philosophy and film very seriously indeed; other art forms, and more or less all of popular culture, come a long, long way behind. Although there have been periodic shake-ups of the editorial board, complete with affirmations of the need to bring in new blood, the members of the core group are now around 70 and so date their formation to those heady days of bringing the news from Paris in the decade from 1958 to 1968.

The fiftieth-anniversary issue includes articles by several of the long-serving stalwarts of the journal—Tariq Ali, Perry Anderson, Robin Blackburn, Mike Davis—as well as interviews or reprinted pieces by iconic figures of the intellectual left such as Eric Hobsbawm and Stuart Hall. These names signify a quite striking element of continuity. Anderson and Blackburn were at the head of the younger group who took over direction of the journal in 1962, after two years under Hall's editorship, and they, together with Ali, Davis, and a handful of others, have been constant or recurrent members of the (overwhelmingly male) editorial board since the 1960s. Anderson was nominally the editor from 1962 to 1983 (the journal has always emphasized its collective ethos, and from the outside it has not been clear how responsibility has been divided between editor and editorial board); Blackburn then took over until the end of 1999, at which point a new series of the journal was re-launched, initially under Anderson's editorship once more; Susan Watkins has been the editor since 2003. Exact circulation figures have always been hard to come by, as has any reliable information about its inner workings, but its bi-monthly issues are said currently to sell around 10,000 each; the online version gets an estimated 50,000 readers, there is now a Spanish-language edition, and the online archive is in high demand. Although Anderson family money was rumoured to have bailed out the journal in the early 1960s, it has long been self-financing, without grants or subsidies, and over the past five years has even made a modest profit.

But the continuities of personnel mask some dramatic shifts of direction and changes in character. The review was founded in 1960 out of a merger of two existing journals, *Universities and Left Review* and *The New Reasoner*, the former representing an upsurge of political and cultural radicalism in the late 1950s, especially strong in universities, that repudiated the reformism of the Labour Party, while the latter provided a rallying ground for those Communists and ex-Communists who now, post-1956, disowned orthodox Stalinism.

New Left clubs were formed around the country, and the Campaign for Nuclear Disarmament provided a mobilizing and unifying focus. For a brief period, the review was part of a wider movement. But after the 1962 changeover, it focused more exclusively on preparing the theoretical ground for 'Revolution' (it can be hard now to remember what an everyday term 'revolution' was in the 1960s and 1970s). One of *NLR*'s most notable services was its role in importing and disseminating continental European ideas, especially the rich tradition of Hegelianized Marxisms, but also other styles of work in, for example, sociology and psychoanalysis. In 1970 a publishing house was set up—New Left Books, which mutated into Verso—and this helped to make many classic works of European social thought available in English at a time when the expanding system of higher education was hungry for such texts. Established Socialist thinkers such as Isaac Deutscher and Raymond Williams were important to the review in its early years; for a while the example of the Belgian Trotskyist economist Ernest Mandel was influential; at various points there was particularly sustained engagement with the ideas of Antonio Gramsci and Louis Althusser.

In the course of the 1980s, the political imagination of the left had to be refashioned to acknowledge the dramatic transformations of that decade, including the end of 'actually existing Socialism'. This and the following decade saw ructions and resignations at the review itself, as well as attempts to remedy its comparative neglect of now prominent issues such as feminism and the environment. Its denunciation of 'the American empire', especially through the so-called humanitarian wars of the 1990s, was one constant; its attempts to uncover the global operation of the new forms of finance capitalism were another. It has also continued to publish influential work in cultural criticism, notably by Fredric Jameson. But questions about what it now meant, in practical or theoretical terms, to be committed to 'a Socialist future' became more insistent, and invited a more fundamental re-thinking of the function of the journal itself. *NLR* 238, published at the end of 1999, was to be the last of the original series.

The first issue of the new series appeared at the beginning of 2000, with a dramatically improved layout and appearance (high-minded left asceticism had tended to favour journals that looked like cyclostyled parish magazines), a regular book review section, and signed editorials. The first of these consisted of a stern, unsparing assessment by Perry Anderson of the challenges facing the left at the start of the new century. Some readers were shocked by its olympian bleakness. 'The only starting-point for a realistic left today is a lucid registration of historical defeat.' (I can't help admiring the sentence as well as the sentiment here, especially that last phrase, with its indomitable commitment to lucidity about the wreck of one's dreams.) Anderson found 'neoliberalism' triumphant across the globe: no effective countervailing radical force existed. But that, it was implied, is all the more reason to seek a properly explanatory understanding of the forces at work in the world today. Only on that basis—a systematic, deeply informed, international analysis—could even the most tentative steps be taken towards formulating a viable alternative. The message may have been bleak, but the tone was resolute: the guiding principle for the review should be 'the refusal of any accommodation with the ruling system, as of any understatement of its power'.

Over the years, *NLR* had shown a proper regard for Gramsci's celebrated motto, 'pessimism of the intellect, optimism of the will', but many readers thought Anderson's 2000 editorial overdid the pessimism and gave precious little nourishment to the optimism. A French critic, in a reproach that must have stung the famously non-parochial and Francophile Anderson, accused him of viewing things too narrowly from one side of *la Manche*: various forms of resistance, it was suggested, were much more visible in France, while others felt that forms of protest elsewhere in the world were similarly being undervalued. But, a decade on, Anderson's pessimism on this score scarcely seems exaggerated: insofar as the imperium of neo-liberalism is being curbed, which is not far, it does not appear to be primarily the outcome of organized and politically effective opposition.

Anderson also announced another kind of change in the character of the journal, which was henceforth to be open to a greater variety of voices (in the interests of full disclosure, I should say that I have been among those who have made occasional contributions under this new policy). Again, there were murmurs about betrayal and elitism—*NLR* as a virtual club for global intellectuals rather than as a getting-its-hands-dirty helper in local struggles—but maybe such objections mistake what a progressive journal of ideas can and should do. Personally, as a relative outsider to this milieu and (I confess all) an irregular reader, I much prefer the hospitable pessimism of the current *NLR* to the excluding optimism of its more sectarian days. But there's no doubt that its present character raises again the question of what a journal of 'the left' should be aiming at when it is not in constructive relations with any organized radical or progressive movements beyond its pages.

Now, in the fiftieth-anniversary issue, the editorial by Susan Watkins takes stock once more. Attention focuses on the financial crash of 2008 and, still more, on the banks' subsequent recovery. The former might have seemed to offer the left some hope: the 'system' was imploding, as in Marxist or post-Marxist theory it was meant to do. Those famous 'contradictions of capitalism' were coming home to roost. Except, as Watkins coolly insists, they haven't; so far there has been adjustment rather than apocalypse. Moreover, this convulsion of the world's financial system seems to have generated precious little political turmoil or popular insurgency. In one of those steely sentences that the modern *NLR* is so good at, she writes: 'That neo-liberalism's crisis should be so eerily non-agonistic, in contrast to the bitter battles over its installation, is a sobering measure of its triumph.'

So, what is there left to do—and what is there to do that is Left? Plenty, it turns out. If there is no 'immediate practical project', the concern has to be with the *longue durée*. 'To attend to the development of actually existing capitalism remains a first duty for a journal like *NLR*.' Or again: 'A priority for the Review in the coming years should be a new typology of development outcomes in the age of global finance. Another is a map of the global proletariat—locations, sectors, differentials—alive to contemporary makings and unmakings of class.'

To some, this may seem like little more than keeping that 'registration of defeat' up to date, but the commitment to information and understanding seems admirable to me. In the final paragraph of her editorial, Watkins appears momentarily tempted by a form of optimism: 'But perhaps the very rarity of a serious left forum in these times makes a journal like *NLR* more valued.' I think that's true, but a 'forum' is, precisely, a space to meet and talk, an agreed place in which to disagree. The metaphor itself signifies a distance from political action, as well as the distance the journal has travelled from the hopes of the 1960s. 'Can a left intellectual project hope to thrive in the absence of a political movement?', she asks. 'That remains to be seen.' Even 'thriving' may be a lot to ask for. 'Fail better' may be as high as the mark should be set for now, with an unblinking awareness of the piquancy that attends the conjunction of political allegiance and Beckettian motto.

Perhaps a sense of having been chastened by world history is becoming to a journal in middle age. Just occasionally, I still feel queasy when confronted by the familiar abstractions, confidently used in the singular. Even the term 'neo-liberalism' may suggest something more monolithic than the confused and conflicting economic policies of the past few years. And when I'm told, for example, that 'the thought-world of the West' is increasingly determined by 'Atlantic-centred structures of wealth and power', dragging academic disciplines in tow, I find myself feeling that the search for pattern and causation is starting to lose sight of something no less important—the uneven, awkward diversity that is apparent when viewed from a little closer. All intellectual enquiry is a see-sawing between abstraction and particularity, and *NLR*'s inheritance can still make it seem more indulgent to the former than the latter. Interestingly, the language of 'determinants' and 'system' falls away when it comes to self-description. '*NLR* stands outside this world,' writes Watkins, 'defines its own agenda.' Excellent, but might not some other elements in 'the thought-world of the West' be doing the same, in their own way? Still, the audacity is, again, admirable: I like the thought that a specially unillusioned, independent, global perspective on what's happening is to be had from a side street in Soho.

When so much of even the so-called 'serious' media is given over to celebrity-fuelled ephemera and the recycling of press releases and in-house gossip; and when the academic world is struggling to mitigate the worst effects of funding-driven over-production and careerist modishness; and when national and international politics seem to consist more and more of bowing to the imperatives of 'the market' while avoiding public relations gaffes; then we need more than ever a 'forum' like *NLR*. It is up to date without being merely journalistic; it is scholarly but unscarred by citation-compulsion; and it is analytical about the long-term forces at work in politics rather than obsessed by the spume of the latest wavelet of manoeuvring and posturing. Despite its self-description in its guidelines for contributors, the journal is not in any obvious sense 'lively'. It is downright difficult, but none the worse for that. Not, these days, obscure or technical or jargon-laden, but difficult because what it tries to analyse is complex and its preferred intellectual tools are often conceptually sophisticated. It is difficult where being easy would be no virtue, difficult where aiming to be 'accessible' would mean patronizing its readers, difficult where ideas need to be chewed rather than simply swallowed. That's what I admire above all about *NLR*: its intellectual seriousness—its magnificently strenuous attempt to understand, to analyse, to theorize.

So, no balloons, and definitely no Party lines. No cheap consolation, either. But hey, respect: no question.

IV

Radio Four is a barometer of cultural decline. Just ask anyone in Tunbridge Wells. In fact, you don't even need to ask them: they'll write and tell you, especially if you are the network's Controller. For example, when in 1977 Ian McIntyre moved the time of the Sunday omnibus edition of *The Archers*, protest included 'an abusive note and a kipper nailed to the door of McIntyre's son's room at his Cambridge college'. In 1982 it became known that there were plans to give the network over to more news programmes: 'More than 2000 letters poured into the BBC expressing outrage, sadness, distress or incredulity at what was planned—or thought to be planned. "I physically shuddered when I heard they are going to tamper with Radio Four,"' wrote one listener. In 1984, David Hatch experimented with *Rollercoaster*, an unstructured magazine format, and unwisely (and perhaps unnecessarily) invited listeners to send in their views. Of 1,167 letters received, 991 arrived 'swinging mean expletives and plenty of vicious assaults on the Controller's mental state'.

In the course of the 1990s, Radio Four's listeners increasingly coordinated their protests; listener-power played a large part in defeating a plan to remove the network from Long Wave (Alan Ayckbourn, with the hyperbole the network seems to attract, called it 'a victory for civilisation'). And then in 1995 there was a proposal to move the midnight edition of *The Shipping Forecast* by twelve minutes. Not to cancel it or meddle with its content

(Heaven forfend!), just to move its slot by twelve minutes. The result: a debate in Parliament and a slew of leading articles in the broadsheets, together with a protest from a listeners' group complaining that this showed how the BBC had 'totally lost sight of the concept of public service broadcasting'.

It's hard not to think that there's something just the teensiest bit bonkers about all this. It's only a radio station, isn't it? Well, of course it's not (quite apart from standing on its linguistic dignity as a 'network', not a 'station'). It's more than that: for its loyal listeners—and its listeners are loyaller than most, as well as boasting an above-average epistolary strike-rate—it's emblematic of continuity, reassurance, Britain, the state of the language, the state of the culture, the state of the world. Many such listeners may like to pretend that *their* network has ministered to the national soul (no, really: that's how people talk about it) since time immemorial, or at least since they were children, whichever is the longer. But in fact it only celebrated its fortieth birthday in 2007, and so is a good deal younger than its average listener. To mark this anniversary, David Hendy, a one-time producer for Radio Four and now part of the fast-expanding world of academic media studies, has written its history.

You might think this would be an impossible task, since radio is such an ephemeral medium and nothing could recapture the experience of those countless thousands (only occasionally millions in Radio Four's case) who chortled while driving home or bridled while doing the ironing. But that would not only be to underestimate Hendy's talents and resourcefulness as a historian who makes brilliant use of interviews, memoirs, old recordings, and so on, but also to overlook a crucial characteristic of the BBC. As a record-keeping organization, it is right up there with the Inland Revenue and the French state. Among the offices and studios of Broadcasting House, memo spake unto memo, and just as the purpose of cricket is sometimes thought to be the generation of statistics, so one possible rationale for the existence of the BBC could be the creation and maintenance of the fabulous burial-chamber that is its Written Archives Centre, a treasure-trove of sources waiting to be explored. As the more than fifty pages of dense endnotes to this book testify, Hendy has explored those relating to Radio Four in its first two decades very thoroughly indeed (he admits his treatment of the second two decades is much sparer). The result is a long and scholarly book, but one filled with riveting detail and anecdote, constantly illuminating about the peculiar character of Britain's best-loved and most-criticized radio network. It also provides a wonderful case-study of the dynamics of the anxiety produced by social change.

Much about the character and national role of Radio Four can be traced back to its inheritance from the old Home Service. When the BBC began broadcasting in the 1920s, there was only one network, The National Programme. In September 1939 this was in effect divided between a Forces Programme and the Home Service, with the latter still informed by the

Reithian principle that the public should be offered programmes 'slightly better than it thinks it likes'. But the identity of the Home Service was only really fixed in 1946 as part of the fundamental reorganization of radio which saw the introduction of three networks: the Light Programme, intended to be 'easy listening', with popular music and serials; the Third Programme, avowedly devoted to the highest intellectual and artistic standards, anticipating a correspondingly small audience; and the Home Service, falling in between these two cultural poles, burdened with the task of being simultaneously the main news and current affairs network, the biggest broadcaster of drama and features, and, eventually, the home of a range of old favourites, from *Children's Hour* to *Round Britain Quiz* and *The Goon Show*.

By the mid-1960s, the BBC feared that the staid offerings of these three networks, whose very titles seemed redolent of paternalism and austerity, were increasingly 'out of touch with society', and so an even bigger shake-up took place in 1967. There were now to be four networks. Radio One was to broadcast non-stop pop music, aiming to reach the audience previously only catered to by the pirate stations. Radio Two inherited some of the character of the old Light Programme, but was even more given over to soft-centred musical favourites plus some easy talk. Radio Three was to be the successor to the Third, but pruned of its more cerebral and experimental elements, and in practice largely a classical music station. And so, by elimination again, the fourth network became Radio Four. The continuity with its predecessor was emphasized by its self-description during its first two years as 'Radio Four, the Home Service', though this was then dropped. One newspaper characterized the cultural profile of the four networks as 'pop, bop, fop, and sop'.

The 1960s were anxious times for radio. The huge growth in TV ownership in the late 1950s and early 1960s displaced it in the nation's evening routines. 'Pirate' commercial stations met wants which the BBC didn't, and the days of legal commercial radio, following the success of 'independent' television (introduced in 1955), seemed not far away. The decision to permit daytime television was taken in 1972; the first legal commercial radio stations began broadcasting in 1973. The end for the old warhorses of BBC steam radio seemed nighish. And the Corporation itself was suffering acute financial pressures as the licence fee failed to keep up with inflation. Towards the end of the 'sixties, this financial crisis found a suitably symbolic expression: 'By April 1968, even John Snagge's radio commentary on the Oxford–Cambridge Boat Race was affected when he found that the launch he had been given by the BBC was simply too old to keep up and he had lost sight of both teams.'

Defenders of Radio Four insisted that it needed to maintain the 'rich mix' it had inherited from the old Home Service, but to its critics this looked like an incoherent jumble of oddments and antiques. In the 1970s it did have vigilant news programmes such as *The World at One*, chaired by William Hardcastle, which became essential listening for that stratum of society the BBC liked to think of as 'opinion formers', but the network was also identified with several 'national treasures' it had been assigned over the years, such as *Desert Island Discs*, *The Archers*, and *Woman's Hour* (the latter having sufficiently adapted to the times to be described in the 1970s as a 'unique mixture of jam, Jerusalem, and genital warts'). It was bad enough to have any newspaper complaining that the schedule had a 'distinct air of looking backwards, of offering nostalgia for the middle-aged and elderly'; but things had to be seriously awry to be so described in 1971 by *The Daily Telegraph*. (It would be nice to think this was a Pythonesque spoof, but Hendy's book is meticulously footnoted.) Even by 1982, as Hendy records, 'Radio Four still looked too much like the home of the blue-rinsed and purple-faced. There they were, one newspaper said: "Mrs Cosy-sides, knitting to the accompaniment of *Woman's Hour* and poised to seize the blue biro and Basildon Bond every time she hears the word 'abortion' pass Sue Macgregor's lips".' The old Third Programme had been criticized for being too much of a club in which 'don speaks unto don', but Radio Four sometimes seemed in danger of being a reserve in which mastodon spoke unto mastodon.

There was no subject which had Mrs Cosy-sides and her ilk reaching for the Basildon Bond faster than so-called 'bad language'. The use of swear-words on Radio Four was the definitive index of national decline. The letter-writing battalions rarely distinguished between allowing certain words to be used in a radio play as situation or character might demand, and deliberately taking the lead in a vast public conspiracy to debauch the morals of the population. Hyperbole about these matters was, it should be said, not confined to critics of radio: when Kenneth Tynan famously used the word 'fuck' on late-night television, the *Daily Express* columnist declared it 'the bloodiest outrage' he had 'ever known'. Given the accents and sounds of action in some radio dramas, it was not always easy to know quite which words *had* been uttered; in the aftermath of one broadcast, its producer was solemnly asked by the Corporation's Review Board to give 'a firm assurance that the word "bugger" had not been used'. This was the same Review Board which, in 1975, could ask whether 'a discussion which mentioned such matters as "loss of virginity" and "penis envy" was entirely suitable at 6.15 pm'. The confusing mix of liberalism and pre-emptive primness in the Corporation's dealings with 'such matters' was perfectly caught in a characteristic edict by Aubrey Singer, Director of Programmes, about swearing: 'If these words sometimes come up naturally in the heat of the moment, fine. But I will not have people sitting down and *typing them out*.'

Radio Four's weakest moments, then as now, were usually the result of cultural complacency and intellectual timidity. Fond comparisons of the network to a garden, needing to be tended and loved and only gently pruned, didn't help ('it was extraordinary', the editor of *Woman's Hour* once claimed, unironically, 'how good gardeners were always good broadcasters'). Descriptions of it as 'the Broad Church of radio' gave off a similar odour of smugness and aversion to boat-rocking. As one insider nicely put it: 'There is no consensus... but you ignore it at your peril.' Tony Whitby, Controller in the early 'seventies, might have done his Oxford thesis on Matthew Arnold, but he was not always averse to pandering to the philistines. During discussions in 1972 that eventually issued in the arts magazine *Kaleidoscope*, he told producers in the Talks Department: 'I don't care what you call the programme, as long as the word "art" or "critic" isn't in the title.'

The political climate of the 1980s was hostile to the BBC in general, and to aspects of Radio Four in particular, the early morning *Today* programme having now taken over the role of skewering cabinet ministers and other public figures for their evasions and dishonesties. Norman Tebbitt responded with his customary delicacy by describing the BBC as that 'insufferable, smug, sanctimonious, naive, guilt-ridden, wet, pink orthodoxy of that sunset-home of third-rate minds of that third-rate decade, the Sixties'. Clearly, the Beeb was getting some things right if it could attract an encomium such as this from someone who had himself been described 'a semi-house trained polecat'. As it turned out, Radio Four came well out of the 1980s: its coverage of the Falklands War had outclassed television (which had been even more handicapped by the news blackout surrounding the Task Force); its even-handed reporting of the conflict in Northern Ireland withstood intense government pressure to suppress representation of the Nationalist perspective; and it continued to commission controversial and provocative drama.

But a more sinister threat to the network, and indeed to the culture of the BBC more generally, now began to manifest itself. As a young man, John Birt had applied to work as a trainee at the BBC but had been turned down. So when he was appointed to the post of Assistant Director-General in 1987, and then Director-General in 1992, it was without his ever having worked in the Corporation. But he was by then a trained accountant, a devout worshipper of the bottom line, so he soon started to set up 'internal markets', breaking up long-established departments, subordinating radio to television, and generally behaving, as one drama director put it, like the Americans in Vietnam, 'trying to win a war by exterminating a culture'. Once upon a time it could have been said that the BBC was an organization run by bohemians disguised as civil servants; later it sometimes seemed nearer the mark to see it as run by civil servants disguised as bohemians; by the late 1990s it appeared to be run by hit squads disguised as management consultants.

And yet, somehow, Radio Four not only survived into the first decade of the twenty-first century, but even enhanced its position. Despite recurrent proposals to turn it into a 24-hour news station, its programme mix remained fairly stable over the decades, with news and current affairs taking up a little over half the schedule. Similarly, though both the clipboard wielders and the Basildon Bond brigade inveighed, for their different reasons, against the network's commitment to commissioning contemporary drama, Radio Four remained one of the great patrons of aspiring playwrights. Hendy calculates that in the 1970s it was broadcasting 'very nearly as many hours of drama as BBC-1, BBC-2 *and* ITV combined'. Books, both new and classic, have also been well served by the network, with a variety of discussion, interview, and reading formats, including the countless hours of *Book at Bedtime*, which has on occasion featured some distinctly unOvaltinish titles.

In addition, under the cover of their familiar titles, some programmes were actually changing their character for the better. *Start the Week* is a good example. 'The first ever edition back in 1970 had featured a cookery slot and a discussion on pigeons; twenty-six years later it was featuring a three-way conversation between Arthur Miller, Gore Vidal, and Amos Oz.' After some broadcasts, listeners would ring the BBC to ask for advice on background reading on the topics discussed. This genre of serious discussion programme was then taken further by Melvyn Bragg's history-of-ideas slot, *In Our Time*, now the network's most popular podcast. The Reith Lectures have had their highs and lows, but they, too, adapted to more participatory and interactive formats. And although the *Today* programme took some hard knocks, not least during the political inquisition following the 'Gilligan affair' in 2003, it has remained not just required listening for the political class, but one of the main arenas in which politicians seek to make the news as well as figure in it.

So, the story Hendy has to tell is, in some respects, a success story. Much about the network has changed since 1967, he concludes, 'and, if we take the long view, it has generally been change for the *better*'. In fact, 'unusually in media history, we can talk of a service that ends up being generally more *upmarket* than when it began.... Despite the many awkward attempts at popularization that have been charted over preceding chapters, the underlying trend was undoubtedly for Radio Four to become steadily *tougher* over time.' (It would be interesting to know whether the changes since 2007 might lead him to qualify this judgement.) His book should provide an antidote to the tendency to regard Radio Four, cosily and complacently, as one of those cherished but dotty and rationally indefensible British institutions, something of a cross between milky tea and the Changing of the Guard and as eternal as the weather (not that the weather now...). In reality, Radio Four is a relatively recent creation, which has altered and adapted a good deal already; it's a very professional operation—or, rather, series of operations—involving constant effort by a large group of capable people, and one which has several times come close to being abolished or changed out of all recognition. And this is what makes its story so interesting and revealing. 'To write the history of broadcasting', observed Asa Briggs, doyen of the trade, 'is in a sense to write the history of everything else'—a dictum that holds particularly true of a network with Radio Four's range of programmes. So what does the history of this peculiar institution tells us about British society over the past four decades?

First, the history of Radio Four bears out the larger moral that people work better and more creatively in conditions of relative security and cooperativeness than in conditions of insecurity and relentless competition. The BBC has historically attracted a remarkable concentration of talented people, and it has been the freedom to give in-house teams of such people their head that has produced the most amusing, most incisive, and most imaginative programmes. To read Hendy's restrained and dispassionate account of the effect of Birt's managerial Maoism on Radio Four is to be reminded of how much damage has been inflicted on other large national organizations by modish prattle about 'internal markets' and 'performance-related incentives'.

Second, discussions about Radio Four have endlessly reiterated the standard British confusion between social class and intellectual and cultural capacity or interest. In practice, the network's successes have mostly come when it has broadcast programmes that have appealed to the intelligent and curious from various class backgrounds, and its failures have often involved prejudiced attempts to cater to tastes it believes to correspond to the Registrar-General's social categories. Identity politics and 'community'-itis have only made this worse: policy-makers are obsessed with hitting the right 'demographic', when actually people possess multiple identities, some of them defined by what they think and what they imagine, not by some reductive social indicator.

Third, Radio Four is a classic example of an organization that has several times nearly destroyed itself out of paranoia about generational change. Our listeners are middle-aged and getting older; we must attract new listeners; therefore we must have programmes aimed at the young. This is, however, a complete non-sequitur. Those listening now were 'the young' a generation ago, but they don't listen because it provides a diet of what they liked when they were 20. There is, anyway, nothing intrinsically wrong with a radio network that has more old than young listeners, any more than there is with the reverse. Radio executives fret about the former rather than the latter, but in this they are largely victims of advertisers' flawed orthodoxies about the need to capture consumers when they are forming their buying habits.

And fourth, debates over Radio Four have mirrored the wider tendency to assume that greater egalitarianism necessarily entails hostility to articulateness or any form of intellectual authority. One result of this confusion is the assumption that unstructured, inconsequential demotic chatter is more 'accessible' than a well-written talk by someone who really knows about a topic. Ah, but that's 'lecturing' to the audience, we are told, up with which the modern I'm-as-good-as-the-next-man listener will not put. But that's nonsense. As sources of information and comment proliferate, the demand for authoritative, well-informed programmes increases rather than diminishes. There is nothing condescending about treating a topic clearly and intelligently; if anything, it might rather be seen as a sign of respect for one's audience. The great advantage of radio over television for certain purposes is that it is not hamstrung by the tyranny of the visual, and so it is able to make words work harder. This is one of Radio Four's strengths, and the recurring bouts of panicky populism represent a needless loss of nerve.

Still, we must not neglect the element of serendipity or even whimsy that can from time to time enchant even the network's most earnest listeners, so let me end with two symbolic expressions of Radio Four's remarkable national status. In May 1980, during the siege of the Iranian Embassy in London (which was extensively covered, live, on TV of course), a remarkable thing happened. 'At one stage the gunmen had demanded that a message be broadcast on the BBC, and this was eventually done during a Radio Two news bulletin. The gunmen missed the broadcast, however, because they had been tuned instead to Radio Four on 1500 metres long wave.' You never really know, do you, who might be listening, or why. Were they afraid of missing an episode of *The Archers* or were they waiting to catch up on the Test Match? Presumably, subsequent events meant that the Corporation did not receive letters of complaint signed 'Disgusted, Iranian Embassy'.

And then there is the *Shipping Forecast*. 'It's always there, always has been, always will be,' wrote one admirer. Actually, it hasn't 'always' been there; it was transferred from Radio Two only in 1978. And it doesn't, it emerges, play such a large part in protecting the lives of our brave mariners any more: technology now allows ships to get constantly updated weather bulletins automatically, though I suspect some keen yachtsmen would be lost, in every sense, without the radio version. But the tumbrils would roll down Whitehall and guillotines be set up in Portland Place if it were now to be dropped. It has, in a wonderful inversion of 'culture-industry' theories, been transformed from an instrumental to a purely aesthetic phenomenon: it is, in effect, radio's most regular poetry slot. As Hendy puts it, at the end of a bravura section of this endlessly engrossing book: 'The *Shipping Forecast* remained on air for no reason other than it was still wanted by many thousands of people who had no logical purpose in listening to it—other than the most basic purpose of all, of course, which was to make life a little bit richer in some intangible way.' Or as Carol Ann Duffy has it:

> Darkness outside. Inside, the radio's prayer—
> Rockall. Malin. Dogger. Finisterre.

Perhaps only the critical historian, nosing out instances of change masquerading as continuity, would pedantically observe that 'Finistere' was replaced by 'Fitzroy' in 2002. Still, there can be no better note to end on. 'Southeast backing easterly 4 or 5, increasing 6 in the south. Mainly fair. Moderate or good.' Very Radio Four—and largely true of Radio Four, as well: 'Mainly fair. Moderate or good.' Happy birthday!

Part II

Public Debate

8

Moralists

J. L. and Barbara Hammond, R. H. Tawney, Richard Hoggart, R. M. Titmuss

I

The crowd of mourners who squeezed into the church of St Dunstan-in-the-West in Fleet Street on 21 April 1949 were taking part in one of those rituals which periodically reaffirm the solidarities of English cultural life. The occasion, a memorial service for the historian and journalist J. L. Hammond who had died earlier in the month, was the liberal intellectual establishment's equivalent of a state funeral. The address was given by Gilbert Murray OM, Regius Professor of Greek at Oxford, pre-eminent ambassador of the ideal of Hellenism, long-time conscience of intellectual liberalism. The lesson was read by R. H. Tawney, distinguished social and economic historian and doyen of the English tradition of ethical Socialism. The long list of distinguished mourners was led by a representative of Clement Attlee, the Prime Minister who was presiding over the creation of the welfare state by the first Labour government ever to possess an overall majority. Each of these figures had links with Hammond that stretched back over several decades, including conscience-driven protests against the more militaristic manifestations of Britain's foreign policy or conscience-appeasing spells working in the slums of East London. For good measure, the officiating cleric, the Reverend J. R. H. Moorman, was G. M. Trevelyan's son-in-law.

These names might be taken to indicate the gathering of a particular slice of the intellectual elite, but even more they represented the inter-twining of

Section Two of this essay, previously unpublished, was written in 2011 to mark the 100th anniversary of the publication of J. L. and Barbara Hammond's *The Village Labourer*.
Lawrence Goldman, *The Life of R. H. Tawney* (Bloomsbury Academic, 2013).
Fred Inglis, *Richard Hoggart: Virtue and Reward* (Polity, 2014).
Ann Oakley, *Father and Daughter: Patriarchy, Gender and Social Science* (Policy Press, 2014).

deep-rooted ethical and political strains within English culture. A visceral antipathy to the dominant individualism of economic life, reviled as 'selfishness', when combined with a strong sense of obligation to promote the collective good, issued in an overarching moralism and conscience-driven form of politics, the whole underwritten by an interpretation of English history that emphasized the socially damaging consequences of the triumph of commercialism. In his address, Murray placed Hammond's work in what he rightly saw as an extended 'condition of England' tradition, noting how the historical works jointly authored by Hammond and his wife Barbara had documented in anger-stirring detail the ways in which the selfish policies of the governing classes in the late eighteenth and early nineteenth centuries had, in an unfortunate phrase, eliminated 'the better class of peasant' from the English countryside.

The late 1940s can in some ways be seen as the culminating moment of this tradition. The sacrifices and austerities of wartime had intensified and diffused a conviction that the time was right to try, by collective action, to bind up the great wound that had been seared into the flesh of English society by the social consequences of the Industrial Revolution. The radical members of the political and intellectual elite joined forces with the political representatives of the organized working class to put in place measures that would reduce the advantages of wealth and make a decent standard of living available to all members of society. There can, of course, be dispute about whether the measures enacted by the Labour government of 1945–51 really achieved these goals, or whether that government should have done differently or done more. It is also arguable whether the legislative achievements of these years really should be regarded as the implementation of the social idealism that had marked the progressive elements of the educated class from the later decades of the nineteenth century onwards, or whether the policies did not to a greater extent reflect a conjuncture marked by full employment based on the needs of the wartime economy, an extension of the solidarities of the Home Front, and a peak of trade union power. But whatever explanatory priority later historians might assign to these different factors, the symbolic importance of the programme of nationalization and welfare provision as a kind of restitution for the great wrong suffered by the industrial working class over the previous century and a half was undeniable. That moment could also be seen to encompass the spirit of what Raymond Williams was to label the 'culture and society tradition' of social criticism from the late eighteenth century onwards, just as it embraced the distinctively supportive ethos of working-class life that was to be celebrated by Richard Hoggart or the altruistic ideals of 'welfare' that were to be explored by Richard Titmuss—all three bodies of work having their beginnings in the late 1940s. This essay discusses the work of five individuals from these overlapping generations who occupy high places in the pantheon of this very English tradition of ethically driven progressive social commentary.

II

'The Hammonds': in their case the plural form always has priority, a single 'Hammond' seeming a barely sustainable life-form. 'The Webbs' might run them close, it's true, but we know so much about the sharply contrasting personalities and talents of Sidney and Beatrice that, though their *œuvre* remains a shared achievement, we have no trouble treating them as separate individuals. Other progressive couples of the period, such as G. D. H. and Margaret Cole or indeed Gilbert and Mary Murray, are accorded the familiar plural relatively rarely and are certainly not, like the Hammonds, cemented into a union that is so close as to make the proverbial pantomime horse seem, by contrast, to constitute a fractious crowd scene. The Hammonds' reputation has dipped sharply since its apogee in the inter-war years, but insofar as they are now remembered it is on account of their jointly authored historical works, especially the 'Labourer' trilogy, so it is entirely appropriate that the major modern study of their work (by Stewart Weaver) should be entitled *The Hammonds: A Marriage in History*. But just as, following the custom of the time, they are known by a last name that belonged to the male partner, so too there is some danger of the woman's role being overshadowed or sidelined by the familiar plural form of reference. Barbara Hammond had had the more successful educational career, getting a First at Oxford to Lawrence's Second, and she, we now know, clearly did the greater part of the research for the eight historical works they published under their joint names (Lawrence largely did the writing). Her letters and the testimony of contemporaries suggest that she was in some ways the more forceful, and certainly the more acerbic, of the two. But Barbara had nothing like the public career that Lawrence did: he not only wrote a further six books under his own name, but, independently of his historical writing, he was one of the most prominent journalist-intellectuals of the first half of the century, and as editor, leader-writer, and columnist he was an influential voice on the moralizing left from the outbreak of the Boer War to the close of the Second World War. (The fact that Barbara would have been barred from the influential *Nation* lunches before 1914 because they were held in the all-male purlieus of the National Liberal Club suggests further reasons why women sometimes found it harder to establish comparably public identities.) The location of Lawrence's memorial service bore witness to his prominence in this latter role: it was entirely fitting that it should be at a church in Fleet Street rather than in one of the cathedrals or college chapels usually favoured by the social elite. The mourners included the current editor of *The Manchester Guardian*, A. P. Wadsworth, and several members of the Scott family. Lawrence Hammond had been a lifelong contributor to 'the *MG*', working as a full-time leader-writer for substantial periods; C. P. Scott had more than once tried to induce him to make the role permanent and at one point he seems to have hoped Lawrence might be his successor as editor. Early in his career, Lawrence had edited the radical weekly *The Speaker*, and thereafter he refused invitations to occupy the editor's chair at several of the leading radical periodicals of the day. Inevitably, therefore, detailed intellectual histories of the period pay more attention to Lawrence than to Barbara, but when referring to their historiographical contributions it seems right to treat the plural form as signifying an equal weighting.

In retrospect, the Hammonds appeared almost destined to combine forces. Both were the children of politically liberal churchmen, Barbara's father becoming a prominent headmaster; both did Mods and Greats at Oxford in the high Idealist days of that celebrated course; Lawrence's main tutor and inspiration was the radical Socialist Sidney Ball, while Barbara's was his friend, the radical liberal L. T. Hobhouse; both were drawn to good works and liberal causes; both were ardent 'pro-Boers' on the great issue of conscience that divided the educated class at the turn of the century—and, as Hobhouse laconically observed, 'Pro-Boers are like to intermarry'. Barbara worked for the Women's Industrial Council, chiefly gathering information to improve the political and social lot of working-class women. She had a small private income and thereafter she seems never to have held a paid post once she and her husband embarked on their histories. Lawrence had immediately launched himself into a journalistic career: he was ever to have a ready pen in support of good causes. His first book, published in 1903 when he was 31, was on Charles James Fox, a folk-hero of radical liberalism. Lawrence was unquestionably Fox's partisan in the latter's struggles with the repressive political inclinations of the younger Pitt, but he did not abstain from criticism. Fox, he lamented, 'never raised his voice against the rule of the squire which was stifling the civic spirit in the country'. Even the great radical statesman, Hammond suggested, had not understood the changes that from the closing decades of the eighteenth century 'gradually extinguished in England the most stable and the most robust of all elements of a nation'. Fox, like most of the political figures of his era, accepted the rule of the aristocracy, and thus he colluded in the devastation of the old order: its epitaph was written in 'the ruin of the yeoman class in England'. The germ of views that the Hammonds were later to make commonplace is visible here, but it would only have been visible to a highly select readership at the time: in its first eighteen months *Charles James Fox: A Political Study* sold a mere 270 copies.

It may be said that for both of the Hammonds the writing of history was the pursuit of politics by other means, but it is scarcely less true to say that their historical allegiances and identifications helped form their attitudes in the present. Early and late in his career, Lawrence was an ardent Gladstonian, taking the great man's belief in 'the masses against the classes' as the touchstone of political morality. For all their own relative privilege (what they described as their 'simple' domestic establishment enjoyed, during most of the period in which they were writing their radical histories, the labour of a cook, a cleaning-woman, and a gardener), he and Barbara saw themselves as unremitting critics of 'the governing classes'. When Lawrence took the comparative sinecure of secretary to the Civil Service Commission in 1907, it meant temporarily retiring from the fray of active liberal journalism, but he explained to one of his radical friends that 'I shall still hope to conspire with you and . . . other plotters against the governing classes'. Barbara's ironic account the following year of the beginnings of the research for what would become *The Village Labourer, 1760–1832: A Study of the Government of England before the Reform Bill* (1911) was: 'Lawrence and I are busy considering the governing classes, and incidentally learning a fair amount of history.' Their critics were later to insist that this order of priorities, taken more literally, was at the root of the weaknesses of their historical work.

That book, as Tawney later observed, was conceived as part of a study of 'the social philosophy of the English ruling classes'. The triumph of the aristocracy and the driving out of 'the small men' from taking part in the affairs of the locality were central themes. The old peasant class, with its freedom and dignity premised on access to common land, was eliminated. But the Hammonds did allow that English landowners at least remained attached to the land; they 'remained a race of country gentlemen'. Unlike the French, they never became 'mere loungers or triflers, kicking their heels about a Court and amusing themselves with tedious gallantries and intrigues'; they never 'fell into the supreme vice of moral decadence'. And the book ends with something of a tribute to the legacy of liberal ideas, especially on relations between nations, that this class, or at least a minority among them, handed down to their successors. Thus, a book that had so vividly portrayed the savage treatment which the governing classes had meted out to the poor and the dispossessed nevertheless managed to end on a celebratory note, praising this legacy of liberal ideas as 'an important and a glorious part of English history'.

It was in the *Town Labourer* (1917) rather than in the *Village Labourer* that the notion of the 'Industrial Revolution' and its 'catastrophic' consequences was elaborated. Surveying the earlier uses of the term in English, Weaver concludes that 'to all but a few learned specialists . . . the idea of the Industrial Revolution would have been either foreign or unfamiliar when the Hammonds burst on the scene with *The Town Labourer*'. And, as with the earlier volume, the key is provided by the subtitle (sometimes omitted from later reprintings): *The Town Labourer, 1760–1832: The New Civilization*. Although the Industrial Revolution is popularly thought of in terms of the invention of machinery, this was not, in the Hammonds' eyes, the essence of the 'social revolution' it brought about. 'The new power' controlling life in England was not steam, but money, and it was this 'inexorable force' that destroyed the 'customs, traditions, and freedom' of the people. This was, of course, a central claim in the tradition of moral criticism of orthodox economics, and it seems to imply that economic rationality had not operated in earlier periods—that customary rights and arrangements had been allowed to determine lives, not the calculation of profit. The preface to the book, published in wartime, explicitly compared the worship of commercial power to the worship of military power: comparably terrible consequences flowed from accepting the so-called 'iron laws' of 'economic necessity'. 'The turn which social history takes in any age results in part from the ideas and opinions that are in the ascendant,' the Hammonds reminded their readers, and in the present case, the determining ideas were to be found in that 'edifice of gloomy error', political economy—'error' suggesting their Ruskinian and Hobsonian confidence in knowing better. But chiefly theirs was a moral indictment. Profit had replaced justice, selfishness had replaced cooperation, competition had replaced custom, wealth had replaced life. Like so many of the 'progressive' intellectuals of the early twentieth century, the Hammonds had come to see the nineteenth century not as a stage towards the fuller development of a modern industrial society, but as an aberration whose excesses now had to be corrected by policies which would in effect 'restore' the moral balance of society.

The Hammonds' histories involved a direct and in some ways simple appeal to their readers' moral intuitions. They were exercises in persuasion, whose chief purpose, it can sometimes seem, was to arouse a state of righteous indignation. The categories which structured their accounts now appear almost archaic in their uninflected simplicity: selfishness versus concern for others, indifference versus a sense of responsibility, greed versus moderation. As that severer and more professional economic historian J. H. Clapham ironically observed in reviewing *The Town Labourer*: 'Throughout the book one gets the impression that but for greed things could have gone on very well,' and even Tawney could wryly note later that the Hammonds tended 'to write at times as though the fall of man occurred in the reign of George III' . But they intended their work as a warning, they wrote in the preface to *The Town Labourer*, of 'what humanity must lose if it makes a god of industrial power'. Similarly, their best-selling text-book, *The Rise of Modern Industry* (1925), insisted that history is 'a struggle between the robber and the artist in man'. Versions of this same simple dichotomy underlay their judgements early and late. Even when writing about Home Rule in his 1938 book on Gladstone, Lawrence argued that the struggle in 1886 'was bound to leave England either more generous or more selfish'.

Variants of this dichotomy are too familiar from the writings of countless public moralists in late nineteenth- and early twentieth-century Britain to be attributable to any single source, but it is clear from the biographical record that the chief intellectual inspiration in the Hammonds' case could be traced back to T. H. Green and Arnold Toynbee, except that, as transmuted by the Hammonds, it was Green without the philosophy, Toynbee without the economics. The comparison with Toynbee is particularly revealing, since he is usually credited with being the first to provide a systematic account of the disfiguring impact of early industrialism on English society. But Toynbee's work, which was comparatively slight and had to be largely reconstructed from his and his students' notes after his early death, had a different intellectual focus from that of the Hammonds. Toynbee wanted to explain the development of classical political economy as an expression of the peculiar commercial and industrial circumstances of England in the late eighteenth and early nineteenth century; to this extent, his was an exercise in relativizing the universalist claims of what he and his like-minded progressive critics felt was the chief ideological support of the 'selfishness system', which is why, for all the skimpiness of his contribution, Toynbee belongs with the late nineteenth-century group of historical economists. But the Hammonds had no economic theory to propose, indeed no view of classical political economy other than that it was commonly used to legitimize ruling-class self-interest. They were historical moralists, not historical economists.

The Hammonds had an importance that goes far beyond the quality of their histories or their scholarly reputation in the light of later research. Briefly stated, that importance consisted of coming nearer than any other authors to underwriting the long-standing radical critique of the moral squalor of commercial society with a detailed political and social history. It may not seem immediately obvious that they belong in what has been called 'the culture and society tradition', following Raymond Williams's classic work of that title. But their account does rely on a fundamentally similar contrast, though it may be slightly disguised by the fact that, as with so many members of the English educated class of their generation, the preferred embodiment of 'culture' was the ancient Athenian polis. The part played by ancient Greece in the beliefs and sensibilities of so many early twentieth-century radical intellectuals is striking and pervasive. In the Hammonds' case, they also argued that this source of inspiration had been shared by the more enlightened members of the English governing classes at the time of the Industrial Revolution. Faced with unprecedented challenges, the English, they argued in *The Rise of Modern Industry*, were able

> to draw inspiration and guidance from the constructive statesmanship of ages. For education had given to the English governing class an insight into a civilization in which the conduct, the relations, the difficulties and the purposes of social life had been the subject of endless experiment, of penetrating discussion, and of the most exquisite compositions in history, philosophy, poetry, and drama. The best representatives of that class were steeped in the humanism of the classics.

Or again: 'If you ask of education that it should teach how man has tried to make societies, how far his experiments have succeeded, from what causes they have come to catastrophe, the study of the life and literature of Greece and Rome is an experience possessing a completeness that no other culture can provide.' Such phrases suggest they rather cavalierly treated Greece and

Rome as sharing a singular culture, though in practice their emphasis was heavily Hellenic (and tended to scant the centrality of slavery). At times the ancient world can seem to be the source of all that was good in English life of the time. 'For it was from the classics that men of liberal temper derived their public spirit, their sense for tolerance, their dread of arbitrary authority, the power to think of their nation in great emergencies as answering nobly or basely to some tremendous summons.' Thus it was that industry and commerce were regulated, as 'the English people turned to their resources of culture and tradition, in order to bring a standard of conduct into the world of raw capitalism'.

Similarly, *The Age of the Chartists*, originally published in 1930, relied upon this contrast between a tendentiously reductive picture of 'the everyday processes of society' and a gushingly idealized picture of the ancient world. In Greece and Rome, they wrote, 'the class struggle was veiled or softened by the moral influence of common possessions; the practice of social fellowship was stimulated by the spectacle of beautiful buildings, and the common enjoyment of the arts and culture of the time.' They treated the Chartists, not altogether persuasively, as pressing for industry to be tamed in favour of 'culture and amenity' of the kind that existed in Greece and Rome. As their initial emphasis on the worsening material condition of the labouring class in the early years of industrialism came under increasingly critical scrutiny, they shifted their focus onto the question of the loss of 'amenity', and the need to recover forms of 'common enjoyment' such as those encountered in the Greek polis. I would suggest that the structure of these arguments clearly places them alongside the 'culture and society tradition', though their easy assumption that 'the English people's' 'resources of culture' consisted principally in knowledge of the literature and history of the ancient world is a reminder of how far Williams ignored or underestimated the place of the classics when anatomizing this tradition in 1958, three years before Barbara's death.

This attachment to ancient Greece went deep in personal terms, too. In 1929, when they were reeling from the allegations by the Tory critic Anna Ramsay that they had systematically distorted and misreported their evidence, they sought the most powerful form of consolation they knew: 'Too weak physically to attempt to look into her charges, we lay on sofas in different rooms. We found afterward that [Barbara] had been reading the *Agamemnon* and I the *Trojan Women.*' When Lawrence was witnessing the atrocities of the troubles in Ireland in 1921, he wrote to Gilbert Murray that he could think of nothing else, 'though I find I can lose myself every night in the Agamemnon'. As their biographer comments: 'From the murderous disappointments of the hour, Greece, as so often, was his respite.' It was to be so again during the bombing raids of the Second World War when the ageing Hammonds had to crouch in the shelter: 'Your *Aeschylus*', Barbara wrote to the equally ageing Murray, 'gives some dignity to the squalid hours spent [there].' As late as 1938, Hammond was still able to write of Gladstone: 'His study of Greek had convinced him that the spirit of justice lurked somewhere in masses of men still "fierce with freedom" and not yet corrupted by power.'

The Hammonds were certainly not lone voices: many of their views were the common coin of the radical progressivism that bloomed in the Edwardian era, but they brought a larger organizing narrative and a richer density of detail to the historical underpinnings of these views, and they thereby made them both more accessible and more telling. As a result, 'far from being controversial, the catastrophic view of the age of industry was by 1925 if not commonplace, then conventional' according to Weaver. 'The Hammonds' was the accepted wisdom.' This also meant that by the mid-1920s they were 'at the height of their public influence, they were *the* historians of the Industrial Revolution, and as such in a position to comment with some authority when the long-festering grievances of the industrial working class they had many times described finally culminated in General Strike in May 1926'. The labour movement had a long memory and part of what it remembered were the injustices so vividly described in the 'labourer' trilogy.

Something else the Hammonds shared with so many other progressive intellectuals of the period was, relatedly, a persistent idealization of the rural. There are traces of the more political versions of this in the way many pro-Boers saw the Afrikaner-speaking farmers as what Weaver terms 'the displaced remnant of an older, simpler, sturdier, and purer peasant civilization that the forces of progress had recklessly obliterated everywhere in Europe'. Something similar is evident in the form of their marked enthusiasm for France: just as Tawney was pleased to join up in the First World War to fight for the defence of what he saw as a nation of peasant proprietors, so Weaver remarks that 'Hammond's own liking for the rural primitivism of the French had undoubtedly influenced his decision to serve'. To be pro-French or pro-Boer may have suggested being pro-republican in the older, humanist sense of that term; above all, it was to be in favour of smallholdings over estates, agriculture over commerce, country over city.

This coloured many of their responses to domestic politics, too. Representative of that familiar combination of leftish politics and an aversion to many aspects of popular culture and material progress was their response to the proposal in 1931 by the Labour Chancellor, Philip Snowden, to levy a tax on land values. This was, of course, an old radical nostrum, stretching back through Lloyd George's land campaign to the ideas of Henry George and ultimately of J. S. Mill. But what alarmed the countryside-loving intellectuals in 1931 was that the proposal did not discriminate between developed and undeveloped land, and so would, they thought, be likely to hasten the sale of undeveloped land for yet more building. The motor car and the suburb now constituted threats every bit as disturbing as the evils of 'landlordism' had two generations earlier. The Hammonds joined with the Murrays, Hobson, Keynes, Nevinson, Toynbee, and Trevelyan ('a select little lot of fastidious highbrows', in Gilbert Murray's rather defensive formulation) in protesting against this feature of the tax in a letter to, inevitably, the *New Statesman and Nation*.

Stewart Weaver gives an excellent account of the Hammonds' histories, but I am not sure he is quite right to say that they gave cultural legitimacy to a story of 'national decline'. It is true that their earlier work represented the Industrial Revolution as little short of a cataclysm in which so much that was desirable about pre-industrial England was lost, but they also charted something of a recovery across the later nineteenth century as enlightened legislation and the growth of social conscience combined to mitigate the worst excesses of commercial competition. The years between about 1780 and 1840 came to seem the nadir not the new norm; theirs was not really a story of unending secular decline. Where such pessimism does unmistakably appear is in their more personal reactions to the spread of mass culture and the effects of prosperity in the present, a common feature of the educated classes' response in the inter-war period. As their close friend and one-time fellow liberal, G. M. Trevelyan, wrote to Lawrence on receiving his copy of *The Bleak Age* in 1947: 'An age that has no culture except American films and Football pools is in some respects bleaker than the one you tell of. The advent of real democracy coinciding in time with 2 World Wars has done the business—cooked the goose of civilisation.' Even in their old age, the Hammonds did not usually strike quite such a bleakly reactionary note, but there is an undeniable poignancy in reading the comparably irritable outbursts of their later years against the backdrop of a politics that was at last offering some redress for the grievances whose origins they had so passionately chronicled.

III

When Richard Hoggart wrote that R. H. Tawney had 'inoculated' him and many left-leaning members of his generation against the idea of personally owning shares or receiving dividends, he was doing more than acknowledging a significant personal political influence. He was registering a point about the intersection of ethical sensibility with economic life in a particular milieu and period. That sensibility can now seem almost unimaginably remote when, in a 'share-owning democracy', ordinary citizens are besieged with injunctions to 'safeguard your family's future' by placing bets in the global casino that is the stock market. But perhaps that makes the epidemiological resonances of Hoggart's phrase all the more intriguing. What could it have been like to inhabit that sensibility with such conviction that dividends or capital gains could figure as forms of infection? What view of the world did Tawney and Hoggart share that made this moral health warning so effective?

Unfortunately, a certain weariness is inclined to come over some readers now at the sight of the names of Tawney and Hoggart. There is a feeling that, although they were no doubt admirable and impressive in their way, their way cannot any longer be our way. They are seen as too worthy, earnest, even moralistic. And it is assumed that we know, pretty much, what they were at—that we have got their measure, and that in the end, for all the prominence they achieved in their lifetimes, they do not now interest us very much.

The appearance of these two sharply contrasting biographies ought to go some way towards disturbing those complacent preconceptions, yet the likelihood is that nothing much will, or could, disturb them—except, perhaps, some comically improbable revelations showing Tawney to have been a rapacious embezzler and Hoggart a serial pornographer. Yet it is at the very least worth asking how that unenquiring confidence maintains itself in relation to two figures who not only commanded so much affection and respect but who were resourceful and powerful writers across several genres. The initial resistance that any discussion of their claims has to overcome may be an index of a widespread unease with the very idea of the unembarrassed appeal to non-economic human values in public debate, though their example ought also to make us wonder why that is so.

Treating them together risks exaggerating a genuine affinity at the expense of more obvious differences. Tawney came from a comfortably off, academically inclined late Victorian family, and followed the approved route to Rugby and Balliol, which endowed him with social confidence and friendships across the intellectual and political elite. Hoggart, orphaned from the age of 8, grew up in the working-class back-streets of inter-war Leeds, making his way via the local grammar school and Leeds University; he always retained an acute sensitivity to the snubs and injuries of class. The differences of period were at least as important as those of social background. Tawney was 34 in 1914 and brought a late Victorian and Edwardian ethical sensibility to the economic and industrial troubles of the 1920s and 1930s, the decades when his influence was at its height. Hoggart was 34 in 1952, just at the beginning of the decades of affluence and the relaxation of traditional social and sexual constraints, developments he scrutinized with a confidence grounded in the tighter necessities and decencies of an earlier phase of working-class life.

But, for all those obvious differences, there were some striking similarities in their trajectories. Both made their early careers in adult education: Tawney starting the first WEA courses in Lancashire and the Black Country, Hoggart working in the north-east for the Extra-Mural department of the University of Hull. Both saw active service: Tawney in the infantry on the western front, Hoggart with an anti-aircraft artillery unit in North Africa and Italy. Both wrote scholarly first books whose relation to their lifelong preoccupations only became apparent many years later: Tawney's *The Agrarian Problem in the Sixteenth Century* (1912) and Hoggart's *Auden: An Introductory Essay* (1951). Both went on to be rather unconventional professors, working at an oblique angle to the mainstream of their respective disciplines: Tawney as Professor of Economic History at the LSE, Hoggart as Professor of English at Birmingham. And, curiously, both became public figures largely as a result of their membership of bodies that played an influential part in twentieth-century British history, public commissions of enquiry: Tawney played a leading part on the Sankey Commission on the coal industry in 1919, even helping to convert its chairman, Mr Justice Sankey, to the cause of nationalization, while Hoggart played a no less prominent role (including writing one of the central chapters of the final report) on the Pilkington Commission on broadcasting in 1960, which was so clear-eyed about the failings of commercial television.

Yet the fundamental reason why they can be bracketed together without doing undue violence to their individuality is because they both belonged to a tradition it might be too sectarian to label 'Socialist' and perhaps too anachronistic to term 'cultural criticism': a tradition of English social thinking that foregrounded the ethically corrosive power of the financial imperatives at the heart of market societies. Faced with the social destruction wrought by unchecked 'market forces' in recent decades, it is hard to see how anyone could regard the concerns of this tradition as altogether passé.

Although there have been earlier studies of Tawney's life and thought that were broadly biographical in structure, such as those by Ross Terrill and A. W. Wright, Lawrence Goldman's is the first to be based on a full examination of the surviving archives, including family papers hitherto closed to researchers. The resulting book is notably thorough, judicious, and fair-minded. It is also—and this is something that can be said of all too few biographies—informed by a disciplined understanding of the main currents of the political, social, and economic history that provided the setting for Tawney's work. To his credit, Goldman is not inclined to exaggerate his subject's importance: he acknowledges that Tawney's confident sense of 'being right and possessing the truth' was a weakness in him as a 'philosopher' as well as 'disqualif[ying] him for the dialectic of parliamentary politics', and he frankly recognizes that he is 'not a truly great writer on politics' nor (not quite the same thing) 'widely read in courses on the history of political thought'. But, taking off from a lazy remark by A. J. P. Taylor that 'Tawney's life was much like that of any other professor of history', he launches into a bravura aria of justification for his biographical enterprise:

> Professors of history do not usually begin their careers as social workers in London's East End. Relatively few of them go out to teach history and economics to workers. They do not usually fight at the Somme; they rarely devote themselves for several years to the interests of the Miners' Federation of

> Great Britain and to the wider cause of industrial justice. Few of them are parliamentary candidates or sit on royal commissions of enquiry; even fewer write a general election manifesto for one of the two major political parties in modern British politics, or, if they are historians of England, write a classic work on the economy and society of modern China. They tend not to know prime ministers and leaders of the Labour Party, or to find themselves in the British embassy in Washington D.C. at the time of the attack on Pearl Harbour. Their closest friends tend not to be the Archbishop of Canterbury, Temple, or the man who did most to design the British welfare state, William Beveridge, whose sister Tawney married. Tawney was, and did, all these things and more. He was no ordinary professor of history but one who believed that scholarship and the service of society should go together. He was, indeed, no ordinary great man.

It could be said, with only a little oversimplification, that Tawney became a historian in order to try to understand the origins of the distinctive pathology of modern society, namely the priority accorded the pursuit of financial gain. This may seem a needlessly cumbersome formula—why not just say 'capitalism'? But although Tawney was sometimes mistakenly held to be a kind of Marxist, he was not principally interested in analysing a mode of production; and although he was often put in company with Max Weber, he was not chiefly attempting to isolate what distinguished economic development in the West. His focus was on how English society had allowed the unchecked pursuit of individual profit to become the overriding social goal. The period that became known as 'Tawney's century'—roughly, 1540 to 1640—saw, in his view, the beginnings of the crucial retreat of the Church from the regulation of material life. Though he became a professor of economic history, and was active in founding and supporting the *Economic History Review*, his real interest lay at least as much in intellectual as strictly economic history. He was scornful of economic theory and econometric models; what he wanted to know was how *ideas* about the legitimate relations between morality and profit had changed. When the Hammonds published *The Town Labourer* in 1917, Tawney (in a letter other scholars have also quoted) hailed their 'really great work in destroying the historical assumptions on which our modern slavery is based'. He intended his own kind of history to be emancipatory in just this way, and *Religion and the Rise of Capitalism* (1926), in particular, spoke powerfully to those in the late 1920s and 1930s who brooded on what seemed like the great failure of capitalism.

In a fine passage from that book Tawney wrote:

> The distinction made by the philosophers of classical antiquity between liberal and servile occupations, the medieval insistence that riches exist for man, not man for riches, Ruskin's famous outburst, 'there is no wealth but life', the argument of the Socialist who urges that production be organized for service not for profit, are but different attempts to emphasize the instrumental character

of economic activities, by reference to an ideal which is held to express the true nature of man.

This certainly expresses the true nature of Tawney's own Socialism: the argument that production should be 'organized for service not for profit' was the central contention of his *The Acquisitive Society* published five years earlier. Goldman is right to see a tension between the emphasis on moral reform of the individual—'making Socialists'—characteristic of the earliest stage of Tawney's political thinking, and the promotion of collectivist measures of state ownership and control—'organizing a socialist society'—that was more prominent in his work in the inter-war years. But the element of continuity lies in seeking ways to assert the primacy of other human values over the economic realm, rather than the reverse.

Tawney often quoted Oliver Cromwell on his 'plain russet-coated Captain that knows what he fights for and loves what he knows'. Tawney saw Socialism resting on similarly deep, unshakeable convictions suffused with strong emotion. His own moral confidence was a limitation as well as a strength here; as Goldman fairly observes, it could lead him 'to underestimate alternative or opposed arguments, and to overlook the requirement to justify to others those positions that he himself took to be axiomatic'. He expected a lot from 'good will', not always the most abundant commodity in political life, and it might be said that his lifetime knew more progress in introducing measures of public ownership and control than in replacing acquisitiveness with fellowship and a sense of service. Referring in his capacious, confident way to 'all decent people', the young Tawney had declared that 'no political creed will ever capture their hearts which begins by saying simply "we will give you a little more money"'. But maybe 'capturing their hearts' has not been the goal of most domestic political creeds in Britain over the 100 years since this sentiment was confided to his commonplace book. And perhaps, some may feel, politics is all the better for not aiming as high as the capture of hearts.

Goldman rightly places Tawney in the line of cultural critics from Ruskin and Morris, though again this judgement raises as many questions as it answers. He was not simply an 'elegant Jeremiah' (to borrow a term applied to that tradition), certainly not just a thunderer and denouncer. On highly practical matters, such as labour relations or school finances, he put in countless wearying hours drafting documents and haggling in committees. He seemed so impressive to so many people because in some way he managed to preserve the moral grandeur of John Ruskin while working with some of the practical effectiveness of Sidney Webb. But he did share some of the nostalgic yearning for a pre-industrial order that has been taken to be one of the recurring weaknesses of that tradition. In the sketch of history that underwrote *The Acquisitive Society*'s critique of the modern financial order, he declared, rhetorically but also unguardedly, 'the past has shown no more excellent social order than that in which the mass of the people were the masters of the holdings which they ploughed and of the tools with which they worked'. And referring to the country towns in Somerset and Gloucestershire (where in later life he had a rural retreat), he enthused to his wife: 'I love these old towns, that were the great towns of England before modern industry made life hideous and cosmopolitan.' (It should be said that Hoggart, with his different class background and more sceptical sensibility, did not share the particular mixture of left-wing politics and cultural nostalgia that marked so much upper-middle-class anti-commercialism in early and mid-twentieth-century Britain.)

Goldman's biography is largely about Tawney the public man, though it gives a sensitive account of the strains in his marriage and does not altogether scant those tit-bits of arcane information we have come to expect of the genre. Interpretations of Tawney on the limits of competition will presumably not be greatly modified by learning that at school he played fly-half for the house 2nd XV. But we do get a vivid insight into his relations with an older industrial order when we read how even decades later he was not forgotten in Rochdale where he had conducted his earliest WEA classes: the testimonial fund launched on the occasion of his eightieth birthday in 1960 received a cheque for £15 from the Rochdale and District Weavers, Winders, Beamers, Reelers, and Doublers' Association.

Goldman astutely pinpoints the precise kind of mature industrial society that Britain was during Tawney's lifetime: 'The upheavals and instabilities of early Victorian capitalism were behind it; the affluence, deindustrialisation, and growing cultural pluralism of the present age unforeseen.' Tawney spoke to, and often for, an organized working class that was conscious of the historical wrongs it had suffered. He did so out of deep Christian conviction and with patrician self-confidence. It is not clear whether any of these ingredients are as available, or could be as effective, today.

And yet Tawney's name continues to be invoked by politicians and public figures where those of other leading political intellectuals of his generation are not. It might be said that the Webbs accomplished more, or that Laski had the adulation of left-wing students from around the world, or that Cole was closer to the Labour leadership, yet when any group wants to lay claim to be the true inheritors of the best traditions of British Socialism, they invariably (though often implausibly) try to trace their lineage back to Tawney. One of the virtues of this good book is that it should make it a little harder to recruit its subject in this high-handed way. Goldman brings out, for example, some of the respects in which Tawney did not correspond to the preferred profile of contemporary right-minded secular progressivism: he supported war in 1914 just as he favoured the nuclear deterrent and the Atlantic alliance in the 1950s; he argued for the retention of grammar schools after 1945; he seems to have been insensitive to the consequences of sexism, including his own; and he was a practising Anglican.

In his conclusion, Goldman suggests that Tawney may now be remote in even more fundamental ways, allowing himself the speculation that 'we no longer have the words with which to express a personal and moral commitment in our politics.... There can be no prophet without a prophetic language.' 'Prophet' may not be quite right for Tawney, for all his mastery of Old Testament cadences, but there may be a larger point here about cultural change, a development that underlies that weary reaction I mentioned earlier. Yet it may be that the *idea* of Tawney still has resonance in some quarters because there are those still susceptible to the *idea* of such moral commitment, however absent it may be from contemporary political life. It's true that when viewed from up close, many of his writings can seem oddly archaic and unusable; but what he, in some less easily definable way, represents retains an appeal. Perhaps, as Goldman concludes, it is his personal example which remains 'the most powerful element in his legacy'.

Something similar may, I suspect, come to be said about Richard Hoggart. In his case there is even less of a theoretical structure or body of doctrine, yet he has exerted an incalculable influence by the unassuming steadiness of his own personality, actual and literary (they may be less distinct in his case than in most writers). Hoggart has been conscious, indeed proud, of the affinity with Tawney, quoting him often in his work, including in the chapter he wrote for the Pilkington committee ('Triviality is more dangerous to the soul than wickedness'—a proleptically Pilkingtonian sentiment). But Hoggart's career was much less involved with either the Labour Party or the trade unions than Tawney's had been, and, if possible, even more involved with educational and arts organizations. After his return in 1976 from a spell working at UNESCO, he became Warden of Goldsmiths' College, London, but also chaired or sat on the boards of such bodies as the Arts Council, the *New Statesman*, the Broadcasting Research Unit, the Advisory Committee on Adult Education, the Board of Film Classification, and more. The British establishment's standard way of rewarding such service has been to bestow a title, but not the least of the affinities between Hoggart and Tawney was that they both turned down such honours.

Hoggart's life had been transformed by the immediate and lasting success of *The Uses of Literacy*, published in 1957, when he was a 39-year-old extra-mural tutor. It is a famously unclassifiable book, part cultural criticism, part autobiography, mixing participant ethnography with literary analysis. Fred Inglis makes a striking claim about it: 'In his great book, we see and feel how judicious objectivity and loving kindness become synonyms, and feel directly how keen moral sympathy dissolves into historical understanding.' It is easier to construe the second clause (especially if one takes 'dissolves' to suggest both disappearance and re-constitution) than the first. Far from being synonyms, the two qualities identified there—'judicious objectivity' and 'loving kindness'—might rather seem to stand as irreconcilable rivals. And yet, with Hoggart's book as the illustration, we can glimpse a procedural precept here, the recommendation of a kind of methodological charity. Hoggart's work was to be criticized for its lack of adequate historical or theoretical underpinning; the homespun quality of its observations can indeed seem worlds away from the protocols of the relevant academic disciplines. But the book, like his best later writing, undeniably achieved a distinctive kind of understanding (though perhaps it's not best described as 'historical'), and Inglis is surely right to suggest that Hoggart's 'keen moral sympathy' lay at the root of this achievement.

In a sense, Inglis has not really written a *biography* of Hoggart. True, he recounts the main episodes of his subject's life in broadly chronological sequence, but the book is more a discursive reflection on, and celebration of, Hoggart's career and the now-lost world that made it possible. Inglis stays fairly close to Hoggart's own account in his three-volume 'Life and Times' (1988–92), and his study is lightly footnoted. Goldman lists over thirty manuscript collections and his endnotes run to fifty pages; Inglis has consulted the Hoggart papers at Sheffield and gives a one-page list of Hoggart's main publications, though he has also talked to a number of relatives, friends, and colleagues. He says in the preface that he has deliberately kept the book short in order to make it 'above all a good read'.

What makes it so is the author's palpable warmth and his own generous human sympathies. To say that Fred Inglis wears his heart on his sleeve would be to understate his forthrightness. His prose is characterized by what might be called exuberant lyricism. The book proceeds by evocation rather than documentation; it is at times fond, even sentimental; at times angry and indignant at the wanton mutilation of life-sustaining social fabric by those who act as though balance-sheets end all arguments. Inglis more than admires Hoggart; he 'reveres' him, as he acknowledges. The book certainly cannot be faulted for underestimating its subject or falling short in enthusiasm for his various endeavours. In time a fuller, more painstaking biography will have to be written, using a wider range of sources and quizzing Hoggart's own account of events a little more searchingly. But, for now, Inglis has given us a heart-warming salutation to a figure who has all too often been patronized by the massive resources of English snobbery.

At the same time, there is a danger that this warm embrace may rather muffle some of the edgier, less comfortable notes in Hoggart's writing voice. Hoggart once said of himself that he was 'much less sorted out, politically, than Edward Thompson or Raymond Williams', the two authors of very different books about aspects of working-class experience with whom, through the accident of timing, he was always being grouped. It is not hard to see how this was true as far as having an announced political affiliation with worked-out theoretical and historical foundations was concerned. Hoggart was a sympathetic neighbour of the New Left rather than a member. When Inglis says that by the time of the appearance of the third volume of his 'Life and Times' in 1992 Hoggart 'had been appointed spontaneously the prose-poet of dissenting politics', it may be that Inglis, somewhat prone to intellectual hero-worship, is elevating Hoggart to an office he would not have sought and had not, in fact, been awarded.

It is true that Hoggart could be outspoken in identifying the destructive effects of Thatcherism, but he was always too much his own man to be an easy recruit to any party-political campaign. And, more generally, there was something both self-questioning and self-protective about his writing—qualities that, while they made him more interesting than some of his critics allowed, may have made his work less easily usable by others. (The contrast with the considerable influence of Stuart Hall's more analytic critique of Thatcherism may help to make the point.) For all that Hoggart has been taken as the laureate of 'community', especially of cosy, enveloping, all-singing-in-the-pub-together community, he has actually been more the watchful loner, the painstakingly self-correcting writer, the scholarship boy estranged from one class yet not fully at ease in another.

Tawney wrote several books that were important in their day and that scholars will continue to return to. Hoggart risks being seen as a one-book man: *The Uses of Literacy* was so affecting, so distinctive, so fortunate in its timing, and such a runaway success, that all else has been overshadowed, especially because the essays written in the two or three busy decades that followed were sometimes a bit dutiful or bland. Thereafter he had an exceptionally productive retirement, writing some fine books in the late 1980s and 1990s (not just his three-volume autobiography, but also his study of Farnham and his re-framed social criticism in *The Way We Live Now*), though probably none of these would have got much attention, or even been published at all, had he not already been a noted public figure.

If Tawney was, as Goldman proposes, a Christian and a Socialist but not a 'Christian socialist', so Hoggart was a writer and from the working class but not in any simple sense a 'working-class writer'. It's true his class background gave him a kind of reverse-authority in certain situations, but he combined this with a wider cultural inheritance to create a distinctive yet inspiritingly democratic voice. Speaking at a memorial service for Allen Lane in 1970, Hoggart said that 'Penguins have stood for the idea that our potentialities are greater than the pressures of our time', and for that reason he called what Lane had done 'one of the great democratic achievements of our recent social history'. The exact sense of the claim that 'our potentialities are greater than the pressures of our time' may be a little murky, but this is clearly a central Hoggartian theme. One reason why he was able to be such a resolute and effective critic of the deceits of 'giving people what they want'—the slogan trotted out to justify various ways of making profits from peddling worthless and degrading cultural wares—was because he had a firm hold of the contrast between such pap and 'our potentialities'. There was nothing utopian about this, in part precisely because it didn't depend upon any large historical or theoretical apparatus. It meant, above all, 'not selling people short', not treating them as incapable of development, not writing off the bulk of the population as doomed to a life of alienated labour and empty distraction.

For all the obvious differences between these two figures and the eras in which they lived—differences curiously magnified by these sharply contrasting forms of biography—their common affirmation of a number of deep, powerful truths shines through. Profit is a hollow and unworthy goal. The unchecked imperatives of the market deform and destroy human lives. The only force capable of resisting the destructive power of capital is the collective will to give expression to a common good through legal means—or in other words, the state. Though Tawney never lost his concern with the kind of inner self-reformation that changes individual character, and although Hoggart always kept his grounding in the small decencies of local and familial life, they both recognized the obligation to 'do' politics, to engage in public life, to work through institutions. Tawney might have written more history or more political theory if he hadn't given himself to so many good causes, just as Hoggart would surely have written more cultural and literary criticism if he not spent so much of the quarter-century after *The Uses of Literacy* chairing committees and running institutions. Their respective *œuvres*, already substantial, might have been larger, but perhaps their influence would have been smaller. They might not have been any more widely read, but they surely would have been less widely admired. Still, the choices they made in these matters were part of who they were. Integrity has a power which opportunism can never reach, just as faith in an ideal and hope for the future turn out to be more stirring and infectious than any amount of hard-boiled realism or cynicism. In the cases of both Tawney and Hoggart, the exemplary quality of their own characters stands high in all recollections and celebrations of them. Even in the face of the complacent disdain that I mentioned at the outset, it is difficult to come away from these two very different biographies without feeling renewed admiration for their subjects.

IV

Descriptions of Richard Titmuss often drew on the language of otherworldliness. He was 'the high priest of the welfare state' according to an assessment quoted in his entry in the *Dictionary of National Biography*. That entry considers, though judiciously rejects, the frequent characterization of him as a 'saint'; understandably, it does not cite the judgement of Michael

Oakeshott, conservative political thinker and LSE colleague, that he was 'a snake in saint's clothing'. But his reputation has remained tinged with an almost religious aura. Even Titmuss's daughter recognizes that he could be described as 'an ascetic divine', one 'who, with his lean face and compelling eyes, might well have been painted by El Greco'.

Saintliness can be an extremely irritating quality, especially when it seems rather too readily compatible with getting one's own way. Titmuss appears, especially in the second half of his life, to have got his own way a good deal—in his role as Professor of Social Administration at LSE, in his public career as perhaps the most influential analyst of social policy in the three decades after 1945, and in his home life as the traditionally cosseted and deferred-to male breadwinner. After his death in 1973, such irritation may have contributed to some of the more critical re-appraisals of his legacy, encouraged by the larger turn in political thinking away from the collectivist and redistributive ideals of social policy he had championed so eloquently. Even so, a more sympathetic assessment could still conclude early in the twenty-first century: 'Almost thirty years after his death, Titmuss remains the single most important intellectual influence on the study and practice of social policy in the United Kingdom.'

For a figure so widely regarded as pre-eminent in a field with more tangible and measurable social consequences than most, Titmuss had a relatively low public profile during his lifetime, and since his death he has not had anything like the name recognition enjoyed by other leading intellectuals and academics of his generation. Although in 1989 a trio of younger colleagues considered it was 'still difficult to gain the necessary distance to assess fully' Titmuss's contribution, they suggested that he had been 'a dominant figure whose influence may perhaps be compared to that of Keynes in economics or Popper in social philosophy'. That judgement has not so far been reflected in the early attempts to write the intellectual history of Britain in the second half of the twentieth century, and although we have full-length biographies of a substantial number of historians, philosophers, and social theorists, Titmuss remains an under-explored and somewhat shadowy figure. Two factors that may have contributed to this comparative neglect are, first, the opacity, or at least largely practical character, of 'social policy' as an intellectual field, and, second, the fact that Titmuss for the most part pursued his goals away from the glare of wider public attention, through teaching and committees and above all in his formidable, often technical writings. Social policy necessarily involves the union of large principles and small facts, and Titmuss certainly did not scant or disdain the necessary empirical detail: his writings are full of graphs, charts, and statistics. The book that made his name was the unexcitingly titled *Problems of Social Policy*, published in 1950. We have numerous testimonies to the galvanizing power of what the sociologist T. H. Marshall termed 'a flawless masterpiece': 'everyone who read the book shared my excitement', recalled the

American social analyst Eveline Burns. Yet revisiting it today one is immediately struck by its uninviting heaviness and impersonality, by the density of information and the lack of any eye-catching interpretative or polemical claims. It is over 500 pages long, published by HMSO as part of the official history of the 'home front' during the Second World War, and it addresses, with unyielding attention to detail, such topics as the exact division of administrative responsibilities for the provision of ambulance and other first-aid services during the war. Much of Titmuss's later work stayed similarly close to the bureaucratic ground. So how did he come to be so influential and even revered?

The work that may best illustrate the power and appeal of his thinking, and that brought him nearest to achieving wider public attention, was his last book, *The Gift Relationship: From Human Blood to Social Policy*, published in 1971. This was a characteristically detailed and rigorous examination of the provisions made by several different countries (principally the UK and the USA) to ensure the availability of enough human blood to meet modern medical and scientific needs. It was the perfect topic for him, an opportunity not just to display his command of social statistics, comparative analysis, and underlying principles, but also a subject that went to the heart, almost literally, of the question of the nature of the social bond. After all, blood has been widely seen not just as the essential medium of life itself, but as the most elemental proof of a common humanity: 'if you prick us, do we not bleed?' Since it cannot be manufactured, complex arrangements have to be put in place to allow for the transfer of large quantities of this precious fluid from healthy people, whose bodies will naturally replenish their supply, to those in need of more or less urgent transfusions.

A central question, clearly, concerns the terms on which these supplies are to be obtained. Economists are professionally disposed to argue that if there is sufficient demand for a commodity, then a market will arise to supply it, and that in the long run the price mechanism will always be the most efficient way of ensuring that demand and supply coincide. Following this style of reasoning, the most effective system would involve offering healthy individuals sufficient financial incentive to sell their blood, and on this principle some countries, such as the United States, developed an extensive commercial trading system in blood. But other countries, notably the UK, relied almost entirely on voluntary donors, who gave blood as an expression of human solidarity and in recognition of the fact that since we are all equally liable to illnesses and accidents, so we all have a common interest in making the necessary remedies universally available. Part of what was so powerful about Titmuss's careful, thoroughly documented analysis was its demonstration, *pace* the economists, of the greater efficiency of the latter system as measured by all the relevant criteria—purity of blood, availability and reliability of supply, cost, and administration. Though his treatment is restrained and technical, his conviction of the ethical as well as administrative superiority of the donor model is palpable. This is the 'gift relationship', a way of relating to 'the needs of the universal stranger' that was governed by recognition of our common humanity, not by the prospect of financial gain. And in this respect the book was re-stating what, stirred by the ethically driven analyses of R. H. Tawney, had been a governing preoccupation of Titmuss's work for the previous thirty years or more: the need for societies to give effective institutional expression to non-economic values in the face of the tirelessly corrosive power of the profit motive. Employing a dichotomy that had enjoyed such shaping power in British social thinking since the mid-nineteenth century, Titmuss saw the system of blood-donors as a important example of where 'altruism' set bounds to the operation of 'egoism'.

All this might seem to suggest that Titmuss belonged to that long line of upper-middle-class, Oxbridge-educated public moralists who featured so prominently in English intellectual and political life in the late nineteenth and early twentieth centuries. But in reality his was a more remarkable personal story. He came from a much lower social stratum altogether, and when he was appointed to the newly established Chair of Social Administration at the LSE in 1950 he not only did not possess a Ph.D. (commonplace enough at that date) or a BA (unusual, even in those more freebooting days): he did not even possess the equivalent of A or O levels. His only formal qualification was a certificate in book-keeping; his main professional experience lay in working for an insurance company.

Titmuss came from a lower-middle-class family that fell upon hard and then harder times. His father had been a more than usually unsuccessful small farmer in Bedfordshire before moving to the outskirts of north London where he managed to be equally unsuccessful in running a small haulage business. Richard was 15 in 1922 when the move to London took place, and, schooling completed or at least indefinitely interrupted, he was sent to learn basic book-keeping skills. Low-level clerical employment followed. When his father died in 1926, his mother managed to wangle better career prospects for her son as a probationary clerk with the County Fire Office insurance company in central London. For the next eleven years, Richard Titmuss was one of the black-coated army of office workers, commuting from (and helping to sustain) the family home which he only left when he got married at the age of 30. This early employment gave him a hands-on familiarity with the kinds of social statistics upon which insurance companies depend, including the shockingly class-determined incidence of illness and early death. Conforming to long-established (but soon to be much reduced) traditions of self-improvement, he educated himself in some of the larger questions of demography and policy that underlay the figures which were his daily business, and in his early thirties began to publish articles and books on these topics.

The Second World War opened up new possibilities for Titmuss as for so many others whose opportunities had been tightly constrained in the inter-war years. On the basis of his publications and his activities in the Eugenic Society, then a forum for the serious discussion of a range of population-related issues, he was recruited by the historian Keith Hancock to the imaginative project of writing the civil history of the war while it was still in progress, and so at the beginning of 1942 Titmuss left his insurance job to undertake research, under the supervision of the Cabinet Office, on the role of the Ministry of Health and related agencies. *Problems of Social Policy* was the delayed outcome of his wartime researches, though by the time of its publication his temporary attachment to the civil service had come to an end and he was working as a social researcher for the Medical Research Council.

At this point his personal story intersected with what has become one of the neglected byways of twentieth-century university history. In its early years (it was founded in 1895), the London School of Economics had not been a conventional higher education institution, partly because it had largely been founded by Socialists to help promote Socialism, partly because it had retained a variety of informal or unorthodox procedures from its early experimental years, and partly because its concern for social and political practice meant that it offered a variety of shorter or part-time courses leading to diplomas and certificates rather than degrees (as late as 1947 only 37 per cent of its students were studying for a degree). For example, it ran special courses for 'Colonial Cadets and Officers' and for 'Officials of the Exchequer and Audit Office', as well as a notably remunerative course in 'Railway Economics'. In this setting, practical courses for training social workers were hardly anomalous in the School's first half-century. Its commitment to such work was long-standing: since 1912, following an earmarked donation, it had catered for a variety of case-workers and empirical social investigators within its 'Department of Social Science and Administration', later called just the Department of Social Administration. Such work had roots stretching back to the Charity Organization Society of the late nineteenth century and even to the settlement movement in which young, earnest middle-class men and women were implanted into some of the most deprived urban areas. At its heart was 'the case-work method', involving a close personal engagement with the individual or family in distress. By the 1940s this was becoming psychologized, with the social worker's intervention coming to be seen as involving a form of therapy, a turn that has been regarded by later critics as yet another way of side-stepping or playing down the structural determinants of individual need. But alongside the practice of social work there was, as there had been from the department's inception, a commitment to undertaking, and training others to undertake, detailed, small-scale empirical social investigation. Over time, the Edwardian usage of 'social science' to embrace this mixture of social work, social investigation, and practical do-goodery yielded to the more familiar academic usage, but in the mid-1940s the traditional amalgam was still more or less functioning at LSE, and this was to be the setting of Titmuss's first (and only) academic appointment.

However, in the decade following the end of the war, the LSE was beginning to move closer to what was becoming the dominant academic pattern: a higher proportion of students were enrolled for degrees, with a notably large increase in graduate students, and universities were increasingly expected to be centres of approved forms of scholarly and scientific research. Perhaps as a way of nudging the rag-bag Department of Social Administration in this direction, T. H. Marshall was briefly made its head after the war; he liked facetiously to refer to its purpose as 'pouring oil on troubled daughters', a patronizing reference to the large numbers of well-brought-up young women who at the time sought in social work some outlet for their active social consciences. Finding the role an uncongenial burden, and having, like other informed readers, been impressed by Titmuss's volume of official history, Marshall engineered the appointment of a man with no previous experience of higher education institutions in any capacity to a newly created Chair of Social Administration and ex officio headship of the department.

Social Administration has not cut a striking figure in the history of modern academic disciplines: its opaque, faintly bureaucratic title may not have helped, and the temptation has been to see its history in terms of a transition from lame duck to lost tribe. But no small part of the vitality of social science in Britain in the first half of the twentieth century and beyond was due to the mixture of impulses that gathered under this uninformative label, especially in terms of engagement with contemporary social problems as encountered in the local community. The processes of academic specialization and professionalization were not kind to such an ad hoc coalition of practices, and it encountered increasing disdain from more heavily theorized adjacent fields. At LSE, Social Administration's somewhat anomalous status by the late 1940s was compounded by the fact that its staff was overwhelmingly female, frequently women with more practical experience than orthodox academic qualifications, and that its activities depended heavily on funding from external charitable foundations.

When appointed to head this somewhat fragile enterprise, Titmuss was an outsider in several senses—an outsider to the LSE (many of the staff were former students), an outsider to academia, an outsider to social work. And he had another potential handicap as far as relations with his overwhelmingly female staff were concerned: he was a man. Not surprisingly, the departmental teacup was racked by storms through much of the 1950s; ideals, identity, and amour-propre interacted with their usual combustible consequences. Titmuss may have treated some of his inherited staff unsympathetically: the training of social workers was not his priority. With hindsight, one can see that he was attempting to re-shape his department as a centre of systematic (and academically respectable) policy-focused social investigation—in which guise, re-named the Department of Social Policy, it flourishes to this day. He was himself neither a sociologist nor an economist, at least not in any of the professionally recognized senses of those terms at the time ('social economist' was the slightly old-fashioned self-description he had used in his application for the LSE chair). But even though he was hard to pigeon-hole in disciplinary terms, he had a clear view of the distinctive focus of his and his department's work. His subject was the study of social policy, that elaborate network of governmental and non-governmental agencies and measures that determined the 'welfare' of a country's inhabitants (a country seemed a more obvious analytical unit then than it might now). He never produced a general theory to provide the conceptual framework within which such work should be conducted; his hallmark was the strong ethical purpose informing his close and formidably well-informed analyses of how particular policies worked (and how, above all, they often benefited the comfortably-off middle class more than their intended beneficiaries among those on lower rungs of the social ladder). Through his writing and teaching and his institutional role he shaped a whole generation of analysts of social policy who worked in this vein—'the Titmice', as they were known, affectionately or derisively.

It may now be difficult to recapture the excitement that was generated in the 1950s and 1960s by the encounter between social science, then enjoying its vogueish heyday, and the fast-expanding network of services that was dubbed 'the welfare state'. Titmuss was the master of the rigorous statistical analysis of how specific policies worked in practice, while at the same time reiterating the fundamental ethical principles that he believed should govern a properly functioning machinery of well-being. In particular, he insisted on the centrality of the basic conception of universal citizenly entitlement, as opposed to models that justified benefits either as a bandage to staunch the wounds of a social residuum or as something that had been 'earned' through a contributions-based insurance scheme (he was too familiar with the insurance industry ever to have much faith in either its efficiency or its beneficence). The avoidance of stigma was crucial, he argued: we can never disentangle the skein of causality with sufficient clarity to be confident in discriminating 'deserving' from 'undeserving' beneficiaries, yet we cannot simply allow the costs of economic life 'to lie where they fall'. Characteristically, this sentiment combined a basic moral commitment with an acknowledgement of the limits of sociological analysis.

He also influentially maintained that 'fiscal welfare' and 'occupational welfare' needed to be taken into account alongside the conventional understanding of the services that made up 'the welfare state'. For example, on the question of old age he worked, unsuccessfully in the end, to achieve something better than the shocking divide we still have between those with private or occupational pensions that have benefited from extremely generous fiscal treatment and those condemned to struggle through their, increasingly long, old age on the unliveable pittance that is the state pension. Consistently, Titmuss looked to social policy to counter the savage injustices of economic life and to express something of that sense of solidarity which he had identified as so crucial to many of the measures introduced for the first time in the 1940s, in contrast to arrangements such as the old Poor Law and its modern descendants which merely pick up the worst casualties of the market, having first stripped them of their dignity. Titmuss's ideas have subsequently been criticized on various counts, but it is hard not to feel and respond to the inspiriting power of such convictions, even at this distance and in our dismally unpropitious political climate.

Part of what has made Titmuss seem, in retrospect, both influential yet very much of his time is the extent to which his work resonated with sympathetic policy-makers. He and his associates, such as Brian Abel-Smith and Peter Townsend, had particularly intimate connections with the Wilson governments of the 1960s, but their reach was not confined to Britain. They were consulted by more than one foreign government of a broadly progressive persuasion. It is striking that much of the social policy of, for example, Mauritius and Tanzania in the 1960s and 1970s appears to have been drafted or strongly influenced by this English ex-insurance inspector with little or no direct experience either of government or of Africa.

For all the probing, revisionist character of so much of his work on the impact of welfare policy, Titmuss, like most of his contemporaries, took the nuclear family to be the foundational unit of society both analytically and normatively. This, as many later critics pointed out, not only involved over-generalizing a model that was far from universal, thereby marginalizing those who did not fit it in one way or another; it also exhibited the gender-blindness characteristic of the time, the failure to identify the multiple forms of subordination and exploitation that sustained the role of the male 'head of the family'.

In many respects, Titmuss's own family life corresponded to the traditional model assumed in his work. When he and Kay Miller married in 1937, she, five years his senior, was a social worker. In their early years together she helped him with his writing—the title-page of *Parents Revolt*, published in 1942, declares it to be 'by Richard Titmuss and Kathleen Titmuss', though a later edition subtly downgrades that 'and' to 'with'—but after the birth of Ann, their only child, in 1944, and still more after Richard's appointment at LSE, they fell into a wholly conventional pattern. He went out into the world, did important things, and earned the money; his wife stayed at home, did all the domestic chores, and lived much of her public life vicariously through him. Ann Titmuss proved to be a clever if, in her later teens, a rebellious child, who had the experience reported by other only children of simultaneously being the focus of her parents' vigilance while feeling peripheral to their mutual self-absorption. She went on to study sociology and, in a deliberately subversive act, got married while still an undergraduate, subsequently publishing, as Ann Oakley, notable polemical books on sex and gender and on the sociology of housework.

Maybe having a famous parent encourages the constant scrutiny of the success or otherwise of one's own career; certainly, Oakley has been an inveterate autobiographer, publishing her first full-length summation of her life to date, *Taking it Like a Woman*, when she was 40. She has also written fairly extensively, and sometimes critically, about her father's work as well as about his life, especially in *Man and Wife: Richard and Kay Titmuss, my Parents' Early Years* (1996). Ann Oakley turned 70 in 2014 and, prompted in part by having attended the ceremony in which a blue plaque was affixed to her parents' home marking it as where her father lived for the last twenty-two years of his life, she decided to revisit what she calls 'the Titmuss legend' in order to reflect once again on the relations between her own career and that of her famous father. But this description makes the book sound more conventional than it is. This is not an autobiography, though it has many autobiographical elements. Nor is it a portrait of her father, though he figures in it largely and, in more elusive ways, dominates the whole project.

Father and Daughter is an avowedly hybrid piece of writing, perhaps even more hybrid than its author allows. Some chapters are very short and focus on Oakley as she now is, remembering the girl she was fifty or sixty years ago, or else they uncover bits of family history by digging in local record offices. A chapter based on reading her mother's diaries is especially powerful, streaked as it is with declarations about how 'the emotional wasteland of my and my mother's relationship has always left me floored'. But other chapters shift the register sharply, including fierce indictments of the continuing inequalities between men and women or exposures of the patriarchy that is, in her view, constitutive of academia. More discrepant still, some chapters investigate some contested episodes in the life of her father's department at LSE or the neglected careers of female social investigators; these are based on archival research and are heavily footnoted—they would not be out of place in a learned journal or volume of scholarly essays. Across the book, the writing shifts between scholarly exactness and pungent polemic, between dreamy reverie and pained resentment. Oakley's desire to experiment with a variety of literary forms is attractive, potentially offering unusual insights into the dynamics of career-making in British social science as well as providing a new twist on fashionable understandings of 'life-writing'. But it is not easy to pull off such shifts of register and focus while retaining the reader's confidence, and Oakley may, in addition, be hampered by a certain unsteadiness in her motives for attempting this unusual task.

There can be no simple or transparent stories by children about their parents. Oakley sometimes has a rather brisk way with the styles of thinking that try to explore some of the theoretical or epistemological issues inherent in the telling of all such stories. She says, for example, that she has never wavered in her view

> that what I would later encounter as 'the crisis in epistemology' of Western culture—the suspension of belief in any kind of stable objective reality—is simply a trick of the mind invented by theorists who've got nothing better to do. Reality does exist, and so does the real stress and pain that derive from a completely non-random (unfair) distribution of life-chances.

Much that this last sentence rather breathlessly asserts is surely true, but perhaps some of those 'theorists' were probing what is involved in trying to describe 'reality' in language in the first place, not having found the stories that most people tell to be notably 'stable' or 'objective'. Far from having 'nothing better to do'—an oddly *Daily Mail*ish charge in this context—these derided 'theorists' may be exploring some fundamental puzzles inherent in human attempts to communicate their experience of life, and their probings may have special pertinence for a reflective autobiographer who is attempting to understand the part played in her life by her fractured and unsatisfactory relations with her professionally very successful father.

Alerted by such thoughts, we can't fail to register how the language used in this book may reveal more than its author intends or knows. For example, her prose betrays how the whole enterprise of *Father and Daughter* is shot through with a competitive impulse, a desire simultaneously to please and match her father while also showing some inclination to topple him from his pedestal. Most notable, but least avowed, is the presence of a strong desire to have the world recognize her as an important figure on a par with her more celebrated father. We are told more than once about the sheer quantity of the achievements listed on her c.v. More specifically, she refers to herself as 'the discoverer of gender', and ascribes 'the introduction of gender, its differentiation from sex' as the consequence of the publication of 'my first book, *Sex, Gender and Society* in 1972'. Perhaps these claims might, in modified form, be justified—Oakley's early work was widely noticed and she has long been regarded as an important voice in what is often called 'second-wave feminism'—but it is her insistent assertion of them that causes the reader to recoil somewhat. Then there is the constant pairing of her achievements with her father's in what she terms 'the Titmuss–Oakley case-study': 'Thus, father and daughter both accomplished much of what they are known for within the institutional structures and strictures of academia', or again:

> The story of *Father and Daughter* has settled on two small moments in this convoluted history [of the social sciences]: the separation during the 1950s and 1960s in Britain of social policy from the older linked traditions of social

> administration and social work; and the emergence, since the late 1960s, of gender analysis. The first moment is associated with the legend of Richard Titmuss, the second with the legend of the 'feminist pioneer', his daughter, Ann Oakley.

Even the arrangement of the bibliography seems expressive of this bid for equal ranking: its first heading is 'Richard Titmuss and Ann Oakley: main publications' and two comparable lists of titles are provided.

In a poignant passage she records some of the disruptive things she did as a child to get her parents' attention and reflects that 'for most of my childhood I couldn't work out how to get them to notice the person who was really me'. It's a cry that may find echo in other writers' recollections, yet there's a slight but interesting awkwardness in the phrasing in this case. In wanting her parents to 'notice' rather than, say, to understand or appreciate her, she seems to have been asking for a form of attention or recognition for her achieved distinctiveness, an implication strengthened by the faint syntactical oddity of writing 'the person who was really me' rather than something like 'the person I really was'. Perhaps this book may be thought of as the latest of Oakley's disruptive strategies for getting herself noticed—by her parents metaphorically, by others more literally. In taking the blue plaque as both her starting point and one of her recurring conceits, she may say more than she intends about her preoccupation with how certain individuals obtain due recognition for their achievements and others do not. Richard Titmuss was obviously not any kind of 'saint', but he was a figure of real importance—the 'legend' may have been built up in part of others' fantasies and needs, as legends tend to be, but his achievements and influence seem hard to dispute. Only time will tell whether Ann Oakley's deep wish to be seen as of comparable importance will be gratified, but, sadly, I can't help feeling that this book does not entirely help her case.

9

Migrants

Nikolaus Pevsner, Isaiah Berlin, Isaac Deutscher, Ernest Gellner

I

Few forms of modern poetry can be as immediately recognizable or as widely cherished. 'ST PETER. 1867–8 by *Edwin Dolby*, built for £456. A simple Street-like job in red brick, banded in blue with Bath stone details. Hipped-roofed SE vestry with tiny stone bellecote. Stained glass: SW window, early C20. Two angels.' The brisk knowingness of the summative judgement recruits and flatters us: 'a simple Street-like job'—limiting but not at all dismissive, slightly collusive, briefly alluding to one strand of Victorian architectural history. The details of price, Bath stone, and twentieth-century glass reassuringly imply wide knowledge supplemented by just enough research. And you can be sure that there are indeed precisely two angels.

It is almost a cliché to observe that Pevsner has joined that company of names that have become nouns, signalling a category of things that everybody might have one of. In this respect, 'Pevsner' belongs with Wisden or Kobbé, the 'bibles' of their respective secular cults ('my second Bible', according to the vicar of one church that appears in it), doing for buildings what the *ODNB* does for people and the *OED* for words. At the same time, much of its charm, and certainly much of the affection felt for it by users, is due not to its orderly accumulation of fact, but to that distinctive, recognizably Pevsnerian voice—by turns technical, brisk, judgemental, peppery—suggesting greater kinship with, say, Fowler or Elizabeth David.

Susie Harries, *Nikolaus Pevsner: The Life* (Chatto and Windus, 2011).
David Caute, *Isaac and Isaiah: The Covert Punishment of a Cold War Heretic* (Yale, 2013).
Isaiah Berlin, *Building: Letters 1960–1975*, ed. Henry Hardy and Mark Pottle (Chatto, 2013).
John A. Hall, *Ernest Gellner: An Intellectual Biography* (Verso, 2010).

But just as 'Pevsner' now refers to something larger than the work of one man, so the achievements of Nikolaus Pevsner went far beyond the series of architectural guides which bears his name. He became a significant figure in British cultural life between the 1940s and 1970s, not only through his writing for a wide readership, but through his membership of committees and commissions (and, said some, conspiracies) that profoundly affected the appearance of British cities, the role of industrial design, and the teaching of the history of art and architecture.

For a man with such a talent for addressing a wide non-specialist public in authoritative tones, he perfectly suited his moment, those decades immediately after 1945 when, through such institutions as Penguin Books and the Third Programme, a new hunger for accessible guidance about culture sought and found nourishment. It was in some ways a democratic moment, something Pevsner celebrated, yet also one in which traditional hierarchies, whether social or educational, could still command a degree of deference. And in his case this allowed for what may seem an improbable (though actually far from unique) triumph—a German professor who flourished as an intellectual in a country not usually regarded as well disposed to either of those alien species.

Pevsner died in 1983, and it was only a few years later, Susie Harries tells us in this magnificent biography, that she set out to write his life, all unknowing that it was a project which would eventually take her over twenty years. What delayed and complicated her task, while also contributing to the vivid richness of the resulting portrait, was the discovery not only of extensive surviving correspondence, including intimate letters to his wife, Lola, but of the secret diaries or *Heftchen* that Pevsner kept from his teens onwards. Drawing liberally on this source, but also displaying exemplary thoroughness in tracking down other kinds of material, Harries is able to give us more of Pevsner's hopes, anxieties, moods, and sartorial mishaps than we normally learn about even the best-documented public lives. This makes the book very long, and I have to confess that I found a few passages dragged, as Pevsner and his wife work in excruciating detail through some fresh emotional misunderstanding or conflict, but that may be a small price to pay for the remarkable access this biography gives us to the inner life of a man sometimes accused of not having one. No less impressive are Harries's full and even-handed accounts of the various ventures and conflicts in which Pevsner was involved. It is no small compliment to say that in its attention to detail, its eye for pattern, and its ear for the apposite phrase, this biography is worthy of its subject.

Born in Leipzig in 1902, Nikolai Pewsner was descended from Eastern European Jews. His parents had prospered in Germany and, in a word that came to have tragic or reproachful overtones, assimilated: they did not observe any of the rites of their ancestral religion, they changed their name, they became good German bourgeois. The young Nikolaus, or 'Nika', was intellectually precocious, excelling at school and university. As early as 16 he recorded a 'dream I had been cherishing for some time: to see myself as a professor of art history'. When he was 19 he was baptized a Lutheran. As he recalled later, this did not signal the outcome of a spiritual crisis: 'The act was of course done for me to be normal German' [*sic*]. He began to clamber over the obstacle course that constituted the first stages of an academic career in Germany, including years as an unsalaried dogsbody. His father, we learn, 'effectively paid for the writing of Nika's thesis and would underwrite his career for at least ten more years'. During these years Pevsner married Lola, who was half-Jewish; the couple had three children between 1924 and 1932.

Pevsner's intellectual and professional formation marked him forever as a product of that strain in *Kunstgeschichte* that analysed art and architecture primarily as the expression of the spirit of an age. It was in these terms that he studied Italian Mannerist painting of the sixteenth and seventeenth centuries for his *Habilitationschrift*, and he brought the same framework to his study of the Bauhaus and Modernism, seeing the latter as the proper expression of a rational, democratic, functional society. The thoroughness of his research trip to Italy in 1928 while working on Mannerism also prefigured his later heroic gazetteering; he proudly reported: 'Now I really know what is above every altar in every church in Florence.' His chosen mentor at this stage of his career was Wilhelm Pinder, author of *Geschichte der deutschen Kunst*, who adapted a loosely Hegelian set of categories to explore the relations between national character and *Zeitgeist* in the history of art. Even though Pinder was later tainted by collaboration with the Nazis, Pevsner never disowned his debt, even (perhaps unwisely) dedicating to him a book published in 1940.

Having obtained a post as *Privatdozent* at the University of Göttingen in 1929, Pevsner was sent to England the following year to prepare materials for lectures on English art and architecture. Again one sees indications of greater labours to come, as he wrote back to his wife: 'In the daytime I have to collect all kinds of details . . . generalisations are a luxury for the evenings.' Amid the privations of English cooking and plumbing, there were moments of aesthetic rapture, especially his first encounter with Durham cathedral, which he never ceased to regard as one of the world's great buildings.

By the early 1930s, Pevsner was making a name for himself as a coming man in German art history, while also living the cultivated family life of the *Bildungsbürgertum*. However, Hitler had rather different ideas about who could count as 'normal German'. In April 1933 Pevsner was, as the phrase had it, 'asked not to lecture'; in September he was dismissed from his post. He was not prepared to take up some other, more menial career (then still open to Jews), so in October he set out for England, in search of employment, which at that stage he assumed would be temporary.

The eventual academic or cultural success in Britain of several notable refugees from Nazism can make it seem that the transition was relatively easy and continued intellectual or literary success inevitable. Pevsner's career in the 1930s and 1940s provides a sharp corrective to any such superficial view. Well into his forties he had no regular employment and no sure way to feed his young family. These were desperate years for the Pevsners, with Nikolaus sometimes living in a dingy rented room, anxiously chasing scraps of gainful employment, while Lola scrabbled to keep a semblance of normal family life going in increasingly dire circumstances. His wife and children joined him in London at the beginning of 1936, but they were all homesick for Germany, hoping to be able to return there soon (Harries has a compassionate eye for the difficulties highly assimilated German Jews had in understanding the way things were going in the 1930s, noting that at the end of 1937, 75 per cent of German Jews were still in Germany). It is a telling indication of the problem that relatively unpolitical people like the Pevsners had in taking the measure of events that they continued to send their children back to Germany for the traditional summer holiday, even in August 1939, with the result that their daughter was trapped there for the duration of the war, protected by relatives.

Pevsner's difficulties in establishing himself in his new country and his eventual triumphs point to a complicated story about the receptiveness or otherwise of British society at the time. Prejudice against foreigners, perhaps some anti-Semitism, may have blocked his early efforts to obtain an academic post, but Art History barely existed as a discipline in Britain at that time, and anyway he was scarcely alone in having difficulty finding a job in the 1930s. Moreover, Pevsner never (to his credit) fitted in with the strain of precious, aristocracy-infatuated, country-house-sniffing connoisseurship in the English art history tradition. Yet, all that said, room was found for him, support was provided (not least by the Society for the Protection of Science and Learning), publishers and periodicals proved hospitable, and he became a prominent component of the remarkable émigré fertilization of British intellectual and cultural life after 1933.

Two early books helped to build a reputation that eventually led to other openings. In 1936 he published *Pioneers of the Modern Movement: From William Morris to Walter Gropius.* The subtitle indicates the somewhat polemical thrust of the book, its depiction of International Modernism as descending from the English Arts-and-Crafts tradition (at least, polemical in Britain: Pevsner considered this interpretation something of a truism among German art historians). In the following year he published his report on research he had been commissioned to undertake into the state of design in British industry, *An Enquiry into Industrial Art in England.* One reviewer of the latter book observed that though 'written throughout with the care and precision of a scholar' it was 'animated throughout by the zeal of a second Ruskin'. This may not have been a comparison Pevsner would have cared for: he mostly found Ruskin exasperating. But it is worth reflecting on the extent to which, then and later, Pevsner might nonetheless be thought of as 'a second Ruskin'. In very broad terms, they shared a preoccupation with the social values expressed in art and architecture; there was some of the same emphasis upon the priority of looking, really looking, and some of the same passionate irascibility against heedless developers. But Pevsner, though highly judgemental, was not quite a public moralist in the Ruskinian mould, not quite so given to reading lessons on the state of the national soul. He was, by both temperament and education, more of a scholar and less of an artist than Ruskin. He was also much more of a Modernist, though as Harries reminds us, 'Modernism was to some extent a revolt against the social consequences of the Industrial Revolution—dirt, clutter, ugliness, and inequity—and had at its core commitment to a better society', surely a very Ruskinian recipe. Then there was Pevsner's enormous admiration at this point for Morris, 'not the greatest artist of the 19th century, but the greatest man'. Pevsner is often taken as a leading example of an outsider who, through talent and effort, became an insider, but Harries also brings out his complicated fit with existing features of British culture.

It was during the war years (once released from relatively short-term internment) that Pevsner began to put together the portfolio of roles that was eventually to see him gain security and celebrity in his adopted land. He did various forms of teaching, gaining a part-time post at Birkbeck College in London (where he eventually became a professor in 1959); he wrote books as well as articles for several periodicals; and he did some broadcasting. He even tried out a proposal for a multi-volume guide to the architecture of England, county by county, but the Syndics of Cambridge University Press decided against supporting such a series.

His main breakthrough came from Allen Lane, the ebullient founder of Penguin Books. Lane intuitively recognized Pevsner as someone with special gifts for bringing the fruits of scholarship to a broad public, and commissioned him to write *An Outline of European Architecture* (1942), a short, wide-ranging, opinionated survey that was to become the most successful of all Pevsner's writings (Harries reports the remarkable calculation that 'in the late 1990s, *Outline* was still selling as many copies per year at Penguin as all the *Buildings of England* series combined'). Lane also made Pevsner the editor of the new King Penguin imprint of illustrated books. Pevsner enjoyed the work and, perhaps more surprisingly in view of his reputation for humourless diligence, enjoyed the camaraderie of early Penguin publishing. 'When the series reached its fiftieth volume in 1949', Harries records, 'the team threw a party in the garden behind Pevsner's Gower Street office; whose idea it was to import real penguins, which kept disappearing into the bushes, history does not relate. (The penguins missed the end of the party, returning prematurely to the zoo in disgrace, after one bit a fellow-guest.)'

But by that date Pevsner's life had taken its defining turn. According to the oft-told story, he and Lane were taking a post-lunch stroll in the summer of

1945 when Lane asked his companion what he would like to publish if he had a completely free hand. Pevsner promptly suggested two hugely ambitious projects, each with European models: a multi-volume history of art, and a county-by county catalogue of England's 'significant buildings'. Lane, amazingly, agreed to both, and Pevsner set to work. Harries gently suggests that the *Pelican History of Art*, the first volumes of which came out in 1953, was considered at best an uneven, perhaps flawed, venture, for all that it contained some notable books, but the 'Buildings of England' series enjoyed a far more favourable response (though for many years Penguin lost money on it until rescued by subsidy from the Leverhulme Trust; Lane liked to introduce Pevsner as 'my best-losing author'). For almost thirty years—he started work in 1946, the 46th and final volume was published in 1974—it also provided Pevsner's life with a rigid and gruelling routine of preparatory research, county visits, writing-up of notes, producing text, checking facts, correcting proofs, over and over again. Harries gives an excellent account of the making of this national monument, complete with details of Lola's erratic driving, Pevsner's scarcely credible stamina and discipline, and the obstructive contributions of those owners of grand houses who did not take kindly to a German with a notebook trying to get a foot in the door ('they've come to read the meter, Ma' was one, less common, response).

The remorseless treadmill of the Buildings of England project did not prevent Pevsner from doing much other writing during these decades, or from devoting many hours to various national committees and other forms of public service. He also became a frequent, even a reasonably popular, lecturer and broadcaster. One of his more controversial performances in this role came in his 1955 Reith Lectures, which he published the following year under the Pinder-esque title *The Englishness of English Art*. Not all lovers of English art found the book's identification of traits of national character persuasive, just as not all listeners had enjoyed the experience of being lectured at on this topic in a German accent.

Two other important institutions through which Pevsner acted on the British public were 'the Archie' and 'the Vic Soc'. In the middle decades of the twentieth century, the *Architectural Review* was a lively periodical, not a narrowly trade journal but a forum for the discussion of all kinds of ideas about the relationship of architecture and society. Pevsner found it a congenial home, becoming its assistant editor for a while during the war: several of his most celebrated or controversial writings were first published in its pages, and he remained on its advisory board until 1970. Although Pevsner's own tastes tended to favour the chronological extremes of the medieval and the modern, he wrote appreciatively of the highlights of Victorian architecture at a time when such appreciation was not common, and he devoted some space to Victorian buildings, churches especially, in the 'Buildings of England'. So it was not altogether paradoxical that this ardent disciple of the Bauhaus should become a founding member of the Victorian Society in 1958 and then serve as its chairman from 1964 to 1976. In this capacity he took part in many battles, not all successful, to rescue threatened buildings from demolition ('they've saved a hundred years', reflected one admirer), and his writings contributed to the more general revaluation of things Victorian that took place during these decades.

Pevsner, it should be remembered, was not in any straightforward sense a 'conservationist'. What mattered to him was the living whole, the relation of architectural form to human content, which could involve the harmonious integration of new and old, where neighbouring buildings nodded appreciatively to each other rather than turning their backs or making rude gestures (as he observed of Stirling's assertive History Faculty Building in Cambridge, which sat next to Casson's inventive Raised Faculty Building: 'Perhaps if Sir Hugh Casson had not been so playful, James Stirling might not have been so rude'). Moreover, although Pevsner loved and sought to protect outstanding buildings of all periods, from medieval to contemporary, he retained his early loyalty to Modernism. Or, rather, what he favoured was the idealistic, social-purpose Modernism of the movement's founders before 1939, not the debased, corporate-headquarters modernism of the 1960s and 1970s. He continued to believe in the principles of Gropius and the Bauhaus, but became uncomfortably aware in his later years that his kind of Modernism was itself becoming 'period' architecture. It is one of the peculiarities of the original Buildings of England volumes that they often single out the occasional bold essay in Modernism among civic or educational buildings for extended appreciative comment while in general having relatively little to say on secular and domestic architecture after the mid-Victorian years.

Harries puzzles a little over why Pevsner, not himself an aggressive or duplicitous man, attracted what could seem like more than his share of hostility (she perhaps doesn't allow quite enough for the sneer which can be the default response in England to anyone bearing the title 'professor'). She suggests that 'Pevsner's principal offence . . . may well have been his success', and recognizes that he often served as 'a lightning conductor for more general spleen and discontent with modern life'. Betjeman, Pevsner's almost comically exact antithesis, is the obvious witness to call at this point: 'Art history and architectural history still seem to me to be verbiage written by uncreative people who want to make a name or a faculty for themselves with chairs and incomes attached to it ensuring dignity and a comfortable set of rooms in a college or university.' Dismissal of 'pedantry' could also be a cover for sheer anti-German prejudice, further dressed up as celebration of the virtues of 'the amateur'. 'The Herr-Professor-Doktors are writing everything down for us, sometimes throwing in a little hurried pontificating too,' grumbled Betjeman, singling Pevsner out (inaccurately as well as unfairly) as 'that dull pedant from Prussia'. Auberon Waugh thought that Pevsner's 'bleary socialist eyes' simply could not appreciate the glories of English country houses, though in reality he gives superb architectural descriptions of many of these buildings. His sin, of course, was not to indulge in chit-chat about eccentric ancestors and all the other sentimental snobbery which overcomes some English people when confronted by the links between a few titles and a fine façade.

One of the most notorious attacks came from an ex-student, the Cambridge architectural historian (and fellow of Peterhouse) David Watkin, in his *Morality and Architecture*, published in 1977. Harries carefully documents how, by means of selective quotation from some of Pevsner's more enthusiastic writings about Modernism in the 1930s, combined with unsympathetic innuendo, Watkin constructed a portrait of an almost sinister figure, an authoritarian moralist of the left who wished to subordinate all vernacular English styles to a soulless, Socialist, rationalism. 'Rancorous', 'waspish', and 'spiteful' were among reviewers' characterizations of the book (Watkin's allegiance to a wider, Peterhouse-based campaign to discredit all forms of 'progressive liberalism' was noted), but, as always with such unfair attacks, some mud tends to stick. Watkin's book also had its admirers, it should be said. Paul Johnson commended it to readers of the *Daily Telegraph*: 'All sensible and sensitive people know that modern architecture is bad and horrible, almost without exception. Mr Watkin explains why.' Pevsner had to put up with a lot of this kind of thing.

These attacks were vastly outweighed by the admiration and praise that Pevsner increasingly garnered (in 1969 he was knighted 'for services to art and architecture'), and by the affection felt for him by a surprisingly diverse range of people. One of the forms taken by this last response that Pevsner himself particularly appreciated was parody. '*Smogge Hall.* C18. Offices of Northmet and British Restaurant. 1–2–3 hop 1–2–3 window arrangement. Characteristic double-hollow-chamfered waterspout. Not specially nice.' This was by the *Punch* humourist Peter Clarke, who was also responsible for dubbing Pevsner 'Big Chief I-Spy'. Pevsner himself joined in the fun, one year sending Christmas cards with detailed line drawings of 'The Collegiate Church of St Aldate and St Ursula, Candleford Magna' in Barsetshire.

For all his vastly detailed scholarship, Pevsner knew, and sometimes regretted, that he had not had an orthodox academic career; he described himself as a 'General Practitioner', in contrast to the more specialized 'Consultants' in the history of art and architecture. His most notable achievement involved an improbable marriage between the austere classifying impulse of *Kunstgeschichte* and the discursive judgementalism of the architectural or topographical guidebook. A man schooled in the impersonal discipline of early twentieth-century German scholarship ended up producing a highly idiosyncratic vade mecum with a cherished place in the glove-box or saddle-bag of countless twenty-first-century church-bibbers and country-house enthusiasts.

It is impossible not to admire the magnificent improbability of the original idea: that one man might visit, identify, and characterize all of what he referred to, simply but encompassingly, as 'the buildings of England'.

Despite his youthful fantasies, Pevsner did not dominate and partially reshape a scholarly field in the way a few leading academics occasionally do. He did not, for example, have the impact on Art History as a discipline that his friend and fellow-refugee Ernst Gombrich did. Nor did he, quite, become an unofficial national treasure in the way Betjeman did. Instead, he did something the overall significance and quality of which is peculiarly hard to estimate. Some of the engaging complications of the topic arise from the *trompe l'œil* relation between Pevsner and 'Pevsner'. He conceived the initial series and determined its working methods, its criteria for inclusion, its style, its rate of completion. He did a lot, but not all, of the work, especially not the preparatory work; he did most, but not all, of the on-the-spot inspections (all to begin with, but dividing it up with others in the later stages of the series); similarly, though he did practically all the writing to begin with (apart from some specialist sections on topics such as geology), progressively he shared this labour with co-authors. He employed assistants and secretaries, and Penguin, inevitably, had considerable input into production of the volumes. Moreover, all of this applied to the first editions only: the second editions, and still more the new series of revised volumes, have largely been the work of other hands, partly working within Pevsner's original template and simply correcting and extending, but partly going beyond it to include kinds of buildings he neglected, and, at all stages, greatly expanding the scale of the volumes. In the current revised editions, now published by Yale University Press, many of the counties are sub-divided into more than one volume, which are no longer in the handy pocket format (though some readers of the first series complained that Pevsner must have had coats with exceptionally large pockets). So 'Pevsner' has become not just a noun, but also a brand. The whole series is now, officially but perhaps slightly awkwardly, titled 'Pevsner Architectural Guides', and since 1994 it has been supported by the Pevsner Books Trust whose purpose is to 'promote the appreciation and understanding of architecture by supporting and financing the research needed to sustain new and revised volumes of *The Buildings of England, Ireland, Scotland, and Wales*'.

At the end of this long biography we are left with the conviction that Pevsner himself would have been content to know that he had created something much bigger and more enduring than just the *œuvre* of a single scholar, something at once impersonal yet organic, that goes on living. By way of underlining this last point, I should reveal that the description of the church of St Peter at Headley in Hampshire with which I began comes, not from the first edition, but from the splendid new revised edition (confined to the northern part of the county plus Winchester). As the Acknowledgements for this volume declare: 'In common with all the revised editions of Pevsner's work the aim has been to preserve at the very least the spirit of his style and wherever possible to preserve his descriptions and opinions.' The passage quoted certainly seems to have done that; it sounds like ur-Pevsner. But actually that passage illustrates not just the way in which the Buildings of England series has become increasingly a collective enterprise, but also the fine line separating fidelity, imitation, and pastiche. For if one turns to the original 1967 volume on Hampshire (the whole county, plus Isle of Wight, in one handy-sized book, jointly authored by Pevsner and David Lloyd, but with Pevsner mostly responsible for the churches), the corresponding entry is slighter and, dare one say, less immediately Pevsnerian. 'ST PETER. 1867–8 by *Edwin Dolby*. Brick. Nave and chancel in one; no bellecote. The tender for this church amounted to £456 (GS [i.e. information supplied by Geoffrey Spain from "Victorian technical journals"]).' No Bath stone, no stained glass, and, sadly, no angels. More shocking still, there's that firm denial of the existence of a bellecote. 'Tiny', in the revised edition, comes to seem an apologetic explanation for this omission, perhaps a slight tugging at the master's sleeve as he too-quickly got back in the car to move on to the dozens of buildings that still awaited him that day. Such tactful revision may be the best kind of tribute, a practical acknowledgement of the way in which Pevsner, or at least 'Pevsner', has entered the cultural bloodstream. As he put it in the Foreword to *Staffordshire*, the final volume of the initial series to be published, when he, with genuine humility, issued his usual invitation to readers to point out his mistakes: 'Don't be deceived, gentle reader, the first editions are only *ballons d'essai*; it is the second editions which count.'

II

Is intellectual disagreement ever a legitimate reason to deny a scholar an academic appointment? One view of a university is that it is a partly protected space designed to provide a home for intellectual debate. In the search for wider and deeper understanding, disagreement is here seen as productive, forcing all hypotheses to confront criticism and counter-evidence. On this view of the matter, the fact that individual members of the committee may strongly disagree with a particular scholar's approach must be set aside: the spirit of the proceedings should be that incarnated in the anecdote about the philosopher Henry Sidgwick, pillar of late Victorian liberal rationalism, who, when finding a candidate's work contained passages of what he regarded as cloudy Hegelianism, observed to his fellow-examiner: 'I can see that this is nonsense, but is it the right kind of nonsense?' But the question of what is to count as a 'legitimate' reason for objecting to an appointment may not always be quite so straightforward. What if it is felt that some scholars' approach commits them to systematically neglecting important forms of evidence? What if their manner of argument can be seen as wilfully disregarding standards of consistency or clarity? What if their analyses always seem to end up coinciding with their strong political convictions? The terrain is obviously honeycombed with pitfalls. And then there are the familiar anxieties that a teacher with pronounced commitments of certain kinds may be misleading the young, closing rather than opening their minds. The rival pictures of doom can be presented in stark and familiar terms: on the one side, the substitution of propaganda for scholarship and the perversion of teaching into ideological indoctrination; on the other, the witch-hunt, the persecution and exclusion of various forms of unorthodoxy. But, even when all these familiar considerations are allowed for, could there be cases where the intellectual (or maybe moral?) character of someone's work is such that this would constitute a legitimate ground for opposing their appointment?

Perhaps in March 1963 Isaiah Berlin thought that there could be. Perhaps he thought that Isaac Deutscher, Marxist historian and biographer of Stalin and Trotsky, was not to be trusted with the minds of the young. Perhaps, even though the 56-year-old Deutscher was at this point one of the leading authorities on Soviet Russia in the West, Berlin blocked his appointment to a chair at the new University of Sussex. And perhaps he really did so because of political or personal antagonism.

This allegation first surfaced in the fortnightly radical periodical *Black Dwarf*, edited by Tariq Ali. In its issue for 14 February 1969, the anonymously written 'Dwarf Diary' defended Perry Anderson's recent *New Left Review* essay on 'Components of the national culture' against its critics. Prominent among these, claimed the Diary, had been Isaiah Berlin, who allegedly denounced what he saw as the anti-Semitism implicit in Anderson's concentration on the impact on British intellectual life of the 'white migration' of liberal and conservative European intellectuals (who were nearly all Jewish). The *Black Dwarf* article pointed out, by way of counter-evidence, that Anderson had explicitly praised the contribution of another immigrant intellectual who was also Jewish, Isaac Deutscher, and it went on: 'There are good reasons why Berlin prefers to ignore this. It was Berlin who was responsible for Deutscher being refused a university post at Sussex. He justified it by saying: "You can't have a Marxist teaching Russian history."' At the time, Berlin made no public response, though, as we shall see, his private correspondence reveals him to have been considerably exercised about the affair. The rumour continued to be repeated, but at the time of Berlin's death in 1997 it had still never been decisively substantiated or denied.

David Caute has written a book that is loosely structured around this episode. He recounts the lives of the two protagonists, summarizes their work, and itemizes the various grounds of difference between them—their contrasting loyalties in the Cold War, their rival interpretations of Russian history, their different attitudes to their Jewishness and to Zionism, their contrasting characters and careers. Both, of course, were Jewish immigrants to Britain, but with radically different experiences of that transition. Berlin's family had left Riga for London in 1920, when he was 11: his subsequent education at St Paul's and Oxford, made possible by the success of his father's business, enabled him to penetrate the inner recesses of the English cultural elite. Deutscher, by contrast, had already had a first career in Poland in the Communist Party and in radical journalism before he came to England in 1939 at the age of 32; learning English late, he nonetheless made a successful new identity for himself as a freelance historian and journalist specializing in Soviet Russia. Caute covers all this ground well enough, though his prose occasionally strains to inject additional drama—'For two decades they stood, heavily armed, on opposite banks of a Rubicon coloured red by deposits of mud and blood.' And then he provides detailed documentation of what, as far as the record allows us to know, happened about Deutscher's non-appointment at Sussex. Much of this is drawn from unpublished correspondence, and the almost simultaneous appearance of the third volume of Henry Hardy's heroic edition of Berlin's letters enables us to see the full texts of the prize exhibits for the prosecution. These certainly seem to confirm the verdict briskly reported in Michael Ignatieff's 1998 biography that Berlin's contribution 'put paid to Deutscher's chances'. Here are the facts as we now know them.

In November 1962, Deutscher applied for a Senior Lectureship in Modern History and/or Economics advertised at Sussex. He had made a living as a freelance writer and journalist for almost twenty years, but he wanted to be relieved from the burdens of regular journalism to devote more time to scholarship, especially to a recently commissioned biography of Lenin. It soon emerged that Deutscher would not be willing to undertake the volume of tutorial teaching that the new university, here following the Oxford model, expected of its lecturers, but senior academics in related areas quickly saw that there might be some advantage for the new institution in attracting such a distinguished figure as Deutscher to, say, a chair in Soviet studies, where the demands, in terms of lecturing and promoting the study of the Soviet Union rather than doing large amounts of small-group undergraduate teaching, might be more congenial. Deutscher was invited for an informal discussion with this group; this seems to have gone very well, and in February 1963 Martin Wight, Professor of Modern History and Dean of the School of European Studies, wrote to Deutscher, emphasizing that 'the Vice-Chancellor asked me this morning to tell you how much he hopes that we shall be able to come to a satisfactory arrangement'.

In its early years, the University of Sussex, founded in 1961, was guided by an Academic Advisory Council made up of distinguished external figures. For posts at professorial level, the university's procedures required that the appointing committee include a member of this body. Berlin, then reaching his peak as a much-admired and influential figure in British academic and intellectual life (he had been knighted six years previously), was in this instance the obvious representative from the AAC in terms of fields of interests and expertise. But since all the relevant senior academics already seemed so keen to recruit Deutscher, the Vice-Chancellor, John Fulton, hoped to avoid the cumbersome procedure of a formal meeting, so he wrote personally to Berlin to inform him of the situation and, in effect, to seek his blessing. Fulton had been a PPE tutor at Balliol and knew Berlin reasonably well; at this time a good deal of the business in British universities and other institutions was conducted in this informal, off-the-record manner by people with shared values and backgrounds.

But on this occasion the anticipated endorsement was not forthcoming. Marking his letter 'Personal and Confidential', Berlin studiously avoided mentioning Deutscher by name. That he was more than usually anxious that the matter remain confidential is suggested by his indicating in the letter that he could expand upon his views 'in conversation—I would rather not put them down on paper.' But he left Fulton in no doubt of his opposition to the proposal: 'The candidate of whom you speak is the only man whose presence in the same academic community as myself I should find morally intolerable.' Of course, in the ordinary way, he insisted, he would not wish to oppose an appointment about which the senior academic staff all concurred. 'But I think there is a limit below which lack of scruple must not go in the case of academic teachers.' Berlin also made clear that 'the man in question is the only one about whom I have any such feeling—there is literally no one [else], so far as I know, to whom I would wish to urge such objections', and he illustrated his more general tolerance by noting that he would never consider objecting in these terms were a university considering other notable left-wing figures such as C. Wright Mills or Eric Hobsbawm.

Two things are immediately striking about this. First, there is the clear implication that more is involved here than intellectual or political disagreement: Deutscher's work or way of conducting himself is being tarred as fundamentally dishonest, marked by an unspecified 'lack of scruple'. Second, to declare that his presence would be 'morally intolerable' is to make a peculiar and peculiarly strong claim. One might, conceivably, wish to say something like this if the office down the corridor were to be occupied by a convicted mass murderer or child torturer, but in the present case there is something oddly self-regarding about the wording. It insists that he, Berlin, simply could not bear it, and indeed ought not to be made to bear it. There is something visceral about this, and at the same time the invocation of the most indefeasible general justification. It is hard to see how discussion might go after such a declaration, and perhaps that is what Berlin intended. Martin Wight was deputed to go to discuss the matter with Berlin, but there is no contemporary record of what passed between them.

The upshot was that Sussex did not, after all, offer the post to Deutscher: Fulton wrote him a weaselly letter, not really explaining the *volte-face*, to which Deutscher returned a dignified reply. What, if anything, the latter ever learned about Berlin's role, we do not know. He was to die four years later and does not seem to have referred to the issue publicly during that time. And there the matter rested until the allegation surfaced in *Black Dwarf* in 1969, though it is a reasonable inference that there may have been speculative gossip about the episode.

Berlin reacted with some agitation when the *Black Dwarf* article was brought to his attention. He justified himself to his friend Jean Floud, also named in the article:

> What in fact I said to Prof Wight—the only person I saw on the subject—was that I did not think [Deutscher] was a suitable Professor of Russian History, unless there was somebody else there also professing it, not quite so fanatical, to be able to give at least two sides of the case, that I should almost welcome his presence in a university like Oxford or Cambridge, where [there would be] some debate on the subject, and at least more than one point of view obtained—but that if Sussex University wanted him to hold the job, quite apart from what other electors might do, I should certainly not oppose it, and would not vote against him....

and more in similar vein. Well, perhaps he did say some of those things to Wight, though their spirit is not easy to reconcile with his original letter to Fulton: 'welcoming' his presence at Oxford, for example, strikes a rather different note from declaring his presence in the same institution 'morally intolerable'. Indeed, in this same rather over-strained self-vindication Berlin went on to say:' I disliked him personally, read his books with some admiration, was not prepared to vote against him for any post, and would have voted for him for e.g. a Fellowship at All Souls or Nuffield or St Antony's.' This last claim seems in particularly stark contradiction with what he had said in his letter to Fulton, especially when we remember that Berlin was himself a Fellow of All Souls for the greater part of his adult life. Perhaps he had forgotten exactly what he had written; perhaps he misremembered the precise sequence of events; perhaps he preferred to think that this is how he would have behaved, must have behaved, did behave.

It is possible that his conscience continued to nag at him, or perhaps he wanted to try to scotch the rumours, since Berlin then took the unusual step of writing to Deutscher's widow Tamara, denying the allegation in *Black Dwarf*. Henry Hardy's impeccable edition of the letters enables us to see that Berlin chose to solicit the aid of an intermediary, the Russian-born Anna Kallin, a BBC producer who knew both Berlin and Tamara Deutscher well. His letter to Kallin again emphasizes that he is most concerned that Mrs Deutscher should understand 'that I had no wish to do her husband harm, and indeed refrained from doing so', adding: 'I did think Deutscher pretty awful, as you know, but

I bent over backwards—perhaps unnecessarily—on the few occasions in which I was concerned in anything that concerned him.' Apart, he concedes with a misleading show of honesty, from suggesting that Deutscher might not be the ideal person to write the life of Chaim Weizmann, 'I do not think I offered any obstruction to his career.'

His long letter to Tamara Deutscher went further, emphasizing that he had done, and would have done, nothing to obstruct Deutscher's appointment; he had merely explained to the people at Sussex that it might be desirable to balance Deutscher's appointment with that of somebody who took a different view of Soviet history. The *Black Dwarf* article had imputed to Berlin the view that, as he reported it, 'no Marxist should ever be a Professor of Russian history'. This he vigorously disowned. 'Your husband disapproved of my views, if anything, more strongly than I did of his; nevertheless it would have been a betrayal of every intellectual value in which I believe if I had allowed this to sway my judgement consciously in judging his fitness for an academic post.' And he concluded by reiterating his innocence of the charge: it was distressing to be thought to have acted unjustly to a fellow scholar, 'especially if he were brilliant, courageous, gifted, and had in all probability suffered a good deal for his political convictions'.

The effort to placate, even to please, Mrs Deutscher is palpable, but it is hard not to contrast these phrases with those used by Berlin when writing to other correspondents. The edition of his letters has a sub-heading under the entry for Deutscher: 'detested by IB'. A substantial list of page numbers follows, indicating such passages as 'Deutscher is the least objective and factually least reliable writer among serious writers on politics to be found today', 'Deutscher, whom I detest as a nasty human being', and so on. As Caute indicates, the animus went back a long way; one formative moment came in 1954 with Deutscher's unfavourable review of Berlin's long essay on 'Historical Inevitablity', with Berlin complaining to friends of 'gibes from the horrible Deutscher', 'nastier than I had conceived possible', and so on. He took Deutscher to be an unreconstructed exponent of the kind of 'left authoritarianism' that invoked objective 'laws of historical progress' to justify its callous actions, and characterized the argument of 'Historical Inevitability' as 'directly aimed at his [Deutscher's] own cherished beliefs'. Then there was Berlin's exchange in 1958 with David Astor, proprietor and editor of the *Observer*, on the latter's inviting Deutscher to write an article marking the tenth anniversary of the state of Israel. Here Berlin raged intemperately against 'this still most fanatical of Marxists' whom he thought not just unsympathetic to Israel but capable of believing that the Jews 'deserved ("objectively") to be exterminated'. Berlin was certainly not in the habit of describing his *bête noire* as 'brilliant, courageous, gifted'.

In 1969 Tamara Deutscher's reply suggests she was not wholly convinced by Berlin's protestations, but there was no publicly available evidence with which to controvert his account. When in 1980 Christopher Hitchens reviewed Berlin's *Personal Impressions*, he repeated the allegation about Deutscher's non-appointment at Sussex. This immediately produced a postcard of denial from Berlin, and when Hitchens consulted Tamara Deutscher to see if there were not some evidence to support the accusation he drew a blank (and published a retraction). Only in his memorable assault on Berlin's reputation in the *London Review of Books* in 1998 was Hitchens able, drawing upon the bare acknowledgement of the facts in Ignatieff's newly published biography, to confirm that he (and *Black Dwarf*) had been right all along. The episode furnished an important illustration to support Hitchens's swingeing condemnation of Berlin's reactionary politics, moral evasiveness, and unreliability as a historical source.

The publication of the relevant volume of Berlin's letters together with Caute's more forensic examination of the episode may seem merely to provide corroborating evidence for what is by now a closed case. Yet in some respects the more extensive materials provoke at least as many questions as they settle. Caute contends that 'the deeper you dig into the core values underpinning Berlin's trademark warnings and exhortations, the more you find, or may find, a passionate defence of the status quo, an extended plea that the things we enjoy and value should not be taken from us'. This is made to sound like something of an exposé, the result of 'digging', but I wonder whether the implied indictment of a covert conservatism is altogether justified. After all, the wish that 'the things we enjoy and value should not be taken from us' is not the same thing as a 'defence of the status quo'. Berlin was a man of warm attachments, to places and routines of life as well as to people; the extent to which that is a likely impediment to identifying, and attempting to right, injustices presumably has to be judged in specific instances, otherwise we are all damned as black reactionaries. It is true that there were times when Berlin seems to have decided that silence was the better part of valour, and maybe he can be criticized for not having used his extraordinary prestige to speak out more often against bad policies and bad actions. Still, there is no point in wishing he were some kind of radical socialist of a post-1989 vintage. The Cold War was the enveloping setting of his politics, and he made no bones about being strongly anti-Communist. But that is not all that he was.

Letters are a peculiar kind of literary genre, and in drawing upon them as evidence we need to be attentive to the ways in which different writers exploit or stretch the generic conventions. Berlin was a wonderfully expressive letter-writer; it may be hard to decide how far his seeming to be such a chameleon was a necessary concomitant of this quality. He had a deep need to be loved and well thought of, as well as an only partially controllable urge to please. Here we are peering into that murky region that lies across and between what we feel, what we think we feel, what we say we feel, what we think we said we felt, and so on. What he wrote to any particular individual whom he cared about was no doubt what he thought he felt deeply at that moment, even if the record shows him expressing a directly contrary view to someone else on another occasion. This does not come across as conscious duplicity: it suggests someone who inhabited his own expressiveness with a rare kind of emotional brio, an enjoyment of hitting the high notes and indulging sentiment, an infectious pleasure in dealing in strong feelings. We may at times be inclined to do a little decoding: perhaps 'I felt more reverence for him . . . than for any living man' (on the death of Edmund Wilson) might be glossed as 'I want you to know that I thought highly of your late husband'. In retrospect, we might regret that John Fulton did not have access in 1963 to this rich store-house of Berlin's rococo epistolary habits. If he had, he might have been inclined to paraphrase that damning letter about Deutscher as 'I can't bear the thought of his getting this job; at some level I'd like it not to happen, and at some other level I do not wish to be party to the process at all, whatever the outcome.'

Berlin's verbal forcefulness could be extremely effective in any individual instance, yet somewhat self-defeating when considered in quantity. He risks becoming like the writer of reference-letters who describes several different candidates as 'the best student I have ever taught'. Of course, we all of us have the experience of having got 'carried away' and said things we later realized contained exaggeration or mis-description. Berlin rather cultivated this Dionysiac epistolary state; it made for an intenser experience of living, and anyway perhaps he could do no other (at this stage of his life he dictated many of his letters, and it shows). It was presumably among the things his friends cherished him for, and it can make for wonderfully engaging reading half a century later. But read *in extenso*, his letters reveal patterns of rhetorical surplus, as his various, not always compatible, urges and feelings jostle for expressive advantage.

Much of *Building* is taken up with the founding of Wolfson College in Oxford, of which Berlin became the first President. His social connections were vital to raising the necessary funds and overcoming the inevitable objections. In the UK he successfully wooed the Wolfson family, while in the USA his friendship with McGeorge Bundy opened doors, and coffers, at the Ford Foundation. In all of this he comes across as a very capable man of affairs, energetic in trying to realize what was, in terms of local traditions, a radical vision, resourceful in coping with the inevitable setbacks and crises. But accompanying this activity is the undertow of self-reproach about not completing any 'solid' work: 'As for me I am not doing enough serious work . . . I must really settle down and do something solid.' 'I am terribly unproductive and terribly ashamed of being so,' which may have been only partially true on either count. All this was accompanied by frequent declarations of how much he hated giving public lectures, in practice his main substitute for 'solid work': 'I would rather have a leg sawn off with[out] an anaesthetic than deliver these lectures: why the sustained masochism of my life?'—though he was by almost universal report considered a virtuoso performer. One must have a heart of stone (to adapt Wilde on the death of Little Nell) to read these laments without laughing: '. . . I hate being Professor, I hate lecturing, I hate work . . . ' 'I wish I could be idle all day and read newspapers.' 'I *love* being away from affairs—but am also conscious, as you never, *never*, are, of being an itinerant comedian moving from one one-night stand to another: not *like* a comedian, but literally one . . . ', and more in the same vein. Berlin's correspondence fulfilled many functions, but entertaining his friends and giving vent to feelings at odds with his public roles were certainly two of them, both calling for a certain interpretative tact from the reader before the letters can be pressed into service as historical sources.

As Berlin was indirectly acknowledging in his letter to Tamara Deutscher, his celebrated articulation of a form of liberalism meant that any demonstration of illiberal dogmatism in his public actions would appear especially damaging. But here, too, the letters raise some interesting questions about the relations between views, feelings, expressions, and actions. We can see a certain tension or slippage at work in a wholly innocent, indeed almost comic, case when Berlin was offered the Order of Merit in 1971. For several days he was racked by indecision about whether to accept, troubled by his awareness that many people would think it undeserved ('for services to conversation?', as one of them had teased about his knighthood), and that one or two of his closest friends might be consumed by envy ('My God, I thought, what will Maurice [Bowra] say?'). Having finally, and predictably, accepted, he recounted his inner struggles to David Cecil, explaining along the way that he had no principled objection to honours in themselves and was indeed in favour of anything that made life gayer and more various and more pleasurable, adding reflectively: 'Yet my beliefs are obviously quite different from the way in which I in fact react and behave.' This was not always a discreditable characteristic, but it is something else that needs to be borne in mind when drawing on his letters to support an interpretation of his writings or career.

In the case of Deutscher's non-appointment at Sussex, some debatable points also arise about procedure. Appointments committees are already not a wholly open forum, but what is said there has at least to be argued in publicly defensible terms. Berlin's preferred stage was always fronted with closed doors. Sussex's own early dealings with Deutscher had already been largely informal and private: a group of senior academics had lunch with him and believed that he could be an asset—appointments were often made more informally in those days, especially in such a new institution where the first office-holders had great room for manoeuvre. Fulton attempted to maintain this level of informality (and confidentiality) in his personal approach to Berlin, 'in the hope that we can avoid the necessity for a meeting'. This may have been a mistake: in a formal appointments committee meeting, Berlin would have had to express his personal reservations in a way unlikely to have had such decisive consequences; conceivably, he might not even have been willing to express his views at all. Viewing the initial correspondence from this distance, we may also ask what we think Berlin should have done when he received Fulton's letter. Should he have recused himself from taking any part in the proceedings on the ground that he was already too *parti pris*? Should he have kept his misgivings to himself and concurred with the local view that Deutscher was a distinguished figure who would be a good catch for the university? Or should he have declared flatly that he believed Deutscher to be unappointable, in any role in any university, and then stood by that conviction, in public if necessary?

And then there is the question of the reaction of Fulton and his colleagues once Berlin had lobbed his hand-grenade into their dug-out. Should they have allowed this one outside individual's private letter the force of, in effect, a veto? Might the right course of action not have been to convene a formal meeting of the committee, and let Berlin present his objections there? Caute conjectures plausibly that at the regular meeting of the AAC three weeks later the question of Deutscher's candidacy may have been discussed, but if so there is no record of it. So the appointment was dropped, even though the senior figures in all the relevant fields were in favour of it and they had the backing of the Vice-Chancellor. That fact may bespeak the remarkable influence of Berlin in British academia at this period; it may also suggest a too-cosy group of senior figures with Oxford connections (not for nothing was the new university known as 'Balliol-by-the-sea'). Against this explanation would have to be set Sussex's proud record in its early years of recruiting a number of figures with irregular professional histories, several of them European émigrés, some of them controversial in various ways, figures who greatly enriched its intellectual and scholarly life. So why was there not more objection to this blackballing of such a widely published historian? Is it possible that in this case others involved had some sympathy with Berlin's reservations about Deutscher?

There may, I suppose, be those who think that Berlin's objection was well grounded, that Deutcher was an unsuitable person to hold a chair of modern history, still more, perhaps, a chair in Soviet studies. Caute certainly assembles a rather damning list of oversimplifications and omissions in Deutscher's writings that could be grist to any prosecution case about his political bias. But 'bias' can be just the stick that consensus uses to beat off a challenge. It is not self-evident that Berlin should be considered any less 'biased' about the Soviet Union in one direction than Deutscher in another.

Caute's subtitle suggests something both scandalous and systematic: a 'heretic' was being unfairly 'punished' and by 'covert' means. The reality seems to have been murkier and more uneven. Deutscher was in fact accorded numerous opportunities and forms of recognition: he wrote regularly for many of the major newspapers and periodicals, his biographies were commissioned by Oxford University Press, he was invited to give the Trevelyan lectures at Cambridge, and so on. Of course, he was accorded nothing like the recognition and honours that came Berlin's way, but then who was? Their respective careers make for an instructive contrast, but Deutscher's could not really be said to amount to a narrative of 'persecution'. The truth is that any writing on a topic such as this is more likely to have the effect, and often the intention, of discrediting Berlin than of vindicating Deutscher, chiefly because the former has been so widely admired that there is an inevitable urge to take him down a peg or two. Caute acknowledges that his is a 'revisionist' enterprise, likely to be resented by Berlin's many admirers—he speaks of 'the affectionate recall, sometimes breathless adulation, he still engenders'. Both his book and the edition of the letters provide grist for anyone wanting to stay well this side of adulation, but in some ways what they reveal only makes Berlin a more interesting figure than any wholly pure liberal paragon could be. As he himself put it in the course of giving a friend wise counsel in matters of the heart: 'Scars are not vitally important. There is something to be said against totally unscarred lives, too . . .'

But even when all this has been said, the surviving evidence surely suggests that Berlin was in the wrong in the matter of the Sussex chair, and I suspect he half-knew this himself. His standing among British elites in the three decades or more after 1945, and the characteristic modus operandi of those elites, had given him the opportunity to prevent something to which he was viscerally opposed. According to one construction of his liberal principles, he ought to have declined the opportunity, but Deutscher was, for Berlin, a point of intersection of so many strong feelings that to have abstained from comment altogether might well have seemed a denial of existential verities. However, he wanted, as always, not to be blamed. He wanted to be loved, or at least liked, or at least not disapproved of, yet he also wanted his own way. He wanted to bring about a state of affairs (Deutscher not getting the job), yet not to be held responsible for that outcome. His later letters about the matter suggest a man who has constructed a version of the facts that he can live with. The full story, insofar as Caute's reconstruction and the evidence of the newly edited letters allows it now to be known, makes that version no longer tenable.

How much one believes that this outcome matters will depend on many things—not just on one's politics or one's pre-existing attitude towards Berlin and his public standing, but also on how much weight one attaches, in ultimate human evaluations, to inconsistency. As a political theorist and historian of ideas, Berlin had to be committed to prizing a certain consistency in thought and argument, but part of what he brought to those subjects was a deep awareness, at once reflective and intuitive, of how secondary a virtue mere consistency was compared to the powerful currents of emotion and sensibility that shaped any interesting thinker's thought. One of the incidental merits of this spacious edition of his letters is that one can see this intuition being deployed in everyday life and even about himself. In a magnificent letter to Noel Annan about the latter's draft contribution to a memorial volume for Maurice Bowra, Berlin gives spirited voice to his passionate belief in the overriding importance of love, of human sympathy, of openness, and of being in all ways 'pro life', even at the price of glaring inconsistency. In a closely related letter, he cites the line from P. G. Wodehouse that Bowra himself apparently liked to invoke: 'The trouble about you, old boy, is that you haven't a soul, and it's the soul that delivers the goods.' Whatever else may be said about Isaiah Berlin—a long and damning case for the prosecution can certainly be assembled—there's no denying that he had, in this sense, a soul, and that in his own way, especially in the human sympathies he brought to the closest relationships of his life, he did deliver the goods. That doesn't excuse all his actions, nor would he have thought that it should, but maybe it should make us hesitate before rushing to judgement. It should certainly lead us to resist reducing him to a calculating Cold War ideologue. As both these books illustrate, in their very different ways, he was more various—arguably more flawed, possibly more vulnerable, but above all more interesting—than that.

III

When Ernest Gellner was teaching at the Central European University in Prague in 1995, the last year of his life, he cultivated informal social relations with the graduate students there. One student 'confessed to unease when Gellner sat down to watch television with him—saying it was as if Max Weber had dropped by'. It requires only a little familiarity with Weber's vastly ambitious *œuvre* and notoriously austere personality to imagine why that might be an unsettling experience, as well as an unlikely one. Curiously, Perry Anderson, in an essay written three or four years earlier, had also tried to imagine Weber in front of a television set, but in this case as a way of making a contrast between Gellner's complacent-seeming endorsement of post-1945 mass affluence and Weber's more agonized reflections on Europe after 1918: 'It is difficult to imagine Weber, relaxed before a television set, greeting the festivities of the time as a new *Belle Epoque*.'

It is hardly surprising that these contrasting allusions both choose to make their point by invoking the name of Max Weber. Perhaps no other proper name crops up so frequently in discussions of Gellner's work. There was, for all their evident—indeed, almost laughably obvious and incongruous—differences, an important intellectual affinity between the two men as analysts of 'modernity', of the distinctiveness of the West, of the role of the world religions, and as philosophers of social-scientific method. The comparison becomes almost a reflex in John A. Hall's outstanding biography: 'Gellner's understanding and account of modern cognition were profoundly Weberian';

'no modern thinker has stood so close to Weber in insisting that our times must be disenchanted'; Gellner's account is 'Weberian both in according ideology some causal role and in offering a narrative in which different sources of social power mutually condition each other', and so on. In fact, the connection now looks almost fore-ordained, since Hall tells us that Gellner's upwardly mobile father had gone to Berlin in the early 1920s 'to find out more about Max Weber, who had recently died, and whom he came to admire greatly'. Seventy years later, that Prague student's quip was spot-on: the vignette would not have seemed so telling had he chosen to compare his teacher to Marx or Durkheim or Pareto or Parsons or to various other leading names in the history of social thought.

A second-order characteristic that Gellner shared with Weber was the way his work and career fell across several conventionally defined disciplines. An obituary tribute to Gellner pointed up this affinity by quoting Weber's fine remark: 'I am not a donkey and I don't have a field.' Gellner's first academic appointment was as a moral philosopher; much of his professional life was spent in a department of sociology; his final appointment (in Britain, before the brief Prague epilogue) was as a professor of anthropology. This mildly transgressive career trajectory gave him some satisfaction; it was with mock-ruefulness that he noted a possible parallel between his own career and that of R. G. Collingwood, who was 'praised as a philosopher by historians and a historian by philosophers'. Several of his students and admirers responded to Gellner's disregard for academic pigeon-holing: 'It was from Ernest that I learned not to give a damn about disciplinary tribes. He was a *franc tireur* of the disciplines, a zestful poacher who cocked a snook at all fences and all gamekeepers.' Even the briefest description of Gellner's later professional identity requires the juxtaposition of several ungainly abstractions: he was, for what such labels are worth, a social philosopher and a comparative historical sociologist.

Hall retraces the steps that led up to this ambitious job-description with exemplary care and sympathy. His is genuinely an 'intellectual biography', since he is not only exceptionally familiar with Gellner's work (he attended his lectures as a student and went on to become a colleague) but also formidably well read in most of the areas to which his subject contributed, enabling him to provide judicious arbitrations of various intellectual controversies (Gellner was a great igniter of controversies) as well as occasional corrective criticism. But even at the brute biographical level the story he has to tell is an unusually interesting one, beginning with that intellectually self-improving father.

Gellner's parents were assimilated German-speaking Jews, Habsburg subjects before 1919, and thereafter citizens of the new state of Czechoslovakia (where it seemed wise to speak Czech, at least in public). Prague in the inter-war years was cosmopolitan even by the standards of Central Europe: alongside Czech schools, it could boast German Gymnasia, Russian and French

Lycées, and an English grammar school. It was to the latter that his parents sent the 10-year-old Ernest in 1935, perhaps prudently preparing for a time when they would have to flee mainland Europe. They almost left it too late; they were fortunate to make it to England in April 1939, eventually settling in Highgate. Gellner's parents were representative of that stratum of educated, middle-class Jews who, profoundly grateful to Britain for providing them with a home, nonetheless continued throughout the war to speak to each other in the language of the now-hated enemy.

Ernest finished his schooling at St Alban's County School for boys, where a termly report from his History master seemed almost mischievously prophetic of the response the pupil's mature work was to provoke from its numerous critics: 'Ideas brilliant. But he needs to work harder on the facts.' From here, the already intellectually confident boy won a scholarship to Balliol, going up to read PPE in the autumn of 1943. But military service claimed him after one year, and he joined the 1st Czechoslovak Armoured Brigade, serving in northern Europe after D-Day and eventually reaching Prague in May 1945 a couple of weeks after the occupying Russians. He quickly sensed that the prospects for his former homeland were not good, and returned to England, resuming his studies in Oxford in January 1946. He graduated with a First in 1947 (allowed to take a shorter course because of his war service), and then, through the patronage of Balliol's Scottish Master, A. D. Lindsay, Gellner was immediately appointed to a lectureship in moral philosophy at Edinburgh. After two years, he moved to the London School of Economics, where he was to stay for the next thirty-five years.

A photograph of the 26-year-old Gellner, three years into his LSE lectureship, shows a strong, athletic, sexy-looking man, hardened by his passion for mountaineering and skiing as well as by military service. But at some point in his early thirties he began to suffer from debilitating osteoporosis, losing more than four inches over a decade, suffering frequent pain and broken bones, leading him to walk with a stick later in life. That photo also suggests, obscurely, a certain mismatch between the intense, challenging young man who confronts the camera with a stare falling somewhere between steely and sultry, and the professional role which he was coming to occupy. For, to all intents and purposes, he was an orthodox product of Oxford 'linguistic philosophy' in its heyday, publishing articles in philosophical journals on topics such as 'Knowing how and validity'. And the imprimatur of the Oxford philosophy establishment clearly mattered to him: three years after he had left the university, having already been proxime accessit for the John Locke prize, he went to the trouble of sitting for it again, this time successfully.

But his professional identity was not wholly orthodox even at this stage, since at the LSE he had been appointed in the department of Sociology, where Morris Ginsberg kept alive the flame of Hobhousian social evolutionism, and where Gellner's principal duty was to provide lectures on the history of ethics, a subject which, Ginsberg still believed, would illustrate moral progress. However, Gellner then did something which even Hall's meticulous and thoroughly researched biography cannot quite explain: he stopped publishing philosophy articles and began doing fieldwork among the Berbers of the High Atlas in Morocco, eventually submitting the fruits of his researches for a Ph.D. in anthropology (the basis of his 1969 book *Saints of the Atlas*). Love of the mountains had something to do with it, but so did an intellectual restlessness which left him discontented with the merry-go-round of concepts and eager to try to understand how actual societies functioned.

Whatever the ingredients in his intellectual development in the mid-fifties, they were to issue in something no less striking, in its way, than his trips to remote Moroccan villages, as the young Oxford-trained philosopher publicly and spectacularly bit the hand that had fed him. In 1959 he published *Words and Things*, originally subtitled *A Critical Account of Linguistic Philosophy and a Study in Ideology*, later reissued with the more revealing, though scarcely less wooden, subtitle, *An Examination of, and an Attack on, Linguistic Philosophy*. The book sought to demonstrate that the fascination with the nuances of 'ordinary language' which characterized this style of philosophy amounted to nothing more than 'the Higher Lexicography'. The Wittgensteinian practice of linguistic analysis as a solvent for the misleading puzzles of all previous philosophy resulted, Gellner contended, in triviality. In claiming to reveal the richness of everyday language-use, the 'Narodniks of North Oxford' had invented a mode of anti-philosophy that left the world undisturbed, reducing a once-radical form of enquiry to a pastime fit for comfortably situated gentlemen. The book bristles with a kind of displaced class resentment: Gellner hated the social assurance of Oxford philosophy, and he particularly hated its cultivation of indirectness and implicitness. The closing words of the book, parodying Wittgenstein's *Tractatus*, were: 'That which one would insinuate, thereof one must speak.'

The reception of the book shaped Gellner's career in two ways. First, Gilbert Ryle, senior Oxford professor and editor of *Mind*, the leading trade journal, decided the book did not merit a review. Bertrand Russell—whom Gollancz, ever the enterprising publisher, had persuaded to write a sympathetic preface for the book—sent a letter to *The Times* denouncing this as a form of professional censorship. The usual squall in a correspondence-column teacup followed (the episode was given wider currency by Ved Mehta in a *New Yorker* article, later re-published in his *The Fly and the Fly-Bottle*) and Gellner's name was made. At the same time, the book gave offence where offence was due; after its publication, records Hall, Gellner was 'effectively expelled from Britain's philosophical community'.

He was, however, by now launched on the distinctive path of his life's work, becoming (in Hall's words) 'the philosopher of industrialism and the sociologist of philosophy'. His abiding concern hereafter was to try to understand the distinctive character of what he—but not, of course, he alone—termed 'modernity' (of which more later). The first major fruit of this enterprise was his hugely ambitious 1964 book *Thought and Change*, which laid down a theoretical and historical scheme within which much of his later work is contained.

For Gellner, human history fell into two eras, divided by the coming of industrialism. Once the Industrial Revolution had transformed the leading societies of Western Europe—or at least once the benefits of this transformation had become widespread and fully apparent, which did not happen till after 1945—there could be no going back to the stable societies of scarcity alleged to have existed before (and still existing in other parts of the world). 'The crucial premiss is simply that men in general will not tolerate a brief life of poverty, disease, precariousness, hard work, tedium and oppression, when they recognise that at least most of these features can be either obviated or greatly mitigated.' He regarded science as 'the form of cognition of industrial society': it differed from all previous forms of natural philosophy in its ability to transform material reality, and it is the conjunction of industrialism and science that marks what he confidently speaks of as 'the transition' in human history—'the transition from ignorance and superstition to knowledge and control, from poverty and tyranny to wealth and at least the possibility of freedom.' Philosophies which do not take the measure of this change are, as he put it with the over-statement that lay somewhere between deliberate provocation and unnoticed habit, 'worthless'.

Thought and Change is an extraordinarily confident and assertive book, insisting on a single major change in history without giving much evidence of knowing a lot about the history of anywhere in particular. Some years later Gellner co-organized at LSE what was at the time a celebrated seminar on 'Patterns of History', inviting anthropologists, archaeologists, and 'specialists on every period of all major world civilizations'. The level of abstraction of that phrase seems to me to signal the character, and the drawbacks, of Gellner's intellectual ambitions. *C'est magnifique, mais ce n'est pas l'histoire.* Few historians, surely, would think of themselves as 'specialists on a period of one of the major world civilizations'. When polemicizing against the Wittgensteinians or, later, the Geertzians, Gellner often said that human beings were not merely 'concept-fodder'—that is, that there were determinants of action other than language and culture—but perhaps his own intellectual practices tended to treat the more thickly textured work of colleagues in history, literature, and so on as just so much 'theory-fodder'.

It also seems a sign of something awry with Gellner's cultural antennae, as well as an indicator of an obvious affinity, that he could describe C. P. Snow's (thin and tendentious) 'Two Cultures' lecture as 'one of the most important philosophical essays to appear since the war'. He not only shared Snow's enthusiasm for industrialism as the route to improving the human condition, but he endorsed the lecture's intense antipathy to the 'literary intellectuals' (or 'humanists' in Gellner's classification) and its cheer-leading for science. Not, in Gellner's case, any actual science (about which he did not seem especially well informed), but about a certain philosophical and sociological idea of science—a mode of enquiry, a methodological icon. He had first read Popper's *The Open Society and its Enemies* in 1946 and Hall describes it as 'the book which was to influence him more than any other'. It is noticeable that Gellner did not seem to relativize science in the way that Weber had relativized the pervasive process of 'rationality': he treated it, instead, as the 'decisive' intellectual advance in human history. As Perry Anderson put it, 'the material affluence afforded by scientific reason' is his theory's 'epistemological trump card'. As this brief summary suggests, much turned on the nebulous and essentially ahistorical category of 'modernity' and its necessary twin, 'traditional society', categories that risk barring the way to the nuanced understanding of actual historical change in any specific time and place. (My limited sympathy for this enterprise may partly reflect the fact that so much of what is of interest to a literary critic or intellectual historian of recent centuries simply disappears in the undiscriminating capaciousness of the category of 'modernity', figuring only as a series of illustrations of the contrast with the 'pre-modern'.)

Over the next thirty years, Gellner went on to make important contributions to an impressively wide range of topics, notably his studies of Islam, his theories of nationalism, and his critiques of those ideas or intellectual fashions which he saw as attempting, illegitimately, to 're-enchant' the world—thinkers who 'offered more moral warmth and harmony than they can deliver'. Cultivating a form of anthropological detachment and structural-functional explanation, he was a powerful critic of those ideas and movements which he regarded as essentially intellectual fashions, indirectly expressive of certain social needs but fundamentally misleading about the nature of reality. For him, linguistic philosophy, psychoanalysis, ethnomethodology, and post-structuralism all fell into this category. But he was also a notably robust commentator on the appeal and weaknesses of large ideologies, such as Marxism and conservatism. He never succumbed to, for example, the seductions of the form of conservatism promoted by his LSE colleague Michael Oakeshott, observing tartly that 'tradition may be elegance, competence, courage, modesty and realism . . . it is also bullshit, servility, vested interest, arbitrariness, empty ritual'. Gellner didn't do ideological enthusiasm, but he was at the same time scathing about all forms of relativism. 'The argument of his social philosophy as a whole,' Hall summarizes, 'is that we do indeed know certain things. Social science is not an abject failure.'

Running through Gellner's work, and a source of its remarkable fertility, was the constant urge to seek a wider understanding of forms of life than was held by the social agents themselves. This, it might be said, has been the urge informing the very project of the social sciences. For him, the sociological 'explanation' of ideas was bedrock. I hold 'explanation' in the tweezers of quotation marks here simply to signal how curious this familiar enterprise is, or ought to be. Ideas are argued to be 'functional' (more tweezers) for a particular social group, and the identification of that level of correspondence is held to be deeper, more explanatory, than any merely intellectual characterization of those ideas. Actually there was some tension or unsteadiness in Gellner's practice, since he was too interested in ideas to treat them merely as epiphenomenal flotsam in this way, so we get subtle analyses of what are and are not good reasons for thinking one thing rather than another. But he then always reverted to the sociological perspective of trying to explain why some reasons seemed good reasons to a particular group of agents because of features of their social organization and economic practice. In this respect, Gellner was a peculiar kind of fundamentalist: a sociological fundamentalist.

This has been seen by some of his critics as a damaging limitation of his account of nationalism in particular. *Nations and Nationalism*, published in 1983, was his best-selling book, one which was widely translated and which has generated a small industry of critical comment. The general thrust of his argument can be seen as an application of his wider theory. Nationalism is not a timeless feature of human societies, but something that arose as a consequence of the dislocations of 'modernity'. In these circumstances, rule by one's co-culturals comes to seem the only legitimate form of government. Intellectuals and proletarians come together to self-identify as members of a particular historical ethnos, but it is the need of the society for some principle of homogeneity, not the pre-existing cultural traditions, that creates the distinctively modern phenomenon of nationalism. The book is full of arresting insights, drawn, as ever, from wonderfully disparate sources, but Gellner's taste for emphatic assertion has laid him open to charges of rigid functionalism, as, for example, when he writes that nationalism 'springs, inevitably, from the requirements of a modern economy'. Critics such as Anthony Smith (once Gellner's student) have argued that this determinedly modernist account underplays the role both of actual historic continuities and of the emotions that make nationalism more than a set of bureaucratic edicts. Or as Anderson puts it: 'Where Weber was so bewitched by its spell he was never able to theorise nationalism, Gellner has theorised nationalism without detecting the spell.'

This connects to a recurring criticism that Hall permits himself, when he says (he puts it in different ways at different points): 'Gellner's account of the forces operative in the age of nationalism is essentially apolitical.' One of the ways in which Gellner can seem rather unWeberian is in his comparative neglect of, even lack of interest in, political agency. He talks up the role of contingency in abstract terms, but the unpredictable swerves of fortune and play of personality that make politics the embodiment of contingency seem to have left him cold. It may be of a piece with this that I came away from this long biography not knowing anything much about Gellner's own politics in a party sense or how he voted, if he did. Anderson, ruminating on Gellner's uncharacteristically alarmist reaction to labour unrest and oil price rises in the 1970s, speculated: 'One imagines a Conservative vote in 1979,' though he would have seemed a likely Labour supporter before that, especially during the Wilson 'white heat of technology' years. As with some others of his generation, an early anti-communism seems to have mutated into an enthusiasm for 'liberalisation' that could appear to neglect or downplay the systemic injustices inherent in market capitalism.

Of the various lesser controversies in which Gellner participated, the one that has remained greenest in the academic folk-memory is his spat with Edward Said in 1993. Gellner published a highly critical review of the latter's *Culture and Imperialism* in the *TLS*, disputing the role Said ascribed to imperialism in blocking the development of Muslim societies and challenging Said's enveloping condemnation of 'orientalist' prejudices in two centuries of European scholarship on the Arab world. In his reply, Said largely ignored the main challenge, concentrating on what he regarded as the defects of Gellner's own scholarship on Islam, pointedly emphasizing that it was undertaken without knowledge of Arabic or Berber (this was in fact not true: Gellner had become proficient in Berber in the course of his fieldwork). The exchange went through another couple of rounds, marked by the usual increase in animosity and decline in relevant argument. Robert Irwin, in his *For Lust of Knowing: The Orientalists and their Enemies* (2006), concludes that it was 'one of the finest intellectual dogfights of recent decades'. I'm not so sure. Neither protagonist comes out of it all that well, with Gellner becoming increasingly mocking or flippant and Said seeming simply incapable of acknowledging his own mistakes.

Hall remarks of the exceptionally favourable reception of *Conditions of Liberty*, published the year before Gellner's death, that 'it was recognition that he had become a public intellectual'. I wonder. It was certainly recognition that he had become a major figure, one whose work, now much translated and reprinted, stood near the centre of several large issues in the understanding of modern societies. Yet Gellner's direct participation in public debate, beyond academic circles, was patchy and comparatively slight. He stood aloof from contemporary politics, and did not court media exposure. Reversing Noel Coward's dictum, he seems to have regarded television as a medium for watching rather than appearing on. And although he wrote prolifically for more than thirty years, a close examination of his complete bibliography reveals rather little writing clearly directed to a non-academic readership. The nearest he came to doing this with any regularity was as a contributor to the *TLS*. He did a few occasional pieces for the weeklies, plus a scattering of broadsheet reviews, but his preferred genre was the essay or conference paper which, by the standards of conventional professional practice, may have been informal and cross-disciplinary—full of ideas, wit, and provocation, not necessarily overladen with references—but which was obviously directed at other scholars who were willing to engage with the large questions (often theoretical or comparative questions) that exercised him. He was the reverse of the narrow specialist, and he was a living reproach to parochialism, yet he was not, at least not quite, what has come to be understood by the imported American label 'a public intellectual'. His peers were figures such as, say, the anthropologist Jack Goody or the social theorist W. G. Runciman—theorists of great conceptual and empirical range, but not primarily contemporary political and cultural commentators—rather than media-friendly academics such as, say, A. J. Ayer or Hugh Trevor-Roper.

The very enterprise of comparative historical sociology, magnificent though it is in its tireless attempt to find pattern and explanation across societies and millennia, is bound to take a somewhat aerial view, and perhaps that, too, helped distance Gellner from the preoccupations of his local culture. It is also noticeable that although he had fruitful intellectual relations with an exceptionally wide range of scholars in different disciplines, historians figure surprisingly little in this biography, and scholars of art and literature appear scarcely at all. In principle, a compensating level of detail might have been provided by anthropology, by the meticulous ethnography of a particular, often very small, social group, but for Gellner the chief function of such detail was to test hypotheses about social structure, kinship patterns, religious belief and ritual, and other very large, meta-sociological categories. Perhaps for this reason, some of his most attractive writing is to be found in the form of occasional essays and reviews, where the potentially Procrustean demands of theory were often less in play.

This intellectual biography makes Gellner seem attractive and admirable in so many ways that I am slightly puzzled not to find myself more wholly in sympathy with the tenor of his work. In person, he appears to have been wry, witty, irreverent, loyal to friends; professionally, he was unmoved by disciplinary tribalism, bored by administration, endlessly supportive to graduate students; in public matters he was unyieldingly secular, sexually tolerant, instinctively liberal; intellectually he was restless, sceptical, constantly driven to enlarge the circle of understanding; he was the enemy of cant, uplift, and pretentiousness, the critic of the simplifications of 'identity', the champion of the duties of intelligence; and in addition he was a stylish, amusing, and productive writer. What's not to like? Not a lot, actually: there is genuinely much to admire. Yet somewhere in the mix there were elements that make one pause—a streak of, if not exactly philistinism, then aesthetic mulishness; a marked intellectual impatience; a too quickly dismissive attitude towards radical social criticism; and, underlying everything else, that slightly relentless sociological reductivism. Methodologically, Gellner could seem like a curious mixture of Karl Popper and E. Evans-Pritchard; in substantive historical content, he at times appeared to be an unholy combination of Karl Polanyi and C. P. Snow. The datedness of those names says something about his trajectory as well as about his affinities with a style of brisk Austro-English positivism in social science.

And yet that description is itself too brisk, and in particular it underplays his stylishness and fleetness of foot. Perry Anderson, in the essay quoted earlier, speaks of Gellner's 'insouciantly reconnoitred forays . . . travelling light over the most variegated terrain to unexpected theoretical effect'. That manner could, sometimes, be very winning (just as it could, at others, be merely irritating), and the variousness of the terrain is, without question, hugely impressive. But there was something about that imperious 'theoretical' intent, something about the way in which empirical detail was subjugated to conceptual forcefulness, that has evidently left other readers besides myself uneasy. I admire, as Hall clearly does, the intellectual honesty with which Gellner confronted his life and his world, but I wonder whether he did not at times succumb to the pathos of austerity, to the note of self-congratulation that can haunt the insistence on being unillusioned. Perhaps an element of existential drama, like the risk of explanatory high-handedness, comes with the territory if one aspires to be a comparative historical sociologist, the analyst of a disenchanted world. The vignette about watching television with his student may suggest an attractive lack of self-importance, but the student's playful allusion to Weber may also suggest that Gellner did not lack a sense of the elevated company he was trying to keep during working hours.

10

Historian-intellectuals?

Eileen Power, Herbert Butterfield, Hugh Trevor-Roper

I

The category of 'the intellectual'—or, as it has increasingly become, under the influence of American usage, 'the public intellectual'—is a peculiarly vexed and treacherous one. I have tried to pick my way carefully through this semantic minefield on other occasions, principally in *Absent Minds: Intellectuals in Britain* (2006), so I shall not labour the terminological complexities here. Suffice it to say that for the purposes of historical analysis it is more fruitful not to think of the term 'intellectual' as referring to a type of individual or to a given socio-economic role. It is better understood, rather, as the description of a relation—a relation between several variables: an individual's intellectual achievement or standing; a desire and a capacity to address a non-specialist audience; the acquisition of reputation and the means of access to such audiences; and the expression of views which bear on some feature of the general life of those audiences. It is, therefore, a relation into which, historically, various figures have entered to greater or less extents, with greater or less success. It is, necessarily, a matter of degree, not a binary matter of either being or not being an intellectual.

Quite properly, the label is always likely to provoke a sceptical response: on the basis of what relevant qualification or expertise do those who fill the role of public intellectuals tell their fellow-citizens what to think? The tensions involved in this feature of the role go back to the earliest days of the modern usage of 'intellectual' as a noun, as in the celebrated gibe of the French man-of-letters Ferdinand Brunetière against the professors who championed Dreyfus's

Section II of this essay, previously unpublished, was written in 2015 to mark the 75th anniversary of Eileen Power's death.

Michael Bentley, *The Life and Thought of Herbert Butterfield: History, Science and God* (Cambridge University Press, 2011).

Adam Sisman, *Hugh Trevor-Roper: The Biography* (Weidenfeld and Nicolson, 2010).

innocence (the moment when the term gained currency in French): 'I do not see what claim to govern his fellow men a professor of Tibetan has.' And even if we do not begin from a position of such reductive sarcasm, there is always the teasing question of the connection, or lack of it, between the *content* of the primary scholarly or scientific activity and the kinds of topics about which the intellectual holds forth to non-specialist publics. Most straightforward may seem to be those cases where the intellectual is drawing on a relevant body of learning or reasoning about which they are an acknowledged authority and whose implications for present public concerns they are good at spelling out. But, more frequently, those who become established in the public eye usually end up holding forth on topics far removed from their particular area of scholarly or creative expertise. It requires some ingenuity to demonstrate that, say, Noam Chomsky's criticisms of American foreign policy follow from the propositions of transformational linguistics.

When historians step into this role, they may seem to possess both an immediate advantage over their colleagues from other disciplines and an immediate disqualification. The advantage is that they deal with the great questions of society, politics, and culture and write about them for the most part in a non-technical vocabulary, deploying familiar assumptions about motivation and causality. The disqualification is that what they know about must, by definition, be out of date. With historians, too, we can distinguish between those who contribute to wider debate in the role of expert—the historian of the Middle East, for example, asked to comment on the background to current events in the region—and those who, by whatever means, have built up a certain kind of cultural standing which goes beyond the relevance of their specialism and which is taken to license them to talk about all manner of other issues. One of the difficulties here is that some of the strengths of the best historians—judgement about the comparative weight to be given to interacting causes, a sense of the complexity of motive and the ironies of unintended consequences, a constant alertness to the power of anachronism—translate rather poorly into the rough-and-tumble of the controversialist's trade. In fact, to make a really successful name as a public intellectual, it may help if the historian is not too inhibited by the scepticism and the scruples which contributed to their building up a distinguished professional reputation in the first place.

One revealing and little-explored way to understand the mechanisms by which this relation is entered into in the most successful way—or, in other words, of understanding how individuals become prominent intellectuals—is to consider the careers of those who, despite appearing to have many of the requisite qualities and opportunities, did not in fact consistently exercise their cultural authority with a general public in any markedly successful or extended way. Obviously, there will at any given moment be large numbers of scholars, writers, and so on who show no great inclination or aptitude for playing this role in the first place, including many of those who have made the most original or lasting contribution to particular fields. My interest here is, rather, in those who did possess some of the inclination and capacity, but whose relatively limited performance in the role of intellectual may help us to identify distinctive features of the requirements and constraints in a given setting. More particularly, I focus on three historians, all significant figures in the profession who also reached out to various kinds of non-specialist public. In each case, I suspect my discussion may offend their most ardent admirers precisely because I am exploring the limited degree to which they occupied the role of intellectual as I have identified it, and since that label is sometimes regarded as an honorific or term of praise I may be felt to be diminishing their standing by trying to account for their only partial success in this role. But in my own view acting as an intellectual is certainly not obligatory for writers and scholars; indeed, some of those who have achieved the widest celebrity as intellectuals may seem to have done so by betraying or abandoning the standards and qualities that are most to be admired in those who attempt to live the life of the mind. So I see the less clear-cut ways in which these three figures partially or occasionally occupied that role as no dishonour whatever. Rather, my interest is in pinning down the distinctiveness of each career and exploring the relation between different kinds of achievement.

For convenience, we can start with a simple, even simple-minded, little grid of types of historian before going on to see where we might place my chosen figures. We might begin with a rough-and-ready distinction between academic and non-academic historians, and then for each group distinguish between those who do engage with wider public issues and those who on the whole do not. And then, moving down the imaginary flow-chart, we might distinguish, among those who do engage, between historians who do so as experts on a specific region or question and those who do so as broader public commentators. After all, reaching a wide readership does not in itself amount to playing the role of the public intellectual. Lively, colourful writing about the past may attract a wide readership, without thereby participating in public debate on broader issues. So, we might say, thinking of those who were roughly contemporary with some of the figures discussed here, that C. V. Wedgwood could be an example of the non-academic who reached a wide audience but did not engage directly with public issues, and Arthur Bryant an example of one who did, or attempted to do, both those things.

Obviously, we could take any number of people as examples of the category of academic historians who do *not* so engage, but it is not difficult to think of figures from the first two-thirds of the twentieth century who achieved, in some form, both professional standing and a public voice. We might begin, for instance, with one of the historians whose name has been best known to a wider readership, G. M. Trevelyan. Trevelyan would, of course, have barked at the label itself as suggestive of Stracheyesque degeneracy, yet he constantly insisted on the need for historians to address an extended non-specialist public and he did not hesitate to draw liberal conclusions from his early writing about

Italian patriots and conservative ones from his later writings about English social history. Or we might think of R. H. Tawney and his way of making the past, especially the Tudor and Stuart past, a resource for the moral criticism of the greed and inequality of the present (as briefly discussed in Chapter 8). Or, on a much grander scale, Arnold J. Toynbee (nephew of the historical economist also discussed in that chapter), who gave generations of non-specialist readers a framework within which to think about the rise and fall of civilizations, including their own. Toynbee's name raises the question of how far this role can be successfully sustained if the historian in question does not continue to command respect among professional peers. The normal expectation is that there will be some detailed work of high quality which underwrites and licenses the reaching-out to wider topics. The limiting case here occurs when *both* the scholarship comes to seem too doubtful and too thinly spread, *and* the opinions come to seem too idiosyncratic and merely personal, so that the figure in question ends up commanding the respect of neither the professional nor the non-specialist audiences. Some sobering reflections of this kind can be derived from contemplating the later career of A. L. Rowse.

Among those who managed, at least for a time, to sustain both scholarly and public standing, the names of A. J. P. Taylor, Hugh Trevor-Roper, and J. H. Plumb come immediately to mind, obvious rivals as mainstays of the broadsheet review pages. Or, slightly older, Herbert Butterfield, who, as we shall see, somehow managed to make his gnomic thoughts about the workings of Providence the basis for a public role interpreting international relations, though he shied away from the vulgarer seductions of media celebrity. Or, in a different vein, we might think of Eric Hobsbawm, like Plumb something of a late starter, but one whose work was strikingly more European and more ideological (and, one is tempted to add, exhibited more staying-power). And we might even move forwards to a slightly younger figure such as E. P. Thompson who encouraged readers to draw rather different political conclusions from the history of the poor in the eighteenth and early nineteenth centuries from those drawn by a long line of historians from Trevelyan onwards. Clearly, the sub-divisions, and the possible illustrations, are almost endless, but this brisk retrospect may be enough to enable us to ask where we should situate the intriguingly different but not wholly incomparable figures of Eileen Power, Herbert Butterfield, and Hugh Trevor-Roper.

II

I can easily imagine, had I been born at the right time, falling in love with Eileen Power. Several men did, it seems, and that is not at all surprising. Clever, talented, warm, good-looking, gregarious—all the surviving descriptions concur in emphasizing her compelling attractiveness. These qualities have also helped to turn her into one of the heroines of twentieth-century academic culture, partly as one who excelled in some of the most technical and demanding forms of scholarship while also reaching out to wider readerships on a range of issues, partly as a woman who was professionally and intellectually successful in what was still a very male-dominated world. In addition, she did the one thing most likely to turn her into an icon, more venerated than scrutinized: she died young, at the age of 51, with the result that she could be seen simultaneously as an impressive, even precocious, over-achiever and a talent tragically cut off before its full flowering. All this tends to intensify posterity's admiration for what she did achieve while allowing us to play the game of imagining what she might have done.

For a half-century or so after her death in 1940 historians paid tribute to her memory, occasionally in a rather star-struck way, but the biographical accounts of her were few and somewhat scrappy, mostly based on acquaintance rather than research. But then in 1996 the economic historian Maxine Berg published the first full-length study, *A Woman in History: Eileen Power, 1889–1940*, a book rightly lauded for its careful scholarship and its imaginative sympathy. I am certainly indebted to this excellent biography, but in what follows I want to use some of the evidence it makes available to question one of the claims it advances on behalf of its subject—the claim that Power became one of Britain's leading intellectuals. Berg puts the case for this wider role in emphatic terms: 'Eileen Power's fame and significance reached far beyond the academic enclosure. She also participated actively in the life of literary London: she reviewed frequently in the weeklies, and was a popular lecturer and pioneer radio broadcaster. She combined her work as a historian with journalism and lecturing on contemporary politics from a progressive liberal and socialist stance.' There is much truth to this, but while the description accurately captures some of what makes Power seem so interesting in retrospect, it risks overstating her public impact at the time. Power was, without question, an outstanding historian and an impressive person, but only to a very modest extent, I would argue, was she one of Britain's leading intellectuals. Why was this?

Born in 1889, the daughter of a Manchester stockbroker, Power read history at Girton between 1907 and 1910, followed by periods of study in Paris and at the LSE, working on the history of the Middle Ages. She returned to teach history at Girton throughout the years of the First World War, chafing at the restricted society of the place and the limited opportunities for women scholars. Something of a turning-point in her life came with the award of a Kahn travelling fellowship in 1920, which enabled her to spend a year travelling round the world, fostering her already growing internationalism and feeding her comparative interest in non-European societies, China above all. She had begun to cultivate a wide acquaintance in the previous decade, especially among progressive and feminist circles, and her travelling built upon and enabled her to extend this range of contacts. For example, she and

Dora Black had briefly overlapped as Fellows of Girton, and she now met Dora and her new husband, Bertrand Russell, in Peking and spent some time travelling with them. On her return to England in 1921 she took up the post of Lecturer in Economic History at the LSE and moved to London. This geographical move was an important fact in itself for the development of her career. The 32-year-old Power, by this point a magnetic and sociable woman, set up house in Mecklenburgh Square in the heart of intellectual Bloomsbury, where she held parties and receptions at which figures from various walks of public life gathered. She became the founding secretary of the Economic History Society in 1926, and thereafter devoted much time and energy to this professional body and its allied journal, the *Economic History Review*. In 1931 she was appointed to the Chair of Economic History at the LSE, a position she retained till her death from a sudden heart attack nine years later.

When, at the age of 31, she set off to travel around the world, Eileen Power had made no mark with any public beyond the readers of specialized articles in medieval history. She endorsed a range of progressive causes without taking a leading part in their enterprises: she supported women's suffrage and the League of Nations, and she lectured for the WEA. A couple of articles on women in the Middle Ages for the *Cambridge Magazine* were the extent of her non-professional publishing at this date. In the course of the 1920s she began to reach wider audiences, though still largely by popularizing her work on medieval women, especially in the form of public lectures for various non-academic groups. She also undertook what her biographer calls 'extensive reviewing on medieval and other historical topics for the *Nation and Athenaeum*, the *Times Literary Supplement* and the *Spectator*. This lecturing and reviewing in the weeklies helped to establish women's history as a new and popular subject.' It is not clear quite how 'extensive' this reviewing was—available bibliographies only list selected items—and the reference to its effect in helping to establish a new 'subject' still suggests a primarily academic frame of reference. Moreover, at this date writing for the *TLS* only extended one's standing among the limited circles of the cognoscenti, since the reviews were published anonymously. There is no doubt that Power was committed to trying to reach a more than professional audience, and in her reviews she urged her fellow-historians to write in ways that would be accessible and attractive to the general reader rather than simply 'to throw a card index in the public's face', something she thought 'American professors' were particularly guilty of. Her first substantial monograph, *Medieval English Nunneries c.1275 to 1535*, was a long and heavily documented work of research, published by Cambridge University Press, and clearly addressed primarily to other scholars. But her next (and always her best-known) book was *Medieval People*, published by Methuen in 1924, which attempted to recreate in an imaginative and self-consciously literary way the world of representative 'ordinary people' in the Middle Ages and which was addressed, as she made clear in the preface, to 'the general reader'. There is no question but that Power triumphantly succeeded in making medieval history accessible to a broader readership than one confined to her fellow-professionals.

But any case for Power as a public intellectual figure obviously needs to go beyond this. According to Berg, 'Power's social history was her response to the First World War. Social history was an intervention in internationalist politics.' Although this may be true as far as the association of these activities in Power's own mind was concerned, it is less clear that a general audience at the time recognized her social history as any kind of 'intervention' in politics. Power insisted, in both her writing and teaching, that history should be approached comparatively and sociologically, and to this extent she was committed to seeing history encourage an internationalist perspective which went well beyond the traditional emphasis on high politics and wars. Considering her role as an intellectual, the question would be how far she managed to bring this commitment to bear on issues of topical concern to a broader public, and here more, and different, evidence is required.

From this point of view, two things need to be said about several of the sources used to substantiate the case for the close interweaving of political and scholarly purpose in Power's work between the wars. The first is that much of this material is in the form of drafts or of notes for lectures, material that remained unpublished in Power's lifetime. The second is that the main genre through which Power voiced her larger concerns seems to have been the public lecture, and this raises an interesting question about the historically varying role of different media. In the inter-war period public lectures retained considerable importance in what was still in practice a pre-television world (in the early twenty-first century public lectures on the whole only attain this level of importance when they are reported in another medium, such as the press or TV). The lecture is also a particularly clear instance of the dialectic at the root of the building of cultural authority: as a figure starts to earn a reputation, they become more likely to attract invitations to take part in activities which carry some cachet, which participation in turn boosts the reputation, and so on. But, against this, it has to be recognized that the lecture, unless otherwise reported, only reaches the audience actually present on that occasion, and very often a lecture audience reflects a high level of self-selection. By comparison to, for example, publishing in the general daily or periodical press, there is a far greater tendency for lectures organized by political or campaigning bodies to consist essentially of preaching to the converted. Power did acquire a reputation in the inter-war years that went beyond the confines of the professional study of medieval history, but it was a reputation limited in both extent and kind.

The same could be said of another area in which Power made some impact—the teaching of history in schools, as in her editing of the New

World History series. She joined an international committee which was attempting to steer school text-books away from purely national themes. The problem of the negligible public impact of unpublished material comes up again here: her 'An introduction to world history' was intended to be a rival to H. G. Wells's *Outline of History* but, for reasons which are not clear, it remained unpublished at her death. (In terms of public impact, there is also the question of her lack of direct engagement with recent and contemporary history; her 'Introduction to world history' stopped at the end of the eighteenth century.) With her sister Rhoda, Power wrote a series of children's history books, and she particularly excelled in the exploitation of a new medium in the BBC's broadcasts for schools, helping to devise and deliver major series on history through the mid-1930s until several differences of opinion with the BBC producers ended her participation (characteristically, she refused to collaborate on any series confined purely to British history). The broadcasting was, in its own terms, important work, but it was not the route to significant national impact, and there was always the danger that addressing children might be undervalued as work peculiarly appropriate to women. Perhaps if she had lived on into the Golden Age of radio as a medium for intellectuals, the 1940s and 1950s, she might have extended her reputation through imaginative and topical talks.

As part of her commitment to internationalism, Power lectured for the League of Nations Union. She also drew up a suggested course of reading (published under the auspices of the Women's International League for Peace and Freedom) for the school-teacher who wished the teaching of history to foster a sense of world-citizenship, and she argued that social history brought out the similarities and links between societies more than the emphasis on political or military history did. She continued to support the League of Nations through the 1930s and, unlike many of her pacifist-inclined friends, she opposed appeasement in 1938. Here again, Berg rightly finds Power's historical and political concerns coming together, the principal source being an interesting lecture on the parallels between the threats to civilization in contemporary Europe and those which finally brought an end to the civilization of the ancient world. But, once again, there is the problem that this lecture was delivered to the limited forum of the Cambridge History Club in 1938, and that it remained unpublished (a shortened version of it, entitled 'The precursors', was eventually included by her husband, Michael Postan, in the 10th edition of *Medieval People*, twenty-three years after Power's death). Writing half a century later, a biographer quite properly finds this an illuminating source for understanding the delicate interplay of scholarly and political impulses that informed Power's work; it provides no evidence that any kind of genuine 'public' at the time took her to be making a significant comment on the implications of Munich.

The character of Power's career can be brought out by comparing it with that of some of her close friends and colleagues. Two immediately obvious comparisons are with historians discussed in Chapter 8: R. H. Tawney and the Hammonds. Tawney became one of her most intimate associates at LSE, with whom she worked closely on various projects in economic and social history. But three very obvious contrasts can be made immediately. First, nothing in Power's career remotely resembled Tawney's long-standing role in the Labour Party and his active participation in various trade union and working-class organizations. To take merely one detail: Tawney had a large hand in drafting the Labour manifesto for the 1929 election; it would have been unimaginable for Power to have been asked to do anything comparable in that domain. Secondly, in addition to being a leading social and economic historian, Tawney was a notable social critic and political theorist. Books such as *The Acquisitive Society* and *Equality* engaged in a level of analysis of *contemporary* society which Power never essayed. Thirdly, Tawney did a large amount of journalism, reaching a variety of general publics through daily and weekly papers as well as more specific (but still wholly non-academic) publications. Again to illustrate with just one detail: Tawney wrote no fewer than 117 articles on the subject of education alone in the inter-war years (the period when his and Power's careers may legitimately be compared), as well as dozens of other articles sub-divided in his bibliography under such headings as 'industry', 'religion', and 'general political articles'. Tawney was a commentator on contemporary affairs in a way Power never was.

An illuminating contrast of a different kind is provided by the Hammonds, of whom Power also became a close friend. As historians, the Hammonds never held any academic position and their impact on the practice of social history by a subsequent generation of professional historians may well have been less than Power's. But the Hammonds' work enjoyed much greater public standing, partly because their history was widely seen to engage with contemporary debates. Several of their books were frequently reprinted during their lifetime, and their bearing on, for example, the land question in the years immediately before 1914 or on social policy at the end of the war were explicit and acknowledged as such by their reviewers. Moreover, it has to be remembered, as emphasized in Chapter 8, that Lawrence Hammond was a prolific political journalist, a full-time editor and leader writer for substantial stretches of his life, and never less than a frequent contributor during those other periods when he was concentrating on his books. Indeed, he was, as we have seen, at various points invited to become the editor of leading papers like *The Nation* or *The Manchester Guardian*; this alone indicates a quite different kind of career from that represented by Power's occasional contribution to the weeklies. Noting the explicit political message of the Hammonds' books, Berg remarks: 'Eileen Power, too, believed in using her position as a historian to attack militarism and nationalism. But she sought to do so through encouraging comparative and social history.' This may, once again, be an accurate description of Power's own sense of purpose, and it may also be a justifiable characterization of the spirit informing some of her surviving work. But in considering her performance in the role of intellectual one has also to ask how far this connection was evident to a wide contemporary readership, and how far it brought her further opportunities to deploy her scholarly authority in preaching her anti-militarist and anti-nationalist views. The evidence suggests that it was not very far on either count.

Two further comparisons which may be briefly touched upon are with two other historians mentioned earlier: Arnold J. Toynbee and G. M. Trevelyan. Power and Toynbee were exact contemporaries who knew each other well, moving in the same liberal intellectual social circles, and they shared an interest in large-scale cross-cultural comparisons. As the volumes of Toynbee's grandiose *A Study of History* started to come out in the 1930s, he briefly commanded a wide reputation as a 'sage' capable of discerning the meaning of history. Power's ventures into comparative history were far more circumspect and rigorous, and never impinged on the consciousness of the kind of 'Book-of-the-Month-Club' readership which Toynbee reached; conversely, she never forfeited the respect of the leading historians of the time in the way Toynbee did with his increasingly mythopoeic reading of the history of civilizations. Trevelyan was another contemporary historian (in this case a decade older) who enjoyed a far greater level of popular success than Power ever did, though he managed to combine this with the distinctive form of professional recognition represented by the Regius Chair at Cambridge and the Mastership of Trinity. Trevelyan was in several respects a much more conservative, indeed deliberately old-fashioned, historian than Power. For one thing, he chose to write in the colourful narrative vein of the nineteenth-century literary historians, with none of Power's explicit borrowing of the concepts and methods of the social sciences. For another, Trevelyan wrote overwhelmingly about *English* history, whereas Power always repudiated any such narrowly national concentration (it was, as Berg points out, ironic that Trevelyan should have dedicated his hugely successful *English Social History* to Power's memory since social history as she conceived it was irreducibly hostile to taking such politically defined units as the focus of one's history). But Trevelyan's example raises an interesting question about the advantage enjoyed, as far as gaining a wide readership is concerned, by the historian who writes the history of his or her native country, especially one who writes, as Trevelyan did, in a largely celebratory tone. The larger public and political bearing of his work was for the most part only oblique; it was at its most pointed, perhaps, in its laments for the passing of a pre-industrial England. But in this way Trevelyan was a contributor to the 'condition of England' question, and, as I argued earlier, that subject ensured that an intellectual in Britain was able to command a kind of public attention which few other topics could guarantee.

The contrasts I am drawing here are, as ever, matters of degree not of kind. For example, the very fact of holding a chair at a time when professors were few and were still accorded considerable social respect meant that Power had a form of cultural authority to deploy not available to non-academics, not even perhaps to otherwise distinguished figures such as the Hammonds. When, for example, in 1934 William Beveridge, as Director of the LSE, was threatening to gather public support for sanctions against Harold Laski, Professor of Political Science at the school, on the grounds of his 'objectionable' political views, Power joined with four other LSE professors (Tawney, Charles Webster, Theodore Gregory, and Robert Chorley) in writing a letter to *The Times* to protest against this threat to academic freedom. In such a case, her office and her professional standing endowed the expression of this view with a relevant kind of authority. There is also the intractable question of how far any given individual may 'overspend' his or her 'cultural capital' (the limitations of this particular, and particularly fashionable, metaphor are soon reached). Laski himself was probably the best-known political intellectual in Britain in the inter-war period, enjoying a degree of public exposure that has, arguably, been unmatched by any subsequent figure. But he was an acknowledged and, at times, extreme partisan as well as a fluent rhetorician with an uncontrollable tendency to exaggerate and misrepresent. Power enjoyed nothing like the 'visibility' of her LSE colleague and friend, but it is a moot point whether she did not thereby accumulate a reputation for impartial and serious scholarship which she could, had she chosen, have deployed on issues on which Laski could not have commanded comparable credibility.

'Had she chosen'—the phrase suggests that it was essentially a question of inclination and temperament, and that Power preferred to devote the greater share of her energies to her scholarly and professional pursuits, or, in other words, that she had no great desire to play the part of the intellectual in the sense in which I am using the term here. Her biography suggests that there is some truth to this, but it perhaps leaves other possibilities unexplored. One is that, although she was clearly a gifted expositor, able to bring history alive with deft, imaginative touches, she may have had no exceptional gifts as a social critic or moralist, still less as a political commentator. Another possibility is that the largely male-dominated world of journalism, politics, committees, and campaigns simply did not take women seriously as potential contributors to this kind of public activity. This could, in principle, be compatible with the undoubted fact that Power was socially far better connected to the leading spirits in these worlds than many of her male counterparts. The position of women in the Middle Ages was one of Power's areas of scholarly concern, and this may have brought with it some risk of being undervalued by a male world confident of knowing what 'counted', though the greater part of her later work was devoted to impeccably orthodox topics such as the history of trade. Nor were her public interests by any means confined to matters too easily classified as 'women's issues'; her engagement with the traditionally 'masculine' topics of nationalism and international relations were sufficient proof of that. Perhaps she made more frequent and diverse kinds of public contribution than I am allowing; perhaps on many occasions she declined invitations to write something or participate in other ways; or perhaps she never seemed quite the right contributor on a given public issue in the first place. The process by which particular names come to mind when editors want to commission contributions and organizers need to find speakers will necessarily remain one of the great dark areas of intellectual history.

Berg's biography of Power protests against what is described as the slighting or undervaluing of Power's scholarly achievements after her death, and the failure of the historical profession to accord her the kind of standing it has given to, for example, Marc Bloch, who preached and to some extent practised a similarly comparative and structural kind of medieval social history. The issue is complicated, and the specific comparison may raise too many other questions to be entirely helpful, but one might certainly agree that the kind of inclusive, comparative social and economic history promoted by Power was not the predominant form of economic history in Britain in the decades after 1945. Nonetheless, looking at the question from another angle, one might equally conclude that her posthumous reputation seems *greater* than appears to be justified by her far from abundant legacy of published work. Berg regrets that so many of the obituaries and later tributes emphasized her personal qualities (her beauty, love of parties and travel, etc.), yet in some ways it seems to have been these qualities that helped establish a greater reputation than she would have had on the basis of her scholarship alone. Both in reminiscences and in later portraits, there is something of the fondness that is also found in accounts of a greater historian, F. W. Maitland—who also appears to have been personally lovable, who also died early, who was also a stylish writer, but who was also primarily a historian's historian, and who was also (for this is surely true of Power) the kind of hero the profession likes to have. It may indeed be true both that the type of work Power promoted fell from fashion for some years after 1945 and that the position of women in economic history declined during that time, but these later developments obviously did not affect Power's standing during her lifetime, nor do they appear to have diminished her reputation in the long term.

One can clearly overdo 'explanations' of Power's limited impact, not least because hers was a more successful career than most. It is also all too easy to think of individuals who shared her putative disadvantages but who nonetheless made a greater mark (Orwell was even younger when he died, Virginia Woolf was a woman who shared many of Power's 'advanced' causes, Laski had to encounter a quite different kind of prejudice as a Jew, and so on). But this is to be led along an ultimately fruitless path or to descend into a style of analysis which is, at best, post-prandial. Power, after all, only partly courted the public role of intellectual and it is not therefore very surprising that she only partly filled that role. She did not, a generalized feminism and anti-militarism apart, engage in direct and critical ways with contemporary society; she did not appear to have a distinctive message about life in the way that figures such as Wells or Russell were perceived, rightly or wrongly, to have. And the fact is that if we subtract two categories of her work addressed to specific, if very different audiences—her professional writing in medieval economic history and her history-writing for children—it becomes clear that she did not actually publish that much. She left a lot of unpublished work, and she was quite active in several organizations, some of them purely scholarly, some with a wider remit, but in both cases this was for the most part that kind of unseen work that does not contribute to the building of a wider public reputation. Power was, as I have emphasized, a distinguished historian who enjoyed considerable professional and personal success: there is no dishonour in having been in addition only an occasional and rather minor public intellectual.

III

For someone who failed to bring so many announced projects to publication, Herbert Butterfield has received a generous amount of critical attention. It no doubt helped that as (eventually) Regius Professor of Modern History and Master of Peterhouse, Cambridge, he exerted significant influence over institutions that occupied a prominent place in the intellectual life of mid-twentieth-century Britain. It mattered, too, that he published several shorter or occasional works that either made a mark at the time (for example, his set of lectures on *Christianity and History*, which appeared in 1949) or have retained a place in that small library of works on historiography and historical method to which later generations still make reference (above all, his brisk polemic on *The Whig Interpretation of History*, first published in 1931). But although when he died in 1979, the same age as the century, the bibliography of his writings ran to several pages, it contained relatively few examples of the kind of original, substantive, detailed work that usually wins historians their enduring reputations. No doubt most careers contain more promise than achievement, and a sense of having outlived one's moment may be an uncomfortably common experience, but Butterfield's reputation was already registering a sharp decline by the time of his death, a trajectory which the ensuing couple of decades did nothing to arrest. The treatment of him in Noel Annan's *Our Age* (1990) was representative: 'A Methodist with a twinkling eye, a fascinator whose chief pastime was academic intrigue, Butterfield scorned every orthodoxy.' The hint that that twinkling eye may have led him into conduct incompatible with orthodox morality, let alone the strictest tenets of Methodism, may have encouraged gossip; it did nothing to dispel the accusation that he had been devious and hypocritical on more than one front, including national just as much as university politics. 'By 1943 he was advocating a separate peace with Germany,' Annan claimed, 'and saw nothing odd when visiting Dublin . . . in going to parties at the German Consulate.'

Recent years, however, have seen the appearance of several studies that take Butterfield much more seriously. The most substantial, by some distance, was C. T. McIntire's *Herbert Butterfield: Historian as Dissenter* which appeared in 2004, shortly followed by Keith Sewell's briefer, more analytical account, *Herbert Butterfield and the Interpretation of History*; there has also been a small flurry of articles (I discuss McIntire's work in ch. 11 of *Common Reading*). McIntire's book had been long in the making, drawing upon interviews he had conducted with its subject: it followed a chronological course through Butterfield's life, though it was more an exposition of his writings than a traditional biography. Still, one could have been forgiven for thinking that, with these studies in place, there really wasn't much left to say, and certainly not enough to justify a full-length biography in the near future. Michael Bentley's rich and stylish book triumphantly shows just how wrong such an assumption would be.

As someone who has already written well-regarded works on historiography and on British political history of the past two centuries, Bentley is particularly well placed to take the measure of Butterfield. As someone responsive to the claims of Christianity and drawn to the abrasive form of anti-liberalism associated with Maurice Cowling (who was himself initially something of a protégé of Butterfield at Peterhouse), Bentley is also disposed to be sympathetic to his subject's sensibility. But, even so, not all good historians have it in them to become good biographers (successful translation in the reverse direction may be still rarer). Bentley, however, displays exemplary patience, tact, and imagination in reconstructing his subject's personality and thinking, as much from scrappy and inconclusive jottings as from conventional records such as letters and diaries. His chief resource has been the very extensive collection of unpublished material held in the Cambridge University Library, a source which no other scholar has mined in anything like this detail. Bentley's heroic labours here give us many engaging glimpses of the nearly lifelong dialogue Butterfield conducted with himself on paper. This material has been supplemented by a lesser collection of more personal papers entrusted to him by the Butterfield family. But, beyond all this, Bentley has discovered the biographer's Eldorado: a large and revealing cache of letters to the woman with whom, hitherto unknown to history, Butterfield had a passionate affair in the mid-1930s.

Butterfield had been married for five years (following a long engagement) when in 1934 he met Joy Marc, a single, university-educated school-teacher five years his junior. 'Joy Marc was the love of Herbert Butterfield's life and he of hers.' Bentley confidently announces this on the basis of his reading of Butterfield's many letters to her over the next five years (he destroyed all her letters to him): it may be some time before anyone can be in a position to take a different view, because although Bentley has been allowed to quote from them, they are not to be made available to other scholars. Apart from the intrinsic human interest of the story they have to tell, these letters are invaluable for anyone interested in reconstructing the movement of Butterfield's mind in the mid- and late 1930s, since he wrote freely to Joy about history, politics, and religion as well as about love and sex. (Among the topics that Butterfield viewed with new eyes as a result of this relationship were the constrained lives of women in the narrow village world in which he had grown up: 'Spinsterly, thwarted views on Sex make people sadistic and catty in social life and cruel to their children.') At about this time he abandoned the practice of regular Methodist preaching which he had sustained for his first fifteen or so years in Cambridge; it now seems that discontent with the unrealism of the churches' teaching about sex may have been an element in his decision.

Bentley handles the evidence with much sensitivity and sympathy, though some may find him, on this as on other matters, insufficiently critical of Butterfield. It risks a slightly false note to announce that he has 'suppressed any sexually explicit material in this account, both on grounds of taste and in consideration of the feelings of Joy Marc's family', especially since the evident sexual happiness she and Butterfield brought each other seems not the least of the reasons for thinking that Joy comes out of the story with some credit. Bentley does later allow himself to report of a clandestine visit to Vienna that 'they made love on an epic scale', though he cites no evidence for the computation. Several of their assignations appear to have been enabled by Butterfield's duties as an external examiner, leading his biographer to pen such rare phrases as 'Oxford examining again proved unusually exciting for the external examiner' ('this time in a pub at Goring, which both he and Joy would always remember'—though 'We'll always have Goring' doesn't quite match up to *Casablanca* standards). Dwelling on the relationship with Joy may seem to give disproportionate attention to one episode in Butterfield's life (it had petered out into unhappiness by the outbreak of war), but it deserves its prominence. Not only is it Bentley's one indisputable *coup de biographie*; by drawing on so many letters written when Butterfield seemed most alive and responsive to the world, he is also able to exhibit a more expressive and appealing version of a figure who, in his defensively layered public persona, tended to appear chilly as well as opaque.

This biography amplifies our understanding of Butterfield's early years without radically altering the well-established account of the poor boy from a small Yorkshire village who won a scholarship to Cambridge. It is interesting to learn that the young Butterfield wanted to read English, but since Cambridge colleges did not offer scholarships in the newly established subject he had to settle for History: 'it seemed to offer the only opportunity of becoming a writer,' he reflected many years later, not necessarily a reliable retrospect, but a plausible indication of an only partly realized aspiration. As he wrote in his commonplace book when a young don in the mid-1920s: 'I would like to do a creative thing, to throw out as a challenge to the sky—to put my footprint on the world and to justify my life before the high gods.' Translating this soaring ambition into the form of a deeply researched, archive-based piece of political or diplomatic history of the kind that earned approval from professional historians at that time was no easy task. Butterfield experimented with several historical genres over the next half-century without, perhaps, ever quite realizing his ambition or winning unqualified professional admiration.

While Bentley will rightly win many plaudits for his reconstruction of the hesitations, tensions, and contradictions within Butterfield's thinking, his estimation of the cogency and significance of his subject's published work is likely to encounter more resistance. There is a sense in which he makes Butterfield more interesting than Butterfield himself always managed to do—no mean feat—but that cannot retrospectively improve Butterfield's standing during his lifetime and it also cannot altogether dispel the doubts and objections that many readers of the published work will continue to register.

Part of the challenge in trying to assess Butterfield's achievement is deciding quite what weight to allow to the many projected but unfinished books. Perhaps the major project which Butterfield publicly committed himself to but never finished (and possibly never made any great progress with) was a life of Charles James Fox, and this, as Bentley shows, was part of a wider failure ever to get his deeply learned thoughts about eighteenth-century English politics into satisfactory form. Form was in some ways the central issue. He could not be content with a conventional 'Life': 'I still feel the awful futility of mere political biography.' But nor did his attempts at more analytical political narrative ever quite come off. After conceding the unsatisfactory character of Butterfield's 1949 book, *George III, Lord North, and the People, 1779–1780*, Bentley comments: 'he would never write substantive historical analysis again.' There are numerous essays and lectures, but it's an oddly patchy record of publication.

Another might-have-been was an edition of the letters of Lord Acton, a predecessor to whom Butterfield was strongly drawn despite obvious social and confessional differences. After carefully surveying the fragmentary evidence, Bentley observes: 'Had he persisted, the world would now see Butterfield as the great Acton scholar of the twentieth century; and its failure as a project should not obscure the seriousness of his intention and delude readers into believing that the occasional pieces he produced on Acton represented the sum of his interest.' In many ways, that sentence may stand for the very considerable achievement of this biography: it gives us a far richer, more compelling

Butterfield than is suggested by his publications alone. But, of course, the sentence can also be reversed: the seriousness of his intention, as posthumously reconstructed from his unpublished papers, should not obscure his failure to produce more than a few occasional pieces on Acton. (As Bentley allows of the equally unpublished Gifford lectures on historiography: 'It is hard to report on the influence of a series of typescripts that remained in a drawer.')

Quite aside from questions of temperament, Butterfield created inhibitions for himself as far as writing history was concerned with his worries about how 'technical history' and 'general history' were to be related. He was surely right to see these two forms, however characterized, as mutually implicated—no matter how minute the historian's focus in a given case, 'there is always', he insisted, 'an assumed "general history"'—but his awareness of this necessary tension appears to have frustrated rather than enabled his own ambitions as a writer. It seems possible that Butterfield's difficulties were contagious. Bentley nicely observes that his immediately posthumous reputation may not have been helped by the fact that of the two men to whom he had been closest, one (Brian Wormald) 'could not bring an essay to any conclusion', while the other (Desmond Williams) 'could not bring an essay to a beginning'.

As Annan's remark, quoted earlier, suggests, Butterfield's reputation also suffered from allegations that he had been, at best, insufficiently patriotic during the Second World War or, at worst, pro-Nazi. Bentley traces the volatile character of Butterfield's responses to European politics in the late 1930s in some detail. 'What made him more hopeful than he could and should have been about the new politics of Italy and Germany,' Bentley concludes, 'was a misplaced faith that they might supply, possibly despite themselves, a form of moral discipline without which the civilization of Europe would wither beneath the suffocation of atheistic Communism and the cupidity of modern capitalism.' Butterfield was not alone in responding in this way in the 1930s, of course, though we may feel that he was led into a kind of unrealism, ironically enough, by his assumption that there could be no 'moral discipline' without a Divine foundation. Even in October 1939 he seems to be imagining, as Bentley remarks with admirable tartness, that 'the war could be fought on humanitarian, eighteenth-century principles', and 'he misses entirely the sense of ideological drive within Nazism'. It has also been held against Butterfield that during the war he cultivated close links with University College Dublin, an institution, Bentley reminds us, whose 'President, Michael Tierney had been a Blueshirt and now presided over a college amused as much as outraged by Nazi aggression against England'. Butterfield's judgement of how such associates might be perceived in England was not always of the best, even allowing for his habitual desire to shock. However, Bentley is surely right to conclude that Butterfield was not in any real sense a Nazi sympathizer: rather, through an unattractive mixture of wilful cynicism and puzzling naivety he allowed himself to deliver quite a few provocative remarks about European politics, and like some of the more simply reactionary members of his adopted class he may have thought that it was better to have mainland Europe dominated by Nazi Germany than by Soviet Russia. Whatever the attractive complexities of the private man, as a commentator on contemporary international politics Butterfield at times exemplified the moral hollowness of self-consciously worldly balance-of-power thinking. His close friend Betty Behrens shrewdly termed him a 'mystifier'; he was good at debunking the too-easy certainties of the day, less good at holding on to the fundamental truths that such certainties over-stated.

But Butterfield was nothing if not complex, and before the war was over he was to be found publishing a little book whose pious patriotism would have passed even the most demanding tests. Bentley appears uncomfortable with the rather conventional opinions expressed in *The Englishman and his History*, which came out in 1944, and he tries hard to minimize the apparent contradiction with the debunking purpose of *The Whig Interpretation of History*, but there is no way round the fact that the later book did signal a marked change of tone and a noticeable loss of critical edge in comparison to its predecessor. 'The greatest kindness to bestow on his book', concludes Bentley, after some pages of slightly strained apologetic, 'takes the form of indulgence towards Butterfield's purposes and the ambiguities that he allowed into print.' There may be a touch of Butterfieldian 'mystifying' about this sentence itself; many readers may find themselves inclined to be rather less indulgent. It is interesting to learn along the way that Butterfield wrote this topical essay (it is under 35,000 words long) in order to strengthen his not outstandingly strong claims to the Chair of Modern History at Cambridge which was due to be filled in March 1944, and that, for all the book's evident weaknesses as well as the fact that he had only completed it the month before the electors met, it seems, as Bentley puts it, to have been 'good enough'.

Another aspect of Butterfield's reputation where even Bentley's best efforts cannot go very far towards dispelling familiar reservations concerns the role he ascribed to Providence. As usual, Bentley is both imaginative and generous in construing meaning in Butterfield's sometimes deliberately gnomic reflections about religion, and there can be no doubt that whatever he understood by 'God' lay near the centre of his life. He was evidently drawn to Acton's definition of Providence as 'the continual extraction of good from evil'. But despite Bentley's subtle exegeses, there is no escaping the sense that, in Butterfield's hands, 'Providence' just turns out to be a way of referring to those unintended consequences which come up trumps in the long run. For example: 'The industrial revolution and the rise of the capitalistic system are the best that Providence can do with human cupidity at certain stages of the story.' It is hard to know whether to respond to such claims by asking inconvenient questions (Couldn't Providence have tried a bit harder? Has Providence gone to sleep on the job since then?) or humming *Que sera, sera.*

Providence becomes particularly prominent, and therefore particularly problematic, in Butterfield's contribution to the study of the relations between states. Bentley is surely right to say that the story of Butterfield's thinking about this topic 'silhouettes the degree to which his version of International Relations owed little to the new discipline gathering itself around those capital letters and everything to the mental field of forces confined by his interweaving of history, science and God'. For Butterfield, the point of studying the history of international relations was to 'nourish a sense of the human condition under God's governance'—a goal that idioms drawn from systems-theory and other bits of applied social science were always unlikely to reach. The problems with Butterfield's loftier perspective come into sharpest focus when Bentley contrasts his views with those of a leading American exponent of the 'realist' approach to international relations, Kenneth Waltz. Waltz apparently tried to strip states down to their 'capabilities' and to treat them as 'units' of force; Butterfield, by contrast, clung to a perspective that acknowledged 'the tragic element' in conflict, which enables us to see strengths and failings on both sides. Then Bentley adds: 'And of course we also see God, to whose enhanced capability across units Waltz has remained oblivious.' I'm not sure what this means, but I assume it's an appropriately Butterfieldian reproof to Waltz and other 'realists'. I am tempted to read it as an ironic pastiche at Butterfield's expense, but in general Bentley seems committed to endorsing his subject's views, on Providence as on other matters, rather than ironizing them.

Butterfield operated with a conception, Bentley reports, of 'History as a divinely sponsored master-narrative'. Again, I confess that there is not much I can do with this phrase other than poke it with quite a long stick; it is difficult for the unbeliever to get from such language any clear sense of the character of the Sponsor's involvement with everyday events. The undertow to all Butterfield's mischievous demolitions of conventional opinions is the hint that he does indeed possess the key to understanding the universe—it's just that for the moment he's left it in his other jacket. Bentley sternly reproves any such sceptical murmuring: 'To regard the Augustinian predicament in Butterfield's conception of international relations as mere obfuscating dogma is . . . seriously to detract from its importance in Butterfield's thought as a whole.' This must be right: these concerns went deep in his mind, and anyway it is rarely a good idea to treat such convictions as 'mere' obfuscating dogma. Whether those who do not share this Augustinian conception will feel that that was, nonetheless, its effective function in much of his writing about international relations is another question.

Sad to say, especially of one who made notable contributions to intellectual history and to the study of the eighteenth century in particular, Butterfield was not above a certain amount of cheap Enlightenment-bashing, and Bentley seems a little quick to indulge him here, as well as occasionally descending to his own Cowlingesque gibes against the 'sanctimonious judgement' of 'secular liberalism' and more generally at 'custodians of the modern liberal conscience'. Whatever targets these rather tired phrases are shooting at, they don't do a very good job of recommending an alternative to the necessary, and admirable, task of trying to understand and improve the world in secular terms.

It would be a pity, however, to let such lapses distract us from the unusual merits of this book. At one point Bentley challenges those who have wanted to insist that 'Nonconformist churchmanship [can] account for every recess in Butterfield's mind.' Such a view, he concedes, may make for 'a far more continuous narrative, certainly, but it obscures the tangles of a powerful, cynical, *hard* mind by converting them into soft pleasantries and pieties'. It does not detract from this admirable honesty about his subject to wonder whether Bentley himself does not find the cynicism and the hardness far more attractive than any hint of soft pleasantries and pieties. This shared sensibility may discourage some sorts of criticism: viewed from a greater distance, Butterfield's cynicism seems a disability rather than a strength, as it does in those historians in Peterhouse who may have taken some inspiration from him. But, undoubtedly, Bentley's partial identification with his subject enables him to treat both Butterfield's convictions and his feelings with more whole-hearted empathy than a biographer critical of these dispositions might be likely to do.

This has emboldened him to essay several novelistic flourishes in recreating a troubled, elusive inner life. One of the most successful is a rather touching prose snapshot of a man, known publicly as a driven scholar and earnest Methodist preacher, mooning around the streets of Cambridge on a wet Sunday in February 1937, killing time by drinking coffee and reading the papers, before turning to the piano and then a trashy detective novella to see out the day. 'I wish you were here', he writes plaintively to Joy: 'I feel like a sex-starved bank-clerk who has to turn to fretwork or naughty stories or religion to relieve his feelings.' This may not be the voice that most readers of *Christianity and History* associate with its author any more than it was the view of him held by those who later in his life encountered only the reticent professor and cagey academic politician, but whatever reservations one may retain about the case Michael Bentley makes for Butterfield's public and historiographical significance, he has without question succeeded in painting a delicately shaded and humanly appealing portrait.

IV

Few scholars have been on such intimate terms with that tricky duo, Hubris and Nemesis, as Hugh Trevor-Roper. It may appear absurdly inflated to invoke Greek tragedy to describe the life of someone who, rather than being a statesman or general or artist or other traditional 'great man', was a historian and therefore a member of a tribe whose deities might seem to be scepticism and caution. Yet in reading his biography it is hard to escape a feeling of horrified fascination as, over and over again, the stakes rising at each new turn of the wheel, the over-confidence engendered (at least in part) by his prodigious talents led him to court, and eventually encounter, disaster.

Nothing in his childhood, as the eldest son of a modestly successful country doctor, suggested what was to follow, except perhaps the combination of intellectual precociousness and lack of love. Public school and Oxford accentuated both aspects of his upbringing; a perceptive school-teacher reported, 'The only thing I at all fear is his facility; I sometimes wish things caused him a little more difficulty.' His experience of these exclusive institutions in their inter-war form also fostered in him an enduring susceptibility to the social, sporting, and alcoholic tastes of the English upper classes. Precociousness became almost his trademark. In 1940, at the age of 26, he published an obviously clever if overly provocative first book, on Archbishop Laud. A war spent largely in top-secret intelligence work was not wholly disagreeable: Gilbert Ryle and Stuart Hampshire were among his closest colleagues, and his duties did not prevent his riding to hounds at least once a week. As a result of his role in wartime intelligence, he was called upon to investigate the circumstances surrounding Hitler's death, with the result that, when he was 33, he wrote an international bestseller, and perhaps minor historical classic, *The Last Days of Hitler*. By the time he was 41, he was being paid a handsome retainer by *The Sunday Times*, just entering its great days, to write 'special articles' for them, which he did for over thirty-five years. He married the daughter of an earl and was on visiting terms with heads of state. He was made Regius Professor of History at Oxford when 43. And by contrast to the insularity of so many of his colleagues, Trevor-Roper was, as Sisman observes, 'cosmopolitan, and a fluent reader of French, German, Spanish, and Italian, with enough Romanian, Portuguese, and Serbo-Croat to read the occasional historical work in these languages, and of course Latin and ancient Greek.' Was there anything that he couldn't do?

'Complete a major work of history' was the answer his contemporaries increasingly gave. Trevor-Roper failed to finish a truly remarkable number of books. His biography is studded with abandoned manuscripts and unfulfilled publishers' contracts; his non-completion rate rivalled and perhaps even outclassed that of such an acknowledged master of the art as Butterfield. He tackled the big subjects, always in an original and combative way: the causes of the English Civil War, the relations between Protestantism and Capitalism, the European witch-craze, as well as Hitler and the origins of the Second World War. He published some dazzling essays on these and other topics, but there were so many other things to do, so much money to be earned, so many duchesses to meet (he had a terrible weakness for duchesses), so much journalism, so much travel... Only in his seventies did he begin to publish in any quantity collections of revised versions of the long historical essays at which he excelled. It says a lot about both his productivity and his underachievement that in the years since his death in 2003 his executors have already brought out nearly as many books under his name as he himself saw through the press in his lifetime.

Something else he conspicuously failed to do was to win universal affection. He could be superior, sharp-tongued, and downright dismissive. He made enemies with reckless abandon: sometimes they were bores, sometimes they were fellow-scholars (two categories he was prone to conflate), but sometimes they were whole social groups—he was pretty offensive to Christians, especially to Catholics (he couldn't be received at some of the best Catholic country houses, much to the chagrin of his snobbish wife), and for a while he came close to being Public Enemy Number One in Scotland (he was very rude about Scottish history, and extremely rude about Scottish historians). Some of this was high spirits; some was love of the witty phrase (his own, anyway); some was the solipsism of the very clever; and some, it seems, may have been the expression of a certain emotional awkwardness, a deep self-protectiveness that few were able to penetrate. But when you have A. L. Rowse, of all people, asking, 'Why *are* you so *nasty* to people?', you should realize all is not well with your character.

In his distinctive way, Trevor-Roper achieved as high a public profile as any historian of his generation. The long 'special' articles he wrote for the *Sunday Times* often became objects of commentary and controversy in their own right. In 1957 he joined the television version of 'the Brains Trust'. In 1961 he covered the Eichmann trial for the *Sunday Times* and wrote about the controversy surrounding E. H. Carr's *What is History?* for *Encounter*. In 1962 he gave a series of television lectures on 'The Rise of Christian Europe', which subsequently appeared as a glossy book. Alongside a quantity of regular broadsheet reviewing, he had been a frequent essayist in *Encounter* in its high days and he became a favoured contributor to the *New York Review of Books*. One historian expressed particular gratitude for a favourable review from him because, as he put it with flattering hyperbole, 'you have a following comparable (in numbers) to that of a major pop singer'. More public roles followed, including membership of the board of directors of *The Times* during its period of greatest turmoil in the 1980s. In that decade he was also one of the historians, selected as much for assumed political sympathies as for historical expertise, to advise the Prime Minister; to his credit, he seems to have been willing to tell her things she didn't want to hear—and, to her discredit, she seems to have robustly dismissed such donnish obstructiveness. But across these crowded decades he never completed his projected three-volume *magnum opus* on the English Civil War, though he drafted substantial sections of it. In fact, what makes his case 'especially tantalising', remarks Sisman, 'is the number of books he brought to the brink of completion and then abandoned'. In one case, the fee for a set of public lectures he had been invited to give was conditional upon publication, but even this goad proved ineffective: Trevor-Roper gave the lectures and never received his fee.

Nemesis lurked at Trevor-Roper's elbow in part because he was always so severe on other people's scholarly errors while being so prone to commit a few of his own. He was a sharp-tongued as well as prolific reviewer—perhaps a *sine qua non* for developing that 'name recognition' that is one of the essential steps towards becoming an acknowledged public intellectual—and a magnificent controversialist and pamphleteer. He had a notable, and intellectually fruitful, passage of arms with Lawrence Stone over the economic history of the seventeenth-century gentry in relation to the causes of the English Civil War. He had a high-profile spat with A. J. P. Taylor about the origins of the Second World War, a spat conducted in two representative media of the time, *Encounter* magazine and a BBC TV debate—indeed, it may now seem striking how much public attention such detailed historiographical disputes received in the couple of decades after 1945. And he courted international controversy by challenging the Warren Commission's report on the assassination of President Kennedy (he always believed he was a better detective than the professionals).

Having been ennobled by Mrs Thatcher in 1979 (as Lord Dacre), he took the Tory whip in the Lords, but he was at heart a kind of maverick Whig—allergic to pieties of all kinds, cultivating Gibbonian irreverence. When he unexpectedly became Master of Peterhouse, Cambridge, in 1980 (as successor-but-two to Butterfield), he soon found himself at odds with the more notoriously reactionary of its fellows, casting himself in the unwonted role of modernizing reformer. (This chapter in Sisman's book should be skipped by anyone of a delicate disposition: the ugliness of the behaviour exhibited by his opponents in these storms was in inverse proportion to the laughable tininess of the teacup.) It looked as though it was to be a sadly inglorious final stage of his career. But there was much worse to come.

As a result of the world-wide success of *The Last Days of Hitler*, Trevor-Roper had frequently been asked to adjudicate on the authenticity of various documents allegedly written by the *Führer* or one of his inner circle. He enjoyed exercising his considerable forensic skills; he enjoyed being treated as an authority; and he enjoyed receiving large fees for relatively little labour. In spring 1983, the German magazine *Stern* claimed to have discovered Hitler's diaries, and the syndication rights were offered to *The Times*. If the diaries were genuine, this would be a scoop to end all scoops. Trevor-Roper was flown to Zurich to examine the documents held in the vaults of a Swiss bank. Circumstances dictated that he had to arrive at a decision quickly: he decided that they were the real thing, and *The Times* went ahead with the deal, with extracts to be serialized in *The Sunday Times*. The advance publicity was mountainous, and Trevor-Roper was very publicly staking his reputation on this one, rushed decision.

Others were more sceptical; the evidence started to look shakier; even Trevor-Roper's normally assured confidence began to waver. At a little after the last minute, he havered and made himself look foolish, even donnish, itself a defeat for someone who had always soared above such stereotypes with his mixture of intellectual and social entitlement. But it was too late for him or *The Times* to pull back. It was a case of publish and be damned—and, boy, were they damned. When the 'diaries' were revealed to be the work of a fraudster, Trevor-Roper was swept away in the mud-slide of gloating. His reputation never properly recovered; *The Times*'s own headline on the day of his death twenty years later was 'Hitler Diaries Hoax Victim Lord Dacre Dies at 89'.

As Sisman reflects at the end of this hugely detailed but consistently engrossing biography, that was unfair and will surely not be how posterity rates him. Sisman has some of the partiality of the biographer who knew his subject and was given the run of his huge cache of personal papers (whatever else might be said about Trevor-Roper, he would have to be recognized as one of the great letter-writers, not out of place among the epistolary stylists of the eighteenth century). But he has done his subject a great service, both by putting together such a detailed narrative almost entirely from archival sources, and by giving us glimpses of a more ardent, more melancholy, even in his later years more lovable, figure than the public image. Trevor-Roper's work receives somewhat scant attention in places, but otherwise the thoroughness, fairness, and frankness of this biography are exemplary.

Yet it still remains frustratingly difficult to take the measure of Trevor-Roper's performance in the role of historian-as-intellectual. Both the merits and the appeal of his writing are undeniable. As his friend and former student Blair Worden said in a memorial encomium, he deserved to be remembered for 'the achievement of his writing in making sophisticated historical thinking accessible and enjoyable to a lay audience'. This was no small achievement when others who aspired to reach such an audience too often assumed they must first simplify their thoughts. But Trevor-Roper may have been too independent a thinker and too maverick a personality ever to mass his literary artillery in support of an advance on any front in particular. Irreverent conservatism can be enjoyable for both performer and audience, but it can, as the witticisms and epigrams clear, seem a form of private self-indulgence rather than a sustained attempt to nudge the thinking of one's fellow-citizens in a humanly more fruitful direction.

In advance, I had expected that reading a life of Trevor-Roper would stir a kind of envy in me—envy of his opportunities and of his moment, but also envy of his confidence and courage, and above all envy of his gifts as a historian and a writer. It certainly does that, but, quite unpredictably, one of my chief feelings on concluding this very long but interest-packed book is a kind of sympathy, almost of pity. There is the obvious tragedy of a man burnt by the flame of celebrity, but there is the deeper pathos of someone driven to shine, someone whose intellectual development in the first half of his life so outstripped his emotional development that he formed habits of insensitivity and egotism from which he never fully recovered. He was too clever and too knowing not to realize that his boundless ambition was at times sabotaged by the ease with which he could deploy his rich talents, including his talent to wound, and this knowledge is part of his pathos.

The peak of that ambition was to write a book that 'someone, one day, will mention in the same breath as Gibbon'. Anyone who confesses to such an ambition is obviously not shy about chatting up Hubris and so has to accept that Nemesis may come along and rough him up sooner or later. Trevor-Roper never completed his *Decline and Fall*, and maybe that was a minor tragedy of sorts, but he did write a lot of long analytical essays that had enough ideas in them, and enough arresting and elegant turns of phrase, to keep several seminars-worth of lesser historians plodding in his tracks for years to come. (As Sisman shrewdly observes, the paradoxical effect of Trevor-Roper's starting to publish collections of such pieces towards the end of his career was that 'his standing within the profession steadily rose, at the very time when the public could hardly esteem him less'.) And, as this biography reveals, he lived a life that was, for a scholar, unusually rich and varied in its achievements and gratifications. Anyway, nothing, I suspect, would have galled him more than the thought of lesser mortals feeling sorry for him. But then, perhaps Nemesis never quite turns out to be what you expect.

11

'New Orwells'?

Christopher Hitchens, Tony Judt, Timothy Garton Ash

I

Winning is very important to Christopher Hitchens. Dr Johnson was said to 'talk for victory', and by all accounts it seems the same might be said of Hitchens. He certainly writes for victory. His preferred genre is the polemic; his favoured tone mixes forensic argument with a kind of high-octane contempt. And no one can accuse him of only picking on boys his own size: he is happy to take the ring against tubby, bespectacled, former diplomats and little, shrivelled old ladies as well as against (special contempt here) relatively fit joggers. His indictments of Henry Kissinger, Mother Teresa, and Bill Clinton have been among the glories of the prosecuting counsel's art in recent years. Taking the global village as his courtroom, Hitchens asks us, the jury, to stare with wonder and loathing at these singular specimens of human depravity who are united in being economical, indeed positively parsimonious, with the truth and in being the object of some very good jokes.

From his early Trotskyist days on the *New Statesman*, through extended spells as a columnist for *Vanity Fair* and *The Nation*, and spreading out into contributions to a daunting variety of other weeklies and monthlies, Hitchens has been a prolific journalist, and in addition to his books he has now published four collections of his articles and essays. This is where much of his best writing is to be found—he comes off better in the literary sprints than at the longer distances—and where he can display the range of his literary

Christopher Hitchens, *Orwell's Victory* (Allen Lane, 2002).
Tony Judt, *Reappraisals: Reflections on the Forgotten Twentieth Century* (Penguin, 2008).
Timothy Garton Ash, *Facts Are Subversive: Political Writing from a Decade Without a Name* (Yale, 2009).
The respective dates of composition of the three parts of this essay particularly need to be borne in mind here, not least because Christopher Hitchens died in 2011 and Tony Judt in 2009.

tastes as well as the incisiveness of his literary judgements. Hitchens is one of the best contemporary examples of a species we tend to think of as flourishing in the nineteenth century rather than the twenty-first, the political journalist as man of letters. He would have been entirely at home amid the slash-and-burn style of the early partisan quarterlies, such as the *Edinburgh* or the *Westminster*, disposing of shoddy Romantic poetry and shoddy arguments in favour of the slave-trade or the unreformed House of Commons with equal gusto, in a style two parts Hazlitt to one part Cobbett with a dash of Croker's Tory venom.

It's worth pausing to ask what kind of cultural authority this type of writing can lay claim to these days. It self-consciously repudiates the credentials of academic scholarship; it disparages the narrow technical expertise of the policy wonk; it cannot rest on the standing of achievement as a politician or novelist. Like Oscar Wilde at the US customs, it has nothing to declare but its talent. Knowing the facts is very important; knowing the people helps (there's a fair bit of anecdotage and I-was-there-ism in Hitchens's journalism). But in the end it stands or falls by the cogency of its case, based on vigorous moral intuitions, honesty and integrity in expressing them, mastery of the relevant sources, and a forceful, readable style. Car licence-plates in New Hampshire bear (rather threateningly, it always seems to me, as big SUVs speed by) the state motto 'Live free or die'. In this spirit, the maxim on Hitchens's crest has to be 'Get it Right or Die'.

In the earlier part of his writing career, Hitchens's main way of being always right was to be very Left, but just recently there have been signs that he is casting off this identity, at least in any of its familiar forms. Now, it seems that the infallible litmus-test of whether one is on the right track is whether most people think the contrary. Comrade Hitchens may still be susceptible to the pull of fraternity when embodied by old buddies from *New Left Review* days, but his self-ascribed identity now is as a 'contrarian'. Being 'independent' (of parties, institutions, conventional wisdom, codes of politeness) is the thing. He describes himself in a recent essay as writing in opposition to 'the present complacently "liberal" consensus', where it's pretty clear that what really gets his goat is that it is a consensus and that it's complacent rather than just that it's liberal. In the same piece he introduces a sentence with the nicely self-ironic phrase 'without wishing to seem even-handed . . . ', but it's hard to think of anyone for whom this is less of a risk. Irreverence is now more highly prized than ever (he's always admired Wilde), and he hates cant, especially pious cant, especially pious radical academic cant. This protects him from any risk of being well thought of by the well-meaning, particularly in the United States, and he further insures himself against the danger of being approved of in such quarters by his conspicuous consumption of fags and booze.

Of course, in choosing to distance oneself from a particular 'consensus', especially of the liberal variety, one inevitably appears to be aligning oneself with its other, more traditional, opponents. Hitchens's recent high-profile resignation from *The Nation* illustrates the difficulty. His denunciation of his erstwhile colleagues' too predictable criticisms of US foreign policy—and especially their too indulgent perspective on the understandable response of some of those who suffer the impact of that policy in other parts of the world—can make him look like a recruit to the ranks of those who would have us all line up against 'the axis of evil'. In such circumstances, too irritable an aversion from one's self-righteously 'radical' associates can lead one into some very unlovely company. In this way, the self-contradictoriness of consistent contrarianism can produce odd outcomes. Surely Hitchens is not going to go the way of someone like Paul Johnson, one of the leading attack-journalists (and *New Statesman* stalwarts) of a previous generation, now reduced to indiscriminate barking at all things 'fashionable', while in practice intoning *pas d'ennemis à droite*?

As it happens, I've been re-reading Hitchens's latest collection of essays, *Unacknowledged Legislation*, alongside a couple of other collections that have recently appeared in paperback, Martin Amis's *The War Against Cliché* and Frank Kermode's *Pleasing Myself*. That's a tough poker-table to ask anyone to sit at, and it's impressive that some of Hitchens's best pieces, or at least some of his best paragraphs, don't seem out of place. It's true that he is quite often doing something different from those two contrasting masters of the literary review-essay, something more argumentative and political, but even when allowance is made for that, this company does in the end make his writing seem a bit blowsy or over-pleased with itself, certainly a bit too prone to go for the cheap shot. Amis is, of course, partial to a spot of sitting duck too, but he pays in full for his day's shooting from his wad of newly minted images, while Kermode mostly contents himself with a saddened shake of the head, a devastating weapon in its way, but one that doesn't leave any mess on the carpet. Hitchens *loves* mess on the carpet.

What Hitchens hasn't previously attempted at any length is the positive tribute, the admiring portrait. It has, however, long been clear that George Orwell is something of a hero of his, as of most political journalists with claims to be both essayists and tellers of unpopular truths, and now, spurred by the appearance four years ago of Peter Davison's marvellously thorough complete edition of Orwell's writings (and no doubt with an eye on Orwell's centenary which falls next year), he has written a short book entirely devoted to telling us, as the title of the US edition has it, 'Why Orwell Matters'. One therefore turns with interest to see how Hitchens, as an acknowledged master of the literary bazooka-attack, will acquit himself in the trickier arts of discriminating appreciation.

Orwell's Victory has both a dedication and an epigraph, not unusual things in themselves, but curious and curiously revealing in this case. The dedication is to Robert Conquest, 'premature anti-fascist, premature anti-Stalinist, poet and mentor, and founder of "the united front against bullshit"'. Conquest seems to be being saluted here principally for having been against a lot of things; this seems to be an early signal of the connection between being 'anti' and telling it like it is, of which more in a moment. As a self-professed 'contrarian', Hitchens is all for being against things (and one thinks again of the title of that collection by his close friend Martin Amis), though here he perhaps risks the mild paradox of 'we contrarians must stick together'. The dedication, while playing on the euphemism 'premature anti-Fascists' later used to refer to Communist sympathizers in the 1930s, also seems to suggest that Conquest is being praised for being against certain things before most people were, though the tonal unsteadiness of 'premature' risks, whatever its ironic intent, putting Conquest in the company of babies, conclusions, ejaculations. One seems intended to register the sense of Conquest as, in Nietzsche's sense, an 'untimely man' (contrarians are prone to congratulate themselves on being out of step with their times), or perhaps, to take up the more familiar idiom of fellow Movement poet Philip Larkin, that he has always been one of 'the less deceived'. Although we haven't even got to the contents page yet, we're starting to catch a whiff of the '"no bullshit" bullshit' that is one of Hitchens's trademarks.

The epigraph is from Proust and, being from Proust, is a paragraph long. It is about one kind of genius, genius as 'reflecting power', the kind of genius possessed by those who, though they may not always be those 'whose conversation is most brilliant' or 'culture the most extensive', can 'transform their personality into a sort of mirror'. The reader is naturally led to hear this as the first touch on the tuning fork, striking the right note for the ensuing performance about Orwell. Actually, as one reads and re-reads this passage, its meaning starts to slip through one's grasp. The syntax is not easy to follow (it *is* Proust, and in English, too). The 'men who produce works of genius' are those who have the power to 'transform their personality into a sort of mirror, in such a way that their life, however mediocre it may be socially and even, in a sense, intellectually, is reflected by it, genius consisting in reflecting power and not in the intrinsic quality of the scene reflected'. Taken alone, this might serve as a manifesto both for the purest naturalism (the best mirrors are those which reflect most faithfully and in most detail) and for extreme aestheticism (the subject written about is irrelevant, imaginative intensity is all). But what it doesn't seem, on fuller reflection (so to speak), is a very apt way to characterize *Orwell's* strengths, or indeed those of anyone who, like Orwell and like Hitchens himself, writes about what is going on in the public world and about what actually, despite appearances, makes things happen. Although the passage appears, at first reading, to suggest something about Orwell's self-absenting directness of observation and his much-lauded (and self-lauded) 'power of facing unpleasant facts', it comes to seem quite the opposite, a celebration of an almost Jamesian capacity for infusing a charged intensity of consciousness into the detail of experience. The passage may also prompt an association with Orwell's endlessly quoted dictum that 'good prose is like a window-pane'. This is a formula whose shortcomings don't need to be dwelled upon, but at least it suggests that one looks *through* the window, at the world outside, whereas the defining quality of the mirror is to bounce vision back at the viewer. As with 'premature' in the dedication, one is left a little uncertain what signal the epigraph is intended to send.

The 'Acknowledgements' then begin with thanks to 'my old English master' who set Hitchens to read *Animal Farm* 'and who allowed me to show him my work, late, as an off-the-subject comparison with *Darkness at Noon*: the first decent essay I ever wrote'. It is often said that adult English men tend to be fixated on their schooldays, especially when they went to the kind of minor public school that Hitchens did, and there is an unexpectedly nostalgic tea-and-crumpets flavour to this, as well as a statue-in-the-marble recognition of early signs of later identity (despite the missed deadline), a kind of coming home. It hints at a more personal answer to the question of 'why Orwell matters'.

And then, as the opening to the 'Introduction', we get a poem (there are a lot of antipasti to this relatively slight meal). The poem is by Conquest himself and is entitled simply 'George Orwell'. It praises Orwell as 'a moral genius': 'honesty', 'truth', and 'truth-seeking' structure the citation, and Orwell is lauded for testing words against 'The real person, real event or thing'. Throughout, he is thumpingly commended for directing our attention to 'reality', as in the rather Empsonian-sounding line 'Because he taught us what the actual meant'. Orwell figures in this poem as an early (perhaps 'premature') member of 'the united front against bullshit'; or, in other words, as one of Hitchens's precursors in the 'no bullshit' bullshit.

When we do finally get going with Hitchens himself writing about Orwell, the effect is a little anti-climactic. This is partly because one has a pretty good sense in advance of the kind of thing Hitchens would want to say about his hero. 'The three great subjects of the twentieth century were imperialism, fascism, and Stalinism'; Orwell 'was essentially "right"' about these issues; and 'he was enabled to be "right" by a certain insistence on intellectual integrity and independence'. So far, so familiar. (It is interesting to note in passing that Hitchens, loyal to aspects of the Trotskyism he has for the most part abandoned, always says 'Stalinism' where most people would say 'Communism'.) This is very much a political journalist's view of the 'great subjects'; from other perspectives it wouldn't be hard to make a case for, say, the mechanization of agriculture, the development of global communications, and changed attitudes towards sex—or, indeed, a whole variety of quite different 'subjects', though it's harder to see what being 'right' would mean in such cases.

It is also a rather romantic view of the 'independent' intellectual. Orwell, Hitchens announces, 'faced the competing orthodoxies and despotisms of his day with little more than a battered typewriter and a stubborn personality'. Most versions of 'writers versus Leviathan', to borrow Orwell's own terms, seem prone to hit this over-dramatic, David-versus-Goliath note, including the mandatory weapons-upgrade from slingshot to 'battered typewriter' (it somehow wouldn't do for the typewriter to be newish and in quite good nick). Orwell does seem to have been a brave man when put to the test, but to speak of him 'facing' despotisms from behind his desk ratchets up the register in a rather empty way. The lone protestor in Tienanmen Square, in the unforgettable image, certainly 'faced' the tank in a dramatically uneven contest, but those who write about orthodoxies and despotisms, especially from the distance of another country in the latter case, don't seem to merit the same verb. Similarly, isn't it the case that most writers who address such topics do so with 'little more' than their typewriters and their personalities, battered, stubborn, or otherwise? Of course, Hitchens needs to play up Orwell's complete 'independence', partly because he shares with him the animating illusion that to be out of step with a large body of opinion is in itself the most likely indicator of being right.

It is not easy to write a good book about Orwell now. He has been written about so extensively, and sometimes so well, that to justify devoting a whole book to him one would really need to have discovered some new material or be able to set him in some new context (not that this will deter publishers eager to cash in on his centenary). The main problem with *Orwell's Victory* is that Hitchens doesn't have enough of his own to say about Orwell to fill a book, so he writes as, in effect, Orwell's minder, briskly seeing off various characters who have in some way or other got him wrong. This is the structuring principle for a series of chapters on 'Orwell and Empire', 'Orwell and the Left', 'Orwell and the Right', and so on. Some of the offenders clearly deserve what they get, but there's something repetitive and relentless about it, as though the duffing-up were more important than dealing with Orwell's own writing. Raymond Williams is taken behind the bike sheds for a particularly nasty going-over; repetition of another kind adds to the problem here, since the substance of this long section was first delivered at the Hay-on-Wye literary festival in 1999 (as the Raymond Williams Memorial Lecture, if you please), then published in *Critical Quarterly* later that year, then re-published in *Unacknowledged Legislation* in 2000. It's a fair specimen of the Hitchens polemical manner—inveighing against 'the over-rated doyen of cultural studies and Cambridge English' and his 'almost deliberate obtuseness', accusing his writing of being 'replete with dishonesty and evasion', and so on—but reading it again is a vaguely dispiriting experience, rather like watching an old video of a one-sided boxing match.

As always with Hitchens's work, one gets the strongest possible sense of how much it matters to prove that one is and always has been *right*: right about which side to be on, right that there are sides and one has to be on one of them;

right about which way the world (in the rather narrow, political journalist's sense of that term) is going, right about which policies will work and which regimes are wicked; right about the accuracy of one's facts and one's stories; and right when so many others, especially well-regarded or well-placed others, are demonstrably wrong. There is a palpably macho tone to all of this, as of alpha males competing for dominance and display.

That one's facts should be right seems desirable from most points of view, but since Hitchens makes so much of others' failings here, one is driven to a spot of murmuring about stones and glass houses. For example, he describes Friedrich Hayek as succeeding 'Orwell's old foe Laski in the chair at the London School of Economics', but he didn't; Michael Oakeshott did. He quotes from C. P. Snow's 'Two Cultures' lecture, ascribing it to 'the mid-1960s', though it was delivered and published in 1959. He, most bizarrely, even mangles an extremely well-known line of Orwell's, his tirade about 'every fruit-juice drinker, nudist, sandal-wearer . . . ' and so on. Hitchens notes, rightly, that Orwell included 'feminist' in this list along, he goes on to say, 'with the fruit-juice drinkers, escaped Quakers, sandal-wearers, and other cranks'. 'Quakers', yes, but '*escaped* Quakers'? Escaped from where, exactly?

Trying to characterize for myself a certain tone that seems to be becoming more and more marked in Hitchens's recent writings, I recalled that in Martin Amis's baroquely footnoted *Experience*, there is a relatively brief note on Amis's almost filial relation to Saul Bellow, in which, having clarified that although he was not Bellow's son he was Bellow's ideal reader, Amis added: 'I am not my father's ideal reader, however. *His* ideal reader, funnily enough, is Christopher Hitchens.' One can see why that could seem odd or unexpected, but the more Hitchens I read the less unexpected it becomes. To be the ideal reader of Kingsley Amis, one would need, among much else, to be responsive to the pleasures of being bloody. Hitchens doesn't actually list 'giving offence' as among his hobbies in *Who's Who*, but perhaps that's only because it's not a hobby. It's interesting, too, that Martin Amis can be the ideal reader for Bellow despite the obvious cultural differences; it is unimaginable that Kingsley Amis's ideal reader could be anything other than deeply English.

Of course, 'deeply English' is the accolade that one group of Orwell's admirers are keenest to bestow on 'Saint George', and Hitchens, though properly suspicious of Tory evocations of 'deep England', does not dissent from this description or its positive force. At one point he concludes a nice little riff on the resemblances between Orwell and Larkin by acknowledging their front-runner status 'in the undeclared contest for most symbolic Englishman'. What particularly strikes one here is the way in which Hitchens, wanting to identify with a kind of Englishness that is at once authentic and radical, free from the taint both of 'heritage' kitsch and of a class-bound nostalgia for social hierarchy, aligns himself with a tradition that goes back to Tom Paine, John Milton, and the Diggers. This move has structural similarities to the 'Norman Yoke' theory of the seventeenth century which claimed that the ancient, popular liberties of the Saxons had been (temporarily, i.e. for several centuries) suppressed by the alien laws of a conquering aristocracy. And the comparison brings out how much Hitchens, cosmopolitan man of letters and geo-political analyst though he may be, is also a kind of 'country-party Whig', quick to sniff corruption at court or abuses of power by over-mighty governments. This affinity almost declares itself when he quotes Orwell endorsing Milton's invocation of 'the known rules of ancient liberty'. Here is an 'English tradition' with which he, like Orwell, is proud to identify.

Part of what is attractive and persuasive about Hitchens's take on Orwell in this book is his insistence on the way some of the latter's most admirable positions represent a kind of triumph over himself, as he educated himself into more liberal convictions against the grain of his inherited attitudes and temperamental inclinations (here 'Orwell's victory' can be understood in a more personal, less world-historical sense). One can't help wondering whether there isn't something of this in Hitchens, too, and whether, as with Orwell, we don't sometimes get a glimpse of the attitudes which the son of Commander Eric Hitchens RN might have been in some ways expected to hold (i.e. roughly those of his other son, the *Mail on Sunday* columnist Peter Hitchens). As Christopher Hitchens perceptively, but maybe also self-revealingly, says of his subject: 'George Orwell was conservative about many things, but not about politics.'

One of the qualities he claims Orwell managed to 'suppress' in himself was his 'anti-intellectualism'. Yikes! If that's how he wrote after having 'suppressed' his anti-intellectualism . . . Perhaps he means 'suppress' in the sense in which he suppresses his own tendencies in this direction, as when he speaks of 'the intellectual rot . . . spread by pseudo-intellectuals'. In the (mercifully short) chapter called, ominously, 'Deconstructing the Post-Modernists', he finds the source of contemporary 'intellectual rot' in 'Continental' thinkers and their American disciples. Taking up a comparison between Orwell and Adorno suggested a couple of years ago by James Miller (head of the department at the New School in New York where Hitchens teaches a course), Hitchens reflects how both men might have been surprised that 'only half a century or so after the Hitler–Stalin pact, every major city in Europe would be able to claim a free press and a free university', and he goes on to speculate that 'this outcome owes something to both men but more, one suspects, to the Englishman than to the Frankfurt theorist'. I'm not sure either of them would be quite as confident as Hitchens that the press in some of these cities can so readily be described as 'free', but it's hard not to hear a bit of a nativist growl as he awards the palm to 'the Englishman' over 'the Frankfurt theorist'.

At his best, Hitchens is a telling writer, but the occasional appearance of this almost blimpish strain means that he is not always at his best in this book. For example, in referring, with extreme briskness, to the vogue in Britain and the

United States for certain European philosophers, he speaks of Althusser's doomed project 'to re-create Communism by abstract thought', 'terminating in his own insanity and by what I once rather heartlessly called his application for the Electric Chair of philosophy at the *École Abnormale*'. If heartlessness were the quip's main failing the self-quotation could almost amount to an apology, whereas in fact by being still so obviously pleased with his schoolboyish *mot* he condemns himself twice over. But this is just the kind of gag about 'abroad' that Kingsley Amis might have liked, the affinity not serving either of them very well in this case. It's so strange that at the very time when Hitchens is telling audiences in the United States that we need to jettison the inherited categories of the twentieth century, including those of 'Left' and 'Right', if we are to make sense of the radically different world of the twenty-first century, he should also be sounding more and more like *le bloke moyen sensuel* of England in the 1950s.

The sight of Hitchens view-hallooing across the fields in pursuit of some particularly dislikeable quarry has been among the most exhilarating experiences of literary journalism during the last two decades. He's courageous, fast, tireless, and certainly not squeamish about being in at the kill. But after reading this and some of his other recent writings, I begin to imagine that, encountering him, still glowing and red-faced from the pleasures of the chase, in the tap-room of the local inn afterwards, one might begin to see a resemblance not to Trotsky and other members of the European revolutionary intelligentsia whom he once admired, nor to the sophisticated columnists and political commentators of the East Coast among whom he now practises his trade, but to other red-coated, red-faced riders increasingly comfortable in their prejudices and their Englishness—to Kingsley Amis, pop-eyed, spluttering and splenetic; to Philip Larkin, farcing away at the expense of all *bien-pensants*; to Robert Conquest and a hundred other I-told-you-so's. They would be good company, up to a point, but their brand of saloon-bar finality is only a quick sharpener away from philistinism, and I would be sorry to think of one of the essayists I have most enjoyed reading in recent decades turning into a no-two-ways-about-it-let's-face-it bore. I just hope he doesn't go on one hunt too many and find himself, as twilight gathers and the fields fall silent, lying face down in his own bullshit.

II

'*The past has nothing of interest to teach us.*' That, fears Tony Judt, is the presiding assumption of the early twenty-first century. The speed of social and economic change, the exhaustion of the twentieth century's dominant ideologies, and a desire to put the horrors of that century's carnage behind us, all conspire, he believes, to encourage a culture of forgetting. And this belief frames and justifies his sense of his own role; he appoints himself the Reminder-General in contemporary society (or at least in the United States), a particular version of the historian as public intellectual.

He had already played this role for some years before 2005 through his contributions to the leading periodicals of cultural and political opinion in the United States and Britain and his direction of the Remarque Institute at New York University, but his standing and authority were considerably enhanced by the publication in that year of *Postwar: A History of Europe since 1945*. This massive volume was acclaimed for its extraordinary synthesis of more than half a century of the history of an entire continent. In it the big questions and the big countries properly receive the greatest share of attention, but the book is in some ways more remarkable for showing us where, say, Norway or Portugal or Bulgaria fit into the larger picture. A work of synthesis on the scale of *Postwar*, in which, inevitably, some ruthless decisions have to be made about selection and emphasis, benefits from being organized around a small number of large themes; a strong controlling argument has its drawbacks, but it helps keep the potentially disruptive heterogeneity in line. The most successful collections of essays, by contrast, are likely to exhibit other qualities: a sensibility responsive and sympathetic to a plurality of voices may be one such quality, an engaging and persuasive authorial presence may be another. But there is the danger that essays which may have seemed forceful when initially published can come to seem forced when brought into the company of other, unnervingly similar, performances. In *Reappraisals*, Judt has collected twenty-three of his review-essays from the years 1994–2006, the great majority of them having first appeared in the *New York Review of Books*, so the book's publication allows us to take stock of his performance in the related role of historian-as-essayist.

In his introduction, Judt claims that two main themes run through the book: first, 'the role of ideas and the responsibility of intellectuals'; and second, 'the place of recent history in an age of forgetting'. I'm not sure that these are, in practice, the salient themes, but the announcement does fairly represent the insistent, exigent tone of what is to follow—'the role', 'the responsibility', 'the place'. It might be more accurate to say that the dominant concerns of the volume are, first, the primacy of the political when evaluating ideas; second, the defining significance of attitudes towards the Holocaust and towards Communism; third, the value of transatlantic comparisons and contrasts when thinking about the state; and fourth, the distinctive contribution of Jews to understanding modern history.

Some of the best essays in this collection display the same power to identify and analyse the interplay of political power, cultural identity, and socio-economic change that characterized the strongest sections of *Postwar*. Learned and illuminating essays on Belgium and on Romania are good examples of Judt's capacity to grasp, frame, and narrate. And, as we might expect from someone who began his career as a specialist in French history, there are some good explorations of the distinctiveness of France and its peculiar forms of 'backwardness'—France was, 'of all the countries of Western Europe, the one which had changed least until very recently'. His strengths as a political analyst and polemicist are also on display in several fine essays, including those on American foreign policy and on the role of the state in the global economy. (And, speaking as an outsider to the debates to which he has contributed, I find his essays here on Israel sympathetic and perceptive, though I well realize that some other readers will not share that judgement.) In all these pieces, Judt gives a master-class in the role of the historian as public intellectual, informing and educating his readers, getting behind the headlines and stereotypes to pinpoint the real forces that are at work in determining policies and shaping societies.

But there are also deeper continuities with his previous work. *Postwar* ends with an epilogue entitled 'From the house of the dead: an essay on modern European memory'. In it, Judt's concerns about public forgetting take a highly specific form. What needs to be properly remembered, he insists, is the Holocaust. 'Holocaust recognition is our contemporary European entry ticket,' and not just to the European Union: 'The recovered memory of Europe's dead Jews has become the very definition and guarantee of the continent's restored humanity.' This is a highly eccentric construal of European identity, one that is rather belied by the more complex history of social, economic, and political change recounted in the book's previous 800 pages. But in Judt's eyes, this topic, above all, confirms the public role of the historian. He quotes Yosef Yerushalmi on how mere 'memory' is inadequate to the task of maintaining a proper grasp on the enormity of the Holocaust: 'Only the historian, with the austere passion for fact, proof, evidence, which are central to his vocation, can stand guard.' And Judt concludes: 'If Europe's past is to continue to furnish Europe's present with admonitory meaning and moral purpose—then it will have to be *taught* afresh with each passing generation.'

One response to this passionate credo is to feel not just that it may exaggerate the present place of the Holocaust in European societies, but that it risks turning history into too narrowly didactic an exercise, as though the main purpose of an interest in the past were to provide us with 'admonitory meaning and moral purpose'. And this may be a danger in the role of 'historian as public intellectual' more generally. The pressure of public debate demands clear messages, 'lessons' from the past, whereas that 'austere passion for fact' will usually tend towards the recognition of complexity and often the absence of anything that might qualify as a 'lesson'. The temper of historical analysis necessarily leans to the sceptical; its effects tend to be corrosive of all pieties, and those may on occasion include the admirable civic values Judt and other public moralists would have it validate.

Judt's ready embrace of that public role means that there is no shortage in these essays of lessons for the present, often trenchantly stated. A particularly powerful example is provided by the theme of the function of the state in twenty-first-century societies. 'The state, as the history of the last century copiously illustrates, does some things rather well and other things quite badly. There are some things the private sector, or the market, can do better and many things they cannot do at all.' This line of reasoning leads him to conclude in the final essay on 'The Social Question Redivivus': 'Only a state can provide the services and conditions through which its citizens may aspire to lead a good or fulfilling life.' And he goes on to spell out what a social-democratic ideal revised in the light of a realistic appraisal of both the weaknesses and the strengths of global capitalism could look like:

> For some years to come, the chief burden on the government of any well-run national community will be ensuring that those of its members who are the victims of economic transformations over which the government itself can exercise only limited control nevertheless live decent lives, even (especially) if such a life no longer contains the expectation of steady, remunerative, and productive employment; that the rest of the community is led to an appreciation of its duty to share that burden; and that the economic growth required to sustain this responsibility is not inhibited by the ends to which it is applied. This is a job for the state; and *that* is hard to accept because the desirability of placing the maximum possible restrictions upon the interventionary capacities of the state has become the cant of our time.

This is, clearly, a minimalist prescription. In many European countries it would be widely assumed, including by some regarded as being on the right, that the state ought to be playing a broader and more constructive role than this, helping to shape the framework within which social and economic activity is carried on, not confining itself to providing a safety-net for the losers in the great scramble. Judt himself agrees that the task for 'the Left in Europe' is to 'reconstruct a case for the activist state'. But in an American context, simply to spell out this minimalist case in such measured terms as the inescapable conclusion to be drawn from an intelligent analysis of recent history may be to perform an important public-intellectual service.

The topic on which Judt's reading of the lessons of history has generated most controversy in recent years is, of course, Israel. That topic occupies a relatively minor place in this collection, but the same outspokenness and trenchancy are in evidence when he does touch upon it. For example, in the course of an admirable essay written in 2004 as an introduction to a posthumous collection of Edward Said's writings on the Middle East, he declares: 'After thirty-seven years of military occupation, Israel has gained nothing in security; it has lost everything in domestic civility and international respectability; and it has forfeited the moral high ground forever.' Even those who broadly share this view may jib a little at the sweepingness of 'nothing', 'everything', and 'forever', but we should recognize that in the contemporary United States it takes courage to express this view in such downright terms. Judt has already been vilified for his position on Israel; indeed, he has been subjected to a quite shameful level of denunciation, something that makes his steadiness under fire in these essays all the more admirable.

In some of the other pieces he writes more in the vein of the prosecuting attorney, relentlessly forensic. Here, his touchstone tests of giving rightful preeminence to the Holocaust in modern European history and of being properly vehement in one's condemnation of Communism start to grate in the way over-ground axes always do. (It may be relevant here to note that Judt, who was born and spent the first thirty-five years of his life in Britain, describes his provenance in these terms: 'Coming from that branch of East European Jewry that had embraced social democracy and the Bund (the Jewish Labor organisation of early twentieth-century Russia and Poland), my own family was viscerally anti-Communist.') Several of the essays in this style are about individual intellectuals, and although Judt has written extensively about French intellectuals in the past, I have to say that the topic does not seem to me to play to his strengths. This is partly because he focuses so narrowly on the *political* bearing of their ideas, a focus which in practice often tends to reduce to whether they were (culpably) sympathetic or (properly) hostile to Communism. As political critiques, they are always forceful and usually intelligent, but as intellectual portraits they sometimes feel rather thin and monochromatic.

Consider his discussion of the figure often now acclaimed as 'the world's most famous historian', Eric Hobsbawm. Though at points Judt praises Hobsbawm's gifts, he generalizes a damning indictment from the fact that Hobsbawm, mainly out of loyalty to his old comrades and their shared ideals, never resigned his membership of the Communist Party of Great Britain. This allows Judt to conclude that Hobsbawm 'has somehow slept through the terror and shame of the age'. Even the briefest glance at Hobsbawm's celebrated history of the 'short twentieth century', let alone his many other writings on modern history, is sufficient to demonstrate the absurdity of this judgement (condemnation of the 'brutal and dictatorial' Soviet system and the 'murderous absurdity' of Stalin's policies pepper Hobsbawm's pages). But its substantive and stylistic exaggeration is not an isolated instance. Moving to his peroration, Judt thunders: 'The values and institutions that have mattered to the Left—from equality before the law to the provision of public services as a matter of right— . . . owed nothing to Communism. Seventy years of "real existing Socialism" contributed nothing to the sum of human welfare. Nothing.' The table-thumping repetition here seems eerily reminiscent of the

Commissar at the Party meeting, yet to whom are these rhetorical excesses addressed in Judt's case? Perhaps to those left-deviationists who, reprehensibly, don't think that a vehement display of anti-Communism is the overriding indication of historical intelligence?

This note becomes disturbingly insistent in his remarks, in the course of a very positive assessment of the Polish philosopher Lezek Kolakowski, about another British historian, E. P. Thompson. In 1973 Thompson addressed an 'Open Letter' to Kolakowski, expressing dismay at the latter's repudiation, since his arrival in the West, of the kind of independent Marxist thinking he had bravely upheld as a dissident voice within Poland in the 1950s and 1960s. 'The "Open Letter"', writes Judt, slipping into adjectival over-drive,

> was Thompson at his priggish, Little-Englander worst . . . patronising and sanctimonious. In a pompous, demagogic tone, with more than half an eye to his worshipful progressive audience, Thompson shook his finger at the exiled Kolakowski. . . . How dare you, Thompson suggested from the safety of his leafy perch in middle England, betray us by letting your inconvenient experiences in Communist Poland obstruct the view of our common Marxist ideal?

From the outset, Judt's laboured sarcasms start to backfire: even someone who had not previously heard of, let alone read, Thompson's letter begins to sense from the over-kill of 'worshipful', 'leafy', 'inconvenient', and so on that Thompson is here facing a firing-squad rather than a critical appraisal. Judt goes on to pronounce that Kolakowski's reply 'may be the most perfectly executed intellectual demolition in the history of political argument. No one who reads it will ever take E. P. Thompson seriously again.' The history of political argument is a long one and can boast some celebrated intellectual demolitions: why would anyone claim they were *all* outranked by Kolakowski's response, a document which, to be sure, makes some telling local points, but which on the whole talks past Thompson as well as down to him, in a heavy-handed display of misplaced condescension? And '*no one*' who read it will '*ever*' take Thompson '*seriously*' again? This is stump oratory, not one distinguished historian's appraisal of the achievements of a, surely, no less distinguished colleague.

Even in cases where Judt's criticisms seem broadly right, there is often a betraying exaggeration in his swelling address to the jury. For example, in writing about the French Marxist philosopher Louis Althusser, who enjoyed great esteem among many on the theoretically inclined left in the 1960s and 1970s, he jabs his finger in the juror's chest: 'What does it say about modern academic life that such a figure can have trapped teachers and students for so long in the cage of his insane fictions, and traps them still?' I find Althusser's theories no more compelling than Judt does, but 'trapped', 'cage', 'insane'? And can the current interest on the part of a tiny minority of university teachers in what is by any measure a complex and highly abstract body of thinking really be read as damningly symptomatic of something as extensive as 'modern academic life'?

Critics usually write more winningly about those authors they admire than about those they abhor, but even with these figures Judt can sometimes intrude the political judgement too soon and too insistently. The lead essay in the collection is entitled 'Arthur Koestler, the Exemplary Intellectual'. This was originally published as a review of a biography of Koestler, and Judt scores several good points against the parochial and anachronistic judgements made by the biographer about, for example, Koestler's voracious sexuality and his ambivalent attitude towards Zionism. But as the essay goes on, one increasingly wonders how anyone could now think of Koestler as 'the exemplary intellectual'. Judt fairly acknowledges that many of Koestler's books 'were panned by specialists for their idiosyncratic speculation, their searching for coherence and meaning in every little coincidence and detail, their abuse of analogy, and the overconfident intrusion of their author into matters of which he was comparatively ignorant'.

On what grounds, then, could we regard such a figure as an 'exemplary' intellectual? Principally, it seems, on the strength of his having written *Darkness at Noon*, which is 'widely credited with having made a singular and unequalled contribution to exploding the Soviet myth'. Even Judt recognizes some of the weaknesses of that book, and he acknowledges that it 'seems curiously dated today'. But the failings of this and Koestler's other writings on the same theme are, somehow, part of what makes him 'the exemplary intellectual'. 'His obsession with the fight against Communism (like all his other obsessions) brooked no compromise and seemed to lack all proportion. . . . This made Koestler an uncomfortable presence, someone who brought disruption and conflict in his train. But that is what intellectuals are for.' Is that really true? Like most one-liners about what intellectuals are 'for', it has a certain snappy charm, but, if we are being serious rather than merely provocative or epigrammatic, do we really want intellectuals, any more than any other category of our fellow-citizens, to 'lack all proportion' and bring 'disruption and conflict in [their] train'?

Judt's (qualified) endorsement of Hannah Arendt displays some of the same characteristics. He again notes that other critics have found her to be 'inaccurate in argument and to make a parade of learned allusion without any detailed enquiry into texts', but he endorses her nonetheless because, in his view, 'she got the big things right', namely her insistence that genocide was the 'basis' of Nazism and that 'the Stalinist era was not a perversion of the logic of Historical Progress but its very acme'. And in his discussion of Arendt, the themes of not forgetting and of being Jewish come together in a revealing way. Although she was a wholly assimilated product of the German culture of 'Bildung' and 'Wissenschaft', Judt takes the fact of her having been born in Königsberg to indicate her kinship with the members of the 'lost cosmopolitan communities' of Europe, intellectuals who hailed from 'vulnerable cities that were at once central and peripheral—Vilna, Trieste, Danzig, Alexandria, Algiers, even Dublin'. And so, he argues, Arendt, like other cosmopolitan 'survivors', felt a special obligation to combat the tendency to forget. 'In Arendt's case the responsibility, as she felt it, was made heavier by a conscientious, and perhaps distinctively Jewish, refusal to condemn modernity completely or to pass a curse upon the Enlightenment and all its works.' I am still not quite sure I understand what he is saying in this sentence, but on the face of things it is hard to see anything 'distinctively Jewish' about 'refusing to condemn modernity completely or to pass a curse upon the Enlightenment and all its works'.

We may get some clarification of his thinking here from the conclusion of his essay on the Central European polyglot writer Manès Sperber, whom Judt describes as by origin 'a shtetl Jew from Galicia':

> The extermination of the past—by design, by neglect, by good intention—is what characterizes the history of our time. That is why the ahistorical memory of a marginal community that found itself in the whirlwind may yet be the best guide to our era. You don't have to be Jewish to understand the history of Europe in the twentieth century, but it helps.

That closing *mot* is lightly turned, but it may speak volumes not just about Judt's preoccupation with Jews and Jewishness, but about his particular construal of the advantages of 'marginality'. The implication is that homelessness, exile, and displacement sensitize one's social and cultural antennae, perhaps that the best cultural analysts (and maybe the best historians?) are those who have moved on from their country of origin or who belong to a group which never felt at home there in the first place. It's a fashionable assumption, but there's no good reason to think it's true. Displacement and grievance narrow as well as enlarge horizons, and even being a European Jew in New York may bring with it parochialisms of its own.

Judt's essays become both more important and more troubling for being brought together in one volume. The publication of *Reappraisals* certainly confirms, were any confirmation still needed, his standing as a significant figure in the public intellectual life of the contemporary United States. I salute the range, the command, and the courage displayed in his writing. But spending a prolonged spell in his literary company also leaves me feeling a bit uncomfortable. I feel that I would be forced into banging the table in my turn if I wanted to enter the conversations whose terms he partly sets. We need historians to play the role that Judt so ably does, but perhaps we need them also to be a bit less at ease with that role. The best works of history rarely yield unambiguous support to any political cause or affiliation, and we look to the vocabulary, register, and cadence of good historical writing to communicate that chastened sense of complexity which otherwise can struggle to get itself heard in public debate. That's not everything, of course. But it's not 'nothing', either.

III

Towards the end of his life, George Orwell declared that his overriding aim had been 'to make political writing into an art'. The more we ponder this celebrated phrase, the more problematic it comes to seem. There is the initial question about what it could mean to make such writing into an art ('into an art', not 'into Art', suggesting something nearer to cookery than to ballet). Orwell's syntax also makes us wonder what this sort of writing had been before, such that he needed to effect this transformation on it (or is it just the transformation of his own earlier political writing?). Any writer can, needless to say, have more than one goal in mind at the same time, but the phrase also prompts us to consider whether this was the best, or even an appropriate, way to describe, say, Orwell's revelations about the Communists in the Spanish Civil War or his denunciations of the 'Russo-phile intelligentsia' at home. What relation had this overarching aesthetic project borne towards the more immediate purposes of getting some facts known and some untruths exposed? Is more artful or artistic political writing likely to achieve these goals more effectively, or the reverse? Orwell was famously the apostle of 'plain speaking', telling it like it is, but perhaps, we come to think, that is not quite such a straightforward matter. Perhaps it requires no little art if we wish to be plain.

'Political writing' is the label Timothy Garton Ash applies to *Facts Are Subversive*, a selection of his work from the past decade, and he is explicit about his indebtedness to, and admiration for, Orwell. Garton Ash identified his own life's work with some precocity. 'In the long summer after I took my first degree at Oxford, I read the whole of Orwell's work, read him self-consciously as example and guide for a would-be writer.' He then sought out some very Orwellian subjects to write about—East Germany in the grip of the Stasi, Poland in the heady days of Solidarity, Czechoslovakia during the 'velvet' revolution of 1989. He wrote from the front line, having become friends with several leading Eastern European dissidents, but he also wrote as a trained historian. In the 1990s he went on to cultivate this dual identity in relation to other political and military hot spots in Europe, notably the Balkans. By this point he held a fellowship at St Antony's, the Oxford post-graduate college which specializes in the politics and cultures of, essentially, the non-anglophone world, and he had begun to contribute long, vivid, well-informed essays to the *New York Review of Books*. In addition to more detailed historical monographs, he also published collections of his occasional writings, beginning in 1989 with *The Uses of Adversity*, followed ten years later by *History of the Present*. The latter volume contained a spirited defence of the 'hybrid' enterprise he was engaged in, falling across and between journalism and scholarship, usually combining first-hand reporting with in-depth analysis.

Since that last collection, he has extended his geographical range well beyond Europe, writing increasingly about the United States (since 2000 he has held a part-time appointment at the Hoover Institution at Stanford), but also about Brazil, Iran, Burma, and elsewhere. Above all, the last decade has seen him addressing the many cultures and questions folded into the term 'Islam', whether pondering sympathetically the plight of poor immigrant communities of Muslims in Europe or the larger geopolitical questions focused around 'terrorism'. And since 2002 he has had a regular column in *The Guardian*, a column which is syndicated to various publications across the world. So, he is now acknowledged as an influential commentator on international politics, invited to advise heads of states almost as often as he is asked to speak to packed auditoria around the globe.

The appearance of this third collection is an occasion for asking how far Garton Ash has made political writing into an art, and indeed, to what extent that is a desirable goal. American readers may be forgiven for thinking that it is a kind of writing in which the English have something of a corner—though, interestingly, few of the leading contemporary practitioners are in fact Anglo-English. For example, Ian Buruma is Anglo-Dutch, Perry Anderson is Anglo-Irish, Tony Judt grew up in England as the child of Russian Jews before spending the later decades of his life in the USA. Garton Ash is at least as cosmopolitan as any of his peers (a better linguist than many, better travelled than most), though he is the only one who is Anglo-English and who has maintained his connection with Oxford. This company also helps identify some of Garton Ash's distinctiveness: he is, for example, less of a story-teller than Buruma, less analytical and olympian than Anderson, less angular and polemical than Judt. His forte is the exceptionally well-informed, vivid account of the personal, cultural, and geopolitical elements at work at a moment of political decision in a country most of his readers previously knew little about. His writing is more personal and more dramatic than that of most historians, but more scholarly and more comparative than that of almost all journalists.

For all his admiration of Orwell, Garton Ash is a very different type of animal. He is a historian-journalist, not a novelist-journalist (or at least, if he does write fiction he has yet to publish any of it). He is an academic, albeit of an unconventional kind, as well as, increasingly, a familiar of those who exercise power. It is almost impossible to imagine Orwell as a professor at an Oxford college or hob-nobbing with world leaders. Though an Old Etonian, Orwell contrived to view the world from the bottom of the social heap as often as he could, living as a tramp in England, a *plongeur* in Paris, a volunteer in Spain, and cultivating a spiky isolation, ultimately retreating to the remote Scottish island of Jura. Garton Ash is far more *mondain*: his is the view from the top table, though with a hot-line to the leading dissidents (even then it's the *leading* dissidents). He nicely refers at one point to Orwell's 'sandpapery charm', but his own is silky smooth, scarcely ever abrading the reader's sensibilities. I wonder whether he is not a little torn between the glamour of being acknowledged as one of the world elite, rubbing shoulders with the powerful at the World Economic Forum at Davos and so on, and the alternative glamour of being the graduate student who was spied upon by the Stasi (this is his equivalent of Orwell's bullet in the throat on behalf of the Republican side in the Spanish Civil war).

A figure whom he admires scarcely less than Orwell is Isaiah Berlin. In reviewing a collection of Berlin's early letters, Garton Ash probes the identity of the almost ostentatiously Anglicized, indeed Oxfordized, Russian Jew, citing Berlin's own sense of himself as a 'Metic' (an alien living in an ancient Greek city who was not a citizen). And then suddenly Garton Ash breaks in with: 'Often the difference between an academic and an intellectual lies precisely in this stubborn grain of alienation. All intellectuals are mental Metics.' It's a common enough contention (we have just seen a version of it in Judt); the second sentence only needs 'Discuss' after it to become an ageless exam question. But is it true of Garton Ash himself? I know nothing of his biography except what is easily available in the public domain, and there may be deep rather than merely contingent explanations behind his having a Polish wife and spending much of his late twenties and early thirties in Central Europe. But just going by his published persona, the 'stubborn grain of alienation' would be hard to identify. It's true he is more international in his outlook than many educated Englishmen of his generation, but scarcely unique in that, even if exceptionally impressive in his range. In Garton Ash's case, I suspect (this is pure speculation on my part) that his 'alienation', such as it may have been, was less from the norms of educated English culture than from the limitations of academic research. Not—as he makes clear a little too frequently and insistently—that he has been at all tempted by any postmodern playfulness about the status of objective truth; the title of this volume bespeaks his continuing empiricist confidence on that score. But he appears always to have possessed the kind of restless curiosity, literary energy, and fascination with the here and now that might have found the protocols of conventional historical scholarship a little too constraining. In this, as well as in his cosmopolitanism and his confidence, he may resemble another of Berlin's great admirers, Michael Ignatieff (though without the latter's electoral ambitions discussed in Chapter 12).

To range oneself alongside such figures as Orwell and Berlin is to declare oneself a certain kind of 'liberal', as well as, perhaps, a particular kind of anti-communist insofar as that is still a relevant identity. Garton Ash speaks up eloquently for legal and political freedoms in places where they are conspicuously lacking (most obviously in Burma and Iran), but he is a little less forthcoming about his understanding of the relations between liberty on the one hand and economic forces on the other. He eschews any theorizing about this, reasonably enough given the constraints of journalism, but his passing comments suggest that he believes that 'free markets' are the essential precondition of 'free individuals', a view that may be axiomatic at the Hoover Institution, but that, from the standpoint of some other (European?) traditions of political thought, may seem closer to the IMF than to J. S. Mill.

Ruminating on capitalism's global triumph, Garton Ash observes: 'Most anti-globalists, *altermondialistes* and, indeed, green activists are much better at pointing out the failings of global capitalism than they are at suggesting systemic alternatives. "Capitalism should be replaced by something nicer" read a placard at a May Day demonstration in London a few years back.' He ends his paragraph there, without offering any further comment on the placard's slogan. This led me to wonder why he had quoted it. Does it seem to him to clinch his argument, to sum up the ineffectual yearning behind most anti-capitalist sentiment, self-condemning in its feebleness? Or, assuming wit and playfulness on the part of the slogan's author, does he quote it to endorse a rueful or knowing sense of being stymied, sending up one's own lack of realistic proposals? (Does he, for that matter, rule out the possibility that it was the work of an anarchist infiltrator, satirizing and thus hoping to subvert the protest?) Does Garton Ash himself, I wonder, really want capitalism to be replaced by something nicer? Most of the time he seems pretty happy with capitalism as it is.

Although his reach is now global, Garton Ash still writes with particular authority on Germany and Eastern Europe (his essay on Gunter Grass's belated revelation of his time in the Waffen-SS is perhaps the most compelling piece in the book, clear-eyed about the damage to the novelist's moral stature yet charitable about the pressures and confusions behind this representative German experience), and the anti-communist movements of the late Cold War era remain important points of reference. '1989 established a new model of nonviolent revolution that now often supplants, or at least competes with, the older, violent model we associate with 1789.' He also writes well about the European Union, why it's necessary and how it's flawed. He argues that it doesn't require some additional kind of 'Euronationalism' or historical myth on the lines of 'From Charlemagne to the euro' to make it work better, but it may require more democracy. He astutely emphasizes that the power of the EU is at its greatest over those states which are on the point of being considered for membership and are therefore keen to acquire the necessary democratic and liberal credentials. And he has a lovely little tongue-in-cheek riff on the country that would make 'the perfect EU member', the country that already has all the ideal political, economic, and cultural qualities, including a commitment to using two of the major European languages, a willingness to contribute to peace-keeping, and a suspicion of encroaching American influence. Also its people are notoriously nice, though they do live rather a long way away from Europe. (If anyone hasn't got the joke yet, just keep reading.)

Since 'political writing' is not itself a single form, we have to recognize that this collection in practice comprises examples of three genres: the longish review-essay, the public lecture, and the regular newspaper column. They involve different opportunities and constraints, each requiring a different 'voice' or relation to its implied reader. Garton Ash is very good at all three, spectacularly so with the review-essay, but they do not all translate equally well into book form. There is no problem with the longer review-essays. The lectures mostly survive the transition well enough, though readers of the book version are bound to feel that they are hearing an echo of an occasion that had its own remit and its own intimacy. But the columns? The column is the adrenalin-shot of opinion that we fuel up on at breakfast or on the commute to work; it's the fast-food of the mind. Served hot, it has a useful function; but served cold . . . ?

Contemporary 'serious' newspapers carry a lot of columnists, and perhaps, as breaking news becomes easily available in other forms, the columns will be more and more the Unique Selling Point of the individual paper (perhaps they are already). The column is a handy pulpit, but the requirement to preach when the appointed day comes round, whether or not the columnist has anything new or important to say, can be damaging to one's intellectual and literary judgement. The condition diagnosed as Compulsive Columnist Disorder may set in: the writer can't help expressing confident and authoritative-sounding views upon almost any subject. Garton Ash often has something important to say, and he strikes me as one of the best exponents of this peculiar craft currently writing in the British press (I speak here as a regular reader of *The Guardian*). But maybe even he cannot altogether escape the *déformation professionnelle* of the trade.

Garton Ash has always been an accomplished writer, and his virtuosity is frequently on display in this collection. For example, on seeing young men in Burma wearing Western clothes: 'A few already wear their baseball caps reversed: globalization's moronic meme.' The deft use of the colon adds a kind of laconic force to the sigh here, the better to allow the alliteration to do its rhythmic work. Or again, he describes how, reading his own Stasi file, he was 'deeply stirred by its minute-by-minute record of my past life: 325 pages of poisoned madeleine'. But it is a question, to say the least, whether the ready availability of a column has had a beneficial effect on Garton Ash's style. His sentences now tend to be short enough and clear enough to win approval from the most grizzled sub-editor, but this is not always a virtue. I have to say I frequently had the opposite reaction to the one we all tend to have when reading Henry James: I longed for a few subordinate clauses. For example: 'The facts themselves must be checked against all the available evidence. But some are round and hard—and the most powerful leaders in the world trip over them. So can writers, dissidents and saints. There have been worse times for facts.' And so on. There's nothing technically wrong with these sentences (journalism can stand a few 'sentences' that contain no finite verb), but the effect starts to become monotonous and uninflected. There is this. There is that. And there is something else.

Even Garton Ash occasionally displays some of the secondary symptoms of columnitis, as an uncharacteristic trite phrase or tired cliché insinuates itself into his prose. At the end of his admirable discussion of the need for European citizens of non-Muslim background to forestall the slide into disaffection and extremism by everyday acts of welcome and respect, he asks whether it is still possible that they will rise to this challenge, and answers: 'Yes, but it's already five minutes to midnight—and we are drinking in the last chance saloon.' In this case, the double cliché is doubly disturbing: the jacked-up alarmism of the columnist is bad enough, but in addition the slackness of the clichés undermines the moral strenuousness he is attempting to encourage. Or again, when reflecting on the changes that have come over Europe in the past half-century, he writes: 'Most Europeans now live in liberal democracies. That has never before been the case; not in 2,500 years. It's worth celebrating.' Well, perhaps, but what could the ringingly emphatic gloss 'not in 2,500 years' actually mean? There weren't exactly a lot of 'liberal democracies' around for the first 2,300 years of that period, indeed the concepts of 'liberal' or 'democracy' were scarcely current except in peculiar and now archaic senses of the words. Not only does this seem triumphalist whiggism of an uncharacteristically simple-minded kind, but it echoes the cadence of electioneering oratory.

It is hard not to feel, in reading the shorter pieces gathered here, that a certain forced punchiness is the stylistic correlative of his confidence that there is a right course of action in world politics and that we (whoever 'we' are) are the ones to undertake it. To his credit, he reproduces the piece he wrote for the *Guardian* on the eve of the decision to invade Iraq, in which he summarized the arguments for and against, concluding inconclusively that 'I remain unconvinced of the case for—and doubtful of the case against'. With hindsight, he now concedes that the arguments against invasion have stood up to analysis, and to events, a hell of a lot better than the arguments for, and he acknowledges that many Iraqis believe that things in their country are worse now than under Saddam. Nonetheless, he reflects—and I respect his honesty as well as his principles here: 'I still defend the right of the commentator not always to take sides, but in this case I got it wrong. Next time, I shall need a great deal more convincing. I'm not alone in that.'

So far, so admirable. But the brevity of the form leaves us wondering whether he endorses what appears to be the implicit premise, namely that the United States, or any other powerful country acting unilaterally, has the right to play the role of the world's disciplinarian. In his original article he took Tony Blair to be acting as 'a Gladstonian Christian liberal interventionist'. That's a pretty fancy gloss on what looked to many people even at the time to be unjustified, over-confident, disregard for the lives of innocent citizens of another sovereign state with whom Britain was not at war. The matter was, needless to say, very complex, but perhaps the quoted phrase obscures rather than illuminates the real issues. Insofar as one can draw parallels, one can perhaps imagine Gladstone authorizing a military expedition to protect British subjects or to help rescue persecuted Christians, but that's a long way from the desolation visited upon contemporary Iraq largely because Britain's more powerful ally felt it needed to do *something* in the wake of the 9/11 attacks.

Garton Ash, I should make clear, is very far from being one of the intellectual cheerleaders for Pentagon hawkishness. He is not to be counted among those liberals who were Bush's 'useful idiots', and since 2003 he has been emphatic in his negative verdict on that administration's foreign policy. He recognizes what is so misleading and so dangerous about the idea of 'a war on terror' (at most, 'it's a war to prevent such people wanting to become terrorists in the first place'), just as he will have no truck with those calling for a secular jihad against 'Islamofascism'. His views are measured and thoughtful, even if they do not always command agreement. What I am pointing to is not a ground for disagreement, especially in this particular case which involved a difficult decision, one about which opinion was very divided at the time. What I'm pointing to, rather, is the brisk confidence with which he draws up the moral balance-sheet on very complex issues and the taken-for-grantedness of the assumption that there exists a power with the agency, and the right, to try to arrange the pieces on the global chessboard to produce the 'correct' answer. He emphasizes that he favours the 'promotion' of democracy, and does not think we should 'sit on the sidelines and jeer' at the United States when its attempts turn out badly. But if we re-state this sentiment in less pejorative language, do we not think it *is* one of the tasks of the independent commentator to remind governments of the limits of their knowledge and the frailty of their designs? This is not the same as head-in-the-sand irresponsibility or purer-than-thou moralism; it is, rather, a matter of being true to one's intellectual vocation. There may be times when it might be better to decline the invitation to pronounce or to advise the powerful, not just because a region or a problem may be beyond one's competence, but also because briskly identifying the lesser evil tends to be habit-forming, working at the expense of that more extended brooding on a subject that not only probes beneath the surface of the evidence but also starts to put pressure on one's own intellectual categories.

This is not about the seductions of power; it is about the seductions of the regular column. In an ideal world (perhaps that same world in which Canada could, in his earlier spoof, become a member of the EU), one might imagine Garton Ash taking a sabbatical from opinion for a while, a vow of journalistic silence. Perhaps he could withdraw to a (well-appointed) cave in North Oxford and brood on questions of agency and causality, on issues of language and description, on the relations between the roar of the world and the whisper of thought. Perhaps a different form of that 'stubborn grain of alienation' would help here. After all, the Slow Food movement needs its Slow Thought counterpart. There are few better practitioners of the genre of 'analytical reportage', as he calls it, than Timothy Garton Ash, and I admire the boldness and energy with which he has cultivated this particular métier. Perhaps I would admire him still more if his journalism now gave a little more room, as his best essays do, to the hesitations and ambivalences that must be part of the attempt to understand on this heroic scale. And that may, in turn, suggest that, when assembling one's essays in book form, few even of one's most notable columns should be subjected to the rigours of a curtain call.

12

Politician-Intellectuals?

Roy Jenkins and Michael Ignatieff

I

'Wanted: philosopher-king of impeccably social-democratic credentials; the successful candidate must also have a liberal disposition and attractive human characteristics; upon appointment, the post-holder will draw enthusiastic support from intellectuals.' Three desires or dreams have played important parts in modern progressive politics in Britain (and elsewhere) in the decades after 1945. The first expresses the hope that even in contemporary mass democracies a figure will come to the fore who can both work the political machine and at the same time embody intellect, sensibility, and liberal values, someone who can both win power and then exercise it in the name of reason and enlightenment. The longing on the part of those with intellectual and radical inclinations themselves to be governed by someone who shares those qualities can, of course, encourage the investment of unrealistic hopes in potential candidates: having been the bearer of others' overreaching desires, the chosen champion then becomes the target of unreasonable blame.

The second, sometimes contingently related dream is what may be called the fantasy of the middle ground. This depends, logically as well as practically, on the tacit model of a spectrum. The spatial metaphor exerts its own semantic pull, so that those placed at either extreme of the spectrum must be described as 'extremists'—those characterized as zealots, ideologues, and so on. By contrast, those nearer the middle must be more 'moderate', characterized by good sense, willingness to compromise, lack of fanaticism. All this is reinforced by the conventional wisdom of the pollsters; being 'too right-wing' or, especially, 'too-left-wing' is taken to be synonymous with 'unelectable'. The

John Campbell, *Roy Jenkins: A Well-Rounded Life* (Cape, 2014).
Michael Ignatieff, *Fire and Ashes: Success and Failure in Politics* (Harvard University Press, 2013).

terms are relational or structural, not stable descriptors of political content, but they acquire evaluative force. 'Centre-left' is taken to signify the marriage of progressive inclinations with the pragmatism necessary to acquire and exercise power; 'far-left' automatically signals a preoccupation with ideological purity and a lack of realism. If only—so goes the dream in its classic form—those of good will from all parties could be brought together on this middle ground, the wasteful hostilities of traditional sectarian warfare could cease and the sensible administration of business begin.

Then there is a third dream, of a rather different kind—one that perhaps exercised a special hold over the imagination in Britain in the decades after 1945: the dream of the politician who transcends class identity, who moves away from defining origins not just to enjoy wider worlds but to take the wider view. This is also in its way a dream about enlightenment, but this time figured as the logic of a life-story: its hidden premise is the thought that those who most emancipate themselves from their inherited class identities are best placed to be swayed by reason and evidence rather than tribal affiliation. This is different from the cherished picture of the working-class boy or (less often) girl who rises through education but then devotes a political career to fighting for the interests of 'their people'. It is, rather, a fantasy about not having one's own 'people', about not being bound to the chippy defensiveness of a lower class or the insouciant selfishness of an upper class. If traditional politics is seen as more about belonging than agreeing, then, by contrast, the imagined form of this trajectory is of a release into the free upper air where good arguments are sovereign.

II

It was the fate of Roy Jenkins more than of any other recent figure in British politics to serve, both during his life and even in some ways since his death in 2003, as the point of intersection of these dreams. Over and above his actual achievements and failures, Jenkins carried the burden of embodying the 'centre-left's' idea of its best self, the emblem for all those hopes that politics might be that little bit more rational and enlightened and, well, agreeable than it actually is. He appeared to meet several of the job-specifications for the role of social-democratic philosopher-king (or, in his case, biographer-king—actually a very telling difference). And his own trajectory, moving easily from a South Wales grammar school via Oxford to Parliament and high society, becoming Chancellor of the Exchequer by the age of 47, meant that he not only seemed unstoppably destined for the highest political office of all, but also that he could be seen as the champion of a cultivated liberal progressivism that was not tarnished by the stale stereotypes of cloth cap versus top hat.

But that, of course, was not how it turned out, and so then Jenkins became a prize exhibit in another cherished category: the nearly-men—those who, for all their talents, don't quite make it to the top, and who then have another set of qualities projected onto them. They are judged to be not quite ruthless enough, perhaps too self-indulgent, and not sufficiently in tune with the mainstream elements within their parties. For all his early achievements, Jenkins's later political aspirations were not to be crowned with success: he failed to become leader of the Labour Party, failed to become Prime Minister, failed to 'break the mould' of two-party politics, failed to get Britain to join the Euro, failed to replace the first-past-the-post voting system. Inevitably, given the hopes that had been vested in him and the fantasies that had partly worked themselves out through him, these failures were seen as more than personal. As Jenkins's career subsided into jowly grandeeism, a set of political hopes could be seen as subsiding with him. The stubbornly unbroken mould was taken by many of his admirers to indicate that politics remained tribal not rational—and by many of his critics to confirm the deserved fate of those who desert their party.

All this makes it hard to see Jenkins in himself, stripped of the dreams that attached themselves to him. In choosing 'a well-rounded life' as his subtitle, John Campbell risks some obvious jibes about his increasingly portly subject, but he delivers on its promise. It is a persuasive, if at times indulgent, portrait of a life rich in satisfactions, with enough 'hinterland' (as the currently favoured metaphor has it) to give depth and character to half a dozen contemporary identikit politicians. Judged by the most exacting political criteria, Jenkins's career is frequently described as a form of failure even though he enjoyed more success than most of his peers. But whatever the final verdict on that career, it surely has to be said that he lived a conspicuously successful life. At its heart were a long close marriage and three children, to which were added the pleasures of a varied adult sexual life including at least two extremely long-lasting relationships with intelligent and interesting women. Beyond this, he had an unusually wide circle of friends with whom he enjoyed many of his favoured activities: above all, talk, both serious and gossip, but also travel, attractive houses, good food, even better wine, and so on. And he wrote—and wrote not just more and better than most politicians but more and not noticeably less well than a lot of professional writers. Call no man happy till he is dead, but the photo of a beaming 75-year-old Jenkins in black tie being awarded the Whitbread biography prize in 1995 for his life of Gladstone suggests a life well rounded in many senses.

And yet, some nagging questions about Jenkins's politics and political leadership—and, indeed, about the shape of modern British politics more generally—turn out not to be quietened or resolved by this meticulous and perceptive biography. If anything, these questions become more pressing in the light of what we learn about the decisions and beliefs of a man who, though never crowned as philosopher-king, became for a while the Crown Prince of social democracy. Nor are these questions merely of historical interest, since the interpretation and assessment of Jenkins's career continue to frame our sense of progressive political possibilities for the early twenty-first century. Were the travails of the Labour Party in the later decades of the twentieth century contingent upon local circumstance and individual personality, or did they represent a structural fissure in the political project of being, under the circumstances of an increasingly global and rapidly de-industrializing economy, both left-wing and electable?

One term often used now in disparagement of Jenkins, as of some other intellectuals of the Labour Party of his generation, is 'patrician'. We know well enough what we're supposed not to like about anyone to whom this term is applied—their condescension, assumption of superiority, and unreflective class attitudes—but perhaps there is something too touchy and too quickly dismissive going on here. After all, there are ways in which leaders and teachers—and, remembering the root of the word, parents, too—*should* assume that they 'know better', however much that grates on our ostensibly egalitarian (or, in practice, simply relativist) sensibilities. Jenkins's 'patrician' confidence helped to make him a notably liberal Home Secretary, an unwavering champion of the European ideal, and, in the final phase of his career, a valuable Chancellor of Oxford University. In these cases, one of his most impressive features was his willingness to act repeatedly upon the truth that politicians should lead as well as follow. Such action is an acknowledgement that politics cannot only be about satisfying aggregated expressed preferences in their current form. Of course, in the case of any individual politician, too much may depend on an under-examined inheritance of social and cultural confidence, and this may partly have been true of Jenkins, especially as he aged. But at the same time, he was able, at least in the first half of his career, to put this confidence to good radical purposes, and in this he was representative of the relation between his generation of Oxford-educated Labour politicians and the wider electorate.

One of the central tensions in Jenkins's later career turned on this question of political leadership understood in broad terms and not simply as a series of reactive gyrations round the greasy pole. On various social, moral, or cultural matters, he had been prepared to defend policies which were initially regarded as unpopular with substantial sections of public opinion—on, for example, decriminalizing most forms of homosexual activity, or on ensuring proper rights to abortion, or on not reinstating capital punishment, all matters which he supported as Home Secretary even though he did not, as is sometimes thought, initiate legislation on them. Although public opinion on the question of joining (or, later, of staying in) some form of European union tended to be more volatile, it was again the case that Jenkins was prepared to take a stand on what he believed was right, even in the face of hostility from considerable sections of his own party as well as of the country at large.

But on the central questions of the relation between social justice and economic and fiscal policy, broadly understood, Jenkins seemed less willing to try to educate public opinion in a more radical direction. It is possible to account for this contrast in his record in more than one way, but it does raise the question of whether he had comparably intense convictions about these questions as he did about matters of personal behaviour or historic identity. At the beginning of his career, in the late 1940s and early 1950s, he endorsed what were at the time the conventional Labour positions on nationalization and redistribution as essential steps in the pursuit of greater social justice. Later, he seems to have retreated from these positions, and to have done so a good deal sooner than many of his contemporaries in the party. Later still, he disowned Socialism as the label for his beliefs, speaking and writing rather little about questions of economic inequality. Was this, as some of his critics alleged, to be explained largely in terms of his own increasing social and financial success, his obvious delight in the company of the moneyed and titled, and the waning of an inherited political faith which had always served him better than he had served it? Or was it, as the defenders of his memory prefer to argue, that the 'Socialism' from which Jenkins was increasingly estranged had become an anachronism and that he was helping to fashion a politics better adapted to what is now called 'an aspirational age'?

In making the case against erstwhile colleagues whom he now deemed to be on the 'far Left' of the Labour Party, the later Jenkins frequently took his stand on the need to appeal to the middle ground of the electorate. But not only may this insistence, as indicated earlier, risk allowing spatial metaphors too much traction; it also tends to treat existing expressed beliefs as largely immutable. Why, after all, might the project not be thought of in terms of trying to get inhabitants of that middle ground to change their minds? In considering the relationship between political leadership and the movement of public opinion during Jenkins's lifetime, it can be instructive to reflect on the marked and widespread shift in public attitudes towards sexual behaviour, and especially what used to be regarded as sexual morality, that took place in the course of two or three decades after the 1960s. This did not happen solely, or perhaps even principally, as a consequence of leadership by an enlightened elite, but legislation that was in some cases ahead of public opinion played a vital role, most obviously on the issue of homosexuality. The idea that one should aim to capture or represent the 'middle ground' of opinion on this topic would, during these decades, have in fact been a conservative option. Taking a properly progressive position that people should not be prosecuted or stigmatized for their sexual activities may, in these circumstances, have played a part in helping to educate public opinion without, in the medium term, losing public support. (Something similar might be said about the abolition of capital punishment.)

One of the questions provoked by reflection on Jenkins's later career is how far something analogous might have been—might still be—successfully attempted about issues of social and economic justice. Why should radical prescriptions pilloried (by some) as being 'far Left' not have played a similar role in economic as in sexual matters—initially at odds with a lot of inherited or unexamined conviction, but with a good prospect of helping in a process which would lead to their being seen as the received wisdom of the next generation? In actuality, the shift in public attitudes in the 1980s and 1990s was, in contrast, further to the right on these matters, but it is difficult to disentangle the causality—the influence of right-wing governments and right-wing media in both Britain and the USA in the 1980s cannot be discounted, and so, therefore, the counter-factual possibility of politicians and opinion formers of left-wing convictions having a comparable role in moving opinion in the opposite direction cannot be discounted either. Broader social and economic changes were, of course, also in play here, but the case for certain kinds of economic organization as the expression of a commitment to human freedom and dignity can be made as compellingly as the case for certain kinds of protection for sexual or cultural tastes, and it is not obvious that a progressive politician should despair of the possibility of making that case successfully. Endorsing received attitudes on these questions may concede too much to the powerful interests that, in unidentified or unexamined ways, will tend to steer opinion rightwards in a class-divided society.

But what, by the time he was in a position of political leadership, did Jenkins actually believe about the economic determinants of social justice? His critics said that his idea of a centre party represented little more than a coalition of the well intentioned, a fantasy that flew in the face of the adversarial nature of politics in general and of the British electoral system in particular. Rather than leading from the left, endeavouring to persuade the majority of voters that the attempt to tame capitalism in the name of social justice is both right in itself and in their interests, a self-consciously 'centrist' political leader risks taking the present disposition of political conviction (or prejudice or apathy) as given, positioning himself at the mid-point of that imagined spectrum. In place of a political philosophy, a centre party of this kind simply relies on the psephological equivalent of a tape-measure. Could this be said of Jenkins in his later career, and if so what kind of inspiration can he continue to provide?

These are not questions that John Campbell raises, at least not in this explicit form, perhaps feeling they are incompatible with the task of producing a readable biography. He may also admire Jenkins too much to want to take this distant, quizzical perspective. He records that 'Roy Jenkins was the first public figure I was aware of and always the one I most admired'; having served as 'an enthusiastic foot-soldier in the SDP', and published a short biography of his hero in 1983, Campbell 'continued to admire him almost without reservation'. In addition, this is the authorized biography (a task first assigned to Andrew Adonis and then handed on), written with the full collaboration of Dame Jennifer Jenkins. Although Campbell is too intelligent a writer to be content with any kind of hagiography and too well informed about recent British politics not to recognize Jenkins's centrality to the 'painful' story of 'the retreat of social democracy in Britain', perhaps he cannot be expected to call into question the basic premises of his hero's later career. Nonetheless, the story he tells so skilfully is susceptible to more than one reading, and on the principle of trusting the tale not the teller it is possible to draw some rather more analytical conclusions from his account.

Although Jenkins's social trajectory has sometimes been represented as a classic rags-to-riches story, the reality was more complex (to his credit, Jenkins himself mostly did not attempt to play the proletarian card). It is true that his father began his working life as a miner, but he soon moved into trade union activity and was the miners' agent for his region, as well as a county councillor and governor of several local schools, by the time Roy, an only child, was born in 1920. His socially ambitious mother also engaged in local public life, eventually becoming a magistrate and supporter of various charities. In the 1920s and 1930s the family lived in fairly prosperous comfort, enjoying the services of a live-in maid (not uncommon far down the scale of the middle and even lower-middle class at the time). Just as Jenkins never made it to the equivalent of the White House, so, it is clear, he never started from the equivalent of the log cabin. In 1935 Arthur Jenkins was elected to Parliament for the mining constituency of Pontypool, and his son soon got used to meeting leading Labour figures, as well as seizing every chance to listen to debates in the Commons ('as a schoolboy, I was an assiduous gallery-sitter in the House'). Jenkins senior was close to Attlee in the late 1930s and early 1940s, leading to appointment as Under-secretary in the Ministry of Town and Country Planning in 1945. But then in 1946 he died at the age of 63. Violet Attlee, the Prime Minister's wife, collected the grieving Mrs Jenkins and her 25-year-old son from the hospital and took them back to Downing Street with her for the night, which proved to be, as Campbell nicely observes, 'the only time in his life that Roy slept in Number Ten'.

After only modest success at the local grammar school, Jenkins spent a year at University College Cardiff attempting to prepare himself for Oxford entrance examinations. He failed to win an open scholarship, but was offered a place; it would seem that his father found a way to support him financially. At Balliol between 1938 and 1941 Jenkins's overwhelming focus was the Union, though (foreshadowing things to come) he twice failed to be elected President. The old quip that 'life is just one damned Balliol man after another' was to be true of his political career from the start; Edward Heath and Denis Healey, for example, were a couple of years ahead of him in the college. But the most important figure in Jenkins's Oxford years was the dashing Tony Crosland, a year older, with whom he had a passionate relationship for a while, and with whom he maintained a close and at times rivalrous friendship for almost forty years until the latter's early death in 1977. Crosland was the more obviously brilliant of the two, with more theoretical interests (he briefly became an economics don after the war), but Jenkins was already displaying that ability to master and organize quantities of information that was to serve him well in his ministerial roles. He duly got a first in PPE, despite allegedly getting the lowest mark in philosophy obtained by a Balliol man since that degree was first examined in 1924. Jenkins then had a somewhat miscellaneous war, ending up as a captain, working with the code-breakers at Bletchley. In 1940 he had met an attractive, capable, independent-minded Girtonian called Jennifer Morris, daughter of the Town Clerk of Westminster; the couple were married early in 1945—the reception was at the Savoy; Attlee made the principal speech—and it remained a close, mutually supportive marriage, albeit of a distinctly traditional kind, for the remaining fifty-eight years of his life. When their first child was born in 1949, Attlee and Crosland stood as godparents.

From his teenage years, Jenkins had had one consuming interest and goal: a parliamentary career. It says much about his single-mindedness at this stage that while he was doing his basic training in the army he subscribed to just one publication, which he read avidly—*Hansard*. After a few false starts, he entered the Commons in 1948 as member for Central Southwark (Attlee's support certainly didn't hurt), becoming the baby of the House. Since his constituency was due to disappear in a boundary change, Jenkins found himself a safe Labour seat at Birmingham Stechford, which he represented from 1950 until he went to Brussels as President of the European Commission in 1976.

As Campbell rightly notes, MPs during Jenkins's long first spell on the opposition benches (1951–64) enjoyed a very considerable amount of autonomy, spending much less time on constituency work than is now the norm and not called upon for particularly onerous duties by their parties (and, it's important to remember, practically removed from the constant and immediate media scrutiny now common). This suited Jenkins well, since he had already embarked on his second career as a prolific journalist and author. Campbell claims (mimicking his subject's taste for ranking and comparing) that 'no other front-rank politician besides Churchill has ever written so much—or so well'. Whatever the truth of that claim, Jenkins certainly exercised his talents during these years. After well-received books on the parliamentary crisis of 1910 and on Charles Dilke, he undertook a labour of love by writing a biography of Asquith, a figure he admired and identified with—Campbell supplies a long list of Asquith's characteristics that Jenkins shared, including a 'lack of interest in speculative thought'. His own standing as a serious journalist was attested by the offer in 1963 of the editorship of the

Economist. After some hesitation, he turned it down: 'Politics is my life. I've never wanted to do anything else.'

Just occasionally, Campbell, to his credit, permits himself some critical assessments of Jenkins's writing, with its tendency to favour surface polish over deeper analysis. Quoting a representative example, he writes: 'The long sentence is superbly constructed and reads impressively. Yet it contains no thought that is in the least original; rather a catalogue of solidly conventional judgements complacently accepted as received truths,' adding, 'he wrote quickly and disliked revising what he had written, because he thought in images rather than ideas'. Received truths, writing quickly, not thinking in ideas—this sketches the flip side of Jenkins's much-praised intellectual manner, suggesting some of the reasons why he was never likely to make a mark as a radical political thinker.

What Jenkins loved, and excelled at, was a traditional form of parliamentary debate, to which he brought a resourceful eloquence and a responsive historical sensibility. Oratorical or forensic triumphs in the Commons represented some of the high points of a career not light on achievement. For Jenkins, this was a lifelong romance, going back to those teenage years in the gallery and forward to his biographies of Gladstone and Churchill, the outstanding parliamentarians of their respective epochs. If he came to seem a somewhat old-fashioned figure in the later stages of his career, that was due in part to the fact that he still at some level identified with what he regarded as Parliament's Victorian and Edwardian heyday.

At the time of the 1951 election, Jenkins was still willing to call himself a Socialist, but in the internecine war between Bevanites and Gaitskellites by which the Labour Party was riven in the 1950s, he became a firm Gaitskell man and was soon identified as being on the right of the party. Gaitskell's early death in 1963 was a deep personal and political loss for Jenkins; he kept the former leader's photograph on the mantelpiece of his Oxfordshire house for the rest of his life. If it can be said that Hugh Gaitskell was his adored political elder brother (perhaps Attlee was nearer to being his political father), then, Campbell suggests, Tony Blair was to be his favoured political son—a thought which raises further disturbing questions about the political legacy of Jenkinsite social democracy.

In some ways, the statement that best represents Jenkins's politics when he was still a rising star was written not by him but by Crosland. It is hard now to recover the confidence about political and economic progress that underlay Crosland's *The Future of Socialism*, published in 1956. It serenely declared, for example, that 'the national shift to the Left, with all its implications for the balance of power, may be accepted as permanent'. And it held that economic prosperity, too, could henceforth be taken for granted, so that 'we should not now judge a Labour Government's performance primarily by its record in the economic field'. Instead, other goals should become the focus:

'personal freedom, happiness, and cultural endeavour; the cultivation of leisure, beauty, grace, gaiety, excitement, and all the proper pursuits, whether elevated, vulgar, or eccentric, which contribute to the varied fabric of a full private and family life'. In a much-quoted swipe at the Fabian tradition of the Webbs, Crosland wrote: 'Total abstinence and a good filing-system are not now the right sign-posts to the socialist Utopia: or at least, if they are, some of us will fall by the wayside,' and the book's concluding words were: 'We do not want to enter the age of abundance, only to find that we have lost the values which might teach us how to enjoy it.' Jenkins shared Crosland's commitment to the fuller expression of human personality, which helped make him such an appropriate and successful Home Secretary in the 'swinging sixties', but he also shared the optimism that economic growth would be a benign force, tending to reduce the worst forms of social injustice, and this belief may have had a bearing on the later phases of his career.

Taking this optimism into the 1960s, Jenkins declared that the aim of politics should be 'to use prosperity as a means to a more civilised and tolerant community', which led him to this revealing statement of belief: 'One of the central purposes of democratic socialism is to extend throughout the community the freedom of choice which was previously the prerogative of the few.' This could be interpreted as expressing real radical intent, though 'freedom of choice' is a slogan any Socialist may do well to be wary of, and Jenkins's phrasing may seem to suggest leaving the prerogatives of the few unaltered, while giving others the chance to share them.

Perhaps someone who was always so excited by, and enthusiastic about, the United States was anyway unlikely to identify the extremes of inequality as the principal social evil. Like several others of his generation, Jenkins was drawn to the openness, informality, and sense of opportunity characteristic of American society, not least because those features contrasted favourably with the still deeply class-conscious and hierarchical character of British life before 1960. His admiration for FDR and his affinity with well-connected progressive Democrat intellectuals such as Arthur Schlesinger Jnr. and J. K. Galbraith sufficiently indicate his distance from the doctrinaire ideologists of laissez-faire, but even so he seems never to have subjected the fiction at the heart of the 'American dream' to really searching analysis or to have been unduly disturbed by the social and political as well as economic consequences of the fact that American capitalism has been a great engine for making the few wealthy by profiting from the labour of the many. Campbell refers to 'Jenkins' close identification with the post-Roosevelt Democratic Party: classless, progressive, liberal and outward-looking, his model of what the Labour Party could be, if only it would shed its antiquated commitment to old-time socialism'. The adjectival overkill here ('antiquated', 'old-time') expresses Campbell's enthusiastic identification with his subject, but such language can also suggest a similarly limited analysis of the real determinants of life-chances in a contemporary capitalist society. There has, after all, been no shortage of voices suggesting that a little Socialism, 'old-time' or otherwise, might have helped transform the Democrats into a more genuinely progressive party over the past half-century.

The Labour governments of 1964–70 marked the apogee of Jenkins's career within the party. Following his successful tenure at the Home Office, he became Chancellor of the Exchequer in November 1967, after Jim Callaghan had appeared hapless in the face of a sequence of sterling crises eventually leading to devaluation. It was not an easy time to be in charge of the nation's finances, but Jenkins was widely reckoned to have played a bad hand well. Going into the 1970 election, he seemed the obvious choice to succeed Harold Wilson as Labour leader, and Prime Minister, whenever the latter chose to stand down. But after Labour unexpectedly lost the 1970 election, the question of entry into Europe became a live political issue once more. Jenkins, believing that Britain should be part of what eventually became the European Union, felt he had no choice but to vote with the great majority of Heath's Tories in favour of entry; he saw the issue as, in Campbell's words, 'bringing together all the sensible people in public life in a common cause'. A considerable portion of his own party was opposed, and many never forgave him for what was seen in some quarters as a betrayal, an interpretation that drew sustenance from his lofty manner and expensive tastes. In 1973 three Bradford councillors complained in the *Labour Weekly*: 'The truth is that Mr Jenkins is indistinguishable from the liberal wing of the Conservative party.' There was enough truth in this to be damaging, and it prefigured his hopes for a coalition of the right-minded in 1981. He clearly preferred the company of enlightened Tories such as Peter Carrington or Ian Gilmour to many on the left of his own party. He was a frequent guest in grand houses and a constant luncher at Brooks's and other haunts of the well born, well connected, and well oiled. While in opposition, he could pay for his high life by doing even more journalism. His salary as Chancellor had been £8,500, but in the tax-year 1972–3, when out of office, his total declared income was over £35,000 (getting on for £400,000 at today's prices), only a fifth of which came from his salary as an MP. Even his tastes in fiction, where his favourite modern authors were Evelyn Waugh and Anthony Powell, suggested the claret-loving socialite rather than the mining-bred Socialist.

During his second spell at the Home Office in 1974–6 he oversaw important legislation promoting gender and racial equality, while also introducing a much-needed independent element into the system for investigating complaints against the police (at the time the Commissioner of the Met, Robert Mark, was attempting to tackle corruption in his force, offering the memorable definition that 'a good police force is one that catches more crooks than it employs', which has continued to prove a demanding benchmark). When

Wilson unexpectedly announced his decision to stand down as Prime Minister in March 1976, triggering a contest for the party leadership, Jenkins decided to throw his hat in the ring, though by this point he had alienated a good many people in the party (the story was told that 'when one of Jenkins' supporters tried canvassing a group of miners' MPs in the tea-room he was met with a kindly brush-off: "Nay, lad, we're all Labour here"'). He came third in the first round of voting among Labour MPs, behind Michael Foot and Jim Callaghan, and promptly withdrew. He then withdrew from domestic politics more comprehensively by accepting the offer of the presidency of the European Commission, spending four years in Brussels with limited power and abundant perks.

Jenkins raised the profile of the Commission and enjoyed consorting with heads of state. His grand manner, and imperfect French, led one wag to dub him 'Le Roi Jean Quinze'. He certainly had a regal way of doing things. For example, he knew that he ate and drank and smoked too much, so while he was in Brussels he briefly took up running as a form of exercise. But he did it in his characteristic manner. Initially, he would walk through the Bois de la Cambre to a lake not far from his Brussels residence and jog a carefully timed 14-minute course there, before being picked up by his official car and driven back. 'After a while, he started being driven to the Bois as well as back.' (Similarly, his way of dieting, briefly, involved drinking white wine rather than red at lunch.) On the major policy question, he took the debatable view that 'monetary union is more likely to be the cause of economic convergence than the result of it', and pressed for this. But all the while he was still brooding on the configuration of domestic politics in Britain.

Reflecting on Jenkins's already evident 'centrist' leanings in the mid-1970s, a friend observed: 'I don't think that in his heart of hearts he cares—or knows—much about the trade union movement.' This proved to be one of the chief weaknesses of his position within the Labour Party in the 1970s (for all that he was the son of a miners' MP), especially as he came more and more to believe that the unions were part of the problem facing current economic policy rather than part of the solution. Campbell refers more than once, and quite accurately, to Jenkins's 'journey from socialism' during these years, and Jenkins described himself at the end of the 1970s as 'an extreme moderate'. He believed, as Campbell puts it, that Labour 'could not afford to be a narrow socialist party imposing unpopular left-wing nostrums on the basis of a minority vote, but must aim "to represent the hopes and aspirations of the whole leftward thinking half of the country ... A broad-based, international, radical, generous-minded party."' But again this forecloses rather than stimulates analysis: of course 'broad and generous' will seem to trump 'narrow and unpopular', but only because the verbal deck has been stacked in advance. Why, turning the negatives into positives, should Labour not have aimed to be 'a broad socialist party carrying out popular left-wing policies on the basis of a majority vote'? It says something about how far Jenkins had travelled in the previous few years that when late in 1979 he showed the first draft of his Dimbleby lecture to his friend Ian Gilmour, the latter—at the time a junior Tory minister—objected on the grounds that it was 'too right-wing'.

The Dimbleby lecture was, in effect, Jenkins's rallying-call to form a new left-of-centre party (perhaps more centre than left). Campbell's account of the founding of the Social Democratic Party is naturally sympathetic to Jenkins's own perspective, but far from one-eyed. This is well-trodden ground, though he does add engaging details, including that the only place that could be found on a Sunday to photocopy the celebrated 'Limehouse declaration' by the Gang of Four (Jenkins, David Owen, Bill Rodgers, Shirley Williams) for distribution to the press was the Savoy hotel. Initially, the new party, in a semi-formal alliance with the Liberals led by David Steel, enjoyed a heady surge of popularity. A Gallup poll in December 1981 put the Tories on 23 per cent and Labour on 24 per cent, but the new Alliance on 51 per cent. Jenkins triumphantly re-entered Parliament by winning Glasgow Hillhead in March 1982, though the Alliance's frothy lead in the polls was already beginning to diminish. But the biggest blow came the following month: perhaps the individual with the single greatest impact on the immediate fate of the SDP was General Galtieri. When Thatcher was able to go to the polls in 1983 as the victor in the Falklands (as well as presiding over a reviving economy), the SDP was never likely to be able to turn its early popularity into a substantial number of seats. Campbell loyally suggests that, on the eve of the 1983 election, 'while still far from looking like an alternative government, the Alliance did begin to look like an alternative opposition'. But critics at the time maintained that analysis of voting patterns in that election confirmed their reservations: by attracting the overwhelming bulk of its votes from former Labour supporters and scarcely any from former Tory supporters, the SDP's impact was effectively to split the anti-Tory vote, with disastrous consequences. Jenkins's supporters retorted that the Labour Party of the day had made itself unelectable, and that the future lay with a coalition of those who were committed to a viable form of social democracy.

Jenkins was by some way the most senior of the Gang of Four and in these years he still had the aura of a political heavyweight. In a 1983 lecture he suggested that what was needed now was 'some of the rational panache which Keynes showed nearly fifty years ago', and 'rational panache' is not a bad description for Jenkins at his best. But his best now increasingly seemed in the past. In the 1987 election, he lost Hillhead (Mrs Thatcher lamented the rejection of a figure of such stature, adding, 'It tells you something about the Scots'). On the broader front, the Alliance vote played much the same role it had four years earlier. 1987 was effectively the end of the road for the SDP, especially since it led to David Owen's vain (in both senses) attempt to maintain it as a separate party after the bulk of his supporters had endorsed merger with the Liberals. For the most part, Campbell is admirably fair-minded in discussing Jenkins's colleagues and opponents across his career, but Owen is one figure to emerge from this biography looking pretty tarnished. (Norman Lamont is another, but that is a more straightforward case.)

Though Jenkins went on to serve for some years as leader of the Liberal Democrats in the Lords, his active parliamentary career was now largely over. For all his romance with Parliament, even he began to tire of the mixture of town-council tedium and prep-school rowdiness. But his election earlier in 1987 as Chancellor of Oxford University gave him a congenial stage for some late theatrical flourishes, and he did his best to carry out his pre-election promise to 'oppose the philistinism and short-sightedness which now colour prevailing attitudes towards the universities'. For the most part he seems to have won golden opinions for his performance in this largely ceremonial and advisory role, though Campbell does record the occasion when, conferring an honorary degree on Gorbachev in 1996, Jenkins—'having perhaps lunched too well with Robert Harris'—referred to him throughout as 'Mr Brezhnev'. His last important political role was as the author of a 1998 report proposing an alternative to the first-past-the-post voting system, a long-held passion. However, the complex balancing of various alternative mechanisms that he proposed in his report failed to persuade those committed to the existing system and failed to satisfy those who wanted radical change. Blair made a polite show of welcoming the recommendations, but the report was consigned to the longest of the long grass, to Jenkins's bitter disappointment.

Well before his death in 2003, Jenkins had come to seem an increasingly dated figure in many ways. He was good at lengthy formal speeches and elegantly turned articles and essays—the traditional genres in which his political heroes from earlier generations had also excelled—but his somewhat antique Asquithian style of oratory seemed out of place in the slanging match of the late twentieth-century House of Commons and he did not come across well on television. No less of its time was his taste for a lot of wine with lunch (in addition to a lot of wine with dinner). Campbell is admirably uncensorious about Jenkins's tastes, drink and sex included, but the simple fact of recording numerous instances of his alcoholic consumption has the effect of making it seem likely that a more abstemious age will be shocked. No less dated were his assumptions about domestic responsibilities, where he was about as far from being a New Man as it is possible to be. He seems to have disqualified himself from even the most minimal practical tasks: in 1994 he fell off a table when attempting to change a light bulb. Various possible explanations come to mind, as do several variants on an old joke.

What he did continue to do was write—and at an extraordinary, Trollopian rate. His prize-winning 700-page life of Gladstone was researched and written in just under three years, but even that feat was put into the shade by his

1,000-page biography of Churchill. After five months' preliminary reading, he began writing this just before his seventy-eighth birthday and finished it very shortly after his eightieth (including 1,076 words on Christmas Day 2000—he always kept meticulous records of his daily production). Asquith he had admired almost without reservation; Gladstone had fascinated yet puzzled him; Churchill he came to respect even above his predecessors, and there were obvious elements of identification at work: 'I was . . . increasingly struck by Churchill's extraordinary combination of an almost puritan work ethic with a great capacity for pleasure, even for self-indulgence. I found that combination rather attractive.' His readers evidently found his attraction attractive: published in October 2001, the book sold 100,000 copies in hardback before Christmas and a year later sales in the UK and the USA had reached half a million.

In all his writing (and, apparently, conversation) Jenkins loved reputation-bibbing, loved all kinds of ranking, especially of politicians; he also loved emphasizing personality and the play of contingency. In Britain there seems to be a particularly highly developed tradition of this kind of connoisseurship where political history is concerned, though presumably other countries have their own versions. It involves an obsessive focus on individual character, a delight in awarding and withholding marks, a rather narrow and parochial focus on Westminster and Whitehall, and an untroubled passage between past and present. The register of such talk is unmistakably male, redolent of the brandy-and-cigars part of an evening. For initiates, it retains a deep fascination; for everyone else, it seems clubby and boring. Jenkins adored such conversation and, by all accounts, excelled at it. Several of the appreciative reminiscences of him repeat that he had no interest in 'abstract theories or general speculation'. This is usually recorded with approval, being part of his much-applauded delight in 'contingency' and 'personality', but it can also, of course, be a limitation. Perhaps it is a characteristic quite frequently found in both politicians and biographers, 'abstract theories' seeming to be at odds with the demands of their respective vocations. But this brings us back to those fundamental questions raised earlier about Jenkins's legacy for progressive politics.

Apart from the special circumstances of 1945–8, successive Labour governments in the second half of the twentieth century, and possibly beyond, struggled to square the circle of introducing measures that make for a less unjust society while not risking any diminution of prosperity. The difficulty of doing this was compounded by the fact that from the 1950s onwards there was an established expectation of a constantly rising level of consumption; competition between the parties became increasingly centred on ways of meeting this expectation. Until the 1970s it seemed possible for Labour governments to do this while also using the power of the state to reduce certain forms of inequality. It is arguable that for a progressive politics to be successful in the long term the electorate would eventually have had to be persuaded that a somewhat reduced level of prosperity for the majority together with a substantially reduced level for the very wealthy might have to be the short-term price of running a decent society and retaining enough autonomy to make the decisions necessary to sustain it. But that, understandably, was not how it seemed to most actual or potential Labour leaders at the time.

It was certainly not how it seemed to Jenkins, though he became less and less inclined to elaborate any kind of theorized alternative, and it is here that the optimistic assumption that abundance will do away with the worst aspects of inequality could become a limitation. Jenkins treated economic growth as an overwhelmingly positive force, eventually bringing plenty to all; even in our less optimistic times 'growth' has remained the governing shibboleth, treated reverentially by politicians of all parties. But growth, as the markets understand that process, makes the rich vastly richer since they are the ones best placed to take advantage. Left to itself—this has become more evident as governments of all stripes have increasingly been inclined to leave the markets to themselves—economic 'growth', although it may make life at the bottom of the heap a little less desperate, serves to increase inequality, and increasing inequality involves increasing injustice. In believing, or affecting to believe, that 'a rising tide lifts all boats', too many politicians since Jenkins's time have persuaded others, and perhaps themselves, that a widely diffused prosperity will render most questions of social justice irrelevant. Any other view is stigmatized as 'levelling down', as though Socialism, especially through the action of nationalization or redistributive taxation, were simply a matter of taking away, reducing some of the wealth and traditional privileges of the rich out of a kind of mean-minded envy or spite. But attempting to limit the power that those who control capital have to shape or ruin the lives of those who don't is not levelling down. It is a deeper form of the same logic that Jenkins used to increase human dignity and autonomy by his reforms as Home Secretary, though he seems not to have been drawn to theorizing that logic, and his later political career might be seen as a testament to the difficulties always likely to ambush any progressive politician whose policy prescriptions are not underwritten by an analysis of the determining power of capital.

The question of the effective agency actually available to a modern politician has been given a sharper edge in recent years by the popularity of a more bleakly pessimistic analysis than Jenkins was ever confronted with. On this view, the much fought-over questions of policy and ideology are ultimately not what matter any longer because what now determine the fate of all contemporary politics are the convulsions of global capitalism. The rival political parties are like tiny dinghies tossed on mountainously rough seas. One recommends using the paddle to try to move in one direction, one in the other. But however furiously they paddle, their efforts are of little consequence; the tide and the swell really determine their movement, and at any moment a huge wave may reveal their impotence and irrelevance. From this perspective, any ideal of 'social justice in one country' is an illusion. National politics has lost its autonomy everywhere: investment bankers and foreign-exchange traders are more powerful than any politician. As a result, the bodies of successive pretenders to the crown of the social-democratic philosopher-king are doomed to be strewn on the savage rocks of international finance capitalism.

The pessimism of this analysis contrasts starkly with the confidence in the efficacy of government that was so widely shared when Jenkins came of political age. But even if the now-fashionable argument exaggerates the powerlessness of national politics, as it surely does, we can still ask whether Jenkins needed to adapt his more optimistic understanding of the relation between the state and the economy to the changing character of structural exploitation. And those who now look to Jenkins's example for inspiration about the prospects for any form of social democracy may have to ask harder questions about this topic than his admirers, rightly celebrating other aspects of his achievements, usually seem disposed to do. This could involve re-describing the long agony of the Labour Party in the late twentieth and early twenty-first century, as it ceased to be the political expression of the industrial working class and failed (thus far, at least) to become the representative of all those whose lives are blighted by the new forms of finance capitalism. The latter may in fact be a substantial majority of society, but a local version of the American dream—the dream that seduces people into believing capitalism might work for them—has been increasingly successful at diverting energies away from developing the necessary consciousness of shared interest.

It could be said, therefore, that the lesson to be drawn from the final phase of Jenkins's political career had less to do with moments of tactical misjudgement or those contingent cultural tastes journalists loved to harp on, and more with that much-lauded distaste for general ideas. In the absence of a developed analysis of the changing character of capitalism and thus of what a progressive party should or could represent in a financialized world, it was harder to appreciate that one of the principal tasks of such a party had to be to combat the class that collects an economic rent from its control of finance. Members of that class are not the 'owners' of the means of production in the old sense; but their influence and their rewards come from their commanding place in a structure in which the rest of economic life is determined by the decisions of the controllers of vast capital sums. Enough people can be bribed by the promise of increased personal prosperity to make the maintenance of this structure seem a viable political project for the right. Extending throughout society 'the freedom of choice which was previously the prerogative of the few' cannot, in these circumstances, be an adequate goal for the left.

If those who wish to audition for the role of Jenkins's successor as the next best hope of progressive political leadership are not to end up crucified by the demands of an unanalysed conception of 'growth', then they may, metaphorically speaking, first have to write an updated version of Crosland's *Future of*

Socialism. But perhaps what now needs to be superseded is not the killjoy bureaucratism of the Webbs, but rather the grinning compliance of 'Britain is open for business'. In the mid-1950s Crosland stressed the virtues of 'enjoyment', and rightly so, but in a more hedonistic age we may need to turn the notion of enjoyment in a broadly Aristotelian direction, thereby including such values as citizenly participation in a society whose logic is not shameful, and the development with others of ways of life that conduce to human flourishing rather than stunting it. If that case could be persuasively made, there would then be no need to alter the final sentence of Crosland's book, which might also serve as an ambivalent verdict on Roy Jenkins's later political career. 'We do not want to enter the age of abundance, only to find that we have lost the values which might teach us how to enjoy it.'

III

In late 2005, Michael Ignatieff was a 58-year-old professor at Harvard. His career up to that point had been spent in academia and journalism, largely in Britain and the United States. Though Canadian by birth, he had spent all but two of his adult years living abroad and he had no first-hand experience of politics at any level. And yet, within little more than a year he had become, extraordinarily, a member of the Canadian parliament and deputy leader of the Liberal Party. Some two years later, he became the party's leader. In spring 2011 he precipitated a general election, in an attempt to unseat the ruling Conservative Party. The outcome was catastrophic for the Liberals, who were reduced to third place and a rump of only thirty-four seats. It was the worst result in the history of the Liberal Party, the worst result in Canadian history for an incumbent Official Opposition party, and the first time since Confederation in 1867 that the Liberals had failed to finish first or second. Ignatieff lost his own seat, and immediately resigned as leader. Since then he has resumed his academic career in Harvard and Toronto.

These bare facts suggest a remarkable story that might be interpreted in several different ways. In *Fire and Ashes*, Ignatieff has chosen to write a personal memoir of the episode which aspires to double as a set of reflections about the nature of politics. The model of Machiavelli, dismissed from office but still donning his robes to turn his experience into the knowing maxims of *The Prince*, is never far from the well-stocked mind of this long-time teacher of political theory. *Fire and Ashes* is scarcely longer than Machiavelli's classic, and its subtitle indicates a similar aspiration to use the ashes of defeat to fertilize some evergreen thoughts about the timeless nature of politics itself. The book is stylishly written, as one would expect of an author who is a novelist and journalist as well as a widely published academic. The phenomenology of the experience, what it felt like to be there in the middle of things, is engagingly rendered. But as it moves into more general reflections we start to have the unnerving feeling that the author may not, even now, have gauged the true significance of the extraordinary tale he has to tell.

Before his political adventure began, Ignatieff was already a well-known public figure, principally on the basis of his writing and speaking about human rights and international relations, but also because of an earlier career presenting ideas programmes on British television in the 1980s and 1990s. He was, in addition, exceptionally well connected within the previous generation of the Canadian political elite: his father had been a senior diplomat, only one step away from becoming Governor-General, and Ignatieff himself had been on close terms with the former Prime Minister, Pierre Trudeau, and his circle. Ignatieff's glittering educational journey had taken him to Oxford and Cambridge as well as Harvard; he cultivated friendships with figures such as Isaiah Berlin, whose biography he wrote. But with this background and education, not to mention his very considerable confidence and charm, there was obviously the possibility, to say the least, that many voters would feel he gave off an offensive sense of entitlement and opportunism.

There are moments when *Fire and Ashes* seems to grasp the centrality of this theme, but they are undercut by the book's more settled disposition to lament a form of politics in which such accidents of background and perceived identity could be decisive. Academic teacher of political theory that he is, Ignatieff cannot resist invoking the shades of those other unsuccessful or disappointed politicians who attempted to distil some universal political wisdom from the bitter experience of failure—not just Machiavelli but Cicero, Burke, Tocqueville, Mill, Weber. Yet although he couches his own observations in a form that aspires to timelessness—'great politicians have to be masters of the local', 'self-dramatization is of the essence of politics', 'there are no techniques in politics'—his account is in practice structured by an implicit assumption of decline. Ignatieff constantly uses phrases which reveal that he really feels that although politics used to be a properly conducted process in which arguments were put before citizens by eloquent spokesmen and judged accordingly, the whole thing has now gone to pot. He laments that 'nowadays, partisanship has degenerated from the rough-and-tumble jousting of former days to really venomous character assassination', and complains that 'political allegiance is no longer a tradition, it's just a preference'; he refers in passing to 'the degraded politics we are enduring', and fondly calls the kind of campaigning he enjoyed 'politics, old style'.

Quite when this change is supposed to have happened is not clear. But the structuring presence of this assumption makes his otherwise wry and engaging reflections not just obliquely self-justifying—he clearly thinks his talents would have been better suited to the politics of the day before yesterday, which may well be right—but also of questionable relevance. If politics (politics in Canada? politics everywhere?) has become (in the last ten? twenty? thirty? years) little more than a kind of unscrupulous, money-driven advertising campaign which works mainly by subliminal association, then do his more high-toned injunctions to the next generation to pursue the 'noble' art still apply?

As things turned out—though was it really so difficult to foresee that something like this would be the case?—one advertisement by his Conservative opponents, endlessly repeated, outweighed all Ignatieff's arguments and eloquence: it simply said 'Michael Ignatieff. Just visiting.' And the trouble is that, however much one may admire his courage and respect the seriousness of his own sense of commitment, one can see that there was an irreducible element of truth in that hostile ad. He *had* played no part in Canadian politics or even Canadian life before being parachuted into his seat, and he *does* look to have returned for good to academia following his defeat. He *was* 'just visiting', even though he genuinely aspired to be Prime Minister of his country. It is not obvious that we learn any new truths about politics as a result of having seen this improbable meteor rise and, predictably, fall.

Indeed—and this is what may make his book more poignant than he intends—it is not obvious that Ignatieff himself has learned that much about politics from this experience. Of course, he can now write about and teach the subject with both the benefit of first-hand anecdotes and the authority of the battle-scarred veteran. But he repeatedly uses the verb 'learn' when referring to things he either must have been fully aware of beforehand or else not properly have understood since. He writes, for example: 'I learned that you can't take refuge in moral purity if you want to achieve anything,' but did the close student of Machiavelli really have to wreck the fortunes of the Canadian Liberal Party to learn that? He declares that 'I took a long time to understand what politics should be about,' but his book leaves one with the suspicion that he has the same normative ideas about what politics 'should' be about as he had at the outset. There is also the suggestion of mock-humility about some of this: I submitted myself to the judgement of my fellow-citizens and I was found wanting, but in the process I learned to respect their judgement. But actually he doesn't respect it. He can't conceal his disdain for the low animal cunning of Stephen Harper, his victorious Conservative opponent ('a transactional opportunist with no fixed compass other than the pursuit of power'), yet he somehow wants to endorse the process by which Harper was preferred by the voters.

Fire and Ashes may seem to be yet another case-study of 'the intellectual in politics', but if so what it illustrates is nothing to do with the traditional themes of innocence or a lack of capacity for business: Ignatieff was evidently a fast learner who became quite a skilful political operator in some respects. It illustrates, rather, the way that an intellectual who is driven by a compelling need to turn experience into prose is always likely to exhibit a kind of double-consciousness about popular politics: he professes to believe that the process by which 'the people' choose their leaders is, at bottom, a noble and right one, yet at the same time he cannot conceal his conviction that the majority of his fellow-citizens make their choice not just for bad reasons but on grounds that he would not recognize as reasons at all.

'Eggheads of the world unite,' as Adlai Stevenson famously quipped, 'you have nothing to lose but your yolks.' Perhaps Ignatieff is a bit more hard-boiled now, or at least would like us to think he is. But surely in this case something else *was* lost, and lost by all those Canadian citizens who stood to gain from having a more successful Liberal leader defeat a Conservative Party bent on the kind of market-driven policies that blight the lives of the vulnerable everywhere. Ignatieff may show admirable resilience in coming to terms with his own personal defeat, but that does little for the millions whose lives may be somewhat worse for the failure of his experiment, and this points to an irreducibly egotistical element in this testament.

Fire and Ashes is at some level a 'how-to' book, but it is not about how to do politics. It is more like a piece of existential moral exhortation about how to live a life. Its true teaching is that one should embrace experience, stretch oneself, go for it. 'A defensive life is not a life fully lived,' he writes, with all the authority of the brave man who tried something hugely ambitious and risky. The ethical worth of this disposition not to shirk experience is ultimately what underwrites this *Apologia pro Vita Sua*: I gave it my best shot. Fine, but urging others to do this in Scout-leader tones ('In politics, as in life, the challenge is how you learn from your mistakes') doesn't really help recommend the disposition. Like the authors of countless self-help books, he insists that we should 'strive for success and don't allow any excuses for failure, but above all learn equanimity'. Unfortunately, hearing the echo of Polonius only a few syllables away does not help one to treat this with the seriousness it clearly craves.

Nonetheless, it is impossible not to be touched by the romance of his story. The Prince sweeps down from the clouds, pulls the sword from the stone, and the reign of enlightenment begins (the mixture of metaphors accurately reflecting the melange of desire and fantasy invested in his candidacy). It is appealing to think that a very clever, very talented, decent, and well-intentioned man could step out of the study door and persuade his fellow-citizens to entrust the leadership of their country to him. Perhaps Ignatieff came close to pulling this off, unexpectedly close; no doubt we should admire him for trying. But the moral which this short, stylish book suggests to me is not the announced insights into the 'nobility' of the democratic process. It is, rather, that to succeed in a professional business you have to be a real professional, and where politics is concerned every 58-year-old expatriate professor may have left it too late to be that.

13

Social Analysis

'Aspiration', Attitudes, Inequality

I

Historians have long had a taste for labels which aim to capture something about the character or spirit of a period—*The Bleak Age*, *The Age of Equipoise*, or, in a recent work on the inter-war period, *The Morbid Age*. It will serve early twenty-first-century Britain right if it becomes known as 'The Aspirational Age'.

To those who can still use 'aspirational' without wincing, such a label might seem high praise. It connotes endeavour, making something of oneself, trying (as an older idiom had it) to better one's station in life. Glossed in that way, the term might seem to describe a blameless and near-universal human disposition, but in the past few years 'aspirational' has been used to pick out something more specific, something symptomatic of a particular moment in the development of social attitudes in Britain. There is now, according to some commentators, an 'aspirational class', rather uncertainly located within a traditional hierarchical social structure, but composed of people who probably had working-class parents, who hope to have professional- or managerial-class children, and who want more of 'the good things of life'. But they want, it is said (on what authority is not clear), to attain these goals without taking on the outward trappings and associated snobbery that historically went with moving into a higher social class. An edge of *ressentiment* lurks under 'aspiration', not quite of the old truculent 'Jack's as good as his master' kind, which acknowledged social position while claiming it was not the whole of life, but of a more swaggeringly relativist kind, confident that 'no one has the right to say what someone else ought to do or think'. Any other view of the matter is damned as (in another word currently suffering trial by popularity) 'elitist'.

Unleashing Aspiration: The Final Report of the Panel on Fair Access to the Professions (Cabinet Office, 2009).
British Social Attitudes: The 26th Report (The National Centre for Social Research, 2010).
An Anatomy of Economic Inequality in the UK (Government Equalities Office, 2010).

The widely remarked decline of deference here takes a more chippily self-assertive turn. Although the practical goals aspired to may seem very familiar—a better job, a better house, a better education for one's children—the manner of pursuing them is at once insistently egalitarian and aggressively competitive. As these attitudes increasingly assert and impose themselves, we are encouraged to talk not merely of an aspirational class but of 'the aspirational society'.

Politicians of all parties are committed to giving 'the aspirational society' more of what it is thought to aspire to; indeed, there is an inflationary tendency in our public language by which each of the various objects of desire is successively elevated to the status of 'a right'. Much of this may seem to be simply the verbal flotsam thrown up by the tide of market populism that followed from the Thatch–Lab pact of the 1990s. But it also has to be seen, at least in part, as evidence of a deeper shift in the ways we conceive of our social relations. The very recent emphasis on 'aspiration' is one symptom of the effective, if disguised, abandonment of what have been, for the best part of a century, the goals of a progressive politics. For, when looked at more closely, 'the aspirational society' expresses a corrosively individualist conception of life. In trying to understand the relation between this conception and the reality of contemporary British society, we get help of different kinds from the three semi-official publications under review. Taking them in turn, they might be said, epigrammatically, to throw some light on what we're told to want, what we think we want, and what we can want.

II

In January 2009 the government announced the creation of a 'Panel on Fair Access to the Professions', chaired by Alan Milburn, a Cabinet minister during the Blair years. It has now published its conclusions in a report unfortunately (but perhaps predictably) entitled *Unleashing Aspiration*, suggesting we all have some inner Fido currently subject to unnecessary restraint. The panel's task was to 'help ensure that everyone, including those on moderate and middle incomes as well as the wealthiest, has a fair chance to access careers in high-status professions'. We may let pass the statistical absurdity involved in using 'moderate' as a euphemism, and focus on how the task is a highly, perhaps artificially, circumscribed one. The start and end points are given and, apparently, immutable: people come from very different economic backgrounds, the professions in question are indisputably desirable goals, and so the issue is how to ensure a 'fair' chance for those trying to get from the one point to the other. Although both the title and the remit of the panel suggest a self-evidently laudable ambition—who, after all, would want to stand up for unfair access to the professions?—the case is deeply ideological, grounded in the politics of market populism. Even though the panel emphasizes its independence from government, this report is all about making the right noises and promoting popular changes rather than about deepening our understanding of social processes. In other words, the report is, unsurprisingly, a piece of politics, not a contribution to social science.

In one of those phrases we have heard so frequently in the last two or three decades that we no longer register their absurdity, the Milburn report says we need to see how parents 'could be empowered with a new right to choose a better school for their children'. But what can such a piece of electioneering populism actually mean? A 'right' is something universal, something everyone in the relevant category (in this case, parents) has. But if *all* parents have a right to choose a 'better' school for their children, won't we have to maintain in each locality a number of ghostly 'worse' schools to which no children are actually sent, but whose function is to show that the 'better' schools are better than some others? The rhetorical pattern to which this conforms has become depressingly familiar in recent years: each individual has a 'right' to something 'better', where 'better' tends, in practice, to mean 'better than someone else's'. Over and over again, the Milburn report uses the empty and misleading rhetoric of a race in which 'everyone' is 'entitled' to have a 'fair chance' of 'winning'. But if there are winners there must be losers, and sporting metaphors such as this one are intended to deflect attention from the basic fact that, by and large, the most important determinants of who ends up in which category are not some miraculously independent qualities of 'ability' or 'effort' on the part of the individual, but the pre-existing distribution of wealth and power in society.

The ideological functions of this language are most tellingly exhibited these days in the widespread use of the metaphor of 'the level playing-field'. Milburn uses it all the time ('We will not create a mobile society unless we can create a level playing field of opportunities', and so on). Of course, we know, or think we know, more or less what this phrase means. It's a way of saying that everyone should have a chance to compete on equal terms without things being tilted either against them or in their favour from the start. But language carries its own DNA, which then works itself out without our intending or even being aware of it. So, we might begin by noting that sports that are contested on a 'playing-field' are nearly always between two teams. Already the brave individualism of 'opportunity' takes a knock; indeed, the metaphor suggests something as old-fashioned as the conflict between two classes. And then, in most sports that I can think of that take place on a playing field, the teams change ends at half-time. If there is a slope, it affects both teams equally. But the most important limitation of the metaphor, which almost entirely undermines the purpose for which it is normally cited, is that what happens on the playing field, however level, is heavily determined by things that happen off it. Recruitment, wealth, facilities, time, training . . . there's almost no end. Taking a spirit-level to every inch of the pitch is not going to even up a contest between Manchester United and a local pub team.

A part of all of us rebels against attending to the phrase this closely, finding such analysis either too literal or too literary-critical: surely we know that such a phrase just means a fair fight with no unfair advantages built in from the start? How to decide what such phrases 'mean', however, is a complex business, and a highly contextual one. When used as a metaphor, the phrase 'level playing-field' brings in various sporting connotations which the writer may or may not intend, but which affect readers' uptake. Pretty obviously, 'a fair fight' is another such metaphor: using it as a gloss does not help us escape from the de-stabilizing associations of language—quite the contrary. 'A fair fight' suggests observance of certain rules or perhaps conventions by two boxers (originally) who have already been roughly matched by weight. A 'level ring' is not the same thing as a 'fair fight', nor does the emphasis on the direct winner–loser confrontation of 'fight' sit well with the Milburnite 'more shall have prizes' mentality. And anyway, what are 'unfair advantages'? Competitors never come to 'the starting-line' with identical histories, and the fact that, in any kind of 'race', some people seem to be able to run faster than others could be seen as the very epitome of an unfair advantage—just as much an accident of birth as being the eldest son of a duke.

The endeavour of radical critique has to be, as so often, to say that we need to start the analysis from further back. By the time the teams or athletes get onto their level playing fields and race-tracks, unfairness has already done the greater part of its work. Moreover, these sporting metaphors conjure up a very simple, end-stopped activity as a model for the vast complexity of social life. Becoming a successful barrister, say, is not like running a hundred yards or kicking a ball into a net. There's no start line, no referee, no set finish time, and so on. What is a 'fair' advantage? Being confident and having clear articulation may be very helpful attributes for a barrister who has to plead in a crowded court, but we have to ask where these capacities come from, who is likely to have them, and so on. These are all familiar arguments, or at least they *were*. I'm rehearsing them here only because the relentless cultivation of individualism by governments of both parties over the past thirty years has somehow started to make them seem extreme or obstructive.

In its confusions as well as its idiom, the Milburn report faithfully expresses the character of contemporary public debate in Britain. For instance, as sufficient demonstration of its claim that 'the UK's professions are among the world leaders in their fields', the report declares: 'The UK is a global leader in healthcare. For example, the pharmaceutical industry is the biggest investor in research and development (R & D) in the UK, valued at £3.3 billion in 2005.' Even if we leave aside the symptomatic equation of 'world-leading' with money spent, and the still more problematic equation of 'healthcare' with the activity of a big pharmaceutical corporation, it is surely obvious that being the biggest anything in the UK cannot in itself be an indicator of leading the world.

But it is in its handling of its central category of 'social mobility' that the report most tellingly reveals both its sloppiness and its indicative status. The phrase 'social mobility' has become, it should be said, a difficult term to use with any precision. In different settings, it is now deployed to refer to one (or more) of the following three things:

1. The trajectory of individuals in the course of their lifetime away from a starting point defined by their parents' socio-economic position.
2. The changing patterns of advantage and disadvantage between social groups in comparison to the patterns among the previous generation.
3. The changing structure of employment or rewards in a society across generations such that a larger proportion of the population comes to be in 'higher' occupations.

Clearly, these changes do not all entail one another, and one may take place at the expense of the others. A long-familiar criticism of the 'scholarship-boy' model of individual mobility was that it left the relative position of the social classes entirely unchanged, even reinforcing existing hierarchies by siphoning off some of the outstanding talents of the lower classes into the higher classes. Conversely, the third type of 'social mobility', structural change in employment over time, may result in, say, many manual jobs being replaced by white-collar jobs without the relative status and scale of rewards of most of the class filling those jobs being significantly altered. In 1951, one in every eight jobs was classified as 'professional'; by 2001 over one in three jobs were so classified, but the *relative* position of the groups who filled the various levels of job may not have changed very much.

Colloquially, and in practice in the Milburn report, social mobility is always upwards. The report speaks of it as unequivocally desirable. But it takes only a moment's reflection to see that where many of the things being 'competed' for are positional goods, upward mobility for some can only be achieved at the expense of downward mobility for others. The Milburn report's obsession with the question of who fills what it calls 'the top jobs' deflects attention from this. If more of those jobs are filled by individuals belonging to social classes whose members practically never filled such jobs in the past, then, we are told, we have social mobility. The report is entirely silent on what happens to the people who would otherwise have occupied these jobs but have now been pushed out by the upwardly socially mobile. And the report is almost entirely silent on what happens to all those who are left behind in their original class when the 'talented' and 'able' have sped off along the highway of success. The Milburn report seems to envisage society as a kind of lifelong 11-plus, but with the majority ending up in grammar-school occupations and the minority in secondary-modern occupations.

Unleashing Aspiration is only able to maintain the obligatory upbeat tone by fudging the senses of 'social mobility'. Its picture of the future is one in which nearly everybody gets a better job and some people get a much better job. 'At its simplest, social mobility means better jobs for each generation so that our children can do better than us.' It manages, or tries to manage, this juggling act by shifting between the first and third senses distinguished above. Some of the time, it seems to recognize that what is involved is structural change in the economy, with manual and routine jobs being replaced by managerial and professional jobs. This is said to be what happened in 'the first great wave of social mobility' (roughly the 1950s to the 1970s). And this is what will happen in the near future: we are told that 'up to nine new jobs in ten created over the next decade will be in professional and managerial sectors' and thus that 'seven million new professionals may be needed'.

But on this showing, the Milburn report's problem will solve itself: if these really are *new* jobs, then there will have to be massive recruitment of employees not from professional-class backgrounds, and that is what is here counted as 'social mobility' and the 'realizing of aspiration'. Of course, as a general mechanism for social mobility, this is inherently inflationary. In subsequent rounds, the number of new professional jobs that would need to be created to exceed the supply of professional-class offspring available to fill them increases exponentially, and very soon social mobility comes to an end because everybody then fills a job at the same 'top' socio-economic level as their parents did (and there's nobody to empty the dustbins). In practice, the report's attention is not mostly focused on this kind of structural change, but on the characteristics of the individuals recruited to fill the 'top jobs' in the existing occupational structure. The task is to make sure that all the 'top jobs' (can they all be 'top' if there are so many of them?) don't go to the same kinds of people as used to get them. That would be the 'closed-shop society'. They must go to 'able' people from groups who didn't use to have them. That is the 'aspirational society'.

The mixture of bounciness and vacuity indicates that the report is largely written in Blairspeak (or, since this idiom is now general not individual, better referred to as 'blahspeak'). In blahspeak, 'social mobility' is equated with 'realizing pent-up aspirations'. There are several absurdities here, but one is that the second phrase refers to subjective experience, the first to an objective pattern. People may realize pent-up aspirations in all kinds of ways without altering their position in the social structure in the slightest. But this slide into the subjective is once again revealing of the individualist assumptions behind the Thatch–Lab pact, marking the transition from do-good to feel-good. Social life is a benign competition in which most shall have prizes.

The report never really confronts these contradictions. Perhaps the most telling, and also most chilling, moment comes when it briefly acknowledges that the idea of a 'meritocracy' as coined by Michael Young had (as it is here chummily expressed) 'downsides as well as upsides', and that 'others point out that social mobility cuts both ways—the more there is, the greater the likelihood is that, as some people climb up the social ladder, others fall down it'. The report does not even blink; the very next sentence goes on: 'The Panel takes a different view. We believe that a socially mobile society is not just a laudable objective. It is a necessity if the UK is to flourish—economically as well as socially', and on into the usual unstoppable gabble of blahspeak. The Panel, we notice, doesn't *argue* against the position stated in the previous sentence: it simply 'takes a different view'. But the very use of the verb 'point out' in that earlier sentence indicates that this isn't something about which a 'different view' can simply be 'taken'. What those others were 'pointing out' was a matter of logic: where positional goods are concerned, some can't go up without others going down. But that's so off-message; clearly, we need to 'take a different view'.

The Milburn report talks the language of optimism and is the very model of a 'Yes, we can' document, but its assumptions actually reveal a profound kind of pessimism. It is a pessimism, first, about there being any way in which society collectively, acting primarily through the state, can re-shape its underlying socio-economic structure. Staggering inequalities of wealth are simply taken to be part of the natural order. Where it used to be said that 'the poor are always with us', eternal existence is now granted to the rich as well. The market distributes wealth; government then tries to see 'fair play' within the resulting (destructively unequal) framework. And it is a pessimism, secondly, about there being any way for people to agree on what is valuable in life other than in terms of market-modelled consumer satisfaction. The only goals people may be assumed to share are a desire to 'get on', to move up some imaginary (but misleading) 'social ladder'. When these two forms of pessimism are combined, we get the hollow activism of 'fair access'. Everyone has an equal right to try to get what they think they want. Wants can't be criticized: that would be elitist. The market cannot be gainsaid: that would reduce prosperity (itself a completely implausible and undemonstrated contention). Prosperity is the only agreed good, and it trumps all other considerations. We are all, apparently, believers in what George Bernard Shaw long ago dubbed 'the Gospel of Getting On'.

III

But how can we know, with any reliability, what 'we' all 'believe' in? The standard answer to this question, an answer that carries weight with politicians and campaigners of various kinds, is that social surveys tell us. Among these surveys, *British Social Attitudes* is pre-eminent. Published annually since 1983, it claims to be 'the authoritative guide to public opinion in modern Britain'. Its 'findings give a voice to the general public, and paint a picture of what Britain *really* thinks and feels, in all its richness and diversity'. And what the 2010 edition tells us about current attitudes towards inequality and injustice is that in the past dozen years 'the public has taken a decisive turn to the right', and again that 'the public, including Labour supporters themselves, no longer has as much belief in the importance of equality and of government action to secure it as it once did'.

There can be no question but that the various contributors to this volume are highly trained empirical social scientists well versed in the professional literature. The kinds of measurement and analysis it involves clearly rest on immensely sophisticated statistical techniques. The appendices are full of such heavy-duty machinery as the following: 'If the design factor for a particular characteristic is known, a 95% confidence interval for a percentage may be calculated using the formula: p ± 1.96 × complex sampling error (p) = p ± 1.96 × DEFT × the square root of p(100–p) over n.'

Yet, for all the elaborate techniques on show, there is no way round the fact that the eliciting and recording of social attitudes is an inescapably verbal business. Even without plunging into controverted philosophical questions about the extent to which attitudes are constituted linguistically, the simple practical point is that all the information contained here comes from asking people questions. There is no such thing as a transparent and neutral medium in which to do this (though social scientists sometimes appear to believe there is): we have to use the everyday vocabulary of a natural language, and we are thus immediately caught up in the not wholly controllable operations of meaning and reference, tone and register, association and resonance, which it would take a reader of Empsonian delicacy to begin to do justice to.

Presumably, computer-geeks were responsible for the useful formulation 'garbage in, garbage out'. Perhaps where social surveys are concerned we need some motto such as 'language in, language out'. As with jokes, so with questions: it all depends how you ask 'em. For example, in one survey reported here, respondents were asked: 'Do you think it is wrong or not wrong... a married person having sexual relations with someone other than his or her husband or wife?' The answers to this question are then said to reveal 'the acceptability of cheating on a partner'. Well, maybe, but 'cheating' obviously introduces associations of covertness and betrayal that are not necessarily triggered by the original question. That question does not specify whether the sexual activity is known or unknown to the husband or wife, or indeed sanctioned or encouraged by them. Some respondents might think it was perfectly acceptable for a husband or wife to have sexual relations with other people if their marriage no longer, for whatever reason, provided them with sexual satisfaction, while at the same time being very censorious about 'cheating' on a partner. (All the questions in this survey, incidentally, assume heterosexual coupledom as the norm.) Others again might think the difference between being 'married' and having a 'partner' was the crucial distinction where having sex at all is concerned, and so on. Still others might detect a moralistic impulse behind the very asking of either of these questions and respond negatively as a result.

Or again, at one point two questions from different surveys are equated: 'People who want to have children ought to get married', and 'It makes no difference to children whether their parents are married to each other or just living together.' But, obviously, the wording in each case mobilizes a different set of associations. Some people might rebel against the prescriptivism of the first question, but also feel that the second is too open-ended to be agreed with. Other respondents might tick the 'disagree' box in the second case because they think that bitterly unhappy couples might be less likely to separate if they were married and so the difference it makes to children in having married parents is likely to be a negative one. But here their answer will have been aggregated as part of those who hold a 'traditional' view of the family. And so on. There is no pure wording, no way to escape from the web of language. Numbers are, of course, science's answer, part of the dream of freeing knowledge from the tiresome inexactness of language. But where 'social attitudes' are concerned, what is quantified has to remain irreducibly verbal through all the relentlessly statistical and tabular presentation of 'findings'. It's all about what we think people mean by what they say they think they believe when asked a particular question.

So, what kinds of evidence are the judgements about the British public's shift to the right based on? One set of data indicates whether respondents agreed or disagreed with statements about welfare benefits such as the following: 'If welfare benefits weren't so generous people would learn to stand on their own two feet,' or 'Many people who get social security don't really deserve any help.' The responses show that under New Labour, the numbers *dis*agreeing with these propositions have fallen fairly sharply. In 1994, 52 per cent disagreed with the first of these statements; by 2008 only 20 per cent did so, while the numbers disagreeing with the second proposition fell from 50 per cent to 27 per cent over the same period. Clearly, these figures can be interpreted in various ways: they may, for example, be related to the actual levels of benefits, or to the numbers in the population claiming them, or to levels of prosperity enjoyed by the respondents themselves, and so on. The authors of the survey very plausibly interpret these and similar figures as showing how the public's attitudes are in considerable measure shaped by government policy and rhetoric. But it is also evident that the questions cast the choices in starkly individualistic and moralistic terms. When a statement describes the existing benefits as 'generous' and characterizes the alternative as 'standing on [one's] own two feet', it requires a certain analytical effort by the respondent not to be carried along by the powerful evaluative weighting. It's possible that many of those who say they *agree* with the statements in the survey might also agree with a differently worded statement which points towards opposite policy conclusions, such as: 'Large-scale changes in the economy mean that some of the least well-off people are going to need welfare benefits at some point in their lives.'

Similarly, we are told that in 1994 support for the government's role in redistributing wealth was as high as 51 per cent, but by 2007 had fallen to as low as 32 per cent (the financial crash has since driven it back up a little). At least, that was the proportion of respondents who said they agreed with the proposition that 'Government should redistribute income from the better off to those who are less well off.' Why, we may wonder, would two-thirds of the population in such a grotesquely unequal society be against this? Do they think of themselves as the 'better off' and thus potential losers? Statistically, most of them must be wrong about that, and anyway, historically a lot of the better off have been among the most ardent champions of redistribution: narrow economic self-interest does not dictate all views. Does 'redistribute' suggest something too indulgent as well as too literal, just giving a chunk of some people's money to other people? Is the emphasis on 'income' significant, as being what individuals 'earn' as opposed to 'wealth', which they may acquire in various ways? Or is it simply that taking money away from those who have 'earned' it to give to those who haven't seems unfair?

I have used quotation marks liberally throughout as a reminder of the extent to which such reported 'attitudes' depend upon and are constituted by linguistic transactions. The rhetoric of our public debate is, for this reason, never 'mere' rhetoric in any dismissive sense: how we talk about these things comes to be part of what we think we 'believe' about them. In the case in question, the danger about such 'findings' is that a political party may then conclude that it would be an electoral liability to support, say, a properly graduated tax system, a conclusion which may not be at all warranted. Nonetheless, the changes over time in positive or negative responses to what have been the same questions is a significant finding of some kind, and it would be hard to disagree with the authors' conclusion: 'In repositioning itself ideologically, New Labour helped ensure that the ideological terrain of British public opinion acquired a more conservative character.'

British Social Attitudes also enquires about many matters that are not conventionally thought of as 'political', and every so often one comes across a priceless nugget. Buried in a table within an appendix to a chapter on 'Religious faith and contemporary attitudes'—the table is, in the fetching parlance of applied social science, labelled 'Responses to dichotomised items in the religiosity scale'—are a remarkable pair of numbers. If we grant the survey method its claims to representativeness, then these two numbers tell us that 48 per cent of the British adult population believe in the existence of 'heaven', but only 28 per cent believe in the existence of 'hell'. The discrepancy between these two statistics is puzzling, even alarming. Heaven and hell, after all, stand to each other conceptually as do 'on' and 'off'. If you believe some are rewarded (whatever that can mean), then you believe that some are not rewarded. Of course, there have traditionally been those Lib-Dem kinds of in-between places, such as 'purgatory' and 'limbo', but these have only functioned as detention centres where various dodgy or unlucky characters are kept until their full entry visas come through. Ultimately, if you believe this sort of thing, there are only two final destinations, but necessarily *two*.

So, what do those people 'believe' who show up here as believing in heaven but not in hell? Is the Day of Judgement for them just a way of sorting the sheep from the sheepish? Is there thought to be a kind of points system, administered by the great Home Secretary in the sky (another reason to be alarmed . . .), in which some people go straight through and some have to wait a while, but get through in the end? But if everyone goes to heaven, then (other conceptual puzzles aside) doesn't that turn us all into potential salvation-scroungers, deprived of the incentive to work for a better after-life? Whooping it up down here might be worth a few aeons in the detention-centre if we have the assurance that thereafter it's all going to be harps and houris for ever. But this is already to over-elaborate: all we know is that 72 per cent of respondents in this particular survey responded 'no probably not' or 'no definitely not' when confronted by the words 'Do you believe in hell?' (Those who answered 'no, probably not' presumably exercised some hermeneutic charity and took that answer to indicate a lack of certainty about hell's existence rather than any uncertainty in knowing what their own attitude was.) Unfortunately, that proportion of them who had already answered positively to the question about 'heaven' were not then asked, 'So what the fuck do you think happens to those people who don't go to heaven?'

Instead of seeing the difference as a theological one between omni-salvationists and selective-salvationists, perhaps we should see these responses as saying something about a 'kind/tough' range. A quarter of the population identifies as 'tough', believing that people should get what's coming to them (for ever), while another quarter identify as 'kind', wanting everyone at the end of the party to get a goody bag (for ever). And in this respect, the discrepancy between the answers, though theologically confused, may be deeply expressive of everyday social attitudes in contemporary Britain. Perhaps heaven functions as another metaphor for the idea of the kind of competition in which there are quite a lot of winners but absolutely no losers. Heaven is where the aspirational aspire to. Hell is a left-over from the old 'closed-shop society'.

'Fair access' has become the new theology. Upwards is, after all, the direction in which we all want to move. Everyone has a right to a better after-life. You can't say fairer than that, can you?

IV

The National Enquiry Panel's *Anatomy of Economic Inequality in the UK* is all about the size of the goody bags we each get in the here and now. It is the report of the panel, chaired by Professor John Hills, which was established in October 2008 under the aegis of the Government Equalities Office. The Hills report is everything the Milburn report is not: analytical, systematic, and free from feel-good rhetoric. What sense of the reality of 'the aspirational society' do we get from its vastly detailed enquiries?

The structure of the report reflects its terms of reference in that it was required to explore the ways in which socio-economic inequalities interact with the 'strands' defined by existing legislation about equality: gender, ethnicity, disability status, sexual orientation, religion or belief, and age. But to do this, the panel needed to establish a finely textured account of the forms and patterns of socio-economic inequality in the first place, using a vast mass of information much of which, it claims, has never been analysed in this way before, and it is this picture of the economic structure of contemporary British society that is so striking. All the more striking for being written, as it says, 'against a back-drop of widespread public ignorance of the scale of inequality in the dimensions we have examined'.

The concentration of inequality at the top end of the scale is what emerges most clearly. The disparities of income among the bulk of society (of those in work, at least) are certainly substantial, but they are not huge: 90 per cent of those in full-time employment earn less than about £46,000; the median income is around £23,000, so even the 90th percentile is only earning twice the median. But where the seriously better off are concerned, the report is full of indisputable conclusions that should stop all current talk about 'equality of opportunity' in its tracks. Take, almost at random, this sentence: 'Households in the top tenth have total wealth (including private pension rights) almost 100 times those of the cut-off for the bottom tenth.' Just in case you haven't yet got your eye in, it is worth spelling out that the 'cut-off for the bottom tenth' is quite a long way from the very poorest in society, since below that point the graph falls away very sharply. Nonetheless, the households in the top tenth are not just two or three times as wealthy (the sort of differential we are used to observing in everyday consumption patterns), and not just ten times as wealthy (the sort of multiplier that makes for wholly different kinds of life-experiences), but one hundred times as wealthy as those who are themselves some way from the bottom of the heap.

This is dramatic enough in itself, but the aggregate figures involved here disguise an even more extraordinary disparity. Within that top tenth, the gap between the 91st and 100th percentiles is huge: the former have approximately four times the median total net wealth of the population, but the top 1 per cent have almost thirteen times that median figure. Repeatedly, the graphic presentation of the report's findings has to record laconically that the income or wealth or other advantages of the top 1 per cent cannot be properly represented visually because it goes 'off the scale of the figure'. All the distribution charts and bar graphs have this absurd appearance, with a huge chimney at the right hand side disappearing off the page.

What the Hills report also establishes incontrovertibly is, first, that this has not always been the case, and second, that it is not the case in other European countries. Its figures show a massive increase in wealth for the top tier of society since the 1980s, and quite staggering increases for a small (but still reasonably numerous) elite since the 1990s. For example, the top 0.05 per cent of the population had seen its share of national income decline pretty steadily from 1937 till the 1970s, as might be expected as societies moved in a broadly social-democratic direction, but by 2000 its share was *higher* than it had been in 1937. And the very rich got richer faster than the merely wealthy. In the 1980s, every group in the top tenth of taxpayers increased their share of national income, but in the 1990s 'the increase in the share of the top tenth was *all* accounted for by the top 0.1%'. Certain occupational groups stand out, and not just bankers, celebrities, and footballers. Between 1999 and 2007, the real earnings of all full-time employees of the top 350 companies in Britain were almost static: but 'the real earnings of the CEOs of the top 100 companies more than doubled (reaching £2.4 million per year) and those of the next 250 companies almost doubled (reaching £1.1 million)'. (According to a calculation by Compass, not quoted in the Hills report, the average ratio of employee-to-CEO pay was 1:47 in 1999; ten years later it was 1:128.) No less striking is the way in which in other leading European countries the top 1 per cent's share of the national income, having declined from the 1930s to the 1970s in a similar way to that in the UK, thereafter remained broadly flat rather than registering huge gains. 'The rise in the incomes of the very top', concludes Hills, 'has not, therefore, been a global phenomenon.' Where it has happened, of course, has been in the USA, whose Croesus-versus-helot economic arrangements the UK seems more and more determined to ape.

The upshot of the hundreds of pages of statistics and graphs in the Hills report is sobering, not least for those who think that, as a political issue, 'equality' principally involves combating inequalities between social groups defined in terms of gender, ethnicity, and so on. However desirable those goals may be in themselves, the fact is that the 'differences in outcomes between the more and less advantaged *within* each social group . . . are much greater than differences *between* groups'. What the Hills report carefully and unanswerably documents—and what the Milburn report over and over again inadvertently reveals despite itself—is that class (in the sense of objective economic position) is a much more powerful determinant of life-chances than any other variable, including gender and ethnicity. The Hills report also shows—this, once again, should not be at all surprising, but again it tends to be lost sight of in the muddy rhetoric of 'opportunity' and 'fair access'—that economic advantage and disadvantage are cumulative, in terms both of further economic advantage or disadvantage and of other kinds of social and cultural advantage or disadvantage. 'Economic advantage and disadvantage reinforce themselves across the life cycle, and often on to the next generation.'

In its conclusion, the Hills report notes that 'for people across a wide political spectrum' the key question is whether individuals' choices are made against 'a background of equality of opportunity'. Its response is all the more crushing for its measured restraint: 'The systematic nature of many of the differences we present, and the ways in which those advantages and disadvantages are reinforced across the life cycle, make it hard . . . to suggest that there is such a background of equality of opportunity, however defined.' It is that 'however defined' that really pulls the rug from under the New Labour house of cards. It says, in effect, that in a society as staggeringly unequal as contemporary Britain, all talk of 'equality of opportunity' can only function as an ideological smoke-screen.

'For many readers', reflects the Hills report in its summary, 'the sheer scale of the inequalities we have presented may have been shocking.' Actually, anyone who takes the trouble to be a 'reader' of this report is probably already primed not to be shocked, especially if, as is likely, they had attended to the discussion of recent studies such as Toynbee and Walker's *Unjust Rewards* (2008) or Pickett and Wilkinson's *The Spirit Level* (2009). But even for such readers what is still, in one sense, shocking is the way in which the officially endorsed language of 'aspiration' occludes the stark facts of economic inequality in so much public debate. It is characteristic of the antinomies of individualism that the rhetorical stress on 'choice', 'respect', and so on has to be ramped up to compensate for the loss of any real prospect of collectively altering the economic structure that shapes and sets limits to all agency. Moreover, as evidence from the USA has long shown, in an aggressively individualist society large numbers of people identify with what they *dream* of being able to do rather than with what they are *likely* to be able to do. (For many, that may, of course, be the only way to cope.) So we have to ask: is the 'aspirational society' simply the most recent ideological reflex of the entrenched inequalities of market individualism?

Some light is thrown on the contradictions within this position by its unsteadiness over whether the fundamental unit is the individual or something inexactly but emotively referred to as 'the family'. This unsteadiness surfaces in attitudes towards inheritance taxes. At the beginning of the twentieth century, a tax on estates ('death duties') was the flagship of progressive politics. It was thought to be a singularly effective weapon in the attack on 'privilege', that visible accumulation of advantages which the rich passed on to their children. At the time, the case for such a tax drew strength from arguments about the need for rewards to be proportional to effort; indeed, the Victorian argument about the deleterious effect of doles on the 'character' of the poor could be paralleled in the case of the children of the rich. Such taxes thereafter had a significant effect on the break-up of great landed estates, especially in times of economic downturn or other upheaval (e.g. 1919–21 and in the years after 1945, generating much Brideshеady nostalgia). In subsequent decades it proved easier to protect assets that were predominantly financial rather than landed, but inheritance taxes continued to have a mildly redistributory effect through the late twentieth century.

In recent years, however, such taxes have been steeply declining in popularity. In the United States, George W. Bush introduced a proposal to abolish federal estate tax altogether, and this proved to be hugely popular. (In fact, 2010 may be the first year since 1916 when no such tax will be levied by the federal government, though Obama has pledged to re-introduce it in 2011.) What makes the popularity of Bush's move all the more striking is that the tax was paid by only the wealthiest 2 per cent of estates. There are signs that inheritance tax is becoming almost as unpopular in Britain, despite the fact that at present it affects only 6 per cent of estates.

This puzzling development may owe something to the increase in home ownership in Britain, and particularly to the increase in the value of the homes owned. For a great many people, one of the most important 'aspirational' goals has been to own their own home, something which has involved not just a shift from rented to owner-occupied accommodation but also to smaller households as people increasingly prefer not to live with relatives (and, additionally, have fewer children). In the past fifty years, Britain's population has increased from 53 to 62 million, but the number of households has grown from 16.7 to 26.6 million, meaning that in 1959 there were on average 3.17 people per household as against 2.3 in 2009 (all figures in this and the following paragraph are from the Halifax Housing Survey published in January 2010). A kind of individualism enabled by prosperity is expressed in another statistic, namely that whereas in the period between 1945 and 1964 only 10 per cent of new properties were detached houses, since 1980 36 per cent of such properties have been detached.

As always, it is crucial to recognize who did and did not benefit from these changes. In the half-century between 1959 and 2009 the growth in earnings in real terms (i.e. adjusted for inflation) was 165 per cent. This represents a huge surge in overall prosperity, though we know (in some detail, thanks to studies such as the Hills report) that an aggregate of this kind masks how unevenly distributed such gains have been. The very, very poor have not done well; the poor have seen substantial gains; some in the lower-middle and middle income groups have seen big gains, some not; and the wealthiest have seen stratospheric gains. But against this aggregate figure must be put the increase in house prices over the same period which, similarly adjusted, was 273 per cent. Taking the two figures together might seem to suggest a disillusioning constraint on aspiration, but it has to be remembered that only certain groups in society are in the housing market, even now. In 1961 only 43 per cent of the adult population owned their own house; the figure is now 68 per cent. (It is also important to remember that as late as 1981 a third of households lived in council housing.) A third of the population currently doesn't own a home, and many of them may be getting less rather than more likely to do so on present trends. Conversely, many of the children of those who already owned a house half a century ago have benefited from a huge inheritance windfall, further strengthening their position in the distribution of wealth.

As political philosophers have long pointed out, the central fallacy of individualism is that what may appear to be rational for an individual acting in isolation is often not what it would be rational for a society to do acting in concert. There is an obvious tension between, on the one hand, our rhetorical emphasis on individual effort and the 'fairness' of competition, and, on the other, the endorsement of the 'natural' urge of parents to help children through the hereditary transmission of wealth and capacity. The language of 'aspiration' attempts to mask this contradiction. Like house-owning, with which it is now closely bound up, giving one's children a 'good start in life' is something to work for, a central meaning-creating narrative. Milburn's aspirational society is made up of people who (altruistically) want their children to 'get on' better than they did themselves and who (competitively) want their children to get on better than other people's children. They want them to have a 'fair chance', but they want to give them a better chance of having a fair chance than other competitors in the race will have. But this transmits and entrenches advantage. Parental levels of wealth and education are by far the most significant single determinant of life-chances (or as the Hills report briskly puts it: 'The evidence we examine confirms that social background really matters'). A recent OECD survey showed that male earnings in Britain were more highly determined by fathers' income 'than in any other wealthy nation'. That is not what most people understand by social mobility. So, on this evidence, most people are in favour of social mobility, but most people are also in favour of passing on their estates to their children. The only way to square the circle is to talk of *everyone* moving upwards across the generations, a rank absurdity, but one which rising general prosperity disguises much of the time. Social mobility as envisaged by the Milburn report all too often seems to conform to what one might call the 'trampoline in the lift' model. The person jumping on the trampoline rises higher than those around them, and feels that it is the outcome of their own effort, but the altitude they gain is trivial compared to the general rise, or fall, produced by the lift. (And since I have been talking about the hidden charges in metaphors, I should remark the most obvious feature of trampolining, namely that the gain in altitude is strictly temporary.)

The subjectivism of 'aspiration' is both its strength and its weakness: it speaks to individuals' sense of themselves as trying to get on, but hides from them the reality and power of the social patterns that determine their ability to do so. Similarly, the emphasis on 'social attitudes' as being both given and sovereign, the bedrock which governments must simply accept, reinforces the tendency to let the operations of the market replace collective deliberation. Attitudes are what consumers have: they must be simply pandered to or exploited. Citizens, on the other hand, need to be given reasons, including reasons to change their attitudes on this or that topic.

Overwhelmingly, the evidence suggests that policy and legislation play an important part in forming attitudes. This has been true of matters as diverse as capital punishment, homosexual activity, or smoking in public places. Equality legislation, especially in relation to gender and ethnicity, has clearly helped change attitudes towards discrimination. The conclusion has to be that politics can lead as well as follow. It is certainly possible that if any government took seriously the task of, first, educating us all about the scale and consequences of the scarcely comprehensible inequalities of wealth in this country (a task to which the Hills report makes an impressive contribution), and, second, of instituting measures to reduce those inequalities, then 'social attitudes' on these matters would change.

References

In the interests of brevity, this list includes only works actually quoted or referred to in the text; it is not intended as list of 'sources' nor as guide to further reading on the topics discussed.

Chapter 1

Matthew Arnold, *Culture and Anarchy* [1869], in *Culture and Anarchy and Other Writings*, ed. Stefan Collini (Cambridge University Press, 1993).
Vincent Brome, *J. B. Priestley* (Hamish Hamilton, 1988).
T. S. Eliot, *Notes Towards the Definition of Culture* (Faber, 1948).
George Orwell, 'The Lion and the Unicorn' [1941], in *Complete Works of George Orwell*, ed. Peter Davison, vol. 18 (Secker, 1998).
Nikolaus Pevsner, *The Buildings of England: Warwickshire* (Penguin, 1966).

C. S. Lewis, *Mere Christianity* (G. Bles [Centenary Press], 1952).
—— *A Grief Observed* (Faber, 1961).
—— *The Problem of Pain* (Centenary Press, 1940).
—— *The Screwtape Letters* (Centenary Press, 1942).
—— *The Allegory of Love: A Study of Medieval Tradition* (Cambridge University Press, 1936).
—— *English Literature in the Sixteenth Century, excluding Drama* (Oxford University Press, 1954).
—— *De Descriptione Temporum: An Inaugural Lecture* (Cambridge University Press, 1955).
Walter Hooper (ed.), *C. S. Lewis, Collected Letters*, 3 vols. (Harper Collins, 2000–6).
George Watson (ed.), *Critical Essays on C. S. Lewis* (Scolar Press, 1992).
A. N. Wilson, *C. S. Lewis: A Biography* (Collins, 1990).

Maurice Bowra, *The Heritage of Symbolism* (Macmillan, 1943).
—— *Sophoclean Tragedy* (Oxford University Press, 1944).
—— *The Greek Experience* (Weidenfeld and Nicolson, 1957).
Isaiah Berlin, 'Maurice Bowra', in *Personal Impressions* (Hogarth, 1980).

Chapter 2

Humphrey Carpenter, *A Serious Character: A Life of Ezra Pound* (Faber, 1988).
T. S. Eliot (ed.), *Literary Essays of Ezra Pound* (Faber, 1954).
A. David Moody, *Thomas Stearns Eliot, Poet*, 2nd edn. (Cambridge University Press, 1995).
Ezra Pound, *A lume spento and Other Early Poems* (New Directions, 1965).
—— *Homage to Sextus Propertius* [1919] (Faber, 1934).
—— *Hugh Selwyn Mauberley* (Ovid Press, 1920).
—— *The Cantos of Ezra Pound* (Faber, 1960).

Peter Ackroyd, *T. S. Eliot* (Hamish Hamilton, 1984).
Jewel Spears Brooker (ed.), *T S Eliot: The Contemporary Reviews* (Cambridge University Press, 2004).
T. S. Eliot, *For Lancelot Andrewes* (Faber, 1928).
—— *Selected Essays* (Faber, 1932).
—— *The Use of Poetry and the Use of Criticism* (Faber, 1933).
—— *Varieties of Metaphysical Poetry*, ed. Ron Schuchard (Faber, 1994).
—— *Geoffrey Faber 1889–1961* (Faber, 1961).
Valerie Eliot (ed.), *The Waste Land: The Facsimile Edition* (Faber, 1971).
Jason Harding, *The Criterion: Cultural Politics and Periodical Networks in Inter-war Britain* (Oxford University Press, 2002).
Anthony Julius, *T. S. Eliot: Anti-Semitism and Literary Form* (Cambridge University Press, 1995).
A. Walton Litz, Louis Menand, and Lawrence Rainey (eds.), *The Cambridge History of Literary Criticism: Vol. 7, Modernism and the New Criticism* (Cambridge University Press, 2000).

Chapter 3

Chris Baldick, *The Modern Movement, 1910–1940* (The Oxford English Literary History, vol. 10) (Oxford University Press, 2004).
C. Day-Lewis, *The Magnetic Mountain* (Hogarth Press, 1933).
—— *Poems in War-time* (Cape, 1940).
—— *Word Over All* (Cape, 1943).
—— *The Poetic Image* (Cape, 1947).
—— *Collected Poems* (Cape/Hogarth, 1954).
—— (ed.), *The Mind in Chains: Socialism and the Cultural Revolution* (Frederick Muller, 1937).
Percy Bysshe Shelley, *A Defence of Poetry* ([1821]; 1st pub. Edward Moxon, 1840).
John Stallworthy, *Louis MacNeice* (Faber, 1995).

Graham Greene, *A Sort of Life* (Bodley Head, 1972).
—— *Ways of Escape* (Bodley Head, 1980).
Norman Sherry, *The Life of Graham Greene*, 3 vols. (Cape, 1989–2004).

Chapter 4

Paul Alpers, 'Empson on Pastoral', *New Literary History*, 10 (1978), 101–23.
William Empson, *Seven Types of Ambiguity* (Chatto, 1930).
—— *Some Versions of Pastoral* (Chatto, 1935).
—— *The Structure of Complex Words* (Chatto, 1951).
—— *Milton's God* (Chatto, 1961).
—— *Complete Poems of William Empson*, ed. John Haffenden (Allen Lane, 2000).
—— *Selected Letters of William Empson*, ed. John Haffenden (Oxford University Press, 2006).

Boris Ford (ed.), *The Pelican Guide to English Literature*, 7 vols. (Penguin, 1954–61).
S. L. Goldberg, *Agents and Lives: Moral Thinking in Literature* (Cambridge University Press, 1993).
Stuart Hall and Paddy Whannel, *The Popular Arts* (Hutchinson, 1964).
Richard Hoggart, *Auden: An Introductory Essay* (Chatto, 1951).
—— *The Uses of Literacy* (Chatto, 1957).
Robert S. Lynd and Helen Merrell Lynd, *Middletown: A Study in American Culture* (Harcourt Brace, 1929).
Francis Mulhern, *The Moment of 'Scrutiny'* (New Left Books, 1979).
Guy Ortolano, *The Two Cultures Controversy* (Cambridge University Press, 2009).
Denys Thompson (ed.), *Discrimination and Popular Culture* (Penguin, 1964).

Chapter 5

John Rodden (ed.), *Lionel Trilling and the Critics* (University of Nebraska Press, 1990).
Diana Trilling, *The Beginning of the Journey: The Marriage of Diana and Lionel Trilling* (Harcourt Brace, 1993).
Lionel Trilling, *Matthew Arnold* (Allen and Unwin, 1939).
—— *E. M. Forster* (New Directions, 1943).
—— *The Middle of the Journey* (Viking, 1947).
—— *Sincerity and Authenticity* (Harvard University Press, 1972).

Stefan Collini, 'Critical Minds: Raymond Williams and Richard Hoggart', in *English Pasts: Essays in History and Culture* (Oxford University Press, 1999).
Fred Inglis, *Raymond Williams* (Routledge, 1995).
R. W. Johnson, 'Moooovement', *London Review of Books*, 12, 3 (8 February 1990), 5–6.
Raphael Samuel, 'Making it up', *London Review of Books*, 18, 13 (4 July 1996), 8–11.
Raymond Williams, *Drama from Ibsen to Eliot* (Chatto, 1952).
—— *Culture and Society, 1780–1950* (Chatto, 1958).
—— *Border Country* (Chatto, 1960).
—— *The Long Revolution* (Chatto, 1961).
—— *Second Generation* (Chatto, 1964).
—— *The Country and the City* (Chatto, 1973).
—— *Marxism and Literature* (Oxford University Press, 1977).
—— *Problems in Materialism and Culture* (Verso, 1980).
—— *Writing in Society* (Verso, 1984).
—— *Who Speaks for Wales?*, ed. Daniel Williams (University of Wales Press, 2003).

Chapter 6

Robert Conquest (ed.), *New Lines* (Macmillan, 1956).
Donald Davie, *Purity of Diction in English Verse* (Chatto, 1952).
—— *Articulate Energy* (Routledge, 1955).
—— *Thomas Hardy and British Poetry* (Routledge, 1973).
D. J. Enright (ed.), *Poets of the 1950s* (The Kenyusha Press, 1955).
—— *Collected Poems*, ed. Anthony Thwaite (Faber, 1988).

Blake Morrison, *The Movement: English Poetry and Fiction of the 1950s* (Oxford University Press, 1980).
Randall Stevenson, *The Last of England?* (The Oxford English Literary History, vol. 12: 1960–2000) (Oxford, 2004).

Kingsley Amis, *Lucky Jim* (Gollancz, 1954).
—— *One Fat Englishman* (Gollancz, 1963).
—— *The Old Devils* (Hutchinson, 1986).
—— *The Amis Collection: Selected Non-Fiction 1954–1990* (Hutchinson, 1990).
—— *The Letters of Kingsley Amis*, ed. Zachary Leader (Harper Collins 2000).
—— (ed.), *The New Oxford Book of Light Verse* (Oxford University Press, 1978).
Martin Amis, *Experience* (Cape, 2000).
Philip Larkin (ed.), *The Oxford Book of Twentieth-Century English Verse* (Oxford University Press, 1973).

Malcolm Bradbury, *The History Man* (Secker and Warburg, 1975).
Henry James, 'The Prefaces to the New York Edition', in *Literary Criticism* (The Library of America, vol. 23) (Cambridge University Press, 1984).
David Lodge, *The Picturegoers* (MacGibbon and Kee, 1960).
—— *Ginger You're Barmy* (MacGibbon and Kee, 1962).
—— *The British Museum is Falling Down* (MacGibbon and Kee, 1965).
—— *Language of Fiction* (Routledge, 1966).
—— *Out of the Shelter* (Macmillan, 1970).
—— *Changing Places* (Secker and Warburg, 1975).
—— *How Far Can You Go?* (Secker and Warburg, 1978).
—— *Working with Structuralism* (Routledge, 1981).
—— *Small World* (Secker and Warburg, 1984).
—— *Write On: Occasional Essays 1965–1985* (Secker and Warburg, 1986).
—— *Nice Work* (Secker and Warburg, 1988).
—— *After Bakhtin: Essays on Fiction and Criticism* (Routledge, 1990).
—— *Author, Author; a Novel* (Secker and Warburg, 2004).
—— *Deaf Sentence* (Secker and Warburg, 2008).
—— *A Man of Parts* (Secker and Warburg, 2011).

Chapter 7

Perry Anderson, 'Renewals', *New Left Review*, NS 1 (Jan.–Feb. 2000).
Carol Ann Duffy, *Mean Time*, 2nd edn. (Anvil Press, 1998).
T. S. Eliot, *The Letters of T. S. Eliot: Vol. 1, 1898–1922*, ed. Valerie Eliot (Faber, 1988).
—— 'A Message', *The London Magazine*, 1 (Feb. 1954).
Mark Morrisson, *The Public Face of Modernism: Little Magazines, Audiences, and Reception 1905–1920* (University of Wisconsin Press, 2001).

Chapter 8

'Memorial service: Dr J. L. Hammond', *The Times* (22 Apr. 1949).
J. L. Hammond, *Charles James Fox: A Political Study* (Methuen, 1903).

—— *Gladstone and the Irish Nation* (Longman, 1938).
J. L. and Barbara Hammond, *The Village Labourer, 1760–1832: A Study of the Government of England before the Reform Bill* (Longman, 1911).
—— —— *The Town Labourer, 1760–1832: The New Civilization* (Longman, 1917).
—— —— *The Rise of Modern Industry* (Longman, 1925).
—— —— *The Age of the Chartists, 1832–1854: A Study of Discontent* (Longman, 1930).
Stewart A. Weaver, *The Hammonds: A Marriage in History* (Stanford University Press, 1997).

Stefan Collini, 'Moral Mind: R. H. Tawney', in *English Pasts: Essays in History and Culture* (Oxford University Press, 1999).
Richard Hoggart, *Auden: An Introductory Essay* (Chatto, 1951).
—— *The Uses of Literacy* (Chatto, 1957).
—— *Life and Times*, 3 vols. (Chatto, 1988–92).
—— *Townscape with Figures: Farnham—Portrait of an English Town* (Chatto, 1994).
—— *The Way We Live Now* (Chatto, 1995).
R. H. Tawney, *The Agrarian Problem in the Sixteenth Century* (Longman, 1912).
—— *Religion and the Rise of Capitalism* (Murray, 1926).
Ross Terrill, *R. H. Tawney and his Times: Socialism as Fellowship* (Harvard University Press, 1973).

P. Alcock, H. Glennerster, and A. Sinfield, *Welfare and Well-being: Richard Titmuss's Contribution to Social Policy* (Policy, 2001).
Martin Bulmer, Jane Lewis, and David Piachaud (eds.), *The Goals of Social Policy* (Unwin Hyman, 1989).
Ralf Dahrendorf, *LSE: A History of the London School of Economics and Political Science, 1895–1995* (Oxford University Press, 1995).
Margaret Gowing, 'Richard Morris Titmuss', *Proceedings of the British Academy*, 61 (1975), 401–27.
Ann Oakley, *Sex, Gender and Society* (Temple Smith, 1972).
—— *The Sociology of Housework* (Martin Robertson, 1974).
—— *Man and Wife: Richard and Kay Titmuss, my Parents' Early Years* (Harper Collins, 1996).
Robert Pinker, *Social Theory and Social Policy* (Heinemann, 1971).
R. M. Titmuss, *Problems of Social Policy* (HMSO, 1950).
—— *The Gift Relationship: From Human Blood to Social Policy* (Allen and Unwin, 1970).
R. M. Titmuss and K. Titmuss, *Parents' Revolt* (Secker, 1942).

Chapter 9

Michael Bullen, John Crook, Rodney Hubbuck, and Nikolaus Pevsner (eds.), *Hampshire: Winchester and the North*, 'The Buildings of England' (Yale University Press, 2011).
Nikolaus Pevsner, *Pioneers of the Modern Movement: From William Morris to Walter Gropius* (Faber, 1936).
—— *An Enquiry into Industrial Art in England* (Cambridge University Press, 1937).
—— *An Outline of European Architecture* (Murray, 1942).

—— *The Englishness of English Art* (Architectural Press, 1956).
David Watkin, *Morality and Architecture* (Murray, 1977).

Perry Anderson, 'Components of the National Culture', *New Left Review*, 50 (July–Aug. 1958).
Anon. [Tariq Ali], 'Dwarf Diary', *Black Dwarf* (14 Feb. 1969).
Christopher Hitchens, 'Moderation or Death', *London Review of Books*, 20, 23 (26 Nov. 1998), 3–11.
Michael Ignatieff, *Isaiah Berlin: A Life* (Chatto, 1998).

Perry Anderson, 'Science, Politics, Enchantment', in J. A. Hall and I. C. Jarvie (eds.), *Transition to Modernity: Essays on Power, Wealth and Belief* (Cambridge University Press, 1992).
Ernest Gellner, *Words and Things: A Critical Account of Linguistic Philosophy and a Study in Ideology* (Gollancz, 1959).
—— *Thought and Change* (Weidenfeld and Nicolson, 1964).
—— *Nations and Nationalism* (Blackwell, 1983).
John Hall and Ian Jarvie (eds.), *The Social Philosophy of Ernest Gellner* (Rodopi, 1996).
Robert Irwin, *For Lust of Knowing: The Orientalists and their Enemies* (Allen Lane, 2006).

Chapter 10

Maxine Berg, *A Woman in History: Eileen Power 1889–1940* (Cambridge University Press, 1996).
Stefan Collini, *Absent Minds: Intellectuals in Britain* (Oxford University Press, 2006).
Eileen Power, *Medieval English Nunneries c.1275 to 1535* (Cambridge University Press, 1922).
—— *Medieval People* (Methuen, 1924).

Noel Annan, *Our Age: Portrait of a Generation* (Weidenfeld and Nicolson, 1990).
Herbert Butterfield, *The Whig Interpretation of History* (Bell, 1931).
—— *The Englishman and his History* (Cambridge University Press, 1944).
—— *Christianity and History* (Bell, 1949).
Stefan Collini, 'Believing in History: Herbert Butterfield, Christian and Whig', in *Common Reading: Critics, Historians, Publics* (Oxford University Press, 2008).
C. T. McIntire, *Herbert Butterfield: Historian as Dissenter* (Yale University Press, 2004).
Keith Sewell, *Herbert Butterfield and the Interpretation of History* (Palgrave, 2005).

Hugh Trevor-Roper, *Archbishop Laud 1573–1645* (Macmillan, 1940).
—— *The Last Days of Hitler* (Macmillan, 1947)

Chapter 11

Martin Amis, *The War Against Cliché: Essays and Reviews 1971–2000* (Cape, 2001).
—— *Experience* (Cape, 2000).

Christopher Hitchens, *The Missionary Position: Mother Teresa in Theory and Practice* (Verso, 1995).
—— *No-one Left to Lie to: The Triangulations of William Jefferson Clinton* (Verso, 1999).
—— *Unacknowledged Legislation: Writers in the Public Sphere* (Verso, 2000).
—— *The Trial of Henry Kissinger* (Verso, 2001).
Frank Kermode, *Pleasing Myself: From Beowulf to Philip Roth* (Allen Lane, 2001).

Tony Judt, *Past Imperfect: French Intellectuals 1944–56* (University of California Press, 1992).
—— *Postwar: A History of Europe since 1945* (Heinemann, 2005).
E. P. Thompson, 'An Open Letter to Leszek Kolakowski' (1973), in *The Poverty of Theory and Other Essays* (Merlin Press, 1978).

Timothy Garton Ash, *The File* (Harper Collins, 1997).
—— *History of the Present: Essays, Sketches, and Dispatches from Europe in the 1990s* (Allen Lane, 1999).
—— *The Uses of Adversity: Essays on the Fate of Central Europe* (Granta, 1999).
George Orwell, 'Why I write' (1946), in *The Complete Works of George Orwell*, ed. Peter Davison, vol. 18 (Secker and Warburg, 1998).

Chapter 12

Andrew Adonis and Keith Thomas (eds.), *Roy Jenkins: A Retrospective* (Oxford University Press, 2004).
C. A. R. Crosland, *The Future of Socialism* (Cape, 1956).
Roy Jenkins, *Asquith* (Collins, 1964).
—— *Gladstone* (Macmillan, 1995).
—— *Churchill* (Macmillan, 2001).

Chapter 13

'Soaring Pay of CEOs' [on a report by Compass], *Guardian* (16 Feb. 2010).
'50 Years of Housing UK', Halifax/Lloyds Banking Group (20 Jan. 2010).
OECD Economic Surveys; United Kingdom 2010 (OECD, 2010).
Richard Wilkinson and Kate Pickett, *The Spirit Level: Why More Equal Societies Almost Always Do Better* (Allen Lane, 2009).
Polly Toynbee and David Walker, *Unjust Rewards: Ending the Greed that is Bankrupting Britain* (Granta, 2008).
Michael Young, *The Rise of the Meritocracy 1870–2033: An Essay on Education and Inequality* (Thames and Hudson, 1958).

Acknowledgements

As I indicated in the Introduction, earlier versions of the great majority of these essays have already been published in some form. For permission to re-use the material here, I am grateful to *The London Review of Books*, *The Times Literary Supplement*, *The Nation*, *The Guardian*, *Prospect*, and *The Independent*. I am particularly indebted to those editors who, in some cases over years or even decades, have continued to encourage me, employ me, correct me—especially Alan Jenkins, Paul Laity, John Palatella, and Mary-Kay Wilmers. I am also grateful to my editor at Oxford University Press, Robert Faber, for a precious combination of commitment and good judgement, and to my literary agent, Peter Robinson, who has persisted in being helpful to such a doggedly unremunerative author. In addition, I thank David Baker for some meticulous practical assistance in the preparation of this volume.

In helping to sustain and improve my writing, a number of my long-serving, long-suffering, close friends have been more important than they are ever likely to realize and more responsible than they are ever likely to acknowledge. The following have read and commented on part or all of this book (more than once in one or two heroic cases), and so must shoulder their portion of the blame: Peter Clarke, Geoffrey Hawthorn, Angela Leighton, Ruth Morse, Jeremy Mynott, Helen Small, John Thompson, and Donald Winch.

Index

Printed and bound by CPI Group (UK) Ltd, Croydon, CR0 4YY